Gender and Fair Assessment

Gender and Fair Assessment

Warren W. Willingham
Nancy S. Cole

Educational Testing Service, Princeton, New Jersey

In Collaboration With
Brent Bridgeman, Carol A. Dwyer, Linda M. Johnson,
Susan Wilson Leung, Charles Lewis, Rick L. Morgan,
Judith M. Pollack, Alicia Schmitt, Gita Z. Wilder

 LAWRENCE ERLBAUM ASSOCIATES, PUBLISHERS
1997   Mahwah, New Jersey   London

EDUCATIONAL TESTING SERVICE, ETS, GRADUATE RECORD EXAMINATIONS, GRE and THE PRAXIS SERIES: PROFESSIONAL ASSESSMENTS FOR BEGINNING TEACHERS are registered trademarks of Educational Testing Service.

ADVANCED PLACEMENT PROGRAM, AP, COLLEGE BOARD and SAT are registered trademarks of the College Entrance Examination Board.

DIFFERENTIAL APTITUDE TESTS is a registered trademark and DAT and STANFORD ACHIEVEMENT TEST are trademarks of The Psychological Corporation.

GMAT, GRADUATE MANAGEMENT ADMISSION COUNCIL, and GRADUATE MANAGEMENT ADMISSION TEST are registered trademarks of the Graduate Management Admission Council.

LSAT is a registered trademark by the Law School Admission Services, Inc.

MCAT is a registered service mark of the Association of American Medical Colleges. STRONG VOCATIONAL INTEREST BLANKS is a registered trademark and STRONG INTEREST INVENTORY is a trademark of the Stanford University Press.

Lawrence Erlbaum Associates, Inc., Publishers
10 Industrial Avenue
Mahwah, New Jersey 07430

Library of Congress Cataloging-in-Publication-Data

Willingham, Warren W.
    Gender and fair assessment / Warren W. Willingham,
Nancy S. Cole in collaboration with Brent Bridgeman ...
[et al.].
Includes bibliographical references and index.
ISBN 0-8058-2331-X (alk. paper)
    1. Educational tests and measurements—United
States–Sex differences. 2. Educational tests and measurements—Social aspects—United States. 3. Academic
achievement—United States—Sex differences. 4. Examinations—United States—Design and construction.
    I. Cole, Nancy S. II. Title.
LB3051.W4996 1997
371.26'01'3—DC21   96-39932
                                              CIP

Books published by Lawrence Erlbaum Associates are printed on acid-free paper, and their bindings are chosen for strength and durability.

Printed in the United States of America

10 9 8 7 6 5 4 3 2

Contents

PREFACE

Two contemporary issues encouraged the undertaking of this book. The first issue involved the need to know more about the test performance of women and men—to be sure we know and understand the basic results about which there has been some debate. The second issue concerned the challenges that new methods of educational assessment pose for fair testing. Together, the two issues led us to ask, "Do we know enough about gender differences and similarities to know where our concerns should lie?" And, "If we knew enough, what should we do with the knowledge in order to design fair assessments for the future?"

Although some may think that enough is known about the performance of women and men on tests, we saw inconsistent patterns in some results. Such inconsistencies have caused a degree of confusion regarding gender differences and similarities in achievement, and have also caused some concerns as to whether the tests themselves may unfairly influence patterns of performance. Considerable recent research on the test performance of females and males makes this a good time to review and extend what has been learned.

New assessments have become more possible and more prevalent in recent years, raising a whole new set of issues about how to design assessments for fairness. Several trends account for the progressive move to broadened forms of assessment. Increasingly, an informed public asks for testing that will lead to more effective education for all students. Researchers are learning more about critical cognitive skills and how to teach and assess them. Technology is expanding the practical alternatives for new assessment methods. Each of these trends leads to assessment options that are more diverse and more complex. It is not only an exciting time for the measurement profession but also a sobering task.

Designing and using more complex tests that are more directly connected with the educational process will require more from all of us. We will have to know more about how people perform on different types of tests and why a particular type of test in a particular situation may be more fair for one student and less fair for another. How can we be sure that new types of tests will be fair to all those taking them? It seems unlikely that traditional, largely technical definitions of test fairness will provide sufficient guidance.

Thus, we have two related objectives: to better understand gender difference and similarity in test performance in order to better insure the fairness of current and future tests. Chapters 1 and 2 provide useful background on the complexities of the topic and the rationale of our study, but we need to make clear a few caveats, especially regarding the limits of this work.

Our first goal has been to understand better the *ways* in which women and men sometimes differ in test performance. *Why* they sometimes differ is also a question of great interest, but a question that engages a vast area of research, extending much beyond the scope of this project. We have given primary attention to those aspects of *why* that are more likely to have implications for designing fair tests; especially the interests, experiences, and education of young women and men. The project did, however, include a broader review of research literature on these and other possible antecedents of gender differences. That report appears in a *Supplement* to this volume, along with other materials of possible interest.

The *Supplement to Gender and Fair Assessment* (Willingham & Johnson, 1997) contains several types of background material: two special reports commissioned by the project, supplemental tables and technical notes, descriptions of test batteries, and selected bibliographies. The two reports were "Antecedents of Gender Differences," a literature review by Gita Wilder, and "The Effects of Sample Restriction on Gender Differences," a model developed by Charles Lewis and Warren W. Willingham. The bibliographies were based on references from this volume, grouped according to a number of topics of possible interest. *Supplement to Gender and Fair Assessment* is available, free of charge, from ETS. Request RR-97-1 from Research Publications, Mail Stop 05-R, Educational Testing Service, Princeton, NJ 08541.

This book focuses on gender because of the interest in the topic and the availability of much relevant research. It is important to remember, however, that tests must be as fair as possible to all examinees. Different individuals and groups may have different fairness concerns or different views of what is fair. Even while viewing fairness issues through a gender lens, we have tried to use gender as a template in order to consider principles of fairness that apply generally to all examinees. Needless to say, this approach leads to the inevitable omission of important fairness concerns that may be specific to other groups of examinees. Similarly, we have attempted to focus on fairness issues that apply to educational tests generally rather than the design and use of particular tests. Here again, there are many fairness issues that we have been unable to cover in any detail.

Finally, tests are sometimes likened to messengers that bring the often bad news about educational performance. Tests themselves can become one of the educational issues when people ask, "Are these results only due to the characteristics of the test or do they come from real individual differences in background, effort, and opportunity?" The data we have reviewed remind us again that tests reflect inequities in the social fabric and in opportunities for quality education overall and in individual subjects. Part of the function of tests is to raise such flags.

Indeed, equity in education is a broader and much more critical concern than tests. When we seek a "level playing field" in testing, we do so knowing that the playing field in education is not level. Inequities exist and affect the learning of students. The best we can do in testing is to seek a level playing field for demonstrating skills. Tests must be valid and fair, but that will never be the same thing as assuring that educational opportunities are fairly distributed. In this book we have not addressed the unlevel playing field of educational opportunities. We are struggling with the far more limited question of making the tests fair.

Producing this book was considerably more difficult and time-consuming than we had expected. What have we accomplished? The question is better answered in Chapter 8, though a few reflections may provide some perspective at the outset. We believe we now have a far better sense of the basic similarities and occasionally important differences in the test performance of women and men than when we started. As expected, it has proven useful to separately evaluate the influence of what the test measures from other factors such as grade level and, especially, the effect of restricting the sample to a select group of students. In the language of the text, it is essential to disentangle the effects of different constructs, cohorts, and samples in order to make sense of gender differences.

We are all the more convinced that fair and valid assessment requires a broad view of talent, which can often be facilitated by variety in the modes of assessment. The need to build more diverse measures that have effective connections with educational goals is a challenge that still looms large in our future. In this regard, the results of this study make clearer that the assessment of writing and mathematics deserves close attention, partly because of their educational importance and partly because they represent diametric strengths for many women and men.

We believe this analysis of gender fairness helps to make the important point that test fairness has many dimensions and is tightly bound with the intrinsic validity of a test. In evaluating the validity of any test, it is essential to look broadly at the social purpose of the test, the context of its use, other measures that come into play, the constraints on the assessment, the pros and cons of possible alternatives. There are always trade-offs. It is usually a serious oversimplification to think of a test as fair or unfair, valid or invalid on the basis of only one or two considerations. This book focuses on gender but, of course, tests must be as fair as possible to all groups. We are struck by the fact that the fairest test may often be the test that is, overall, as valid as possible for each examinee.

ACKNOWLEDGMENTS

An undertaking of the sort described here requires an enormous amount of detailed work, much sound advice, and considerable help. We are indebted to many people. First of all, we are grateful to our collaborators, listed on the title page, who co-authored individual chapters or contributed substantial work that cut across chapters. This group of ETS colleagues was with us throughout, a constant source of shared expertise, good ideas, and good judgment. Our collaborators overlapped substantially with a staff Gender Committee that included Brent Bridgeman, Nancy Burton, Nancy Cole, Carol Dwyer, Charles Lewis, Alicia Schmitt, and Warren Willingham. This group met frequently and played an important role in getting the work off to a sound beginning and keeping it on course.

We are also especially grateful to an advisory group of external colleagues who served as consultants throughout the project. This group included Patricia Campbell, Richard Duran, Robert Linn, Lorrie Shepard, Richard Snow, Floraline Stevens, Carol Tittle, and Janice Weinman. Our consultants reviewed all chapters and contributed much sound advice, constructive criticism, and useful ideas. In meetings at ETS and through mail communications, they brought diverse experience and wisdom to our thinking, and the project benefitted greatly. We are indebted to these esteemed colleagues, but of course they bear no responsibility for the final product.

Another group of colleagues from a wide range of institutions and organizations were gracious and helpful—and often extremely generous with their time—in providing information, data, and advice. We note especially Stephen Cramer, Howard Everson, Jan-Eric Gustafsson, Diane Halpern, Larry Hedges, H. D. Hoover, Neal Kingston, Stephen Klein, Marcia Linn, James Maxey, Karen Mitchell, John Pitman, Mark Pomplun, Edward Slawski, Julian Stanley, and Linda Wightman. We want to acknowledge useful discussions with the ETS Visiting Panel on Research, the College Board Joint Staff Research and Development Committee, and the Graduate Record Examinations Board. In addition, we appreciate the assistance of many people who were helpful in obtaining permission to reproduce previously published material as noted in the text.

We gratefully acknowledge and express appreciation to the following test publishers and test program sponsors for providing test data that were so useful to the project: ACT, Inc. (known as American College Testing Program prior to September 1996), Association of American Medical Colleges, Board of Senior Secondary School Studies—Queensland, College Board, Georgia State Assessment Program, Graduate Management Admission Council, Graduate Record Examinations Board, Kansas State Assessment Program, Kentucky Instructional Results Information System, Law School Admission Services, New Jersey College Basic Skills Testing Program, Psychological Corporation, and Riverside Publishing Company. We were fortunate also to have the benefit of a number of extremely useful public use data tapes based on National Assessment of Educational Progress and other large-scale assessments sponsored and funded by National Center for Education Statistics.

In addition to our collaborators, many other ETS colleagues contributed to this project. Robert Albright, James Braswell, Hunter Breland, Nancy Burton, Warren Day, Chancey Jones, Jerilee Grandy, Eugene Johnson, Ann Jungeblut, Archie LaPointe, Walter MacDonald, Nancy Mead, Leonard Ramist, Donald Rock, and Stanford von Mayrhauser gave us valuable advice about particular aspects of our work. James Carlson, Linda Heacock, Irwin Kirsch, Lee Jones, Anthony Lutkus, Frederick McHale, Rocco Russo, Gloria Weiss, and Lawrence Wightman provided information and data from testing programs administered by ETS. Other staff assisted with a number of special statistical analyses: Steven Isham, Laura Jenkins, Thomas Jirele, Phillip Leung, Norma Norris, Nancy Robertson, and Steve Wang. We appreciate their valuable contributions.

A number of ETS reviewers provided very helpful suggestions, technical and otherwise. Paul Barton, Nancy Burton, Linda Cook, Ruth Ekstrom, John Fremer, Charlotte Kuh, Craig Mills, Nancy Petersen, Lawrence Stricker, and Howard Wainer reviewed one or more draft chapters. We want to thank these colleagues, as well as our collaborators, Brent Bridgeman, Carol Dwyer, and Charles Lewis, who also reviewed extensively. Henry Braun and Samuel Messick are due our very special thanks for reviewing all chapters, but more generally, for their insight and support throughout this project.

Our thanks go to Carol Crowley, Norene Guglielmo, and Joan Stoeckel for their help in producing the report. We are grateful to Linda Johnson for managing the project and for her extensive contributions to many phases of the work: analytical, graphical, and editorial.

And finally we want to want to thank Anna Willingham and Jim Cole who, like many other spouses we are sure, gave much support to this project, both directly and indirectly.

—*Nancy S. Cole*
—*Warren W. Willingham*

1

INTRODUCTION

This introductory chapter frames our topic by addressing briefly three broad questions. First, how does "gender and fair assessment" fit into the larger social context of testing and such obviously related issues as gender equity and assessment reform? Second, what do we mean by test fairness? Judging the fairness of tests is a complex topic in its own right and is not defined that helpfully and consistently in professional literature. Finally, what did this study involve, and how does its telling unfold in succeeding chapters?

There have been many important changes in the participation of women and men in American society over the past quarter century. Tests play a role in those changes by providing evidence of the diverse achievement and proficiency of women and men. Tests aid the learning process, but they also reflect inequalities in opportunity to learn and participate. Tests provide useful information in considering what alternatives in education and work make most sense for us as individuals. They can also influence our views about groups of students, educational programs, and a wide range of issues. For all of these reasons, it is important that tests assess fairly and reflect accurately the ways young people are and are not achieving as well as we would hope.

The test performance of women and men is a research topic of historical interest, and it has received much attention in recent years. Are patterns of performance changing? Why do women tend to make better grades in school whereas men tend to make better scores on tests? Do multiple-choice tests favor males, or is test content sometimes slanted to males? Why, on mathematics tests, do girls tend to score better than boys, although men tend to score better than women? Such questions have generated much confusion. Do the answers depend on what is assessed how and who is assessed when? How can we be sure that tests are designed and used fairly?

Because of increased interest in test performance and test fairness for women and men, there is a great deal of new research and new data available. Our purpose in undertaking the study reported here has been to review this new information with two objectives in mind. One is to clarify patterns of gender difference and similarity in test performance and related achievements. A second objective is to see what implications those findings might have for fair assessment and, as a corollary, examine the assessment process as a possible source of gender differences.

There are many different types of tests. Our interest here is in tests used in education to assess developed knowledge and skill. However, in order to gain a broader view of gender similarity and difference, we also have looked at other types of measures and other characteristics of young women and men. Our hope is to contribute to a firmer basis for ensuring fairness in tests. This objective is particularly important as the measurement field moves increasingly to new forms of assessment with which we have less experience.

Toward the end of this chapter, we describe the structure of this report and give a brief account of what is in each chapter. That description will make more sense following some brief discussion of how we see this topic. First, therefore, we need to comment on the subject from two perspectives: the social context and the complex nature of test fairness.

THE CONTEXT OF THE TOPIC

Issues of gender and fair assessment occur not in a vacuum but in a social context. Context issues enter our considerations throughout this study. Here we note two aspects of the context that are especially pervasive. First, what constitutes fair testing is, in important respects, a social question. So it is useful to consider briefly the social functions of testing and how testing contributes to fairness in educational decisions. Second, testing issues are closely tied to broader issues of equity in educational opportunity. Even the focus on gender fairness in testing may be seen by some as a diversion from more critical issues of educational equity and reform. From that perspective, one might prefer to pose different questions: How can we improve access to quality education, not study it? How can we change tests and the educational system, not risk reinforcing gender stereotypes by studying the present? These contextual questions deserve some comment as background to our study.

The Social Function of Testing

We use tests of ability and achievement to help us enhance learning and opportunity and to improve the effective use of our human resources. Some tests are used in the day-by-day support of instruction; other tests are used to make broader judgments about abilities and achievements that are developed over time. The former are normally developed locally by teachers; the latter are normally developed by external testing organizations. Short-term instructional assessment surely varies in quality from school to school. In that instance, poor assessment is unfair in the sense that it is part of poor schooling.

In this volume, we are concerned with tests that cover learning outcomes over a longer period of time. Such tests are used primarily in employment, counseling, licensing, and education. We concentrate here on educational tests used in evaluating programs and making high-stakes decisions like grade placement, high school graduation, scholarship selection, granting credit, and selective admissions. In high-stakes decisions, assessment has a very direct capacity for affecting individual students. The possibility of such effects is intrinsic to our concern for fairness.

All high-stakes educational decisions involving individuals are con-cerned with *selection* in a broad sense of the word. In such decisions, tests are used—sometimes alone, and often with other measures—to decide (select, if you will) which examinees meet an acceptable standard. The standard may be either a criterion standard defined as what an examinee knows or can do, or a normative standard defined by performance that is typical for some relevant group. Complex decisions tend to invoke complex standards involving judgments about different types of information.

In this book we devote more attention to some types of high-stakes decisions—especially selective admissions—than to others. This choice is partly determined by the availability of data, and partly by the need to limit the scope of our task to manageable proportions. The use of tests along with other measures in making various types of high-stakes decisions often involves similar issues even though the nature of the decision may differ. It is also important to realize that selective mechanisms in society are far more endemic and subtle than the highly visible actions of, say, the admissions committee of a well-known university. Much selection is self-selection or selection mediated through social expectations or the influence of third parties.

Testing is, by its nature, contentious and unpopular when it involves the allocation of limited resources. There are other ways of serving this social function. One alternative is to rely on birthright, connections, or preparing at the right school. The United States largely completed its move away from this form of educational elitism following World War II (McGrath, 1966). Admissions tests that are largely curriculum-free supported that transition in an educational system that lacked the national curriculum, uniform learning materials, and central school-leaving examinations that focus tightly on a designated syllabus—a model long common in Europe (Bowles, 1965). Another alternative would be to downplay admissions standards and let everyone have a go at whatever program they prefer. In spite of some desirable features, this alternative would be costly to society and have disadvantageous implications for world competition (Glazer, 1970), even if it were favored by institutions.

All countries try to develop and channel talent effectively. Our system is meritocratic with some preferences such as alumni ties and the moderating egalitarian influence of diverse educational institutions (particularly in higher education), compensatory programs, and affirmative action. Tests are a small but important part of the enabling mechanisms. The whole educational system is designed for flexibility and access, as well as selection. Compared to education in most countries, it is a quite open system, although quality is uneven. In this process, tests are not immutable. Somewhat different tests might arguably serve with different advantages and disadvantages. The choice of what tests and what other measures to use can also affect individuals and groups differently. The rationale for testing rests principally on the validity of the test—measuring what is intended and serving a useful and fair function. Clearly, in making decisions about testing, the validity of the whole enterprise is the overriding concern.

Equity and Reform

In recent years, there has been increasing national concern about the effectiveness of education generally and the equity issues associated with an obviously uneven distribution of quality education. In this context, the role of tests is hotly debated. Tests are seen by some as a promising means of encouraging educational reform—particularly if tests can be more closely tuned to the curriculum and thereby help to enforce higher standards in education. Others argue the need for prior improvements in the educational and assessment processes before students are held to a higher standard. An added complication is the difference in function and character of a selection test compared to a school achievement test, both of which play a role in the transition of students from secondary to higher education.

What do we try to accomplish with educational tests? The objective is valid assessment of important learning outcomes—assessment that encourages achievement, that is also fair, and beneficially influences the educational system. What reforms are needed in assessment? The most common concerns are related to educational reform and the need to move educational assessment somewhat closer to critical educational objectives, especially assessment that will encourage the attainment of complex knowledge and skills. To many reformers, this means more emphasis on a broader range of tests and test formats, more direct performance measures, better score interpretation, and better connections with learning and instruction.

There is already considerable movement in this direction. Developing new forms of assessment is a different and broader topic than the one we have undertaken. The two are obviously related, however, and one of our hopes in undertaking this study was to learn more about the potential for improvements in testing by using gender and fair assessment as a template for considering similar issues involving other groups or students generally. Thus, in this study we have taken a careful look at gender difference and similarity on different types of tests and testing formats.

Questions about gender difference and similarity often play an important role in the movement to achieve gender equity throughout society. Testing, as well as much of psychological research on gender differences, has something of a double edge in that context. Objective evidence of knowledge and skill can cut through myths about the careers and social roles to which women and men are well-suited. Or more generally, as Eagly (1995) noted, "The knowledge produced in this area of science can be beneficial both in helping women and men to understand their natures and their society and in suggesting ways to enhance gender equality" (p. 155).

In another guise the same evidence may risk reinforcing stereotypes. As Hare-Mustin and Marecek (1988) argued, the primary meaning of gender in psychology has been difference. Research methods also tend to emphasize difference rather than similarity (Campbell & Greenberg, 1993). Furthermore, differences can have exaggerated impact in media reports (Jacobs & Eccles, 1985). Among feminist researchers there has been divided opinion, at best, as to whether studying gender differences serves a useful purpose (Kitzinger, 1994).

For fair assessment, we see studying gender differences as unavoidable. If there were no gender differences, there would not likely be questions about the gender fairness of tests. Because there are gender differences, gender fairness issues are inevitable. In this circumstance, test developers must understand gender differences in order to design tests fairly. Developers need to consider the similarities as well as the differential strengths, experiences, and interests of women and men in order to design and make tests that fairly represent the purpose of the test for each group and ensure that it is not easy or difficult for either group for reasons unrelated to what is intended to be assessed.

THE NATURE OF TEST FAIRNESS

A few decades ago test fairness was viewed mainly as the administration of objective tests under standard and secure conditions to protect individuals from prejudiced or capricious high-stakes decisions. Over the years the idea of fair testing has taken on additional meaning. To "objective and impartial" were added "unbiased," and more recently, "equitable and just." Test fairness has progressed to a broader goal that involves a range of complex values. The topic has multiple aspects and layers. A large body of research on test fairness has addressed a variety of technical topics like differential test validity across groups or ways to identify biased items (Cole & Moss, 1989). Professional codes and standards have developed principles of good practice on the part of testing professionals (American Educational Research Association, American Psychological Association, & National Council on Measurement in Education [AERA, APA, & NCME], 1985; Association for Measurement and Evaluation in Counseling and Development [AACD/AMECD], 1992; Eyde et al., 1993; Joint Committee on Testing Practices, 1988; National Council on Measurement in Education Ad Hoc Committee on the Development of a Code of Ethics [NCME Ad Hoc Committee], 1995). Legislation and litigation have typically addressed broader social issues concerning the permissible uses of tests, often based on arguments concerning justice and consequences (Bersoff, 1981; Sharf, 1988).

Our purpose in this volume is not to address specific issues regarding the fairness of particular tests, but to consider generally the implications of gender differences for fair assessment and to review what we know about the gender fairness of current testing practice. Thus we are concerned with the full range of questions that might be suggested by the topic: What are the principal fairness issues in testing? How should they be evaluated? How is each issue related to the assessment process? How are validity and fairness related? How are different fairness issues and the concerns of different examinees related? These complications suggest the need for some means of organizing the topic.

This section describes a framework for considering fairness issues that follows, in most respects, suggestions offered in more detail by Willingham (in press). The framework emphasizes several ideas. Test fairness is an important aspect of test validity, the overarching technical standard of test quality (Messick, 1989). Anything that reduces fairness also reduces validity. Test fairness has multiple facets that can be effectively connected directly to steps in the assessment process. Finally, test fairness is best conceived as comparability in assessment; more specifically, comparable validity for all individuals and groups.[1] In this discussion and throughout the volume, we use *test fairness* as a general expression to include test bias, culture-fair testing, and similar terms that have been applied to the topic.

Multiple Facets of Test Fairness

As is the case with test validity, many aspects of a test and its use have to be considered in deciding whether it is a fair test. The different aspects are often interconnected in various ways. Proposals that seem to improve a test's fairness from one perspective may have counterarguments from another perspective. Because of this, test fairness issues cannot be viewed in isolation. Test fairness exhibits multiple facets in three ways. There are multiple ways in which tests are used, multiple participants in testing, and multiple steps in the testing process.

A given test is used with various other measures, in many different situations, with different criteria for judging its effectiveness. Often the same test is used for somewhat different purposes—not always the purposes that were intended. There are benefits—and perhaps some drawbacks—that are associated with the immediate use, the long-term effect, and the influence on examinees and the educational system that come from anticipating an upcoming test. Clearly, there are many possible consequences to consider in evaluating test fairness. As is true of test validity, it is not the test or a specific aspect of the test and its use that makes it fair or unfair; the entire situation must be taken into account. As Cronbach (1980) made clear, for example, "The whole selection system is to be justified, not the test alone" (p. 103).

The multiple participants in the testing process can be viewed in several ways. Different parties to testing may have different interests in its nature and outcome—examinees, administrators who use test scores, and teachers who are affected by that use. People have different ideas about what constitutes fairness; for example, "If groups fail a test at different rates, the

---

[1]Since no test is ever perfectly valid, the feasible fairness goal is comparable validity for different individuals and groups at each step in the assessment process. Viewing fairness as comparable validity defines and elaborates the interpretation of test fairness because validity is based on an established system of features and evidence (Messick, 1989). This conception of fairness provides both an organizing principle and a structure that tells us how to look for evidence of comparable validity in places where one might be able to do something about it. Clearly, fairness is a feature of validity and is no less complex or any easier to establish. Evidence regarding fairness must give special weight to use and implications for use because fairness is primarily concerned with the impartiality and justice of actions that are, in the end, social judgments informed by measurement information (Willingham, in press). The task of achieving comparably valid assessment varies somewhat at different stages of assessment for the obvious reason that the validity issues vary.

test is biased." "An accurate predictor is a fair test." "You should test me on what I am good at." There are also different groups of examinees to consider. Modifications in test procedure or content that are intended to make a test more fair for one group may have an opposite effect on another group.

The assessment process offers another perspective on the multiple facets of test fairness. There are many steps in assessment, from the initial design of a test to the eventual effects of its use. The first implication of that observation is that multiple steps suggest multiple ways that something can go wrong. Fairness at one stage of assessment does not guarantee fairness at another. A more useful implication is the connection between fairness issues and what happens throughout the assessment process. We believe that the assessment process is, itself, a useful framework for organizing fairness issues. More important, this framework becomes a practical means for establishing more direct ties between fairness concerns and the choices that are made in developing and using tests.

Four Stages in Assessment

The assessment process includes a number of interconnected steps. All of these steps involve decisions, small and large, that can affect the fairness of a test. Figure 1.1 illustrates four stages in the process: design, development, administration, and use. Each stage is related to each other stage, but as the arrows in the figure suggest, some connections are stronger than others. Design and use are closely related, as are development and administration.

In the design stage one decides what constructs a test should include. In this volume, we frequently use *construct* as a convenient term in referring to a particular domain of knowledge and skills. Constructs can vary widely in their complexity and applicability to different academic fields and careers (e.g., computational skill, knowledge of American history, or academic proficiency). Test design is intimately connected with test use because the choice and nature of constructs to measure in a given test depend on the intended use of the test and the possible effects of its use. For example, an achievement test that assumes a particular syllabus would not be a fair admissions test for students who did not follow that curriculum. Other important decisions concern the general format of the test; for example, a multiple-choice or an essay format, a computer-based test or a paper-and-pencil test. Beyond broad decisions of this kind, the design stage must also result in a more detailed blueprint for development (usually called *test specifications*), including types of questions, what content to cover, how much time will be allowed, methods of scoring, and so on.

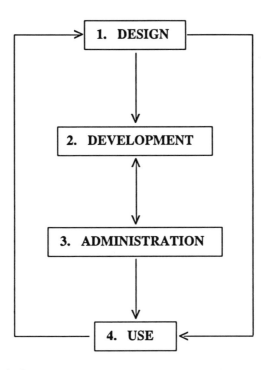

FIG 1.1. Four stages in the assessment process.

In the development stage, specific test material is selected and assembled into an actual test according to the test specifications. The development of a test and its administration to examinees may seem like quite separate activities, but they are intimately related because tests are evaluated and revised partly on the basis of field testing. The final selection of test material, the assembly of several versions or forms of the test, and the development of comparable scores across forms all depend on information obtained in trial administrations. Assessment decisions at these two stages involve carrying out the test specifications faithfully so that all examinees are taking a comparable test, regardless of which version they take or when and where they take it.

Test use involves decisions and actions based on scores along with other relevant information. Use may involve only drawing inferences about the meaning of scores, but such inferences can influence actions—by counselors, admissions officers, teachers, and the examinees themselves. Use also includes broader systemic effects and consequences. This stage in the assessment process is very different from the previous three because it involves a new group of participants—test users—in a wide range of situations. The decisions here concern whether to use the test, how it is used, with what other information, and to what end. At this stage further evidence is gathered regarding the validity and fairness of the test in serving its purpose, all of which feeds back to the design stage for possible revisions.

The various decisions that are reached in these different stages pose somewhat different challenges in order to maintain fairness in the assessment process. In one way or another, they all involve the idea of comparability.

Fairness as Comparability

In designing a test, the primary concern is validity—whether the test will measure what it is intended to measure and whether it will serve a useful function. As we have said, a fair test should be comparably valid for all individuals and groups. The purpose of the test and the effects of its use are key considerations because they determine what types of knowledge and skills are most important for what reasons. Within that framework, *fair test design* should provide examinees comparable opportunity, as far as possible, to demonstrate knowledge and skills they have acquired that are relevant to the purpose of the test. Comparability must always be judged on the basis of all measures that are used with tests (e.g., grades, recommendations, etc.) in making decisions about students, because tests are often not intended to sample from all knowledge and skills that are relevant. In that case, the important fairness question is whether a test, so designed, is likely to lead to fair actions if used as intended.

There may be reasonable alternatives regarding what to measure, and different alternatives may tend to favor some examinees more than others. Also, there may be certain test formats or characteristics of the test or testing situation that make the test more difficult for some examinees for reasons that have nothing to do with the knowledge and skills being assessed. All such design features have a possible bearing on test fairness because they can affect the comparability of the test scores for individual examinees or for groups, including women and men.

In the next two stages of assessment, the challenge to fair assessment is basically similar, although somewhat different from that in test design. *Fair development and administration* of tests should provide tasks, testing conditions, and scaled scores that are as comparable as possible for all examinees taking any version of the test at any location. Most tests have multiple versions that must be comparable to be fair. Moreover, giving students the exact same test does not ensure that it is a comparable measure for each examinee. Achieving such comparability requires a number of steps; for example, selecting test material that does not advantage or disadvantage some examinees for irrelevant reasons, avoiding anything in the testing situation that might add irrelevant difficulty (like undue speededness, or unnecessary technical terms), ensuring that the scoring is equivalent on all tests, and so on.

Fair test use should result in comparable treatment of examinees by avoiding adverse impact due to incorrect inferences or inappropriate actions based on scores and other information normally used with scores. There are a number of ways in which comparable treatment of examinees can be weakened. Using less valid measures than are available will likely mean more decision errors that advantage some examinees and disadvantage others. An inconsistent decision process can have the same effect, as would basing decisions on a limited view of relevant proficiency or systematic underestimation of the proficiency of a particular group. Issues of comparable treatment may reach beyond immediate actions to possible noncomparability in broader systemic effects of testing. Fair test use requires balanced attention to the interests of all individuals and groups. It also requires agreement on what constitutes comparable treatment in a given situation, because there may be competing views of comparability.

The foregoing paragraphs have suggested three criteria for evaluating the fairness of a test: comparable opportunity for examinees to demonstrate relevant proficiency, comparable assessment exercises and scores, and comparable treatment of examinees in test interpretation and use. Comparability is the central principle. Clearly no test can be comparable in every respect for every examinee, but the goal should be to make the assessment process as comparable as possible—as comparable as any practical alternative—on all essential dimensions of validity, such as those outlined in detail by Messick (1989). This principle is elaborated in chapters 6 and 7, which examine the comparability of tests for women and men from a number of different perspectives.

We draw an important distinction between the consideration of specific fairness issues and the broader question as to whether a test is fair overall. Particular fairness issues, considered in isolation, may suggest contradictory solutions or test modifications that have contradictory effects on different groups of examinees. Fairness issues in assessment have to be resolved in relation to possible alternatives. The alternatives usually involve a set of interrelated decisions or issues. The critical question is always how well a test passes these various tests of comparability, considering the context of use that includes other measures and other groups.

Finally, alternative tests or assessment procedures are always evaluated in a broader social context that includes three criteria—not only the fairness of a test but also its usefulness in serving its purpose as well as practical considerations. These three social criteria are discussed in the last section of chapter 5, just prior to the two chapters on test fairness issues.

THE MAIN FEATURES OF THIS STUDY

As we stated at the outset, this study had two objectives. One was to improve our understanding of gender difference and similarity in test performance and related achievements. The other objective was to examine what implications those findings might have for fair assessment, which includes considering what effect the assessment process itself might have on the test performance of females and males. It is useful to distinguish several overlapping methods of studying or understanding sources of gender difference and similarity in test performance.

1. *Early antecedents*—Biological factors, early development, social learning, and role stereotypes.
2. *Patterns of knowledge and skill*—Difference and similarity in the performance of females and males on different types of tests, including differences according to year, age–grade group, ethnicity, and type of sample.
3. *Concomitant evidence and influences*—Differences in interests, experiences, and education, and other achievements that are related to what the tests measure.
4. *Assessment factors*—Variations in design, development, administration, and use of tests that may be associated with gender differences.

Early antecedents of gender differences is a complex topic on which there is a very large literature. It is a topic of considerable interest, although a step removed from our immediate concerns because this level of understanding the evolution of gender difference and similarity is not essential to developing fair tests. Therefore, we have directed our attention primarily to the other methods just listed, which deal with issues that are more proximal and immediately relevant to testing practice. The project did commission a survey of research literature on antecedents of gender differences that provides an informative overview of relevant work and is available in the *Supplement*[2] to this volume (Wilder, 1997).

---

[2] For information on the contents of the *Supplement to Gender and Fair Assessment* and how to order it, see p. viii in the preface.

Improved understanding of patterns of knowledge and skill and the role of concomitant evidence and influences are directly concerned with clarifying gender differences, the first objective of our study. This work is reported in chapters 2, 3, and 4. Chapter 5 provides the logical transition to chapters 6 and 7, which seek to clarify fair assessment issues, our second objective.

Gender Difference and Similarity

In this study our principal interest in understanding gender differences and similarity in test performance is to appreciate possible implications for fair assessment. In order to achieve that objective, it is necessary to understand the differences with some clarity and in some detail, even though they be small. Available research has not been as useful to this end as would be desirable, partly because of some seemingly inconsistent results and partly due to the types of research questions that have been asked.

Consequently, in chapter 2 we take a careful look at recent research on gender differences in test performance in order to determine what additional information would be most helpful from an assessment perspective. A main conclusion of that review was the need to disentangle three sources of gender difference in test data: construct differences (in knowledge and skill), cohort differences (especially by age and grade), and sample differences (especially the selectivity of the sample).

This conclusion led to several others regarding the types of data and analyses that would be useful. One need, we felt, was to study a broader range of tests than has typically been included in previous research. Recent studies of gender differences have primarily stressed mean scores on verbal and mathematical ability tests. Another need was for more reliable samples of data, particularly large samples that are representative of students nationally. Finally, we became convinced that additional statistical descriptors are needed to understand the complex nature of gender difference and similarity. In addition to mean differences, it is sometimes important to understand also any differences in the variability of the scores of women and men, how much the score distributions overlap, and the representation of females and males in a selected group. All this is explained in chapter 2, Research on Gender Differences, which provides a foundation for the analyses reported in chapters 3 and 4.

Chapter 3, Test Performance, presents a considerable amount of data on patterns of female and male performance on widely used current tests. A key analysis in that chapter is the so-called 12th-Grade Profile showing patterns of similarity and difference on a number of tests, all administered to large nationally representative samples of high school seniors. Additional analyses examine gender differences by year in school, over the past decade, within ethnic groups, and within the selected samples of students who take advanced tests.

The analyses in chapter 4 are generally similar, but report data on grades and other measures of interest and accomplishment among young women and men. The data in chapter 4 serve two important purposes. They illustrate, first, that achievement is broader than test performance. In addition, these data provide a useful context for better understanding the observed patterns in test performance. Depending on their purpose, tests may be specifically keyed to certain coursework or educational background. Even so, all students will not have been taught equally well. Test results can only address what has been learned and demonstrated on the test, not the educational context in which the learning occurred. Similarly, tests cannot presume that examinees have identical noneducational backgrounds. Girls and boys come from the same homes and parents, but the data in chapter 4 illustrate how they are similar and different in interests and experiences.

Test Fairness Issues

Following chapter 4, this volume shifts from gender differences to test fairness issues. The transition is bridged in chapter 5, Understanding Gender Differences and Fair Assessment in Context. This chapter examines some of the assessment implications and questions raised by the data in the previous chapters. That discussion centers on what the tests are actually measuring, how gender differences can change with variations in what is measured, and what types of educational and fairness implications may be associated with variations in what is measured. These connections lead naturally to the test fairness issues in chapters 6 and 7. In both cases, our interest is the state of the art and how it might be advanced.

Chapter 6, Fairness Issues in Test Development and Administration, starts with the closely linked second and third stages of assessment in Fig. 1.1, where a test is actually created. Here the central question, with variations, is whether this test creation process has resulted in test exercises and scores that are acceptably comparable for all examinees. The most common question regarding comparability is whether some source of irrelevant difficulty has made the test harder for some examinees than for others. This chapter is based on previous research that bears on such questions.

Chapter 7, Fairness Issues in Test Design and Use, examines fairness issues in the closely linked first and fourth stages, where tests are designed in light of intended use and used in accordance with that design. Chapter 7 differs from chapter 6 in several respects. The lengthier chapter 7 deals with a broader range of issues, engaging questions that call for evidence but also judgment, and often debate over conflicting desirable ends. Fair design and use require judgment as to what assessment objectives are most important and on what basis one should decide when tests afford comparable opportunity and result in comparable treatment.

There are eight topics in chapter 7. The first three concern the possible fairness implications of choosing particular test constructs and formats in test design; a discussion of the design and use of two important types of tests, writing and mathematics, follows. The final topics address three critical aspects of test use: prediction, selection, and using test scores in context with other information. This chapter reviews previous research that is relevant to these topics; it also draws frequently on the findings of chapters 3 and 4 and brings in additional data, especially on performance assessment that was lightly represented in the earlier analyses of current tests.

The final chapter 8 contains a concise summary of findings on gender difference and similarity as well as fairness issues. We offer there our observations on what seem to us the more significant findings. In the final pages we discuss several implications for assessment—all as general issues that we think need more attention than they are currently receiving. None is simple, although we believe all offer good possibilities for improved measurement practice.

2

RESEARCH ON GENDER DIFFERENCES

This is the first of three chapters concerning similarities and differences in the achievement of women and men, and the chapter has two objectives. One is to provide an overview of significant recent research on test performance and some important research questions outstanding. Another is to describe our research methods in studying these questions and to provide necessary explanations for terms and technical aspects of the analyses of data that follow in chapters 3 and 4. Chapter 3 focuses on test performance—mostly traditional tests that are widely used in major testing programs or tests included in prominent national surveys. Chapter 4 reports on similarities and differences between women and men on academic grades, special accomplishments, and personal characteristics that can influence achievement. Together, these three chapters provide descriptive data useful in later discussion of possible implications for fair testing, education, and gender equity more generally.

Gender similarities and differences in test performance and other types of achievement is not a new area of study. The main roots of the topic lie in the psychology of individual differences. In midcentury, textbooks in differential psychology typically included one or more chapters on "sex differences" (Anastasi & Foley, 1949; Tyler, 1947). In their book, Anastasi and Foley cited more than 100 references on the topic, extending back into the 19th century. In recent years there has been an explosion of interest and research in this general area.

In this chapter we provide an overview of the main results of that research. Most of the following discussion is about test performance. When we talk here of ability, knowledge, skill, talent, and so on, it is good to remember that we are normally referring to a test score, and the meaning of the score depends on what is in the test. In this chapter we also give considerable attention to research methods that follow directly from recent work on this topic—methods that apply to test data in chapter 3 as well as other types of achievement that are examined in chapter 4.

Thus, this chapter provides essential background and rationale for the two chapters that follow. First, we describe background literature of more general interest, then take a closer look at some notable studies over the past decade or so. The final section addresses research design: our general orientation as to what types of measures and samples would be most useful to study, specifics regarding tests used in chapter 3, and discussion of statistical methods used in chapters 3 and 4.

Background Literature

In the past few decades the most prominent milestone in research on gender differences undoubtedly has been Maccoby and Jacklin's (1974) comprehensive work, *The Psychology of Sex Differences*. Maccoby and Jacklin carried out an unusually comprehensive study from which they drew a number of clearly articulated conclusions. The book received a great deal of attention and stimulated a heightened level of interest in the topic. They based their analysis on some 1,600 studies in eight areas of achievement, personality, and social relationships.

Maccoby and Jacklin (1974) listed various "unfounded beliefs" (e.g., girls are more social and suggestible but have less self-esteem and motivation for achievement), some other "open questions" on which the evidence was mixed (e.g., which gender is more anxious, competitive, compliant, active, or maternal), and four main conclusions regarding "sex differences that are fairly well established." These main findings were that: (a) girls have greater verbal ability, (b) boys excel in visual-spatial ability, (c) boys excel in mathematics, and (d) males are more aggressive. As we will see, their conclusions have been qualified in various ways by succeeding research (e.g., see reviews and commentaries by Cleary, 1992; Jacklin, 1989; Linn & Hyde, 1989; Linn & Petersen, 1985b; Wilder & Powell, 1989).

In detailed reviews of Maccoby and Jacklin's book, Block (1976a, 1976b) characterized the work as monumental and praised its perceptive contributions, but called it a "controversial portrayal of the field" (1976a, p. 518). Block questioned whether the data and the authors' decision rules in evaluating the data permitted sensible conclusions. She also documented various "slippages," some of which she judged to be of appreciable consequence. These controversies and the methodological problems exposed by Maccoby and Jacklin created a new surge in research and new efforts to achieve dependable results from data with obvious shortcomings. It is a measure of the advances wrought by Maccoby and Jacklin that, after two decades, their study is still widely cited.

Among the vast number of articles and books on gender in recent years, only a limited number are directly concerned with the achievement of women and men. Nonetheless, that limited portion is a sizable literature. Three detailed and useful reviews described gender differences in test performance, but from somewhat different perspectives. Wilder and Powell (1989) focused on test data; Deaux (1985) also included studies devoted to personality and social behavior; Hyde and Linn (1986) based their review largely on results of meta-analytic studies—systematic statistical synthesis of earlier research.

Additional overviews of test performance data—typically less detailed—appear in other books that are useful for their broader coverage. For example, Gipps and Murphy (1994) brought a British perspective to "sex differences in intellectual abilities" within the context of their wide-ranging discussion of what constitutes a fair test. Hyde's (1991) work on the psychology of women embeds discussion of cognitive differences in a variety of salient topics concerning social roles, work, and education, problems women face as women, and so on. On the other hand, a book edited by Baker (1987) includes discussion of cognitive differences with reviews of other aspects of performance; for example, sensory functioning, physiological and anthropometric factors, and cyclical variations.

Such reviews give some attention to the wellsprings of gender differences—environmental, biological, or most typically, both. However, there are substantial literatures devoted specifically to the question of etiology. Benbow (1988b) summarized research on gender differences in mathematical precocity that led her to conclude that biological factors must play a role (see also Benbow, 1986; Eysenck, 1981). Benbow's (1988b) review is particularly interesting due to the large number of accompanying comments published in the same issue of the journal. There and elsewhere, other authors have presented vigorous arguments against biological theories of gender differences in cognitive abilities (Fausto-Sterling, 1985; Kamin, 1981), and counterexplanations from a sociological or educational perspective (Baker & Jones, 1992; Eccles & Jacobs, 1986; Wellesley College Center for Research on Women, 1992).

Similarly, Mickelson (1989) brought a social perspective with her question, "Why does Jane read and write so well?" But as Friedman (1989) commented, "purists of either persuasion [on the heredity-environment dichotomy] are scarce today" (p. 186). Halpern's (1992) book on cognitive abilities illustrates this balanced treatment with what she called a "biopsychosocial" perspective. The review by Wilder and Powell (1989) follows a similar tack, as do Cleary (1992) and Neisser et al. (1996). Wilder's report, in the *Supplement* to this volume, provides a detailed discussion of these various theoretical orientations and lines of research regarding the sources of gender differences.

Other reviews of interest dwell on critical implications of gender differences and similarities. These include especially the influence of real or imagined differences on women's educational and career decisions (Eccles, 1987), and the types of erroneous assumptions that may mislead young women as well as educational practitioners (Linn & Hyde, 1989; Linn & Petersen, 1985b). There are three additional topics that have received considerable attention:

1. Are there differential patterns of development among young females and males (Becker & Forsyth, 1990; Ekstrom, Goertz, & Rock, 1988; Newcombe & Dubas, 1987)?
2. Are gender differences diminishing (Feingold, 1988; Linn, 1992)?
3. Are males more variable than females on measures of achievement (Feingold, 1992b; Hedges & Nowell, 1995; Martin & Hoover, 1987)?

Data presented in the following chapter touch on each of these three topics.

NOTABLE RECENT STUDIES

These various reviews and commentaries are mentioned here in order to provide a fuller view of relevant literature on gender similarities and differences. Because the great majority of research on gender differences in achievement has been based on test performance, we turn now to studies of that character. It is useful to distinguish three types: meta-analytic studies, normative analysis, and national surveys.

Meta-Analytic Studies

The book by Maccoby and Jacklin (1974) illustrates well the problems encountered in a traditional literature review of an important and complex topic where the research interest centers on how experimental treatments or groups under study are similar or different. Often there are too many studies and too much information to sort out and describe in a way that is understandable. This confusion, exacerbated by inconsistent results, led earlier investigators to simply count how many studies showed statistically significant results. This "vote counting" can often yield problematic conclusions because such a simplistic approach ignores differences among studies as to method, sample size, and the character of the results. More important, it diverts attention from the *size* of the difference between groups, which should be of greater concern.

Methods for such research synthesis have been greatly strengthened by the development (Glass, 1976) of a series of related techniques known as meta-analysis (meta, in the sense of transcending or more comprehensive). Simply put, *meta-analysis* is a systematic way of accumulating and making sense of statistical results across a number of studies. By the early 1980s there had been enough progress to justify several books on meta-analysis (Glass, McGaw, & Smith, 1981; Hedges & Olkin, 1985; Hunter, Schmidt, & Jackson, 1982).

The first step in a meta-analysis of gender-related studies is to characterize each independent study or set of data with a measure of gender difference that is comparable across studies. Obviously, an average gender difference of 1 point on, for example, the 5-point scale of the Advanced Placement examinations cannot sensibly be compared with a 1-point difference on the 200 to 800 scale of the Scholastic Aptitude Test.[1] The common way of handling this problem is to create a standard index, D, by subtracting the male mean from the female mean and dividing that difference by the average standard deviation (i.e., the amount of spread in the scores).[2] Thus,

$$D = \frac{\text{female mean} - \text{male mean}}{\text{average standard deviation}}$$

This index D is referred to here as the *standard mean difference*, or simply the *standard difference*. The measure varies about zero. That is, when there is no gender difference, D is zero; if women have the higher score, D is positive; if men have the higher score, D is negative.[3] D is comparable from measure to measure, even if the score scales on the measures are quite different.

---

[1] In 1993 the formal name of the SAT was changed to *Scholastic Assessment Test*. We have used the original name because practically all SAT data used here came from editions with that name.

[2] There are several possibilities for computing the denominator of D (e.g., see Stanley, 1992). We have used the following equation:

$$D = \frac{\overline{X}_F - \overline{X}_M}{\sqrt{(S_F^2 + S_M^2)/2}}$$

One could also use average standard deviations, but it is more common to average variances. Another possibility is to weight the variances in order to obtain a pooled standard deviation. This choice has the disadvantage of making D dependent to some degree on subgroup sample size. In any event, these alternatives make little practical difference because in these data female and male sample sizes and standard deviations seldom differ by very much.

[3] The order of the subtraction is arbitrary (i.e., female − male, or male − female) and is handled both ways in the research literature. In referring to results from other studies, we have changed signs as necessary so that a positive D always means higher performance by women. Similarly, we have consistently referred to ratios of the two genders as females to males (F/M).

For purposes of interpretation, Cohen (1988) proposed these evaluative categories for D that have been widely used: .20 to .49 is a small difference, .50 to .79 is medium, and .80 or higher is large. As we discuss later in more detail, the possible consequences of a difference depend on the situation. In some circumstances a small difference may be important, although as Hyde and Linn (1988) noted, a well-established difference is not necessarily important. Cohen's categories can be misleading in a particular situation, but they do provide a useful frame of reference and point of departure in considering both differences and similarities between two groups.[4]

Figure 2.1 illustrates two score distributions in each of four cases when D ranges from .10 to .50. A difference of .10 is very small but could be important if, for example, it represented a systematic score difference between two groups that was caused by some characteristic of a test unrelated to the knowledge and skills being assessed. At the other extreme among these four cases, one does not frequently find a gender difference in test performance as large as .50 in general populations.

The shading of one distribution in each pair in the figure makes clear that the scores overlap substantially. Even in the case of the larger mean difference, when $D = .50$, the distributions appear much more similar than different. One means of evaluating the degree of overlap is to ask what percentage of the total variation in scores is associated with the difference in group means—in this case, gender. That amount is indicated as %Var next to each pair of curves; for example, when $D = .20$, only 1% of all score variation is associated with gender.

Another way to understand better what such measures mean is to look at some other group differences on a familiar test. Figure 2.2 is useful for that purpose. It shows how a number of groups compared on SAT Verbal and SAT Math scores in 1993. Within each pair of contrasting groups shown in the figure, the group listed first had the higher mean score. Each pair is listed at approximately the level of D corresponding to the mean difference for that pair. The percentage of score variation associated with the group difference (%Var) is also shown at the right for reference.

---

[4]Characterizing group differences with such labels has been strongly discouraged by some writers (e.g., Glass et al., 1981). Nonetheless, they are widely used. Our aim has been to encourage more critical thinking about group differences that takes account of distributional variation, context, and consequences of observed differences.

In characterizing standard differences, we have not limited ourselves to Cohen's language, but we have tried to avoid language that would appear inconsistent with those guidelines. Whether a given difference is worthy of attention is, of course, a different matter. We have not hesitated to interpret and call attention to differences smaller than .20 if they are statistically significant and seem important because they form a pattern, represent a group of tests, differentiate types of measures or groups, or may be otherwise helpful in understanding gender differences or test fairness issues.

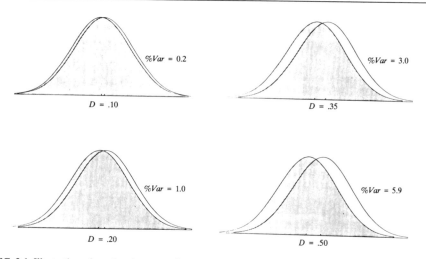

FIG. 2.1. Illustration of overlapping score distributions as the standard mean difference, D, varies from .10 to .50.

Ds can be analyzed in various ways. For example, they may be averaged to determine the overall difference for a number of studies, or categorized to see how D varies for different types of tests or different age groups, and so on. When Ds are averaged, they are often weighted in order to place less emphasis on small samples that give less reliable results. This brief discussion must suffice for now on the matter of measuring gender difference, but there is much more to this topic than readily meets the eye. We return to it later.

Hyde (1981) evidently did the first meta-analysis of gender differences in test performance. She reanalyzed Maccoby and Jacklin's (1974) data on gender differences in verbal ability, quantitative ability, and two varieties of spatial ability. The average Ds were, respectively, +.24, −.43, and −.49 (following the female – male convention in the earlier equation). Hyde also reported the proportion of all variation in test scores that was associated with gender difference. The median proportion was less than .05 for each type of measure.

In the spirit of Cohen's rule of thumb, Hyde's main conclusion was that these "well-established" gender differences were, in fact, all small. That interpretation was later questioned (e.g., Rosenthal & Rubin, 1982b), and as we will see, there are several ways of looking at group differences that may have different implications in different situations. Furthermore, the number of studies on verbal, mathematical, and spatial test performance cited by Maccoby and Jacklin that had sufficient information for meta-analysis was actually rather limited compared to the amount of data available to later such analyses. Nonetheless, Hyde made the important point

D	Groups Compared on SAT-V	Groups Compared on SAT-M	%Var
1.10	Language-Business Intended Major	A average--B average (in H.S.) / Phys. Sci.--Education (intended major) / Masters--Associate (degree goal)	23.2
1.00	A average--B average (in H.S.)	More than--less than 4 years of math / White--Black students	20.0
.90	Masters--Associate (degree goal) / White--Black students / Post grad.--H.S. (father's degree)	Post grad.--H.S. (father's degree)	16.8
.80	Phys. Sci.--Education (intended major)		13.8
.70			10.9
.60	White--Hispanic students	White--Hispanic students	8.3
.50	English--other (first language learned)		5.9
.40	More than--less than 4 years of English	Language--Business (intended major) / Male--female students	3.9
.30		Asian--White students	2.2
.20	White--Asian students		1.0
.10	Male--female students		.3
.00		Other--English (first language learned)	.0

FIG. 2.2. Illustrative differences in SAT Verbal and Math scores for selected groups of students. The group with the higher mean score is always listed first. D = Standard Mean Difference. %Var = Percentage of score variation associated with the difference between the two groups compared. Source: *College Bound Seniors*. The College Board (1993b).

that small group differences, even if reliable, should not color vocational guidance of young women or adversely affect their career aspirations or participation.

A few years later, Hyde and Linn (1986) published a useful book on the application of meta-analysis to understanding gender differences. The introductory chapter by Hyde (1986) gives an overview of the method. A second chapter (Hedges & Becker, 1986) provides an introduction to the technical aspects. Other chapters report on meta-analyses of some interesting characteristics that appear to differ for women and men; for example, Hyde (1986) reported that men tend to be more aggressive in various ways ($D = -.50$); Hall and Halberstadt (1986) reported that women are more likely than men to gaze and smile at other people (D above $+.60$ for adults). An informative meta-analysis in the Hyde and Linn book, more pertinent to test performance, was Linn and Petersen's (1986) study of spatial ability (see also Linn & Petersen, 1985a). This is the first of three types of ability—spatial, verbal, and mathematical—that have been subjected to detailed meta-analysis due to their presumed importance in understanding gender differences in cognition.

Spatial Tests.   Linn and Petersen located 172 studies published from 1973 to 1982 that were suitable for meta-analysis. They categorized each according to the cognitive characteristics of the task. *Spatial visualization* included measures based on questions that are presented in a spatial context but susceptible to solution through a series of analytic steps. Among 81 such measures, gender differences were typically quite small and unrelated to age (mean $D = -.13$). *Spatial perception*, on the other hand, was based on tasks that entail accurate recognition of the vertical or horizontal axis. Males appear to perform this task more efficiently, especially among adults (overall mean $D = -.44$). Tasks for which *mental rotation* in three-dimensional space is the most efficient solution strategy tended to show the largest gender difference (mean $D = -.73$). Vandenberg's test of mental rotation involving groups of blocks in odd configurations (see Linn & Petersen, 1985a) has shown consistently large gender differences on the order of $-.90$. (See Table S-1 in the *Supplement*.)

It may be that the critical aspect of gender difference in performance on spatial tasks is related somehow to the ability to quickly "see" the solution as opposed to reasoning it out, but this distinction is not well-understood or perhaps even accurate. Much of the interest in spatial ability has been due to the speculation (Benbow & Stanley, 1980; Sherman, 1967) that it may be related to some types of mathematical performance. This has proven to be a contentious and complex issue lacking clear answers (Benbow, 1988a; Caplan, MacPherson, & Tobin, 1985; Fennema & Sherman, 1977; Fennema & Tartre, 1985; Linn & Petersen, 1986; Pattison & Grieve, 1984). More recently, there has been interest in the connection of spatial visualization to proficiency on science tests (Hamilton, Nussbaum, Kupermintz, Kerkhoven, & Snow, 1995). More on such possible connections appears in later chapters, but it is performance in mathematics, rather than spatial ability, that has received major attention.

Mathematical Tests.   Proficiency in mathematics has always been recognized as one of the important factors that bear on access to and success in a number of fields (see Chipman, Brush, & Wilson, 1985, for a useful volume on this topic). The observed tendency of women to take fewer advanced mathematics courses and to make somewhat lower average scores on advanced mathematics tests has stimulated much interest and a large literature. Reviews of this literature in recent years appear to be in general agreement that there is little overall gender difference in mathematics test scores in elementary school, some differences appear in junior high (especially among very talented youth), and average differences favoring males are more common in high school, particularly on problem-solving tasks (Benbow, 1988a; Fennema & Carpenter, 1981; Friedman, 1989; Halpern, 1992; Hyde, Fennema, & Lamon, 1990; Linn & Petersen, 1986; Stage, Kreinberg, Eccles, & Becker, 1985).

Meta-analyses of test performance have progressively clarified that pattern. The first such study was the previously mentioned analysis by Hyde (1981), who reported an overall difference, $D = -.43$, favoring males. Friedman (1989) later undertook an analysis of 98 studies published after 1974. She reported a mean D of $-.02$ for 77 studies, largely based on younger students, that she judged not subject to a selection bias. Friedman's group of studies varied widely as to gender difference, and it proved difficult to detect stable patterns in the results as to different types of tests and samples. Overall, she concluded that gender differences on mathematics tests are very small and have decreased over the years.

A more comprehensive and informative meta-analysis was carried out by Hyde et al. (1990). Their analysis was based on 100 studies, including 254 Ds. First, they reported an overall gender difference for general (not selective) samples of $D = .05$ and concluded, "gender differences for mathematical performance are small" (p. 139). The authors went on to say—as both their method of analysis and their results make clear—that, "a general statement about gender differences is misleading because it masks the complexity of the pattern" (p. 151). To help unravel that complexity, mean Ds were computed for various categories of tests and types of subgroups. The authors also carried out a multiple regression analysis to determine which characteristics of data sets had an effect on the magnitude of D (a methodological refinement to meta-analysis suggested by Rosenthal & Rubin, 1982a). That analysis indicated that three variables had an independent effect on D: subjects' age, selectivity of the sample, and cognitive level of the test.

Regarding cognitive level, Hyde and her colleagues reported a small but progressive change in mean gender difference with higher level tests: a small female superiority in computation ($D = .14$), no difference in understanding concepts ($D = .03$), and a slight male superiority in problem solving ($D = -.08$). With respect to the second significant variable, age, the authors reported a small mean difference favoring females in the elementary and middle school years, followed by larger differences favoring males in the high school and college years. Gender differences associated with age and cognitive level were confounded to some extent. As Hyde et al. (1990) wrote, "It was in problem solving that dramatic age trends emerged. The gender difference in problem solving favored females slightly (effect size [i.e., standard mean difference] essentially zero) in the elementary and middle school years, but in the high school and college years there was a moderate effect size favoring males" [$D = -.29$ and $-.32$] (p. 149).

The third independent influence on D was selectivity of the sample, meaning the extent to which the sample is restricted to more proficient, higher scoring students. This factor loomed large. General, moderately selective, and highly selective samples showed Ds of .05, $-.33$, and $-.54$, respectively. Earlier studies had shown a relationship between sample selectivity and male advantage (e.g., Benbow & Stanley, 1980; Rosenthal & Rubin, 1982a). Hyde et al. (1990) appears to be the first study in which this effect on gender difference was so clearly demonstrated in a large and varied collection of test results. It is important to note, however, that sample selectivity is often counfounded with both age and cognitive level.

The authors also concluded that gender difference in mathematics test performance had declined over the years ($D = -.31$ for studies published prior to 1974, and $-.14$ for those from 1974 to 1990). On the other hand, this temporal variable did not come out as an independent factor in their regression analysis. This result suggests that the observed trend over time could have been due mainly to other variables, such as age or selectivity, rather than time per se. Verbal ability is another type of test performance in which there has been special interest in the pattern of gender difference over time.

Verbal Tests.   The major study of gender differences in performance on verbal tests was a meta-analysis by Hyde and Linn (1988). They located 165 studies, including those reviewed by Maccoby and Jacklin. Finding an average D of .11 the authors took a clear position: "We are prepared to assert that there are no gender differences in verbal ability, at least at this time, in American culture, in the standard ways that verbal ability has been measured" (p. 62). This is a shift, of course, from the historic assumption of most that women are more skilled in verbal matters.

These studies in verbal skills were coded in various ways in order to probe further into possible variations in the pattern of gender differences and similarities. Type of verbal test was one of the more interesting classifications. The findings are reproduced in Table 2.1. Some results, notably those for essay writing ($D = .09$), show less superiority by women than have been observed elsewhere (see footnote 6 in chapter 3). This discrepancy appears to have resulted from Hyde and Linn's group of five writing studies being swamped by one study with a small D that was based on a very large and very selected sample—188,811 students taking the College Board's English Composition Test, forerunner to the SAT-Writing Test and required by many selective colleges.[5] The average D for the other four studies was .45.

One important conclusion drawn by Hyde and Linn is that the magnitude of female superiority in verbal ability has declined slightly ($D = .23$ for studies published in 1973 or earlier; .10 for studies published after 1973. This could be an accurate reflection of trends during this period, but here again, the character of the samples may have influenced the results. The single dramatically large sample in the early period had a D of .26. On the other hand, six other large samples in the later period had a median D of .07. Weighting study results in order to avoid overemphasizing unreliable small studies may well be a two-edged sword where sample sizes vary greatly. Linn and Hyde gave witness to that problem by removing SAT results from their analysis because its large sample gave the test undue weight.

TABLE 2.1
Standard Mean Gender Difference, D, for Different Types of Verbal Tests

Type of Test	Number of Differences	Mean D
Vocabulary	40	.02
Analogies	5	−.16
Reading comprehension	18	.03
Speech production	12	.33
Essay writing	5	.09
Scholastic Aptitude Test	4	−.03
Anagrams	5	.22
General/Mixed	25	.20
Other	5	.08
Total	119	.11

Note. From Hyde and Linn (1988). Copyright © 1988 by the American Psychological Association. Adapted with permission.

---

[5]In fact the *English Composition Test* (ECT) was mostly composed of multiple-choice items and is misclassified simply as "essay writing." The point is moot, however, because the highly selective samples taking the ECT consistently show low positive values of D, whether one looks at the essay or the multiple-choice section. This is a quite different result from values in the range of .40 to .60 that are common for such assessments in representative samples in grade 12 (see Table 3.1, and Pomplun, Wright, et al., 1992).

At this point a few additional comments on the strengths and limitations of the meta-analysis method may be useful. There is no doubt that the meta-analytic method, as a general approach to understanding group differences in test performance, is a large step forward (Hyde, 1994). In her very helpful book with Hyde on gender differences and meta-analysis, Linn (1986) reflected on the advantages of the method—systematic analysis, quantification of effects, precision—as well as some of the difficulties one encounters.

Linn discussed methodological problems as factors that lead to inconsistent findings. Factors that cause trouble have especially to do with the uncontrollable variation in the nature of studies that one is able to accumulate. Samples may vary in significant ways, especially in age of subjects and selectivity. Despite tests having similar names, test content may vary in consequential ways. As illustrated at several points in the foregoing discussion, characteristics of samples and measures overlap and interact in ways that often cannot be controlled. Analysis is likely to be confusing because, in the collection of research data that happen to be available, there are typically many holes in the framework of samples and measures one would like to have.

Finally, Chipman (1988) remarked on the possibility that all published studies may be biased or unrepresentative in a similar way because of research convenience or publication biases. Perhaps overstating the matter, she said, "For a question like sex differences in spatial ability or mathematics achievement, one large, nationally representative sample is undoubtedly preferable to the meta-analysis of a hundred local doctoral dissertation studies" (p. 49). In many areas of research where meta-analysis is effectively applied, there is no alternative to analyzing as precisely as possible the findings of whatever studies may have been published. But in the case of test performance, there are valuable alternative data sets of two types: test program norms and national educational surveys. To be sure, such data sources have their own problems, and they have been used in meta-analyses, although not nearly as extensively as they might be. We now move to a brief account of these two types of data and some of the studies based on each.

Normative Analysis

Three types of testing programs produce useful normative information on the performance of female and male examinees. First, there are the dedicated testing programs designed to serve a particular purpose and a selected group of examinees. For example, the Medical College Admissions Test is taken by people interested in attending medical school; the examinations of the Advanced Placement Program are taken by well-prepared students who hope to earn college credits while they are still in high school. Such programs yield important data because the tests bear on significant educational and career decisions, but the samples are obviously not at all representative of the total population. The various reasons why people decide to sit for such elective testing programs are never completely clear, and the character of the sample may change over time in ways that are not obvious. On the other hand, there is usually a good deal of information available about such samples, so it is possible to examine changes over time (see, e.g., Burton, Lewis, & Robertson, 1988).

A second class of test programs are the achievement and aptitude batteries from the major test publishers that are widely used in elementary and secondary schools throughout the country. For example, the Stanford Achievement Tests include 8 to 12 tests of knowledge and skill in various subject areas at several different grade levels from K through 12. Such test batteries are normally revised and renormed every 7 to 10 years in a cross-section of schools, resulting in national norms that are probably reasonably representative of the general population, but undoubtedly fluctuate more than would be expected of carefully drawn samples of students and schools.

State testing programs represent a third category of testing programs that overlaps with the second. Most states sponsor or mandate some type of systematic testing in Grades K through 12. The character of such programs varies considerably, some being contracted to a test publisher, others being developed and administered by a state agency. Some such data find their way into published literature and may be included in a meta-analysis (e.g., the Hyde & Linn, 1988, study of verbal ability). In other instances investigators have included state data by obtaining the necessary statistics directly from the appropriate state agency (Cleary, 1992; Hyde et al., 1990).

There are several advantages to normative information. The availability of large samples is the most apparent. Large samples ensure more stable results, and provide the opportunity to analyze gender differences within ethnic subgroups. Another important advantage of normative data is the availability of results for various types of tests administered to the same group of examinees or results for the same test administered to a generally comparable sample at a different age or grade level or in a different year. It is the possibility of such stratified analysis—without everything varying at once—that is the special strength of normative test data.

A common use of normative data has been simply to describe gender differences across a wide range of tests (Anastasi & Foley, 1949; Clark &

Grandy, 1984; Halpern, 1992; Linn, 1992; Policy Information Center, 1989a, 1989b; Wilder & Powell, 1989). Perhaps the best example is a series of papers by Stanley, Benbow, Brody, Dauber, and Lupkowski (1992).[6] These authors assembled normative data on 86 widely used tests, mostly from testing programs that are moderately to highly selective (e.g., Graduate Record Examinations, Medical College Admission Tests, Advanced Placement Program).

A principal finding of Stanley et al. (1992) was a fairly consistent pattern of larger gender differences (favoring males) in certain subjects with selective samples than are normally observed in tests administered to representative populations. This larger difference was particularly true of advanced tests in science, mathematics, history, and political science. It was also noted that D values favoring males tended to be associated with tests taken by more males than females. Several authors in that series of papers cited the ratio of females to males in the top 10% of the score distribution to illustrate that there may be gender differences of practical significance among high scorers, even when the overall value of D is not large. For example, Lupkowski (1992) noted that there were half as many women as men among the top 10% of scorers on spatial relations tests with a "small" D of $-.22$. She suggested that, "Cohen's verbal categorizing tends to underestimate the potency of an effect size [i.e., standard difference] where one wishes to select at a high score level" (p. 50).

There are several good examples of effective use of normative data to examine questions of considerable interest concerning gender differences. One such question is whether gender differences have narrowed over time (Feingold, 1988; Linn, 1992). Another issue of great interest is better understanding any differential pattern of cognitive development among girls and boys in Grades K to 12 (Becker & Forsyth, 1990; Martin & Hoover, 1987). Possible gender differences in variability of scores is another important question for which normative data has proven useful (Becker & Forsyth, 1990; Feingold, 1992b; Martin & Hoover, 1987). In each of these cases, normative data are well-suited because they are less subject to sampling variation and to extraneous factors than would normally be the case with published reports of studies that follow no particular pattern as to the nature of the sample. We examine the substance of each of these issues in subsequent sections.

---

[6]This group of papers was first presented at the annual meeting of the American Educational Research Association in 1987. Stanley updated his paper for a symposium at the University of Iowa in 1991, and all were published as part of the conference proceedings (Colangelo, Assouline, & Ambroson, 1992).

National Surveys

There are two sources of useful survey data regarding gender differences and similarities: the numerous studies of the National Assessment of Educational Progress (NAEP) and several major longitudinal surveys that have been undertaken over the past 20 years or so. All have been sponsored by the federal government. These two types of survey data share several important advantages. With respect to test data, there is little doubt that such surveys are based on the most representative national samples available of girls, women, boys, and men across the country. They also offer more extensive data than the sources already described; notably, additional information on personal experiences and schooling, developed proficiency, and accomplishments. Finally, because of the nature of the samples and the data available, survey data offer possibilities for cross-sectional comparisons that go considerably beyond those afforded by normative data from testing programs. Aside from these attractive features, which they share, NAEP and longitudinal surveys tend to have complementary advantages as databases.

NAEP has monitored the scholastic achievement of American youth since 1969. There have been two largely independent series of NAEP assessments. One has been based on essentially the same set of Trend Tests in mathematics, science, reading, and writing at ages 9, 13, and 17 (Mullis, Owen, & Phillips, 1990). Another is the Report Card series based on regular assessments at Grades 4, 8, and 12 in those same subjects plus assessments in civics, history, and geography in selected years (Mullis, Dossey, Foertsch, Jones, & Gentile, 1991).

Of the two types of NAEP assessments, the Report Cards are the more comprehensive, with respect to attention devoted to test content, as well as the collection of supplementary information concerning the behavior of students and teachers, characteristics of courses and schools, and other information relevant to understanding the achievement of young people. Detailed information is a major strength of the NAEP data. A great deal of comparative data of this type on female and male students has been analyzed and reported by NAEP in its regular reports and detailed technical documents. NAEP has given little emphasis to special studies and reports on gender, per se, although there have been such efforts by individual investigators (e.g., Armstrong, 1985; Han, Cleary, & Rakaskietisak, 1992).

Comprehensive longitudinal studies of American youth started with Project Talent (Flanagan, et al., 1962) over three decades ago. Starting in 1972 there have been three major studies initiated at 8-year intervals: the National Longitudinal Study (NLS) in 1972, High School and Beyond

(HSB) in 1980, and the National Education Longitudinal Study (NELS) in 1988. A main feature and strength of these studies has been, as the name implies, their longitudinal character. Although there is less emphasis on assessment than is true of NAEP, these surveys—repeated periodically with the same students—have collected extensive information on the educational and career planning and experience of young people.

Gender has not been a primary focus in these studies, although there have been a number of useful reports on the experience and achievement of young women and men (Ekstrom et al., 1988; Hogrebe, Nist, & Newman, 1985; Marsh, 1989; Moore & Smith, 1987; Rock, Ekstrom, Goertz, & Pollack, 1986; Rock & Pollack, 1992; Snow & Ennis, 1996). Two reports illustrate the strength of such rich databases in attempting to unravel complex gender patterns. Snow and Ennis (1996) used various personal characteristics of eighth-grade girls and boys in the NELS sample to explore cognitive differences in mathematics proficiency at different percentile levels. Ekstrom et al. used the extensive HSB database to understand better how such proficiencies develop through the school years.

The Cleary Study

Cleary (1992) recently carried out an extensive study of gender differences in test performance at the University of Iowa. Her work reflects important aspects of each of the three types of studies just outlined. She used selected meta-analytic techniques to examine 704 data sets based on norms from 12 major test batteries, a number of state testing programs, and several national surveys of student achievement. The standard difference, D, was computed for mean scores, and for the female–male difference at the 10th, 50th, and 90th percentile points where the information was available. Cleary examined variation in D in relation to six factors: (a) quantitativeness of the test, (b) complexity of the test, (c) age of the sample, (d) selectivity of the sample, (e) percentile level within the sample, and (f) year the test was administered.

She found that each of these factors, except the last one, was related to level of gender difference—always in the direction of male advantage. Figure 2.3 illustrates such relationships for three of the factors in the case of mathematics tests. With increasing age, males performed better than females. The largest increase occurs at the highest age level, but that change is also associated with a move from an unselective to a selective sample of examinees. The relationship of gender difference to selectivity is also indicated by the fact that D tended to be more negative (favoring males)

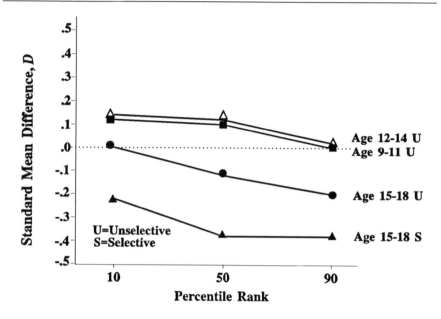

FIG. 2.3. Standard mean differences on mathematics tests for four age groups at three percentile ranks. This figure was adapted from Cleary (1992). She subtracted female from male to obtain *D*, but the order is reversed here and the figure redrawn to be consistent with notation used throughout this book. Reprinted by permission of Educational Testing Service, the copyright owner.

among the more able students at the 90th percentile than was the case for students at the 10th percentile. Regardless of the reason for the gender imbalance at the top and bottom, males will be overrepresented in a selected group drawn mainly from the top.

Cleary included a variety of tests in her study, but prior to her untimely death in 1991, she only undertook analysis of three types of measures—verbal, mathematics, and science. She defined these three types as increasingly quantitative and reported that, in that order, they were increasingly associated with higher performance by males. She also categorized the verbal and the mathematics tests according to degree of complexity of the tasks presented to the examinee, concluding in each case that males did relatively better on the more complex tasks. Her verbal categories did not include writing.

Cleary (1992) emphasized that distributions of male and female scores are more similar than they are different, but she expressed special concern over the lower performance by women on more complex tests—a disadvantage she found to be greatest at the upper percentile levels, and to increase as age increases and as quantitativeness increases. She concluded, saying, "it is imperative that educators try to understand test score differences. Those who are concerned with the education of young women need to develop programs that will enable them to perform better on more complex tasks" (p. 76).

Cleary made several important contributions to the study of gender differences. Her quite systematic analysis of normative data on a wide range of tests clearly demonstrated the advantages of such data. Part of the advantage stems from Cleary's introduction of a stratified method of analysis that enabled her to examine successively the possible effects of each factor and how it might interact with other factors. Her systematic analysis of gender differences at different points on the score distribution also broke new ground as an additional way of studying the effects of sample selectivity.[7]

Cleary's results also posed new puzzles and provoked interesting questions. Three factors appear to play some role in gender differences in test performance: what the test measures, the age cohort, and the selectivity of the sample. But what is the effect of each and how do they interact? Cleary documented the fact that gender differences favoring males are frequently larger at the top of score distributions. She and others have found a larger male advantage on tests taken by more select samples of students at older ages. How important is that apparent connection between score variability, sampling, and age? How does it work? Does test complexity play a role, as Cleary suspected? How might other factors such as different patterns of interest and experience for females and males explain score differences in different subject areas? Such questions greatly aided our thinking in planning the present study, and they run through much of the following three chapters.

Viewing the past 20 years of research on gender differences in test performance, several trends seem apparent. Earlier, the primary emphasis was on overall gender effects. How large were the differences between women and men? Were they changing? Much of the attention was focused on relative performance on verbal and mathematics tests. Increasingly, however, researchers have recognized the complexity of the topic, and have

---

[7]In recent years, Cleary and several colleagues at the University of Iowa were evaluating gender differences at different percentile levels (see, e.g., Becker & Forsyth, 1990). She was the first, however, to examine systematically the relationship of D_{10} and D_{90} to other factors that affect gender difference. This D_P statistic is, in its practical effect, similar to an approach suggested later by Feingold (1992b, 1993b, 1995). The apparent virtue of these two methods—combining the effect of a difference in means with the effect of a difference in standard deviations—seems also to be their main weakness. Both methods trade on the fact that a larger or smaller ratio of females to males in the tail can be indicated with the modified D metric. In a selected group, either a mean difference or a difference in representation may be quite important, for different reasons. The proper interpretation and practical implications of their combined effect is less obvious.

attempted to get beyond mean differences and broad labels that subsume quite varied skills and knowledge. Correspondingly, there has been recent development of new statistical methods that are useful in better understanding the role of individual differences, group variability, and sampling effects. Our study builds on these trends.

DESIGN OF THE PRESENT STUDY

Because research on gender differences in achievement has been largely concerned with studies of test performance, our own work starts from that foundation. Thus, the following discussion springs directly from that preceding, and is related specifically to the data collection and analysis reported in chapter 3 on test performance. As will become obvious, however, many of the research questions raised here apply equally well to the analysis of other types of achievement in chapter 4. The technical definitions and methods of analysis described here have been similarly applied to both types of data.

Three Sources of Variation

Chapter 1 explained the background of our study and its main purpose: to advance understanding of gender differences in achievement in order to better ensure fairness of present tests and to learn more of what we need to know in order to develop new forms of assessment that are as fair as possible. Although gender differences are generally small, our review of previous research suggests a number of ways in which the test performance of boys and men and girls and women can differ. As we have indicated, the various factors that appear to be most useful in describing gender similarities and differences can be usefully grouped into three main sources of variation: (a) the construct, or what the test measures; (b) the cohort, or type of population; and (c) the selectivity of the sample.

Construct Differences. We use the term *construct* in referring generally to the knowledge and skills that a test purports to measure. Tests categorized as to subject knowledge in history, literature, biology, and so on, are concerned with quite different constructs, each broad in nature. It is important to appreciate that a test score represents performance on a given set of items or exercises. Different tests with the same construct label (e.g., history) may vary widely depending on what they contain. Constructs may vary as to the cognitive skills involved and may turn on more subtle and narrow distinctions like math computation versus math knowledge versus math reasoning.

As used by measurement specialists, *construct* may refer to a specific skill or a sharply defined body of knowledge. Most tests in actual use are more complex and reflect several closely related constructs. One can think of two complex constructs as varying in several ways; for example, by representing different knowledge domains, or emphasizing different aspects of a knowledge domain or by using assessment formats that call for somewhat different skills (e.g., essay or multiple choice). Among the three main lines of inquiry described here, an improved understanding of how construct differences are related to gender differences seems most likely to improve our ability to build fair tests.

Cohort Differences.   Descriptive data often include successive cohorts of young people that vary by age or grade, or from year to year. Thus cohorts represent different *populations* of students defined in some such manner. Systematic differences in female and male achievement from one cohort to another may have important educational implications. However, if left uncontrolled in comparing female and male performance, differences among cohorts can easily yield misleading conclusions about construct differences. Examination of gender differences within a cohort—for example, different ethnic groups—can also be helpful in understanding why women and men grow up to be both similar and different.

A given cohort is never represented by a total population—say, all 13-year-olds in 1988. Rather, data are available on random or stratified samples of such students—typically the population of students in school. Ethnic minorities tend to be underrepresented in such populations, but our primary concern here is gender. Girls and boys in late adolescence appear to be reasonably well-represented in school cohorts. In recent years, high school dropout rates have been roughly comparable for females and males (see footnote 2 in chapter 3). Different samples from the same population will typically give somewhat different results. Samples can be unrepresentative in various ways, and small samples are more prone to random fluctuations. When sample is used in this context, we have usually referred to a representative sample or a national sample.

Sample Differences.   In this analysis we are mainly interested in sample differences that come about because a group is selected or restricted in some manner. There are many ways in which a selected sample of test examinees can vary. Three distinctions are important to bear in mind:

1. An "available" sample (e.g., students in a particular school or volunteers for a special study) is likely to be unrepresentative of a national age or grade population in unknown ways.
2. Some self-selected samples, like students who elect to take an admissions test, are clearly unrepresentative of their age group. On the other hand, understanding the characteristics of such groups is important in its own right. There is often a good deal of information about these groups and they may remain relatively stable from year to year but change over time.
3. Selected samples are also subject to systematic influences, such as restriction in the range of scores that usually occurs (i.e., fewer low scores) when groups of students individually elect to take a test.

As we will see, the range of test scores is often not the same for females and males, even in representative samples. If the range varies for women and men, that can cause a selected sample of low-scoring or high-scoring students to show gender differences even though none were observed for a representative sample taking the same test. In summary, some gender differences associated mainly with a particular selected sample may be intrinsically interesting, but differences that come from unknown or random fluctuations are better viewed as "noise" that clouds results and may invite misleading conclusions.

In recent years, researchers have learned a good deal about how different factors influence gender differences in achievement, but it is a complex topic and, in our view, there is still much to learn. Simply put, our main purpose in the analysis reported here was to make further progress in disentangling the effects of construct, cohort, and sample differences. Some success in doing so should help to extend what we know about particular areas of strength and weakness for young women and men, how those patterns are related to developing proficiency through the grades, what changes may have occurred in recent years, and what implications there may be for assessment and for education.

In designing our study of test performance, the main decisions concern the choice of data and the method of analysis. Our interest in disentangling the effects of different constructs, cohorts, and samples had several major design implications. First, to examine the interaction of these three factors requires data on multiple tests represented in each of multiple age and year cohorts, with score scales that are comparable from group to group, so that one factor can be examined in some detail while the others are controlled. Second, the samples need to be stable; this means large and representative, or at least large and reasonably well-understood. Third, it is desirable to have diverse tests of important knowledge and skills. Finally, appropriate metrics and types of analysis are needed to understand gender differences for different students, the implications for various types of test use, and the possible effects of sample variations.

From these considerations, it was evident that we needed a great deal of test data for this task—not data from whatever samples happened to be available, but data on large samples that are nationally representative or otherwise intrinsically interesting because they bear on important educational and career discussions. Needless to say, it is largely traditional tests for which such data are available—more specifically, major test programs and surveys for which one can obtain large sets of data for different ages, years, subgroups, and so on. Our emphasis is on tests and assessments normally associated with educational achievement. In chapters 4 and 7 we add data from representative samples on a broader range of experience and performance, but we have made no effort to canvas the research literature in search of small individual studies that might include test data on interesting skills and proficiencies, but based on unknown samples. That decision was based largely on the lack of comparability and the difficulty in interpreting such studies.

All of the tests of educational achievement included in our analyses are summative rather than formative. That is, we have used tests that represent the knowledge and skill that students have developed, rather than tests that are used in an ongoing instructional process. Thus, the tests in our analyses are largely end-of-course examinations, assessments of educational outcomes, and tests used in various types of selective situations—admissions, placement, and so on. In this context we use the term *selection* quite broadly to include self-selection and influence of counselors, in addition to institutional admissions decisions.

We have excluded employment, certification, and licensing tests, partly because representative national data on such tests are largely not available, and partly to limit the scope of this study to manageable proportions. Finally, in the course of studying work to date, we became convinced that the best hope for further disentangling the various factors that interact to create the observed patterns of gender differences and similarities was to pursue a "stratified" form of meta-analysis somewhat like the approach used by Cleary (1992). It is also clear that any gender difference in the distribution of scores can play an important role, which suggests that an informative analysis must go considerably beyond a simple description of the overall mean difference between female and male scores. With this general orientation, we can now describe the test data sets and the statistical indicators used in the study.

Test Data

The stratified framework of test batteries and samples used in our analyses is illustrated in Fig. 2.4. The five columns correspond to age–grade levels. Data for the test batteries in the first three columns were all based on national samples of students (test batteries 1–15).

Data for test batteries in the last two columns (test batteries 16–24) were all based on program norms; that is, individuals who elected to take each particular test. *Series* is used here to designate a battery from which an examinee would take only one or perhaps a few tests rather than a complete battery. The 24 batteries were as follows:

1. ITBS. *Iowa Test of Basic Skills.* A battery of 13 achievement tests used to assess knowledge and skills in Grades K through 8.
2. TAP. *Tests of Achievement and Proficiency.* A battery of six tests measuring knowledge and skills in Grades 9 through 12, coordinate with the Iowa Test of Basic Skills.
3. STANF. *Stanford Achievement Tests.* A battery of 12 achievement tests designed for Grades K through 8.
4. TASK. *Stanford Test of Academic Skills.* A series of eight tests for Grades 9 through 12, coordinate with the Stanford Achievement Test.
5. NAEPr. *National Assessment of Educational Progress—Report Cards.* The most recent of the comprehensive NAEP surveys of educational achievement in each of seven subject areas, typically at Grades 4, 8, and 12.[8]
6. NAEPt. *National Assessment of Educational Progress—Trend Tests.* A series of assessments in four subject areas at age 9, 13, and 17 that have been administered with varying frequency but essentially the same content since 1969.
7. IAEP. *International Assessment of Educational Progress.* A test in mathematics and a test in science administered to national samples of 9-year-old students and 13-year-old students in conjunction with a multinational study in 1991.
8. DAT. *Differential Aptitude Tests.* A battery of eight ability tests designed for educational and career guidance in Grades 8 to 12.

---

[8]Each of the most recent major NAEP Report Card assessments was included. Depending on the particular subject, these assessments occurred in the years 1988 to 1992 and are designated NAEPr in Fig. 2.4. The NAEP Trend Tests are a separate series administered every few years with essentially the same content in each successive survey. These are designated NAEPt in Fig. 2.4. In order to realize the benefit of these multiple administrations to stability of results, gender differences reported for the NAEP Trend Tests in Table S-4 in the *Supplement* and related analyses are based on average *D*s for 1992 and the previous 8 years (typically, three surveys per subject in that period). Students are typically identified by age level in defining NAEP Trend Test samples and by grade level in defining NAEP Report Card samples. For simplicity as well as consistency with other databases, all NAEP data are here typically reported by grade level. For the Trend Tests, NAEP selected 17-year-olds (or 11th graders in the case of writing), who are more often in the 11th grade. As with other databases, we have referred to all 11th- and 12th-grade data as Grade 12. Report Card surveys are based on independent samples. In the Trend Surveys, mathematics and science tests are administered to the same samples of students. Reading and writing are administered to nearly the same samples, but independent of the math–science surveys.

9. NELS. *National Education Longitudinal Study of 1988*. A national study, including a four-test battery, of a representative sample of eighth-grade students in 1988, retested in the 12th grade.[9]

10. HSB. *High School and Beyond*. A national study, including a six-test battery, of a representative sample of young adults in 1980.

11. NLS. *National Longitudinal Study*. A national study, including a six-test battery, of a representative sample of 12th-grade students in 1972.

12. ASVAB. *Armed Services Vocational Aptitude Battery*. A battery of 10 ability and information tests designed for educational and career guidance of armed service personnel; data here based on a representative national sample of young adults.

13. NALS. *National Adult Literacy Survey*. National surveys of adult proficiency in three areas; 1987 and 1992.

14. PSAT. *Preliminary Scholastic Aptitude Test/National Merit Scholarship Qualification Test*. A slightly shorter version of the SAT used for guidance and scholarship screening at Grade 11. The only battery of the 24 for which both selective program data and national norms data are available.

15. ITED. *Iowa Tests of Educational Development*. A battery of seven tests of knowledge and skills in Grades 9 through 12.

16. ACT. *ACT Assessment*. A battery of four tests used in college admissions (revised in 1990).

17. AP. *Advanced Placement Program*. A series of 29 subject tests based on course syllabi that are used as a basis for granting college credit for college-level work completed in high school.

18. SAT. *Scholastic Aptitude Test*. A battery of two reasoning tests used in college admissions (revised in 1994; now named *Scholastic Assessment Test*). The SAT–PSAT link permits estimation of national norms data for SAT.

19. ATP. *Admissions Testing Program*. A College Board series of 15 tests of subject knowledge and skill used in undergraduate admissions.

20. GRE—G. *Graduate Record Examinations—General Test*. A battery of three ability tests used in graduate admissions.

21. GRE—S. *Graduate Record Examinations—Subject Tests*. A series of tests of knowledge and skill in 16 fields of study used in graduate admissions.

22. MCAT. *Medical College Admission Test*. A battery of four tests used in admission to medical schools (revised in 1991).

23. GMAT. *Graduate Management Admission Test*. A battery of two tests used in admission to graduate management schools.

24. LSAT. *Law School Admission Test*. A single-score test used in admissions by all accredited law schools.

---

[9]The NELS tests (Battery 9 in Fig. 2.4) were essentially the same at Grades 8 and 12. The main difference in the 8th- and 12th-grade tests was the replacement of some easier items with similar, more difficult ones. The tests were administered at Grade 12 to those students still enrolled in the same schools, making this the only national longitudinal retested sample available in recent years and the only one included here. Some students and schools were added at the 12th grade so as to make up a "freshened" sample that would be representative of 12th graders across the country.

	General Population National Norms		Self-Selective Program Data	
Grade 4	Grade 8	Grade 12	College Applicants	Grad/Prof. Applicants
1. ITBS ——> ITBS ——>2. TAP				
3. STANF——> STANF——> 4. TASK				
5. NAEPr——> NAEPr——> NAEPr				
6. NAEPt——> NAEPt——> NAEPt				
7. IAEP——> IAEP				
	8. DAT——> DAT			
	9. NELS ——> NELS			
		10. HS&B		
		11. NLS		
		12. ASVAB		
		13. NALS		
		14. PSAT Norms——>PSAT/NMSQT		
		15. ITED	16. ACT	
			17. AP	
			18. SAT	20. GRE-G
			19. ATP	21. GRE-S
				22. MCAT
				23. GMAT
(——> coordinate tests)				24. LSAT

FIG. 2.4. Data on test performance: Grade levels and connections among the 24 test batteries analyzed.

In a sense the middle column of Fig. 2.4 (Grade 12) is the fulcrum of our database. The 12 test batteries represented in this column include 74 tests, each administered to national samples of students, most frequently in the spring of the 11th grade or the fall of the 12th grade (for convenience, cited as Grade 12, unless otherwise specified).[10] These 12 batteries include: (a) several that are widely used in secondary schools for evaluation and guidance,

---

[10]We have typically referred to this large data set as Grade 12, but there are two qualifications to bear in mind. Some tests are normally administered in the 11th grade, others in the 12th grade, depending on the nature of the program or the subject tested. When test publishers provide national norms, some carry out that norming at both grades, either in the spring, fall, or both. Where possible, 12th-grade spring norms were avoided due to the problem of questionable motivation of examinees in that period when, typically, no important decisions are affected by the score. For our purposes it was often impractical to differentiate 11th- and 12th-grade data and normally not useful to do so. Although these two grades are merged in most analyses reported, this is not to say that their distinction is always inconsequential. For example, there are several lines of evidence that gender differentiation of course selection in advanced mathematics shows up in a widened performance advantage of males at that level. (See change in D from 11th-grade PSAT-M to 12th-grade SAT-M in Fig. 3.9 and discussion in the "Mathematics" section of chapter 7.) The National Adult Literacy Survey (NALS) is a different kind of exception. For this study we used examinees from the NALS representative national sample of adults that were school age (16–24), but the sample was not school based.

(b) the major longitudinal surveys undertaken over the past two decades, and (c) all of the latest round of NAEP assessments. Thus, this large set of data represents a broad profile of standardized test results for the general run of students near the end of secondary school. One consideration in choosing among test batteries was the availability of "coordinate" tests at earlier grades; that is, tests constructed to measure similar knowledge and skills at different grade levels, scaled to permit comparison of performance across grades, and normed in the same school systems. Such data offer a view of how the 12th-Grade Profile develops through the grades; that is, one basis for teasing apart the effects of different constructs, samples, and age cohorts.

Similarly, the last two columns of Fig. 2.4 indicate tests used to evaluate changes in the pattern of gender differences on tests administered to samples of students going on to higher education. An important difference, however, is that these are self-selected rather than national samples. On average, they are high-achieving students, and the samples are not at all comparable from one test to other. The PSAT (Test 14) provides a link between these selective tests and those based on national samples. It is the same test in Columns 3 and 4 but administered to two types of samples: a nationally representative norms sample and a higher scoring group of students who elect to take the test in the annual testing program. As we will see, that linkage will prove useful because the PSAT is a shortened version of the SAT, for which data are often available in samples of students taking other selective tests in the transition from secondary to higher education.

A section in the *Supplement* provides more information about the 24 batteries used and the data available for each: publisher, sources of information, tests included, sample sizes, grade levels, years represented, and subgroup data available. Summary score statistics were obtained for pertinent samples for each of these batteries, in addition to frequency distributions for females and males as available. In many cases we were able to obtain data for both a recent year and for closely comparable tests a decade earlier.[11] Gender data within ethnic groups were also obtained for several major

---

[11]In general, data are based on subtests included in the most recent editions of test batteries. Three test batteries underwent some modification during the past few years: ACT, MCAT, and SAT. In examining trends in test performance through the 1980s (Table 3.8), data from the older battery were compared with data from 10 years later or the most recent year in which the tests were unchanged; that is, ACT in 1989, and SAT in 1992. In the profile of results for selective tests (Table 3.2), several tests from the earlier battery were included because they appeared to be materially different from any of those included in the revised battery; namely, ACT Natural Science, ACT Social Studies Reading, MCAT Chemistry, MCAT Physics, MCAT Quantitative Reasoning, and both the old TSWE and the new SAT Writing, which are adjuncts of SAT Verbal and Mathematics.

testing programs and several major surveys. Gender data from the Graduate Record Examinations Board for 14 graduate fields also proved useful. Some of this information was available in published form, but much of it came from records and data tapes generously provided by publishers and testing programs (see descriptions of the test batteries in the *Supplement*. All told, the data comprise 238 tests in 1,150 sets of data; that is, different tests within different groups defined by grade, year, ethnicity, etc.).

Descriptive Indicators

One signal achievement of the meta-analytic movement, some 20 years ago, was to drive home the idea that it is essential to have some appropriate indicator of the *size* of group differences in order to summarize and make sense of research results from multiple studies on a complex topic. Gender differences and similarities are a prime example. As in many other areas of research, the indicator most commonly used has been D, the standard mean difference between females and males.

That progress established, many writers have warned that it is a mistake to overemphasize D or to rely on that metric alone (Campbell, 1988; Feingold, 1992b; Lupkowski, 1992; Rosenthal & Rubin, 1982a). Individuals in two groups do not all score at their respective group means. The scores spread out, perhaps in different ways for the two groups. One of our objectives in this study has been to look more carefully at different aspects of gender similarities and differences that go beyond one overall number. This goal requires several indicators in addition to D, and close attention to such statistical issues as the nature of the score distribution and the effects of sampling.

There is a dilemma here. On one hand, a measure like D can provide a sensitive barometer of trends or differences that, although very small, may be consequential because they involve a number of tests or affect large numbers of people. Here, as well as in subsequent chapters, we use the term *consequential* to suggest potential importance. On the other hand, individuals vary widely within gender groups, and any single measure of group difference ignores that fact and runs the danger of fostering an inaccurate and potentially damaging stereotype. This dilemma helps to explain why there is frequent disagreement in the literature on gender differences as to how large the differences actually are and whether differences are consequential (e.g., Chipman, 1988; Glass et al., 1981; Hyde et al., 1990; Rosenthal & Rubin, 1982a; Stanley, 1992).

Furthermore, one can ask different questions about how two groups are similar and different. The practical implications may be quite different.

Consider a gender difference of −.25 favoring males on a science knowledge test in Grade 12—a finding not at all unusual. Such a small overall difference is clearly an erroneous basis for advising young women away from the study of science. However, that small difference in a general population might well mean that half again as many males as females score in the top 10% on such a test—an outcome that should certainly be cause for concern to a college science faculty searching for a diversity of well-prepared students.

The example just cited is actually conservative because it implicitly assumes that the scores of women and men follow the same normal distribution. Generally, test scores do follow a distribution that is approximately normal, although the nature of the test can affect the shape of the distribution (see Note 1 in the Lewis & Willingham report in the *Supplement*). In analyzing data it is a useful assumption to start with but not depend on. Let us now consider how an actual distribution of scores might differ from a "normal curve."

Figure 2.5 shows illustrative results for 1,000 females and 1,000 males on a 50-item test. The mean score for both groups was 29.7 and the overall standard deviation was 8.1. The top panel of Fig. 2.5 shows a normal curve reflecting those statistics. Does this curve accurately represent the number of females and males one would actually find at a particular score level?

The second and third panels of Fig. 2.5 show the actual scores. First, it is clear that there is some irregularity. The distributions are approximately normal, but they are not smooth. Although the overall mean score is the same for the two groups, more females than males scored in the 26–28 score range, and more males than females scored in the adjacent range of 23–25. There would be considerably more such irregularity if the test consisted of only a few items or exercises, as would likely be the case with a performance test. The actual data help one to appreciate that a test score represents performance on a particular set of questions. It is never a perfect measure of the intended construct.

One would not ordinarily be especially interested in the number of females and males scoring in a particular score interval. More important would be the number scoring above or below a particular score that, for example, might qualify for a teaching license or advance one's chances of admission to a very selective educational program. How well does the normal curve predict the number of females and males who score above or below a given score? The answer to that question is likely to depend less on whether the two distributions are exactly normal than on whether the female and male scores are equally variable; that is, whether the standard deviations are approximately the same.

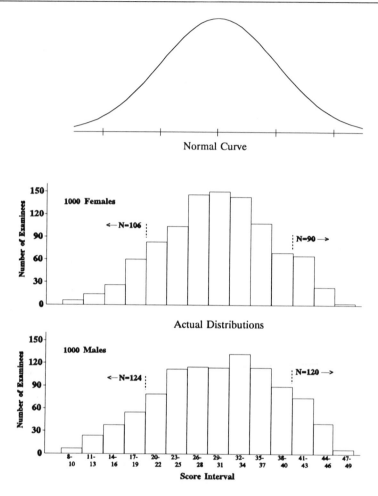

FIG. 2.5. A normal curve representing a total group of examinees and actual distributions of females and males in each score interval.

On the basis of the total group mean and standard deviation (represented by the normal curve at the top of Fig. 2.5), one would predict that 102 females and 102 males would score above 40. As the figure indicates, the actual count above a score of 40 was 90 females and 120 males—33% more males. Similarly, one would predict on the basis of the total group statistics that 115 females and 115 males would score below 20. Again, the actual data show more males and fewer females.

These results reflect what is clear on close inspection of the picture. The male scores tend to spread more. Although the means are the same for the two groups, the standard deviations are not. The standard deviations were

7.7 for females and 8.6 for males. The most important deviation from strictly comparable score distributions for women and men does appear to be a tendency for men's scores to be somewhat more variable. That tendency has important implications for understanding score differences, and we examine it in some detail in chapter 3. For the moment, assume the simple case of two normal distributions of equal size for women and men, as shown in Fig. 2.6.

The two score distributions for women and men in Fig. 2.6 are separated by .40 standard deviation units. Therefore, the first indicator of gender difference here is a D equal to .40—positive .40 because the women's mean score is higher. One can also compute a value for D at any point on the score distribution. For example, D_{90} would refer to the score at the 90th percentile for females minus the score at the 90th percentile for males, divided by the same standard deviation as used for D. This idea is illustrated in Fig. 2.6. Such an indicator was used extensively by Cleary in order to determine whether gender difference on a particular test showed any variation for students at different score levels (see, e.g., Fig. 2.3). As the illustration in Fig. 2.6 suggests, D_{90} is identical to D at the mean when both female and male scores are normally distributed and equally variable; that is, they have equal standard deviations.[12]

Again, how big is a D of .40? Using the guidelines suggested by Cohen, .40 is in the midrange of "small." That is visually confirmed by the fact that the two distributions overlap substantially. It is important to emphasize that, in assessing gender difference and similarity, a D as large as .40 is actually observed only infrequently in general populations, although that value does occur with some frequency in selected populations. Also, other group comparisons may easily exceed .40, as was observed in Fig. 2.2.

In order to add perspective, it may be useful to compare D with two other measures that are sometimes used to indicate the extent of group difference. One is R_{pb}, which is simply the correlation between group membership and the measure in question. Another is %Var, the percentage of all variation in scores that is associated with group membership. A potential problem with both of these measures is the possible suggestion of some functional link between gender and the characteristic in question. Although the measures express a form of association, they are, in fact, based only on mean differences that do not imply attribution or causality to gender.

---

[12]See discussion on pages 4 to 6 in the Lewis and Willingham report in the *Supplement* and accompanying notes and tables.

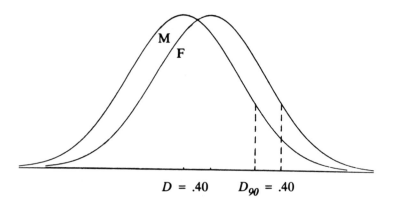

FIG. 2.6. Illustration of the standard difference between scores at the 90th percentile for females and males, respectively, (D_{90}) when D at the mean is +.40 and standard deviations are equal.

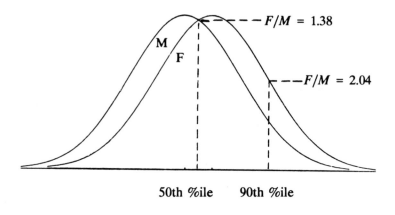

FIG. 2.7. Illustration of the ratio of females to males (F/M) above the 50th and 90th percentiles when D at the mean is .40 and standard deviations are equal.

Table 2.2 shows selected values of these two indicators along with corresponding values of D. Note that if D is negative (i.e., males have a higher mean score), R_{pb} and %Var would have the same values as indicated, although the Rs would all be negative. Although D, R_{pb}, and %Var are all closely related, D has the more desirable characteristics and is the one almost always used in describing gender differences in recent years. Accordingly, we have used D throughout, but we have also used %Var in selected figures because it gives another useful perspective on the degree of group overlap.

Table 2.2 shows that a D of .40 is equivalent to a correlation of approximately .20, which is viewed as a relatively weak relationship in most contexts.

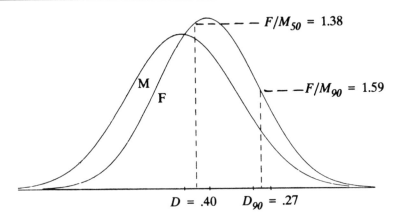

FIG. 2.8. Illustration of gender differences in the upper tail when D at the mean is .40 (females higher) and the standard deviation for females is .90 that for males.

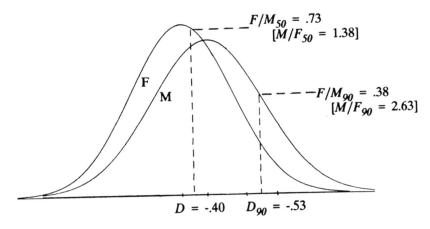

FIG. 2.9. Illustration of gender differences in the upper tail when D at the mean is −.40 (males higher) and the standard deviation for females is .90 that for males.

Similarly, the corresponding value for %Var indicates that in this instance only 3.8% of all score variation is associated with gender. Both observations are consistent with Cohen's characterization of Ds in the range of .20 to .50 as small. However, such general labels can be misleading. As Rosenthal and Rubin (1982b) demonstrated, in evaluating the implications of gender differences it may be important to determine how many females and males score at a particular level, as well as the possible consequences of any discrepancy observed. In this spirit we have used another indicator of gender difference in our analysis: the ratio of females to males (F/M). The F/M ratio has several variations and applications that fall generally into two types:

TABLE 2.2

**Selected Values Showing Relationships Among
Several Possible Indices of Gender Difference**

1. Standard Mean Difference, Female–Male	D	.00	.20	.40	.60	.80
2. Correlation with gender ($F = 1$)	R_{pb}	.00	.10	.20	.29	.37
3. Percentage of score variation associated with gender	%Var	0	1.0	3.8	8.3	13.8
4. Ratio of females to males						
a. Above the 50th percentile	F/M_{50}	1.00	1.17	1.38	1.62	1.90
b. Above the 90th percentile	F/M_{90}	1.00	1.42	2.04	2.95	4.37

1. *Participation*—How many females and males elect a program, take a particular course, engage in an activity, and so on.
2. *Achievement*—How many females and males achieve a given score level, reach a given level of accomplishment, win a particular award, and so on.

Where necessary for clarity, we have identified these two types of ratios in tables or text as F/M_P and F/M_A (see Note S-2 in the *Supplement*). It is the second type of ratio, pertaining to achievement, that complements D and is illustrated in Fig. 2.7. As in Fig. 2.6, scores for females and males are both distributed normally in Fig. 2.7 and are separated by .40 standard deviation units, with the female mean higher. This figure illustrates the ratio of females to males scoring above selected percentile levels. It is clear that the farther out the right tail one chooses to count, the more disproportionate the ratio. This phenomenon results simply from the difference at the mean and the shape of the distribution. If males have the higher mean, one would expect the same gender discrepancies in the tail, but favoring males. Thus, in Table 2.2 we can readily determine the values of F/M that would obtain if D were negative simply by taking the reciprocal of the figures indicated (e.g., $F/M_{90} = 2.04$ when $D = .40$, but $1/(2.04)$ or .49 when $D = -.40$).[13]

Figure 2.7 forcefully illustrates two points. First, consideration of the number of females and males affected (i.e., selected or represented) is complementary to D. We are used to comparing only the mean difference, but as Hedges and Friedman (1993b) argued, representation may in some circumstances be a more relevant indicator of the practical consequences of a gender difference. Second, when there is some overall gender difference on a given measure of achievement, the discrepancy in the actual number of

---

[13]Table 2.2 assumes normal distributions with equal standard deviations and sample sizes. Note S-1 in the *Supplement* shows equations for and interrelations among the indices.

females and males who exceed a given score becomes greater the more extreme the score. This tail effect will vary, of course, if female and male scores do not follow the same normal distribution. In particular, female/male ratios among high (or low) scores will be affected by any difference in female and male variability. The potential importance of that factor requires careful attention.

The Role of Variability

Figures 2.8 and 2.9 illustrate the potential effects of a difference in female and male variability on indicators of gender difference (again, assuming equal sample sizes and distributions that are otherwise normal). In Fig. 2.8 females score somewhat higher on average ($D = .40$). In Fig. 2.9 males score higher by the same amount ($D = -.40$). In both figures, the female scores are slightly less variable; that is, the female standard deviation is .90 that of the male standard deviation, which is close to the average figure we report in chapter 3. Several points are illustrated by comparing Figs. 2.8 and 2.9 with the two previous Figs. 2.6 and 2.7, where there was no gender difference in the variability of scores.

- A difference in variability has little if any effect on gender difference at the mean, but it can have a consequential effect in the tails. This phenomenon is apparent in comparing D_{90} and F/M_{90} in Fig. 2.8 with corresponding values in the two previous figures.
- Greater male variability tends to work to the advantage of males at the top of the score distribution. If male scores are more variable, there is less female advantage at the top than would ordinarily result from a higher female mean (see Fig. 2.8). As a corollary effect, more variable male scores exaggerate any male advantage at the top that would ordinarily result from a higher male mean. This shows up in Fig. 2.9 as a D that is more negative at the 90th percentile than at the mean ($-.53$ rather than $-.40$) and a F/M ratio that is larger in the upper tail (2.63 rather than 2.04) than would be expected if the shape of the two distributions were the same.
- The bottom of the score distribution will tend to show complementary effects if there is greater male variability; for example, an excess of male scores at the bottom when the means are equal or the female mean is only slightly higher. That outcome is illustrated in actual data in the following chapter (see Fig. 3.7). So among low scorers, greater male variability works to the disadvantage of males.

Recognition of such effects has led several writers (e.g., Feingold, 1992b; Hedges & Friedman, 1993b; Hedges & Nowell, 1995; Humphreys, 1988) to urge more attention to the effects of differences in variability in order to understand better the character of gender differences, particularly among more able students. Feingold (1992b) recently provided a useful review of research on gender differences in variability. This is a broad topic with roots in the 19th century. It includes female and male variation in physical, physiological, affective, and intellectual characteristics. At best, the topic has had a checkered history, filled with contradictory findings and controversy. Feingold cited, for example, the writings of Thorndike (1910) and Hollingworth (1914), who tried to demonstrate, respectively, that males were more variable by nature or, conversely, that observed differences in variability were due to social circumstances and prejudice against women.

In her comment on Feingold's review focusing on intellectual abilities, Noddings (1992) described "the social history that aroused fiery passions and induced feminists to call it a 'pernicious hypothesis'" (p. 85). This quite justified reaction of early writers was stimulated especially by an associated theory, which as Dijkstra (1986) characterized the view, cast woman as inherently undifferentiated, lacking in exceptional features, and destined to fulfill a specialized social role.

Although difference in variability has not received anything like the attention of difference in mean achievement, it has not been a totally neglected topic in gender-related research. McNemar and Terman (1936) conducted a review of available data more than a half-century ago, concluding that the evidence was not sufficient to confirm or refute. In their extensive review some years later, Maccoby and Jacklin (1974) concluded, "In summary, we do find some evidence for greater male variability in numerical and spatial abilities but not consistently in verbal abilities" (p. 118). They cited a variety of studies indicating overrepresentation of males at both the top and the bottom of distributions that describe different characteristics of females and how they function. Referring to dysfunction, they noted greater vulnerability of boys to birth injury, childhood disease, developmental problems, mental retardation, and reading problems in the early grades. At the other end of the scale, Maccoby and Jacklin cited the work of Stanley, Fox, and Keating (1972), who were then beginning to report yearly studies that consistently found boys heavily represented among mathematically precocious middle school students.

Recent analyses seem generally consistent, finding somewhat greater male variability on many tests and little if any difference on others. For example, in two analyses of Iowa Tests of Basic Skills and Iowa Tests of Educational Development, most of the subtests show a pattern of somewhat greater male variability (Becker & Forsyth, 1990; Martin & Hoover, 1987).

Cleary (1992) gave close attention to distributional differences in her recent large study of test norms and survey data. She did not report data on variability, per se, but did refer in her discussion to the male variance (a common statistical index that is simply the square of SD) being about 10% higher than the female variance on "almost all tests" (p. 54). Cleary examined the effects of this greater male variability by comparing gender difference at the 10th, 50th, and 90th percentiles. She reported greater male advantage at the higher percentile levels, a pattern that results from more variability among males. That effect is illustrated in Figs. 2.8 and 2.9. Figure 2.3 shows the results that Cleary found for mathematics tests.

Feingold (1992b) did a detailed study specifically to evaluate the variability of women's and men's achievement and ability scores. He used several sets of normative data for each of several standardized test batteries, all based on substantial national samples. He found males to be consistently more variable on tests of general knowledge, mechanical reasoning, quantitative ability, spatial visualization, and spelling. There was no consistent difference in variability on most verbal tests, or on tests of short-term memory, abstract reasoning, and perceptual speed. More recently, Hedges and Nowell (1995) reported results based on large representative samples that indicated that "the test scores of males consistently have larger variance" (p. 41).

These findings confirm that variability does often differ for females and males. Clearly, it is often necessary to take unequal standard deviations into account in order to describe accurately gender differences at different levels of proficiency. It also seems likely that unequal variability is one of the factors involved when the pattern of gender difference in a selected sample is different from that observed in the original group. In light of the obvious importance of variability, we have routinely calculated the female/male standard deviation ratio (SDR) for all test data in addition to the indicators described earlier.[14] The effect of SDR on gender differences in selected samples was examined in some detail in a special study undertaken by Lewis and Willingham (1995). Implications of those effects are discussed in chapter 3.

SUMMARY

There is a long history of research on differences and similarities in the achievements of women and men. Over the past two decades in particular, there have been a number of studies of relative performance on different

---

[14]As Hedges and Friedman (1993b) noted, it is more common among statisticians to use a variance ratio than a ratio of standard deviations. This is largely because variances are additive and the F ratio provides a convenient statistic for testing inferences. In this case, however, we judged the heuristic value of the SDR metric to be more important. SDR gives a more accurate impression of differences in variability than does SDR^2 because SDR is more directly related to range and score scale. We have provided standard errors for SDR, which have advantages over the more traditional F-test.

types of tests. This work suggests that there is no important overall differ-ence in test performance of girls and boys at younger ages, although the pattern of average scores may vary somewhat from one skill or subject to another.

As students get older and approach the end of secondary school, the previous research findings are less clear. It is also true at this age level that distributions of test scores are much more similar than they are different, although there has been a commonly noted tendency for males to pull ahead somewhat on mathematics and science tests. It is frequently observed that males tend to do somewhat better, relative to females, in selected samples at higher age–grade levels. Some writers have seen in research findings a tendency for males to do better on more complex forms of cognitive achievement. This is especially the case in mathematical problem solving.

Modern techniques of meta-analysis have done much to establish such general trends, although limitations in available data and modes of analysis that have been used to date do leave important questions outstanding. Much of the research on gender differences in recent years has focused on verbal and mathematical ability, often not well-differentiated as to type of skill or achievement. Most of the interest has centered on establishing the level of mean difference, often in diverse groups of students with little evidence that they are representative of students generally. Consequently, the outstanding questions concerning gender differences in achievement often turn on confusion as to what construct, cohort, and sample one is talking about. In the main these refer, respectively, to what the test meas-ures, what age–grade or year is involved, and how selected the group is.

The general objective of the current project is to make further progress in disentangling the relationships of different constructs, cohorts, and samples to observed gender differences in achievement. This objective is reflected in two design strategies that are reflected in both chapters 3 and 4, which follow. One is to study performance data on a broader, but more structured range of achievement measures in large samples of stu-dents—nationally representative samples supplemented by selective sam-ples based on key national testing programs. The other is to use additional means of describing and analyzing these data in order to understand better the relative representation of women and men as well as achievement level—in representative as well as selected groups. Our hope is that these further efforts to clarify ways in which the achievement of women and men are similar and different will provide useful insights into ways that assess-ment and education might be improved for all.

3

TEST PERFORMANCE

Warren W. Willingham
Nancy S. Cole
Charles Lewis
Susan Wilson Leung

This is the second of three chapters concerning similarities and differences in the achievement of women and men. We present here the results of a number of analyses of test performance. Readers should consult the previous chapter for an overview of recent research and for explanations of technical terms and procedures encountered here and in chapter 4. Chapter 4 complements chapter 3 by describing grades, accomplishments, and related characteristics of females and males that can influence achievement. In the *Supplement* to this volume, there are two important reports that extend the main text by providing additional information on possible sources of gender differences. A report by Wilder gives an overview of the principal lines of research and theory regarding possible educational, social, and biological antecedents of gender differences. A report by Lewis and Willingham presents a technical analysis of statistical effects on gender differences when samples are selected rather than representative of a general population.

The results of our analysis of gender similarities and differences in test performance are presented in five main sections. First, a 12th-Grade Profile provides a general picture of average performance differences and differences in the overall variability in the scores of young women and men at the end of high school on a wide variety of tests based on national samples of students. Second, we examine how that profile has developed from Grade 4 to Grade 12, giving special attention to changes in the distribution of proficiency. Third comes an analysis of the pattern of gender differences in selected populations of college-going and postgraduate students, and what factors seem to be at work to affect that pattern. Fourth, we look for consistencies and inconsistencies in the nature of gender similarities and differences in test performance within ethnic subgroups. Fifth comes a brief look at stability and change in female and male test performance over the past decade.

A 12TH-GRADE PROFILE

All of the test performance data in this chapter are based on original score distributions and statistics for the various test batteries as described in the previous chapter. Test data sources are described in the *Supplement*. The central portion of the data assembled for this study was based on 12 test batteries normally used with general populations at Grade 12 (Numbers 1–15 given in Figure 2.4, except for 1, 3, & 7). For this 12th-Grade Profile we generally have used the most recent data available.[1] The batteries were administered to 25 independently drawn national samples at the end of high school.

This segment of the total database has several critical characteristics. It is large and therefore stable, but more important, one can assume with some assurance that the data represent reasonably well those 12th-grade students in the country who might normally be expected to participate in national surveys and all-student testing programs. There is currently no indication of any important imbalance in the representation of females and males due to differential dropout rates or graduation from high school.[2] Most of the

---

[1]The 12th-Grade Profile was based on the most recent cohort available at the time data were collected. Typically data came from the period 1988 to 1993. (See test descriptions in the *Supplement*.) The earlier longitudinal surveys (NLS in 1972 and HSB in 1980) were exceptions. As is later observed, there is some suggestion of a different pattern of gender differences in the HSB sample compared to the other 12th-grade national data. This divergence could be associated with the earlier year of administration, but seems more likely due to small differences in the tests or to a sample fluctuation because the pattern is not mirrored in the NLS data 8 years earlier. Another exception was the use of multiple years for NAEP Trend Test data, as explained in footnote 8 in chapter 2.

[2]There are important qualifications to bear in mind. A significant number of students have dropped out of school by the 12th grade. Despite substantial efforts to mainstream as many students as possible, some disabling conditions can be assumed to be underrepresented. Educational folklore, probably accurate in this case, suggests that there is always a certain small percentage of students who are not included in testing programs—some because they are absent for different reasons, others because English is a second language, and others simply because they are not expected to score well and are therefore "overlooked." These various contingencies may be related to gender but seem difficult to evaluate with any accuracy. For example, there are small unaccountable variations in high school dropout rates for White females and males from year to year. Overall, however, there do not now appear to be consequential gender differences in high school dropout rates. In the latest data available, the rate was 12% for females and 13% for males (NCES, 1993, Table 99). Evidently the most recent published data on high school graduates broken down by gender are based on 1991 when there were 1.257 million male and 1.254 million female graduates (Snyder, 1993). Graduation rates for females and males in 1992 were also reported to be "very near 50/50, about 50.5% girls and 49.5% boys" (V. Grant [NCES], personal communication, March 4, 1996).

samples were drawn with considerable care. Despite the emphasis on traditional forms of assessment, the 74 tests included in these 12 batteries cover a wide range of knowledge and skills. Because of its character, the database offers good control of fluctuations associated with age, year of administration, and sample. Thus, the 12th-Grade Profile shown in Fig. 3.1 provides a cross-sectional snapshot in time. We think that attention can be focused on variations in the results for the constructs being assessed, without serious concern that an observed gender difference may actually be due to sampling variations or some characteristic of the groups involved.[3]

A comparison of the average performance of women and men on the 74 tests grouped into 15 categories is summarized in Table 3.1. For each test and each test category, Table 3.1 shows the value of D, the standard mean difference between the scores of women and men.[4] The average D for all 74 tests was .02. This gives us our first general conclusion: Based on a wide variety of tests and a number of large nationally representative samples of high school seniors, we see no evidence of any consequential difference in the average test performance of young women and men.

Figure 3.1 also includes a scale for %Var, directly related to D, which shows what percentage of all test score variation is associated with gender. These percentages are, in general, quite small. Individual differences *within* gender clearly account for most of the variation among scores.

To be sure, this is not a random sample of tests and a different average D might well result from a different selection of tests, but these batteries represent many if not most of the serious national efforts in recent years to assess the performance of young people, and they include tests in subjects and developed skills that informed educators have considered most important.

It is an oversimplification, of course, to say simply that there are no gender differences in test performance. There are some important differences in average performance for individual tests and for some types of tests. The individual tests have been grouped, as indicated in Table 3.1, into 15

---

[3]One way of guarding against unwarranted conclusions is to test every possible difference of interest to evaluate its statistical significance. This approach is not necessarily wise (Cohen, 1994), is not always possible, and given the amount of data involved, would be quite tedious for both researcher and reader. We have sought to achieve the same judicious end by providing standard errors (in parentheses) for the statistics of interest. This mode of interpretation has the decided advantage of keeping the emphasis on the size of the difference rather than its statistical significance. See Note S-3 in the *Supplement* for further details, including equations for the computation of standard errors for standard mean difference, standard deviation ratio, ratios of the numbers of female to male students (actual participation, corrected participation, actual achievement, corrected achievement), the difference between any two statistics, and the mean of a set of statistics.

[4]In order to avoid underestimating standard errors for category means in Table 3.1, no more than one test was used from a given test battery.

TABLE 3.1

Standard Mean Differences, D (With Standard Errors), for Each of 74 Tests Administered to National Samples of Students at Grade 12

ACADEMIC ACHIEVEMENTS			
VERBAL-Writing			
NAEPt Writing		.59	(.025)
NAEPr Writing		.54	(.027)
	Mean	**.57**	**(.018)**
VERBAL-Language Use			
TAP Written Expression		.53	(.044)
ITED Correct. & Approp. of Expres.		.47	(.053)
DAT Language Usage		.46	(.044)
DAT Spelling		.45	(.044)
TASK Spelling		.36	(.036)
TASK English		.33	(.036)
	Mean	**.43**	**(.022)**
VERBAL-Reading			
ITED Abil. to Interp. Literary Mater.		.46	(.053)
NAEPr Reading		.31	(.029)
NAEPt Reading		.26	(.028)
NELS Reading		.24	(.025)
TAP Reading Comprehension		.19	(.043)
ASVAB Paragraph Comp.		.19	(.030)
TASK Reading Comp.		.14	(.035)
NALS Prose Literacy		.11	(.042)
NLS Reading		.06	(.023)
HSB Reading		.00	(.018)
	Mean	**.20**	**(.011)**
VERBAL-Vocabulary/Reasoning			
DAT Verbal Reasoning		.21	(.043)
ITED Vocabulary		.13	(.052)
NLS Vocabulary		.07	(.023)
TASK Reading Vocabulary		.06	(.035)
TAP Vocabulary		.03	(.043)
PSAT Verbal		.02	(.018)
ASVAB Word Knowledge		.01	(.030)
HSB Vocabulary		− .07	(.018)
	Mean	**.06**	**(.012)**
MATH-Computation			
ASVAB Numerical Operations		.19	(.030)
TAP Math Computation		.17	(.052)
	Mean	**.18**	**(.030)**
MATH-Concepts			
DAT Numerical Reasoning		.15	(.043)
TAP Math Concepts & Probs.		.01	(.043)
NALS Quantitative Literacy		− .02	(.042)
NELS Mathematics		− .07	(.025)
TASK Mathematics		− .08	(.035)
ITED Ability to Do Quant. Thinking		− .10	(.053)
NAEPr Mathematics		− .11	(.034)
PSAT Math		− .12	(.018)
NAEPt Mathematics		− .14	(.025)
ASVAB Mathematics Knowledge		− .14	(.030)
HSB Mathematics		− .23	(.019)
NLS Mathematics		− .24	(.023)

NLS Mathematics		− .24	(.023)
ASVAB Arithmetic Reasoning		$\boxed{- .28}$	(.030)
	Mean	**− .11**	**(.010)**
NATURAL SCIENCE			
ITED Analysis of Science Materials		$\boxed{.17}$	(.053)
TAP Science		$\boxed{.02}$	(.043)
NAEPt Science		− .24	(.025)
NAEPr Science		− .24	(.036)
TASK Science		− .27	(.035)
NELS Science		− .27	(.025)
ASVAB General Science		$\boxed{- .36}$	(.030)
	Mean	**− .17**	**(.014)**
SOCIAL SCIENCE			
ITED Anal. of Soc. Studies Materials		$\boxed{.20}$	(.053)
TAP Social Studies		.01	(.043)
TASK Social Science		$\boxed{- .15}$	(.035)
	Mean	**.02**	**(.026)**
GEOPOLITICAL			
NAEPr Civics		− .12	(.043)
NELS History/Citizen./Geog.		− .14	(.025)
NAEPr History		− .19	(.038)
NAEPt Civics		− .26	(.038)
NAEPr Geography		$\boxed{- .43}$	(.052)
	Mean	**− .23**	**(.018)**
STUDY SKILLS			
ITED Use of Sources of Info.		.30	(.052)
TAP Info. Processing		.24	(.044)
TASK Study Skills		.21	(.035)
NALS Document		.06	(.042)
	Mean	**.20**	**(.022)**
OTHER SPECIAL SKILLS			
Perceptual Speed			
ASVAB Coding Speed		.42	(.030)
DAT Perceptual Speed & Accuracy		.31	(.044)
HSB Mosaic Comparisons		.26	(.019)
NLS Mosaic		.23	(.023)
	Mean	**.31**	**(.015)**
Spatial Skills			
DAT Space Relations		− .03	(.044)
HSB Visualization in 3D		− .25	(.019)
	Mean	**− .14**	**(.024)**
Mechanical/Electronics			
ASVAB Electronics Information		$\boxed{- .78}$	(.031)
ASVAB Mechanical Comprehen.		− .83	(.031)
DAT Mechanical Reasoning		− .84	(.045)
ASVAB Auto/Shop Information		$\boxed{- 1.25}$	(.033)
	Mean	**− .93**	**(.027)**
Short-Term Memory			
NLS Picture-Number		.27	(.023)
HSB Picture-Number		.18	(.019)
	Mean	**.23**	**(.015)**
Abstract Reasoning			
NLS Letter Groups		.23	(.023)
DAT Abstract Reasoning		− .03	(.043)
	Mean	**.10**	**(.024)**

Note. Values of D that differ from their respective category means by .15 or more are boxed. Standard errors assume a design factor of 2.

Test Category	No. of Tests	SDR	%Var
			20.0 13.8 8.3 3.9 1.0 .0 1.0 3.9 8.3
Verbal-Writing	2	.96	
Verbal-Language Use	6	.93	
Perceptual Speed	4	.97	
Short-Term Memory	2	.97	
Study Skills	4	.88	
Verbal-Reading	10	.92	
Math-Computation	2	.93	
Abstract Reasoning	2	.93	
Verbal-Vocab./Reasoning	8	.95	
Social Science	3	.88	
Math-Concepts	13	.93	
Spatial Skills	2	.89	
Natural Science	7	.88	
Geo-Political	5	.89	
Mechanical/Electronics	4	.81	

-1.00 -.80 -.60 -.40 -.20 .00 .20 .40 .60

Standard Mean Difference, D

FIG 3.1. Profile of gender similarities and differences on 74 tests in 15 categories, all administered to nationally representative samples of 12th-grade students. SDR is the ratio of female to male standard deviations. %Var = Percentage of score variation associated with gender. The shaded area indicates the region where D is less than $\pm .20$; values of .20 to .50 are often referred to as "small."

categories according to what knowledge and skills each measures. In most cases the appropriate category was obvious from the content of the test. Usually test labels helped; sometimes they confused the issue. The 15 categories serve the practical purpose of sorting the available data into different types of test content, which we often refer to as constructs.

Needless to say, other categories are possible. We were less concerned with whether this was the single *correct* sorting than with achieving a framework for analysis that would be useful in further clarifying gender differences.[5] For example, we distinguished "geopolitical" subjects (e.g., civics, history, geography, comparative government, and economics) from the more socially

---

[5]In general, these 15 categories correspond quite well to selected broad factors (constructs, properly speaking) identified by Carroll (1993) in his exhaustive and authoritative summary of factor analytic studies of cognitive abilities. As is obvious, however, from Carroll's analysis as well as any thoughtful consideration of the complexity of human abilities and achievement, there is much overlap among the categories and somewhat different structuring might be equally useful. Carroll identified vocabulary knowledge as the most frequently occurring measure of verbal ability, but also distinguished several writing factors, reading factors, and others concerning knowledge of English usage and conventions. He commented that a vocabulary test may have a different factorial composition if one has a higher proportion of literary words whereas the other has a higher proportion of scientific words. Verbal reasoning, typified by the verbal analogy item type, is classified in the reasoning domain rather than the language domain, although Carroll noted that a heavy vocabulary load may bring a reasoning test closer to the verbal factor, and vice versa. Thus, the vocabulary tests included here appear to overlap somewhat with the reasoning category because they include some material normally associated with reasoning factors.

oriented subjects within social science (e.g., social studies, psychology, and sociology), because the pattern of gender differences became quite different in these two subject areas in selected samples of examinees.

The 10 "academic" categories in Table 3.1 all have connections to similar tests that students take at an earlier grade. The additional five categories listed as "special skills" are based on other tests that were also included in the batteries we studied. They add interest to the profile, but most were not pursued further. The labels "academic" and "special skills" are used here mainly as a convenient way of designating the two groups of tests and have no particular significance in our analysis. The labels do differentiate with reasonable accuracy, however, tests that are used in conjunction with school-work and tests that are used mainly for counseling and career guidance.

The bar graph in Fig. 3.1 illustrates how much difference there is in the test performance of 12th-grade women and men, *on average*, for each of the 15 categories. Several points deserve comment. Overall, the differences are certainly not large. The majority fall in the gray area from −.20 to +.20, which, according to a conventional rule of thumb (Cohen, 1988), do not even reach the level of "small." Also, %*Var* is 1% or less in that gray area. Thus, among 15 categories of tests on which performance was examined for representative groups of 12th-grade students, the most common result was that individual differences within gender accounted for at least 99% of all score variation and gender differences accounted for no more than 1%.

On the other hand, we have assumed that smaller *D*s or differences of less than .20 between *D*s may well warrant attention in order to understand better the nature of gender differences or possible sources of unfairness in tests. This is particularly true if such small differences represent a pattern of results, different types of assessment, and so on. (See chapter 2 for further comment on interpreting the size of *D*.)

There has been some success in analyzing gender differences in representative populations at the construct level. One example is Backman's (1979) analysis of Project TALENT data on 12th-grade students in 1960. From an examination of "patterns of mental abilities," she found that the gender main effect accounted for zero variance, but that gender was a considerably larger source of variation in patterns of subgroup means (i.e., test × subgroup interaction) than was either ethnicity or socioeconomic background. Insofar as the analysis is comparable, that result seems generally consistent with the findings in Fig. 3.1. Chapter 2 described efforts through meta-analysis to understand gender differences in underlying construct components, especially in mathematics (Hyde et al., 1990) and spatial ability (Linn & Petersen, 1985a).

More recent lines of work show the advantage of examining underlying constructs in addition to observed scores as, for example, they are influenced by different test content or show changing patterns by grade level in representative samples of students. A research group at Stanford has reported on several very useful studies of NELS tests in mathematics and science (Hamilton et al., 1995; Kupermintz et al., 1995; Snow & Ennis, 1996). Other promising studies in Sweden involve the analysis of gender differences on latent ability factors in a hierarchical model (Gustafsson, 1992; Harnqvist, 1997; Rosen, 1995). Several of these studies are described in subsequent sections.

It is also clear that for these 15 types of tests, the performance of females and males is reasonably balanced, although the women do outscore the men somewhat more often. A final obvious point: There are differences—sizable differences—in writing that favor women, and even larger differences in mechanical and electronics subjects that favor men.

These average differences say little if anything about the likely test performance of any one woman or man. A glance back at Fig. 2.1 in the previous chapter shows the substantial overlap of score distributions that differ by .20 standard deviations, which covers most of the categories in this profile. However, small differences overall can accumulate, or they may vary in size and consequence for particular groups—especially high and low scorers. The challenge is to understand the observed differences in sufficient detail in order to be sure that any important implications for limited subsets of students are adequately appreciated, as well as more general implications regarding education and assessment practice.

Gender Difference by Test Category

Table 3.1 gives more detail about each of the 15 test categories in the 12th-Grade Profile. It includes the standard mean difference, D, for each test and the mean for the category as a whole. Standard errors in parentheses indicate to what extent these values of D might be expected to vary by chance. See page 63 for guidelines on interpreting standard errors. Note that the standard errors are small, indicating that the Ds are usually quite stable, especially the average D for each category. A clear advantage of normative and national survey data is that large samples greatly reduce the sampling fluctuations that receive much attention in conventional meta-analyses.

It is useful to think of each category as a complex test construct, although as we shall see, all of the tests are not necessarily true to their category. An interesting question is why some tests show a somewhat different gender difference than do other tests in the same category. If the D for an individual test is enough different to be possibly interesting from a practical stand-point—say, plus or minus .15—there is seldom any question as to whether the difference is statistically significant. Such Ds are shown in boxes. Some variation in test content is the primary suspect in trying to account for such deviant values. Sampling differences cannot be totally discounted, although we doubt that sampling causes much of the differences observed in Table 3.1. (See *Supplement* Table S-2 and Note S-4.) In the following, we comment briefly on the nature of the tests in the 15 categories and the gender differences observed in each.

Interpreting Standard Errors

A few comments are necessary regarding interpretation of data presented in this volume. Any statistic—mean, standard deviation, F/M ratio—is an estimate of the "true" value for a larger population of interest. The estimate will, of course, fluctuate from sample to sample. Most of our results are based on large samples, which means that any difference of practical significance is likely to be a real difference, not merely a sampling fluctuation. Nonetheless, one must always weigh the possibility that apparent differences may simply reflect sampling variation and thus invite misleading conclusions.

Standard errors are provided for that purpose. The standard error indicates to what extent a sample statistic is likely to vary. For example, given a standard error for a particular estimate of gender difference, D, one can say with 95% confidence that the D for the population is within plus or minus two standard errors of the sample estimate. We have routinely computed standard errors for D, for the standard deviation ratio SDR, and for F/M ratios (see footnote 3.) Those values are reported in the text or, in some cases, in the *Supplement*.

A rough rule of thumb may be useful in using the standard error to compare two like statistics; for example, whether one D is larger than another. If the respective Ds are based on independent samples, the following is approximately true. One can say with 95% confidence that two Ds are different if they differ by at least three times their average standard errors.

Verbal—Writing.   Among the 10 categories of academic knowledge and skill that we have examined in this general population of students, the largest gender difference is clearly in writing, a critically important verbal skill. By writing we mean here actual production of an essay, or some similar sample of work. NAEP results have consistently confirmed female superiority in writing over the past decade.[6] Curiously, a point frequently discussed about gender differences in verbal proficiency is whether there is any longer any gender difference of consequence, the conclusion often being that there is not (see chapter 2). An obvious conclusion from Table 3.1 is that the relative level of performance of women and men varies widely among different types of verbal proficiency—some showing no gender difference, others showing a clear advantage for girls and women.

---

[6]See, for example, Applebee, Langer, and Mullis (1986); Applebee, Langer, Jenkins, Mullis, and Foertsch (1990); Mullis, Dossey, Foertsch, et al. (1991); and Applebee et al. (1994). Other recent surveys of student writing confirm these results (Miller & Welch, 1993).

Verbal—Language Use.   This category includes multiple-choice tests that assess a variety of skills and knowledge pertinent to accurate and effective writing: grammatical conventions, expression, punctuation, spelling, and so on. Like writing, these tests of language use consistently showed gender differences in the range of .35 to .50—among the larger of gender differences in test performance. The gender differences on actual writing are more impressive, however, considering that group differences would tend to be somewhat reduced by less reliable essay grades compared to objective scoring of a multiple-choice test (Breland, Camp, Jones, Morris, & Rock, 1987; Linn, 1993a, 1993b; Mazzeo, Schmitt, & Bleistein, 1993).

Verbal—Reading.   Most reading tests, including those examined here, follow a fairly standard format: a reading passage, of perhaps 100 to several hundred words in length, followed by a series of questions on the passage. The character of a reading test may vary in two important ways. First, the content of the passage may be more or less interesting or familiar to the reader. As we see in chapter 6, the subject matter of a passage can affect gender differences in performance even though special knowledge of the subject is not required to answer the question. Second, the questions may address different aspects of reading; for example, comprehension of the central theme, implications, point of view, or embedded facts.

The findings here suggest that the general population of women at the end of secondary school tend to be more proficient readers than men. Table 3.1 indicated some variation in the results for individual tests in this category, but only two Ds clearly depart from the category average. In each case there is an apparent gender tilt in the content. The test with the largest D (ITED, .46) involved interpretation of literary passages from novels, poems, and dramas. The test with the smallest D (HSB, .00) was based on five reading sections, including two on physical science and one on city planning. The test with the next smallest D (NLS, .06) was actually the same test as the HSB.

Verbal—Vocabulary/Reasoning.   Vocabulary tests are a common measure of verbal ability. The more difficult tests often require reasoning beyond simple word knowledge; for example, by requiring the examinee to make logical distinctions among similar words in order to solve verbal analogies or to supply missing words in sentences. The PSAT Verbal more closely resembles this category than any other category, although on this form of the test (for which national norm data were available), 25 of the 85 items were based on reading passages. Overall, tests in this category show little, if any, gender difference. The one that gave the most divergent results (DAT Verbal Reasoning, .21) differed in an interesting way. This test comes in an analogy format and is based on words that are much more common than those normally found in verbal ability tests.[7] Since the test does not differentiate among examinees on the basis of their knowledge of words, it might be more accurately categorized as a reasoning test (Horn, 1972).

Math—Computation.   At lower grade levels it is common to test pupils' proficiency in arithmetic calculations; for example, multiplication, division, fractions, and percentages. This small category of tests is included here because computation is clearly different from higher level math skills, and it can in these few cases be separately identified. To be sure, other math skills also involve computation but in measuring higher skills, test developers normally try to write items that do not call for much computing skill in order to get the right answer. As these results indicate, girls tend to be somewhat better than boys in computing. This difference was well-documented in a national survey some years ago (Flanagan et al., 1964).

Math—Concepts.   Overall, this category shows little gender difference of consequence, but the results vary. There are many aspects of proficiency in mathematics and different ways that it may be assessed. Mathematics tests intended for students in Grades K through 12 include a variety of content: computation, concepts of number, definitions and procedures, quantitative reasoning, applications, problem solving, knowledge specific to geometry and algebra, and so on. The most frequently reported finding has been some increase in male advantage as mathematics content becomes more complex and demanding from a cognitive perspective. Females score somewhat higher on computation, there is little gender difference on general knowledge of mathematics, and males score higher to a varying degree in problem solving and reasoning, depending on the age group and the nature of the problem (Armstrong, 1985; Benbow, 1988a, 1988b; Cleary, 1992; Doolittle, 1989; Doolittle & Cleary, 1987; Dossey, Mullis, Lindquist, & Chambers, 1988; Friedman, 1989; Gallagher, 1990; Hyde et al., 1990; Linn, 1986; Snow & Ennis, 1996).

That same pattern is observed in Table 3.1 for TAP and ASVAB, where different level skills are represented in separate math subtests. A difficulty

---

[7]For example, if one defines words that occur more than 10 times in a million words of text as common and less than 1 time in a million as rare, the word count recently compiled by Breland, Jones, and Jenkins (1994) indicates that the ratio of common to rare words in the DAT Vocabulary is about 29 to 1, whereas the corresponding ratio for HSB Vocabulary is about 1 to 10.

in interpreting some of the data for the "Math—Concepts" category is that the individual tests often include varying proportions of different proficiencies in mathematics that do not necessarily correspond to the names of the tests. It is interesting to note, for example, that the two tests in this category that have the highest and lowest Ds (+.15 and −.28) are the only ones called reasoning tests. Except for the somewhat atypical DAT result,[8] gender differences in this category range from zero to the mid-.20s, favoring males. Chapter 5 examines the possible association of cognitive level of mathematics tests and gender difference in more detail than possible with the data presented here.

Natural Science.   At Grade 12 the science tests taken by general populations of 12th graders do not ordinarily focus on a particular subject like physics or biology. Rather, their content draws from a variety of scientific topics. Consistent with previous findings, males tend to score somewhat higher. The most common D value appears to be in the range of −.25. Two science tests were positive outliers; one was negative.

The TAP and ITED batteries were normed together, so some of the differential gender effect for those two tests may be associated with the particular sample of students, although it seems unlikely that that factor alone accounts for the difference. The content of these two tests seems different from the others in an interesting way. Rather than testing knowledge of scientific facts and principles, the ITED especially, and the TAP to some degree, require interpretation of material that is provided to the student. Thus, these tests appear to place more emphasis on reading comprehension and verbal reasoning, skills on which females tend to do as well or better than males. Another interesting aspect of the ITED science test that may warrant further consideration is the use of integrated parcels of items that question the examinee on different aspects of a scientific observation or set of data.

Social Science.   This category is comprised simply of three tests characterized as social science or social studies. Each of the three comes from secondary school achievement batteries. The D values varied, as did the test content. The content of the ITED items ($D = .20$) mainly concerns social

---

[8]In Table 3.1 here and Table S-2 in the *Supplement*, DAT Numerical Reasoning is the most obvious outlier ($D = .15$). The items are computational in form, which may explain the somewhat different result; or the DAT norming sample may have leaned somewhat to more able female students. That might also help to explain the more positive result for DAT Verbal Reasoning.

issues and other human-interest topics such as health, advertising, and newspaper accounts of the day. In contrast, the TASK Social Science items ($D = -.15$) stress mainly geography, international comparisons, economics, politics, and government. Similar topics are frequently represented in the geopolitical category that follows.

Geopolitical. Tests in this category include history, civics, and geography. At this grade level such tests typically show a modest male advantage in mean score. Geography looks like an outlier because the one such test in our set showed a fairly sizable male advantage ($D = -.43$). There are other indications, however, of a significant gender difference in knowledge of geography. Among the 18,000 school winners in the 1993 National Geography Bee, the F/M (female to male) ratio was .29 (Liben, 1995). As we will see, test programs that are intended for particularly well-prepared students include more specialized tests of additional aspects of this geopolitical domain (e.g., economics and comparative government).

Study Skills. Like Social Science, Study Skills is a test found mostly in K through 12 achievement batteries. The gender difference seems to consistently favor females in the range of .20 to .30, with the exception of NALS, the adult literacy assessment. The NALS Document Literacy scale assesses the ability to interpret various documents from real life (railroad timetables, charts, figures, etc.), and may not fit well with the other tests in this category, which typically deal with skills more clearly relevant to effective schoolwork. Study skills do not appear to have been carefully researched and represented in large-scale testing programs. In the research literature there is much interest, however, in some important and apparently similar higher order cognitive skills in such domains as information processing and self-monitoring (Kuhl & Kraska, 1989; Messick, 1994c).

Other Special Skills. The final five categories in Table 3.1 represent specific abilities or developed skills that are often relevant to career guidance or job placement. These tests come mostly from the DAT and ASVAB, which are frequently used in such contexts. Of the five categories, abstract reasoning is the most general cognitive skill and is perhaps the most applicable to academic work. It shows here little gender difference of consequence. Mechanical-electronics, on the other hand, is the most dependent on accumulated knowledge in a particular area. The large gender difference ($D = -.93$) appears to reflect the well-known strong male interest in such matters.

Spatial tests measure specialized skills that vary in character, depending on the task. Some spatial tests seem more susceptible than others to reasoning what the correct answer might be as opposed to "seeing" it. As noted earlier, mental rotation is the type of spatial skill that seems most clearly to call for such visual capability and also shows the largest gender difference favoring males (see *Supplement* Table S-1). Neither of the two tests listed here includes the type of items that require mental rotation. Being able to visualize an object in three-dimensional space may be an important skill. It would certainly appear to be useful in some professions like architecture and mechanical engineering, but such tests are seldom used in academic settings. There is continuing interest and controversy regarding a possible connection between spatial skills and proficiency in some areas of mathematics (see Kupermintz, Ennis, Hamilton, Talbert, & Snow, 1995, and Lubinski & Humphreys, 1990, for recent positive and negative findings on this connection; see also chapter 2). We have not been able to examine this connection because our database included so little information on spatial tests. This does appear, however, to be an important area for further research because there may be important implications for more explicit training in spatial skills.

Female and Male Variability

As was discussed earlier, a number of writers have noted the potential importance of gender differences in score variability; that is, the tendency for male scores on many tests to have a somewhat larger standard deviation (*SD*), the usual measure of score variability (Becker & Forsyth, 1990; Becker & Hedges, 1988; Humphreys, 1988; Jensen, 1971; Maccoby & Jacklin, 1974; Martin & Hoover, 1987; McNemar & Terman, 1936). In just the past few years, several studies have confirmed this to be the case (Cleary, 1992; Feingold, 1992b; Hedges & Friedman, 1993a, 1993b; Hedges & Nowell, 1995; Lubinski & Humphreys, 1990). International data are conflicting on this point. Feingold (1994) did not find consistent gender differences in variability in international data, although Beller and Gafni (1996b) did find greater male variability in mathematics and science assessments in most countries.

In order to examine the effects of differential variability, we have routinely computed the standard deviation ratio (*SDR*), which is simply the female *SD* divided by the male *SD*. Thus an *SDR* of 1.0 would indicate equal variability; a ratio less than 1.0 would mean more male variability. The third column of Fig. 3.1 shows the average *SDR* for each of the categories of tests administered to national samples of 12th graders. (Table S-3 in the *Supple-*

ment gives results for individual tests.) In 12 of the 15 test categories, the women's *SD* was smaller by 5% or more. Women's scores were not more variable than men's in any category. These results are not materially different from those reported earlier. Although women's scores at Grade 12 show essentially the same variability as those of men on some cognitive tests, the general pattern for women is often less variability. The average *SDR* for all 74 tests was .91. This is essentially the same finding reported recently in an extensive study by Hedges and Nowell (1995).

What is the practical significance of a difference in variability of this magnitude? With normal distributions of female and male scores with the same mean, but a female *SD* that is 91% as large as that of the male *SD*, the distributions appear to overlap almost completely. In this case, one expects an equal number of females and males to score above the mean, but more males in both the top and the bottom 10% of all scores—approximately four females for every five males. If actual score distributions are not normal, the imbalance could be either larger or smaller.

If there is also a gender difference at the mean, the male imbalance would be diminished in one tail and increased in the other, depending on the direction of the mean difference. Looking at the pattern of mean differences and variability differences for the various types of tests in Fig. 3.1, it can be seen that the two factors may often work together at the top of test score distributions because male scores tend to be more variable for tests on which males have the higher average score. The correlation between the mean *D* and the mean *SDR* for these 15 test categories was .81. For the tests with larger positive *D*, *SDR* is often close to 1.0, indicating that there will be little effect of differential variability in the tails. For those with negative *D*, *SDR* is usually smaller than 1.0, leading to an increase in the number of males among the higher scorers.

This relationship between *D* and *SDR* is troubling because it indicates a tendency for greater male representation among the better prepared students than one would expect from looking at overall test score means based on representative national samples. Two types of questions seem particularly important: First, what can we learn about differential variability and how it develops through the school years? Second, in what ways does differential variability influence (a) the number of females and males in selected populations at higher age levels and (b) the observed gender differences in average test scores in those samples? Our data provide some clues on these questions. We move now to an examination of trends in test scores from Grade 4 through Grade 12, which begins to address the first question. Later analysis of gender differences on selective tests speaks to the second.

TRENDS FROM GRADE 4 TO GRADE 12

In examining the nature of gender differences and similarities in achievement, it is quite natural to seek some enlightenment through better understanding of the educational development of young people. To what extent do girls and boys start off with some such gender patterns as we see near the end of high school? Do they get that way, moving through the grades? There has been considerable interest in age trends for certain types of proficiency, especially mathematics (Chipman et al., 1985; Hyde et al., 1990; Marshall & Smith, 1987), verbal ability (Denno, 1982; Hyde & Linn, 1988), and spatial ability (Linn & Petersen, 1985a). Chapter 2 provides an overview of these efforts.

Until recently there have been limited efforts to understand overall patterns of evolving gender differences for multiple measures of achievement for the same students.[9] We were able to undertake some interesting analyses of this sort because, by design, our database includes coordinate tests administered to comparable samples of students at three grade levels—4, 8, and 12. This provides another opportunity—as we said earlier—to disentangle constructs, cohorts, and samples. In this case, cohort refers to grade level and construct refers to test category. We look at construct differences from Grade 4 to Grade 12 from three perspectives: mean gender differences, differences in variability, and changes in the representation of females and males among the highest performing students in each grade.

It is important to distinguish successive cross-sectional analyses from longitudinal analyses. In the following pages we compare cross-sectional data on samples of 4th-, 8th-, and 12th-grade students in the same year. Reasonably good control of sample variation across three grades comes from the fact that all of the data are based on national samples. Notice, however, that differences across these grade groups could be due to developmental differences within children, to social-educational changes that are different for the three cohorts, or to both factors.

---

[9]There are several recent exceptions to the shortage of studies that look broadly at developmental trends in gender differences and similarities. This type of analysis almost requires normative data because of the difficulty in otherwise controlling sample variations. Feingold (1988) provided one useful analysis of grade trends based on several sets of normative data for the Differential Aptitude Tests. Cleary's (1992) extensive study of normative and survey data was the most comprehensive, although in the only report published before her untimely death, there was relatively limited analysis of the data set. Two other studies at the University of Iowa (Becker & Forsyth, 1990; Martin & Hoover, 1987) analyzed age trends in gender differences for the Iowa Test of Basic Skills and a coordinate battery, the Iowa Test of Educational Development. A unique feature of these two studies was the longitudinal sample on which they were based: all students in a statewide testing program who participated in every year of the period examined. The obvious strength was sample control; the less obvious weakness was sample generalizability. The first study, Grade 3 to 8, used 30% of the original third graders; the second study, Grade 3 to 12, used 10% of the original group. Ongoing research in Sweden promises to add to our understanding of gender differences in cognitive development (see footnote 5).

A longitudinal analysis of the same group of students across the three grades would be useful but little such data are available for representative groups of young people. (We later refer to NELS data for Grades 8–12, which are the main exception.) The cross-sectional analyses reported here might differ from a similar longitudinal analysis if successive cohorts of students at the same age level are showing a changing pattern of gender-related test results in recent years. As we will see in a subsequent section, there have been relatively small changes in patterns of achievement for females and males in representative samples over the past decade.

Mean Differences by Grade

Even with the advantages that our database offers, the analysis of gender differences across grades is not without complications. First, it is necessary to restrict the grade-by-grade analysis to the 10 academic test categories in Table 3.1 that have coordinate tests at lower grades. Even in this database there are gaps because some tests are used at only two of the three grade levels. Furthermore, in some cases there are obvious differences between the Grade 12 tests and their coordinate tests at Grade 8 and Grade 4. In order to mitigate these difficulties, we developed a statistical model that uses all of the available data to estimate trends in mean gender differences as accurately as the data permit. See Table S-4 in the *Supplement* for detailed data on the individual tests and grade-to-grade estimates for each of the 10 test categories. The accompanying footnote S-5 describes the approach we used in the analysis.

The results are shown in Fig. 3.2. There are several interesting features to the overall pattern. First, it is evident that there is some increase in gender differentiation from Grade 4 to Grade 12. The differentiation comes from girls improving more in two categories, writing and language use, and boys improving more in three subject areas. For girls their substantial gain in language skill occurs from Grade 4 to Grade 8, after which their relative superiority in this area holds steady. The relative improvement for boys comes later, from Grade 8 to Grade 12, during which time they tend to gain to a smaller degree on tests in mathematics, science, and geopolitical subjects. The other test categories showed no significant changes in relative performance of females and males across this grade span.

These findings help to clarify some apparent confusion in previous interpretations of age trends in verbal test performance by gender. Maccoby and Jacklin (1974) summarized, "It is at about age 10 or 11 that girls begin to come into their own in verbal performance. From this age through the

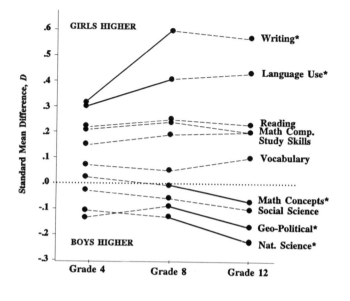

* Solid lines indicate significant trends, P < .001.

FIG. 3.2. Trends in standard mean difference, *D*, from Grade 4 to Grade 12 for 10 categories of tests. See *Supplement* note *S*-5.

high school and college years we find them outscoring boys on a variety of verbal skills" (p. 84). Similarly, Halpern (1992) concluded in her review almost two decades later that most of the evidence supports the view that females are more verbally precocious than males in preschool and through the elementary grades. In the same year, Cleary (1992) described an overall female superiority on verbal tests but no change from early to later grades. Hyde and Linn (1988) reported no consistent changes with age and no consequential gender difference overall in verbal skills.

These inconsistencies apparently arise because prior analyses were hampered by one or more of the following limitations: failure to differentiate writing as an important and distinct verbal skill, lack of control regarding which verbal skills are represented in different age comparisons, or mixing highly selected with representative samples. The results in Fig. 3.2 indicate with little ambiguity that in large representative national samples, girls gain relative to boys to a remarkable degree in writing and language use in the early grades, whereas reading and vocabulary knowledge show little if any change in the relative performance of females and males from Grade 4 to Grade 12.

Over the years, it has been consistently reported that boys tend to improve in mathematics proficiency through the school grades more than girls, especially in more complex skills such as problem solving (Aiken, 1986–1987; Armstrong, 1985; Cleary, 1992; Dossey et al., 1988; Ekstrom et al., 1988; Hilton & Berglund, 1974; Hyde et al., 1990; Maccoby & Jacklin, 1974; Wise, 1985). There has frequently been some confusion as to whether this trend is a reflection of real grade-to-grade gender differences in acquisition of proficiency, differences in sample selectivity, or differences in the construct measured. The results in Fig. 3.2 show similar trends in mathematics test performance as previously reported. With these data (as in those reported by Wise, 1985, and Ekstrom et al., 1988) there is reasonable assurance that the increases in gender difference at the higher grades are not due to changes in the samples. All of the data are based on nationally representative samples and the dropout rate through Grade 12 is currently about the same for girls and boys (see footnote 2). The observed trends may reflect partly a tendency for the 12th-grade tests to place more emphasis on problem solving. The analyses of Ekstrom et al. (1988) and Wise (1985) suggest that math gains in high school are not related to gender, per se, but to number of math courses taken and interest in math.

The increasing gender difference in natural science test performance in secondary school is also consistent with Cleary's (1992) findings. NAEP assessments have shown similar results (Mullis et al., 1990). Limited data are available elsewhere on recent representative samples. It is worth noting, however, that the male advantage in mathematics and science by the end of high school was apparently much larger in earlier years than shown in Fig. 3.2. Project TALENT data from 1960 indicate that mean difference D for achievement in high school mathematics dropped from −.07 in Grade 9 to −.44 in Grade 12. The mean difference for information in physical and biological science dropped from −.41 in Grade 9 to −.60 in Grade 12 (see Table 3.1 in Flanagan et al., 1964).

Data have been reported on performance of women and men on various subject tests like civics, history, and geography; but as far as we are aware, there has been little notice of the tendency for high school males to gain in what we have called geopolitics. These latter trends toward male advantage may largely reflect gender differences in interests among young women and men in secondary school. The likely role of differential interests in gender-related developmental trends is further suggested by grade trends on some tests of special skills. National norms of the mechanical and spatial tests of the *Differential Aptitude Tests* show a consistent pattern of increasing male advantage from Grade 8 to Grade 12 (Feingold, 1988; Lupkowski, 1992).

We examine data on gender differences in interests and possible connections with test performance in the following two chapters.

Variability Differences by Grade

In the earlier discussion of female and male variability, it became clear that equality or inequality in mean scores is not the only question of interest in trying to understand gender differences of potential importance. Other aspects of score distributions may be critical, particularly the ratio of female to male standard deviations (SDR) and the ratio of number of females to males (F/M) among high and low scorers. We now examine those aspects of gender difference and how they change from one grade level to the next.

For these analyses we have relied mostly on composite results from 19 NAEP surveys.[10] Using the NAEP data for these analyses involved two main considerations, both driven by the need for scores that are reasonably comparable across grades in order to evaluate accurately any differential trends in the female and male score distributions. One consideration is the fact that these are the only batteries represented here that have generally similar tests represented at Grades 4 and 8 and Grades 8 and 12. The other batteries are described as having somewhat different combinations of content across those pairs of grades for particular tests. Another consideration is that NAEP takes unusual care to achieve representative samples and scales that are approximately comparable across grades and years.

Figure 3.3 shows the female to male standard deviation ratios (SDR) for each subject at each grade level. Three results are noteworthy:

1. At Grade 4, SDR is reasonably near 1.0 for the six subjects, indicating that there is little difference in the variability of scores on cognitive tests for girls and boys in the early elementary grades.
2. For most of the tests, SDR appeared to decline from Grade 4 to Grade 12, particularly in the first half of that period. The mean SDR dropped from .96 to .91 ($p < .001$), the latter figure corresponding to the mean SDR for the 74 tests at Grade 12 as previously described. For these six subjects overall, this drop in SDR represents a change to about 10% greater male variability by the end of secondary school.

---

[10]The NAEP data comparing Grades 4, 8, and 12 were based on all of the most recent NAEP Report Card surveys that carried out assessments at all three grades. These included the six subjects shown in Fig. 3.3. In four of these subjects—reading, writing, mathematics, and science—NAEP also does trend assessments with independent samples but essentially the same tests every few years. Results for three or four of these most recent Trend Tests were averaged, and then weighted equally with the Report Card results—in all, 19 surveys are thus represented. Test descriptions in the *Supplement* identify the years of these surveys (see also footnote 8 in chapter 2). Because some Trend Tests are administered to the same or overlapping samples, the data are based on 13 independent national samples.

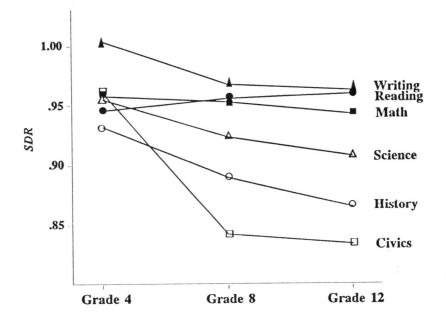

FIG. 3.3. Trends in the ratio of female to male standard deviations (*SDR*) from Grade 4 to Grade 12 for NAEP Assessments in six subjects.

3. At Grade 12 the SDRs suggest a pattern in the relative degree of female–male variability: very small difference in variability in basic academic skills like writing and reading and the largest male variability on tests that are most clearly associated with subject knowledge like history and civics.

These results are generally similar to those reported for national samples in the past few years by other investigators.[11] If the degree of variability in young women's and young men's scores is following a somewhat different track through the grades, one wonders what is happening to variability through those years—not relatively for females and males, but in absolute terms. Figure 3.4 addresses that question for the same set of NAEP data with interesting results.

---

[11]Compared to the results reported here, Feingold's (1992b) data suggest somewhat more gender difference in variability for the California Achievement Tests and somewhat less for the Differential Aptitude Tests. Work by Martin and Hoover (1987) and Becker and Forsyth (1990) suggests somewhat more gender difference in variability for the Iowa Tests of Basic Skills, although their longitudinal sample is not likely representative of students generally. The same pattern of smaller SDRs for subject tests and at higher grade levels is also apparent but less consistent in these more limited sets of data. Cleary (1992) did not give results for standard deviations in her extensive study, although she did report the male SDs to be larger for almost all tests.

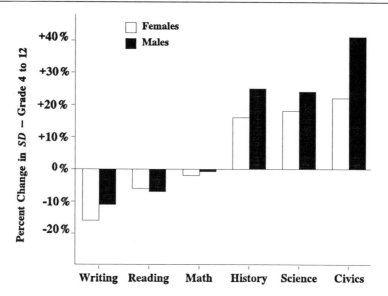

FIG. 3.4. Percentage increase or decrease in score variability (standard deviation) from Grade 4 to Grade 12 for females and males in each of six subjects. Based on multiple NAEP assessments (see footnote 10). All changes in *SD* from Grade 4 to Grade 12 were significant (*p* < .01) except mathematics.

It may frequently be assumed that education serves to bring all citizens up to a similar level of appreciation and understanding; that is, to reduce individual differences. The conventional wisdom among psychologists, however, is more to the effect that education widens individual differences. The results for these six NAEP assessments indicate that individual differences are narrowed from Grade 4 through Grade 12 in the important academic skills of writing and reading, but widened in the more specialized knowledge-based subjects.

This pattern may result from the greater potential impact of differential interests in subject knowledge areas than in more general academic skills like reading and writing. The need and opportunity to develop proficiency in general academic skills is likely more evenly spread than is the case in subjects like science and history, in which greater variations in individual interests likely mean greater variation in committed time and developed skill. If so, these patterns hold for both women and men, but appear to result in somewhat greater variability in males compared to females.[12]

---

[12] Another possible influence on the relative variability at Grade 4 and Grade 12 should be noted. Even though NAEP makes every effort to maintain consistent scales across grade and age groups, there is no way of assuring that the *SD* at the two levels is strictly comparable. Because the scales for the several NAEP subjects are independently developed and all suffer this uncertainty, the interaction in Fig. 3.4 could look different with different assessment or scaling procedures. As a developmental phenomenon, the interaction deserves further research attention and, being substantial, seems unlikely to be explained simply on the basis of a scaling artifact.

Note also that male variability is larger in those subjects where the male mean is higher. As reported earlier, the correlation between mean D and mean SDR was .81 for the 15 test categories at Grade 12. It seems plausible to hypothesize that these two indicators of gender difference have similar roots, although the observed association does not establish that as fact, or say anything at all about what might mediate the differential effects such as schoolwork, habitual activities, social roles, biological factors, and so on. There are a number of rival hypotheses, for example, as to why there tend to be more males at extreme levels of proficiency in mathematics by age 13 (see Benbow, 1988b, and numerous commentaries thereon).

In any event, a typical result of differential variability is a different pattern of gender differences at the two tails of a score distribution. Cleary (1992) examined that possibility by computing the standard difference, D, between female and male scores at particular percentile levels (e.g., the score corresponding to the female 90th percentile minus the score for the male 90th percentile). As she reported, male advantage is typically greatest at the upper percentile levels. This aspect of her findings is clearly discernable in the data on mathematics achievement reproduced in Fig. 2.3.

The same pattern is seen in Fig. 3.5, which is based on the same NAEP data used for the two previous graphs, but here results are averaged across all six subjects. (See Table S-5 in the *Supplement* for detail.) Figure 3.5 shows the standard difference, D, at the 10th, 50th, and 90th percentile for Grades

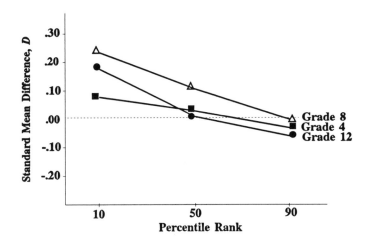

FIG. 3.5. Standard difference at the 10th, 50th, and 90th percentiles—average D for six NAEP Assessments at Grades 4, 8, and 12.

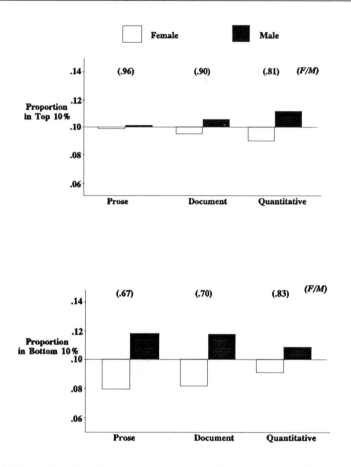

FIG. 3.6. Proportion of females and males who scored in the top and bottom 10% on three adult literacy scales in 1992. *F/M* ratios are shown in parentheses; standard errors for these are all approximately .10.

4, 8, and 12. At each grade level *D* is more negative at the higher percentile. That difference is more evident at the higher grade levels where male scores tend to become more variable compared to female scores

From a practical educational standpoint, an important question is *how many* females and males there are at the high and low proficiency levels. Because we saw earlier that males were noticeably more variable in civics and history, we might expect to find more males in the tails of those distributions, and that is what happened in these two NAEP assessments: On the civics test there were more males among the top 10% of all examinees at Grade 12 and also more males among the bottom 10%. The history test showed the same picture.

This pattern of more males at both the top and the bottom of the score range is not likely to occur if there is much of an overall difference favoring either gender. Also, one might not see as clearly a surplus of males in the lower score range if the test is not designed to measure accurately at that level. For this reason, it is instructive to examine the results of the recent NALS (Kirsch, Jungeblut, Jenkins, & Kolstad, 1993), which was specifically intended to assess the functional skills of the general adult population, in school or out. The data shown in Fig. 3.6 are based on those survey respondents in the 16-to-24 age bracket.

There was almost no *mean* difference on any of these scales ($D = .11$, .06, and $-.02$ for prose, document, and quantitative literacy, respectively), but on each scale, at least to some extent, there were more males in both the top and bottom 10%. This quite different picture at the mean and in the tails well illustrates why it can be insufficient to assess gender difference only at the mean. In fact, there was a noticeable pile-up of males in the bottom 10% on each scale. This overrepresentation of males among low-scoring adults causes one to wonder how and when that pattern developed. The closest parallel to these adult literacy skills at younger age levels would seem to be the three Rs. Figure 3.7 summarizes similar NAEP data for reading, writing, and mathematics assessments in that same year. The relative number of boys and girls scoring at the low end (in the bottom 10% overall) is shown for Grade 4 and Grade 12.

Figure 3.7 shows a somewhat similar picture as that observed in the bottom panel of the previous figure. There were considerably more males than females among low scorers in reading and writing. In these two skills, overrepresentation of males at the low end is due partly to a mean difference favoring the girls and partly due to a somewhat greater spread of male scores (especially at Grade 12). The main change from Grade 4 to Grade 12 was an increase in the number of males among the poor writers. There was little change in the number of low-scoring girls and boys in math across this grade range.

Male overrepresentation at the bottom on important intellectual skills is educationally and socially quite important and should not be overlooked. As Weinberg (1993) said, we must be concerned if there seems to be a shortage of highly qualified females on some skills, but we should also be concerned if there is an excess of males floundering at the bottom tail of the distribution.

Nevertheless, most large testing programs tend to focus on the higher performing students, and it is important to understand issues concerning gender differences and fair assessment at this level. What happens in the top 10%? We move now to a more careful look at that end of the distribution.

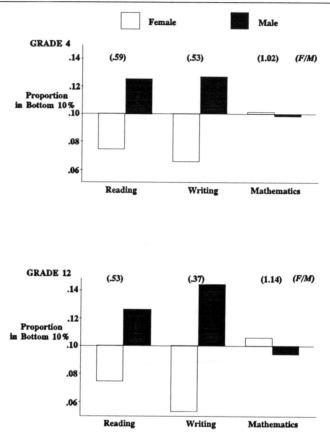

FIG. 3.7. Proportion of females and males who scored in the bottom 10% on NAEP Assessments of three basic skills at Grade 4 and Grade 12 in 1992. Combined results for NAEP Report Card and Trend Tests. *F/M* ratios are shown in parentheses; standard errors are approximately .08.

Representation in the Top 10%

We use "top 10%" here simply as a convenient way of referring to that group of individuals who score high on any particular measure. Because there are different indicators of talent and developed competence, it is neither appropriate nor useful to think of *the* top 10% or 25% as if there were an actual group of such individuals so designated. Nonetheless, understanding grade trends in the pattern of gender difference in test performance of the most able and best educated young people at the end of secondary school is important for several reasons. Possible education and career implications are foremost. The most able high school graduates account for many of those who will enter the most selective undergraduate institutions, the most advanced graduate and professional training programs, and many of the more desirable occupations. On the other hand, current patterns of achieve-ment among this group of accomplished students should not be taken incorrectly to imply any limit on what is possible for young people to attain.

NAEP assessments in the six subject areas are limited, to be sure. They certainly do not represent a full description of developed knowledge and skill at Grade 12, but they do represent a careful assessment, using large national samples and mixed testing formats, in subjects that are considered to be most important for an educated populace. Figure 3.8 shows trends in the representation of females and males in the top 10% on each of these measures from Grade 4 through Grade 12.

Results for students in the top 10% on these various assessments are generally similar to trends in overall *mean* differences from Grade 4 to Grade 12 that were shown earlier in Fig. 3.2. In reading and writing, more of the top students are female; in the other four subject areas, more of the top students are male. Here, as in the earlier figure, females tend to show their relative gain from Grade 4 to Grade 8 and males from Grade 8 to 12. Note, however, that these trends in female and male representation in the top 10% are associated with two factors: changes in the overall means for the two genders from grade to grade, and an increase in male variability compared

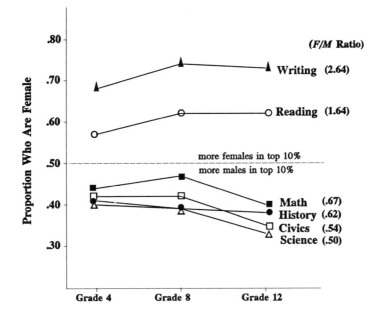

FIG. 3.8. Representation of females and males in the top 10% on NAEP Assessments in six subjects at Grades 4, 8, and 12.

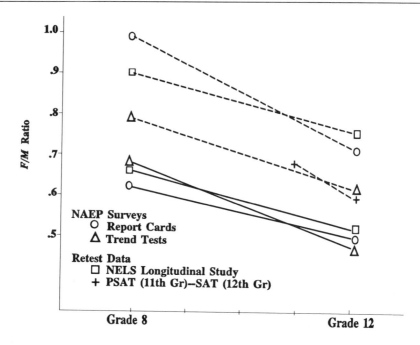

FIG. 3.9. Ratio of females to males in the top 10% on mathematics tests (dashed lines) and science tests (solid lines) for two NAEP surveys and two sets of retest data.

to that of females. The joint effect of those two factors gives a flatter trend line for writing and reading in Fig. 3.8 as compared to the earlier Fig. 3.2. Also, there is a somewhat clearer shift in the relative performance of young women and men in mathematics and science at the upper grade levels.

Women's interest, participation, and achievement in mathematics and science have been the subject of a great deal of attention over the past decade or more (see, e.g., Chipman et al., 1985). We return to this topic more than once, but the data in Fig. 3.7 are worth a closer look. Fig. 3.9 shows the female to male ratios in the top 10% on mathematics and science in Grades 8 and 12 for the two types of NAEP assessments separately (Report Card and Trend Test), along with two other sets of data—the only information we had available from a retest of the same students.

One additional comparison comes from NELS, which followed up a large national sample of 8th graders, administering essentially the same tests in the 12th grade. The other comes from an estimate of female and male performance in mathematics, both early in the 11th grade, when a national sample of students took the PSAT, and midway through the 12th grade, when a large number of these students took the SAT, which is very nearly the same test.[13] All of these data sets showed a similar declining F/M ratio from Grade 8 to Grade 12 among the most able students in these two subjects—to about .70 in math and .50 in science by the end of high school. This troubling trend leads to our next important topic: How do self-selected groups of women and men do on more advanced tests used in undergraduate and graduate educational programs?

ADVANCED TESTS IN SELECTED SAMPLES

In the previous chapter, Fig. 2.4 listed the various sets of test data that were collected for this study. Up to now, the discussion has focused on 74 tests in the first 15 test batteries, all administered to representative school-age samples. We are now concerned with the remaining test batteries, 16 through 24, which are different in two respects. First, this latter group of tests are typically more difficult and advanced as to subject matter. Second, they are taken by selected groups of students going on to higher education, so we do not have data on these tests for representative samples of all students.

At the outset we need to be clear about the term *selected*. We use it simply to suggest that smaller, more select groups are formed in various ways—through self-selection, educational sifting and sorting, the influence of counselors and parents, selective college admissions, and so on. Selected groups are normally more proficient, but in complex ways that reflect how they were formed. The more difficult advanced tests are taken by such selected groups.

Data on standard differences for the advanced tests in selected samples are shown in Table 3.2. Three groups of selective tests are shown in the three columns: 29 subject tests in the Advanced Placement Program (AP), 26 subject and ability tests used in undergraduate admissions (UA), and 29 subject and ability tests used in graduate admissions (GA). We look first at results for the 55 tests in the first two groups that are administered near the end of high school. These 55 test results based on selected samples showed an average standard mean difference of −.15, compared to an average D of .02 for the 74 tests based on representative samples (Table 3.1).

Why this difference? In the general population at Grade 12 the results indicated no overall difference between females and males in mean test

---

[13]In Fig. 3.9 the F/M ratio for the PSAT at Grade 11 and the SAT at Grade 12 are both based on the number of females and males in the top 10% of national norms for the two tests as estimated by Braun et al. (1987).

TABLE 3.2

Standard Mean Difference, D (With Standard Errors), for Various Types of Tests Administered to Selective Samples

Test Type [Grade 12 D][a]	Advanced Placement (AP)	Undergraduate Admissions (UA)	Graduate Admissions (GA)
1. Writing [.57]		SAT Writing .17(.009)	MCAT Writing .13(.010)
2. Language Use [.43]	Engl. Lang. −.06(.011) **−.06(.011)**	ACT English .16(.002) TSWE .13(.002) ATP Engl. Comp. .04(.005) **.11(.002)**	 **.13(.010)**
3. Reading [.20]		ACT Reading .00(.002) **.00(.002)**	MCAT Verbal −.08(.010) **−.08(.010)**
4. Verbal Reasoning [.06]		PSAT Verbal .02(.002) SAT Verbal −.06(.002) **−.02(.001)**	GMAT Verbal −.12(.005) GRE-G Verbal −.23(.004) **−.18(.003)**
5. Math (Mixed) [−.11]	Calculus AB −.17(.007) Calculus BC −.20(.016) Comp. Sci. A −.36(.030) Comp Sci. B −.29(.048) **−.26(.015)**	ATP Math 1 −.38(.006) ATP Math 2 −.42(.008) ACT Math −.25(.002) PSAT Math −.32(.002) SAT Math −.36(.002) **−.35(.002)**	GRE Comp. Sci. −.62(.038) GRE Math −.87(0.38) GMAT Quant. −.49(.005) GRE-G Quant. −.63(.004) MCAT Quant. −.36(.012) **−.59(.011)**
6. Natural Science [−.17]	Biology −.23(.009) Chemistry −.27(.012) Physics B −.36(.018) Physics Mech. −.48(.027) Physics E & M −.28(.038) **−.33(.010)**	ATP Biology −.32(.010) ATP Chemistry −.44(.011) ATP Physics −.62(.017) ACT Sci. Reason. −.29(.002) ACT Nat. Science −.39(.007) **−.41(.005)**	GRE Biochem. −.38(.041) GRE Biology −.23(.022) MCAT Biol. Sci. −.30(.010) GRE Chemistry −.43(.033) MCAT Chemistry −.31(.012) GRE Physics −.61(.043) MCAT Physics −.46(.012) MCAT Phys. Sci. −.49(.010) GRE Engineer. −.62(.038) GRE Geology −.22(.067) **−.41(.011)**

Test Type [Grade 12 D][a]	Advanced Placement (AP)		Undergraduate Admissions (UA)		Graduate Admissions (GA)	
7. Social Science	Psychology	-.09(.026)	ACT Soc. Studies	-.23(.007)	GRE Education	-.01(.051)
					GRE Psychology	-.12(.017)
					GRE Sociology	.15(.053)
[.02]		**-.09(.026)**		**-.23(.007)**		**.01(.025)**
8. Geopolitical	Comp. Gov.	-.12(.028)	ATP Amer. Hist.	-.25(.009)	GRE Economics	-.49(.050)
	Euro. History	-.20(.012)	ATP Euro. Hist.	-.52(.031)	GRE History	-.55(.041)
	Macroecon.	-.35(.023)			GRE Pol. Sci.	-.60(.055)
	Microecon.	-.27(.025)				
	US Gov.	-.24(.012)				
	US History	-.17(.006)				
[-.23]		**-.22(.008)**		**-.39(.016)**		**-.55(.028)**
9. Reasoning					LSAT	-.09(.006)
					GRE-G Analytical	-.18(.004)
[.10]						**-.14(.004)**
10. Lang. & Literature	French Lang.	.00(.020)	ATP French	-.13(.017)	GRE Engl. Lit.	-.17(.023)
	French Lit.	.22(.055)	ATP German	.01(.039)		
	German Lang.	.13(.038)	ATP Hebrew	-.03(.079)		
	Latin-C/H	.08(.062)	ATP Latin	-.26(.037)		
	Latin Vergil	-.04(.042)	ATP Spanish	-.02(.012)		
	Spanish Lang.	.03(.012)	ATP Lit.	.06(.014)		
	Spanish Lit.	.08(.033)				
	Engl. Lit.	.07(.006)				
		.07(.014)		**-.06(.016)**		**-.17(.023)**
11. Art	Art Drawing	-.07(.046)				
	Art General	-.05(.031)				
	Art History	.09(.030)				
		-.01(.021)				
12. Music	Music Theory	-.18(.045)			GRE Music	-.60(.056)
		-.18(.045)				**-.60(.056)**

Note. Statistics for test groups are shown in bold type. In general, data are the most recent available. See footnote 11 in chapter 2.

[a] [Grade 12 D] refers to the average D for tests of this type administered to representative national samples in Grade 11/12 (from Table 3.1 when available).

performance. To what extent is the difference observed in the more advanced tests due to variations in the nature of the tests themselves (the construct), the nature of the selected group (the sample), or the age group (the cohort)? In this section those three possibilities are examined in turn in an effort to shed some light on the question.

Construct Differences

Data in the AP and UA columns of Table 3.2 represent the same grade cohort as the earlier data on representative samples. Considerable information is available on these tests that is useful in evaluating possible reasons why observed gender differences might vary as they do. The sorting of results into the framework of Table 3.2 is a beginning. Insofar as possible, the tests are grouped in the same categories used for tests administered to representative samples of 12th-grade students. We show here for each test the standard mean difference, D, and the standard error of D. The mean D is shown in bold for each group of tests, along with its standard error in parentheses. The average D that we obtained for similar tests administered to representative samples of 12th-grade students (see Table 3.1) is shown within brackets in the first column at the left of Table 3.2 for comparison.

Generally speaking, two types of construct differences could possibly help to explain the appearance of a −.15 difference in the average performance of women and men on the selective tests, compared to a near-zero result in the representative samples. One would be the type of tests represented at each level; another would be what those tests measure. The first of these refers simply to the possibility of a different mix of tests at the selective level; for example, more tests on which men tend to score higher and fewer tests on which women tend to score higher. It is evident in Table 3.2 that the selective tests include fewer tests in the first three categories, on which women often score higher. Is it possible that one would see less change in the average D from representative to selective tests if one focused on tests within the same category?

Figure 3.10 compares the average D for tests administered to representative and selective samples—two profiles, so to speak—for eight test categories where both types of data were available for the same age–grade cohort. Note again, we are talking only about selective tests in the AP and UA columns of Table 3.2, tests administered in the same time period as the earlier data based on representative samples. The main difference in the two sets of data is presumably the selectivity of the samples taking the tests.

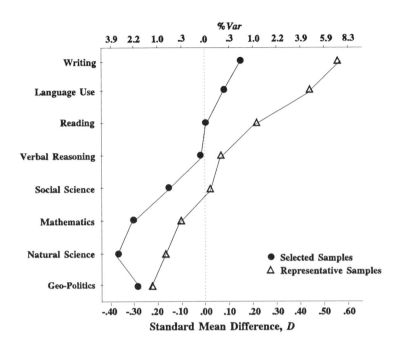

FIG. 3.10. Average *D* for tests in eight categories based on either representative samples or selected samples at Grade 12. *%Var* = Percentage of score variation associated with gender.

The results vary somewhat, but in all categories the value of *D* is more negative in the selective tests; that is, males are getting relatively higher scores. The average *D* for 37 selective tests in those categories was .18 lower than tests in the same category, but administered to representative samples—essentially the same result as obtained with all 55 of the selective undergraduate tests. This finding is consistent with Cleary's (1992) results. She reported consistently more male advantage with more selective samples. Thus, the somewhat negative average *D* for selective tests cannot be attributed simply to a different mix of tests, such as more science and less language. In fact, in these data the language tests show more negative shift in average *D* than do the science tests.

Another type of construct difference could result from some systematic change in the method of testing; for example, the format in which the questions are presented. Such construct changes might appear, of course, in some test categories and not in others, although the negative shift in Fig. 3.10 appears to be fairly general. There is a systematic difference in test format in the case of the AP examinations. All of the AP tests include a free-response section that typically accounts for about 50% of the score, whereas the UA tests are almost all exclusively multiple choice in format.[14]

There is also some difference in the typical gender difference for the placement and the admissions tests. Looking at the AP and the UA tests only in those categories where there is a baseline D for representative samples, the average D for the AP tests was lower by .11; the average D for the UA tests was lower by .24. This outcome raises the interesting question as to what role the free-response format may play in the discrepancy in the performance of women and men on the two types of tests.

Free Response and Multiple Choice.   The AP Program of the College Board is unique in a number of respects. Two characteristics, in particular, may have a bearing on gender difference. This is the only national testing program in which examinations are keyed to specific course syllabi. It is also the only national program in which proficiency in various subjects is separately assessed in both a multiple-choice (MC) and a free-response (FR) mode.

In 27 of 29 subject areas, free-response exercises complement the traditional multiple-choice item type. (Two art examinations contain only free-response material.) The exercises vary within tests and from one test to another; for example, essays, open-ended problems, short answers, and so on. The MC and FR sections are scored separately as part of the assessment process, but combined (most typically with equal weight) to form the reported grade. This makes it possible to calculate a standard mean difference for each section, D_{FR} and D_{MC} and thereby determine whether the form of the examination influences the pattern of performance for women and men.

Table 3.3 shows such results for the 27 tests in 1993, arranged in order of the difference between D_{FR} and D_{MC}. A dashed line separates those at the top on which there was little if any difference in the relative performance of women and men on the FR and MC sections (i.e., within a tenth of a standard deviation), from those at the bottom where there was a more consequential difference.[15] Two aspects of these results are noteworthy.

---

[14]The SAT Writing test is based on a multiple-choice section and an essay. To be consistent with other data on "writing" reported here, the SAT Writing gender difference reported in Table 3.2 is based only on the essay portion.

[15]The standard errors of D_{FR} and D_{MC} are approximately the same as those indicated in Table 3.2 for the total score. For all tests below the dashed line, the difference between D_{FR} and D_{MC} is two or more such standard errors. For most of the tests above the line, the difference is less than two standard errors. Note that the standard error of the difference between D_{FR} and D_{MC} is reduced by the fact that the two measures are positively correlated and based on the same samples. The position of such a dividing line is somewhat arbitrary; it could be placed higher or lower and the implications of the pattern would be much the same.

TABLE 3.3

Standard Mean Difference, (D), for the Multiple-Choice (MC) and Free-Response (FR) Sections of 27 Examinations in the Advanced Placement Program

	Type of Examination		Standard Difference, (D)		
	Mathematics	Natural Science			
	Lang. & Lit.	Geopolitics			
Examination	(X)	(O)	MC	FR	FR–MC
Computer Science A	X		− .32	− .39	− .07
Math—Calculus AB	X		− .14	− .20	− .06
Computer Science AB	X		− .29	− .31	− .02
French Language	X		− .01	− .00	.01
German Language	X		.13	.14	.01
Spanish Language	X		.03	.04	.01
Spanish Literature	X		.06	.09	.03
Engl. Lit. & Comp.	X		.05	.09	.04
Math—Calculus BC	X		− .24	− .19	.05
Music Theory			− .24	− .18	.06
Latin Vergil	X		− .09	− .02	.07
		D similar for FR, MC			
		D more positive for FR			
Psychology			− .14	− .03	.11
French Literature	X		.13	.24	.11
Chemistry		O	− .35	− .21	.14
Art History			.01	.16	.15
Microeconomics		O	− .32	− .17	.15
Biology		O	− .29	− .13	.16
Physics C-Elect. & Mag.		O	− .39	− .20	.19
Macroeconomics		O	− .40	− .21	.19
Physics B		O	− .47	− .25	.22
Engl. Lang. & Comp.	X		− .15	.07	.22
Physics C-Mechanics		O	− .58	− .35	.23
Latin-Catullus-Horace	X		− .05	.18	.23
Gov. & Politics, Comp.		O	− .25	.06	.31
Gov. & Politics, U.S.		O	− .35	− .03	.32
U.S. History		O	− .31	.01	.32
European History		O	− .35	.04	.39
Mean for 27 Examinations			− .20	− .06	.13

Note. Examinations are listed according to the number in the last column: *D* for FR section minus *D* for MC section. For those examinations above the dashed line, *D* differed by less than .10 for MC and FR sections; below the dashed line, *D* for the FR section was more positive by at least .10.

First, the multiple-choice portion of the AP tests showed a standard mean difference of −.20, on average, whereas the free-response portion showed little gender difference (an average D_{FR} of −.06). Although .14 is not a large discrepancy, it warrants serious attention because it represents an average result for a number of examinations and may have an important bearing on fairness considerations in test design.

A second particularly interesting feature of Table 3.3 is the pattern of the results with respect to type of subject matter. Eleven of the 27 examinations showed little difference in the relative performance of women and men on the multiple-choice and free-response sections. Almost all of these were tests in mathematics or tests in language and literature (represented with "X" in Table 3.3). Sixteen of the 27 tests showed a difference of .10 or larger in the Ds based on the FR and MC portions—always in the direction of a more negative D (favoring males) on the multiple-choice section. All of the tests concerning natural science and geopolitics (represented with "O" in Table 3.3) showed this pattern of difference in the MC and FR sections. A similar pattern can also be detected in 1987 AP data reported by Mazzeo, Schmitt, and Bleistein (1991, 1993).

This interesting relationship to subject matter suggests that the difference in relative performance of women and men on multiple-choice and free-response tests may have less to do with testing mode, per se, than with what is being tested. That is, women and men may perform differently in the different testing modes if, and *because*, the nature of the construct differs in the two testing modes. We leave, for now, further speculation along that line. Meanwhile, back to the original question: Does this difference in the character of the AP tests account for the somewhat different average value of D compared with other tests at this level?

To answer that question more precisely, we compared 13 achievement tests in the Admissions Testing Program (ATP) with 13 AP tests in the same subjects (all ATP tests except Hebrew had a reasonably good AP match.) The average Ds were:

Advanced Placement	−.11
Free-response section	−.04
Multiple-choice section	−.17
ATP Achievement Tests	−.25

With matched tests, the difference in the average D for the AP and the ATP tests was −.11 versus −.25. Since the multiple-choice section of those AP tests had an average D of −.17, it appears that almost half of the AP–ATP difference may occur because the AP tests contain a free-response section. What accounts for the remaining difference? Probably not chance fluctuations because, overall, the samples are quite large.[16] Probably not differential selectivity of the samples; AP and ATP seem generally comparable in that

---

[16]The standard error for each of these mean values is approximately .005.

regard.[17] It could be subtle, unknowable differences in the nature of the two sets of tests, or it could be because the AP tests more closely reflect course content. Stumpf and Stanley (1996) speculated similarly. In mathematics, at least, there is evidence that women score relatively higher on tests that better match coursework (Bridgeman & Wendler, 1989).

Summing up, we have found that tests in the same general category and at the same grade level show a negative shift in D of .18 (toward higher male performance) in selected samples compared with representative samples. Thus far, construct differences have not proven to be a fruitful avenue for explaining the change.[18] The difference in the character of the AP tests is apparently related to gender difference, but not in a direction that would contribute to a negative shift for D in selective tests. Nor does the type of tests represented at the two levels suggest any simple explanation. The fact that a similar shift occurred for almost all categories of tests that we could examine suggests that the shift is more likely due to some other change in the situation that is common across different types of tests—such as the selective character of the samples of examinees, which brings us to the next topic.

Effects of Sample Restriction

How selected are the samples of students who take the difficult tests near the end of high school such as the College Board Achievement Tests? Somewhat above average? Very much above average? The question is more difficult to answer than might be assumed because we have no data on these tests that would permit comparing the selected sample with a nationally representative sample. It would be useful to have some other common metric that would allow direct comparison of the selected group with a representative sample of high school seniors. The SAT comes closest to filling that bill because there is available an estimate of SAT score distribu-

---

[17]All students who take AP examinations do not take the SAT. Evidently there is no matched database from which one might ascertain the average SAT score for AP examinees who did take the SAT. However, in 1992 the program located SAT scores for all AP students who made a creditable AP score of 3 or higher and also took the SAT. Such samples who took AP examinations in the subjects represented in Fig. 3.10 had SAT mean scores some 50 to 60 points higher than corresponding samples who took ATP Achievement Tests. Although there is no dependable way to adjust for the fact that the AP samples are truncated at the bottom, it would appear from these data that there is a generally similar level of selectivity in the AP and the ATP samples.

[18]One might also speculate that the somewhat more positive Ds for 12th-grade tests administered to representative samples results from the influence of free-response material in the NAEP assessments. That is not borne out by the data. In Table 3.1 the NAEP assessments actually had an average D slightly more negative than the exclusively multiple-choice tests in corresponding test categories.

tions for high school seniors nationally (Braun, Centra, & King, 1987), and SAT data are often available for students who have taken the selective tests.

Students applying to a college that requires three College Board Achievement Tests for admissions purposes usually have some option as to which tests they take. On what basis would they decide? Presumably, one basis would be the students' interest in putting their best foot forward by taking tests on subjects in which they are most proficient. SAT Verbal or SAT Math scores of those students would give some indication of the selectivity of these groups of examinees, but only in those cases where proficiency in the subject is highly related to verbal or math scores.

Accordingly, for this illustration, we selected the four College Board Achievement Tests that are most highly correlated with SAT Verbal and the four most highly correlated with SAT Math. In Fig. 3.11 the average SAT score for the sample taking each achievement test is indicated on the distribution of SAT scores for representative 12th-grade students. For

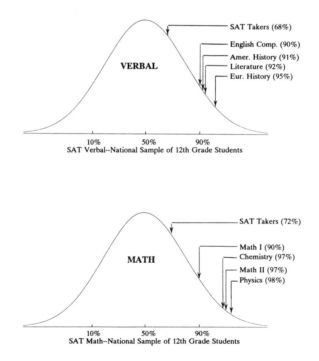

FIG. 3.11. Illustration of the selectivity of samples of students who take the SAT and College Board Achievement Tests—percentile rank of their average SAT scores among all high school seniors. Achievement Tests shown are the four that are most closely related to SAT Verbal and Math, respectively. National norms are from Braun et al. (1987). Other descriptive statistics are based on 1992 program statistics.

comparison, we have also shown where the average score of SAT takers applying to college would fall.

Even allowing for the fact that SAT scores probably underestimate the degree of selectivity of the Achievement Test examinees, they are clearly a very proficient group in their subjects of choice. These samples have *average* SAT scores (i.e., the most relevant score, V or M) that range from the 90th to the 98th percentile among 12th-grade students generally. Samples of students who take AP achievement tests appear to be comparably selective. College-bound SAT takers are above average, but not so markedly.

Seeing that the samples of examinees taking selective tests are definitely restricted, the question is what effect that restriction has had on observed gender differences. There is certainly reason to expect such an effect. We saw earlier that gender differences among 12th graders generally favor males more in the upper tail of score distributions than at the mean (Fig. 3.5). Other investigators have reported extensive data showing the same effect (Cleary, 1992; Feingold, 1992a, 1992b; Hedges & Nowell, 1995). But does sample restriction account for the negative male shift in D that is observed in selective tests? Is it possible to predict the effects of sample restriction on gender differences? If so, what factors are involved? What implications might there be for assessment and educational practice?

There are no simple answers to these questions, but we felt them to be sufficiently important to undertake a special study of the effects of sample restriction. The recent work of several investigators (Cleary, 1992; Feingold, 1992a, 1992b; Hedges & Friedman, 1993a, 1993b) proved extremely valuable in this undertaking. Our study—largely technical in nature—is reported in detail in Lewis and Willingham (1995) and is reprinted in the *Supplement* to this volume.

There are many varieties of sample restriction. We use the following example to illustrate what we see as the main results and implications of our study. Please note that this vignette (about a physics course) is intended only to show how sample restriction can affect gender difference in a selected group, depending on the nature of the selection process. In the following paragraphs we are not attempting to explain the findings in Table 3.2, although we do later get back to Table 3.2. This example omits details and qualifications. Readers should consult Lewis and Willingham (1995) for a more precise account of our analysis and tentative conclusions concerning the effects of sample restriction.

Assume that a selected group of high school seniors elects to take an advanced course in physics. A number of factors may be involved in that decision: interest in physics, previous performance in science courses, advice of teachers and counselors, schedule quirks, competing courses, and so on. Our objective is to consider how the mean gender difference in some relevant proficiency, say a recent test in "science knowledge," would differ among students in the restricted group who take the advanced course as compared to seniors generally. There are actually six factors that have to be weighed in order to answer that question:

- The mean gender difference in "science knowledge" scores for all seniors.
- Any difference in the variability of "science knowledge" scores for all female and male seniors.
- The proportion of seniors who elect the course.
- Any difference in the proportion of women and men who so elect.
- How much weight "science knowledge" has on the decision to take the course (notice that such a "science knowledge" test will reflect, to some degree, students' prior interest and experience in science, as well as their developed proficiency).
- Whether "science knowledge" has more or less weight on the decisions of women compared to those of men.

Assume this is an ideal situation in which we know the relevant charac-teristics of the seniors and how the selection process worked in order to create a restricted sample of advanced physics students. In that case it is possible to predict with considerable accuracy the effects of sample restric-tion on gender difference in "science knowledge" at the start of the physics class. The analyses by Lewis and Willingham (1995) indicate that there are three main components that account for the effects of sample restriction: range restriction, differential variability, and gender balance. These three factors represent the statistical effects of restriction.

Range Restriction.   Range restriction refers to the smaller range of scores that results when the selected group consists mainly of high scorers. If range restriction is the only one of the three factors operating (i.e., when female and male scores were equally variable in the senior class and there is no change in the proportion of females and males in the advanced physics class), then the apparent gender difference will always increase in the selected group. That is to say, if the standard mean difference originally favored men, it will favor them even more in the group taking advanced physics.

Similarly, any difference on any other skill favoring women would also get larger in the selected group. The effect is gender blind. The amount of change in the observed D for science knowledge is directly proportional to the amount of weight science knowledge had in the decision to take physics, and how much difference there originally was in the average science knowledge scores of women and men.

A key fact here is that D always increases even though restriction to the more select group may not actually alter the amount of difference in score points on the original scale. This occurs because restriction reduces the range of scores and the standard deviation in the selected group. A smaller standard deviation means that D, as routinely computed, will necessarily increase even if the mean score difference for women and men does not change. It is arguable, however, as to whether this represents a real change, or only a shift in the standard for evaluating any gender difference between the average scores.

Differential Variability.   The mean difference in female and male science knowledge scores at the beginning of the physics class will be affected by any gender difference in the variability of science knowledge scores in the senior class generally. This effect occurs because differential variability creates a gender imbalance in both low and high scores, even if there is no difference at the mean. In theory it can work either way; whichever group was more variable in the senior class will gain an advantage in the more select physics class. In practice, there appears to be either no gender difference in variability or, as is typically the case with science tests, more male variability. Any given difference in variability will have a constant effect on the mean difference after restriction, regardless of the original difference in science knowledge means or the relative number of women and men in the physics class. Larger differences in variability will have larger effects on mean difference after restriction. The effect always goes in the same direction; for example, if males were more variable, either a positive or a negative D in the full senior class will shift in a negative direction in the physics class. As before, the effects of differential variability can be consequential if science knowledge had a heavy weight in determining who elected to take the physics class, or quite small if it had little weight.

Gender Balance.   When a select sample of good students make up an advanced physics class, an important aspect of gender similarity and difference is the proportion of females to males (F/M) in the restricted group. The F/M ratio in the selected group is not usually determined, or necessarily even heavily influenced, by one variable like science knowledge. Many other factors may come into play: other relevant competencies, a plan to study medicine, or even seeming irrelevancies like whether a friend urges that they take some other course together. However, how many women and men, in this process, decide to take advanced physics can have a strong influence on the standard mean difference, D, on science knowledge at the outset of the physics course.

Thus, gender balance is not only itself an important aspect of gender difference in the restricted group, but also the third main component in the effects of sample restriction on any observed change in D. We illustrate this principle with the following example involving two selection scenarios, but as we move to that, notice that in having identified three components of sample restriction—range restriction, differential variability, and gender balance—we have not actually introduced any new ideas. All three components are intimately connected with the standard deviation ratio and the female to male ratio—two metrics that we incorporated into our study design because there was so much recent work indicating their importance.

Two Selection Scenarios.   In our earlier analysis the most typical D for science tests in representative groups of high school seniors was −.24 (median value, Table 3.1). The most typical standard deviation ratio was .89 (median *SDR*, Table *S-3* in the *Supplement*). Assume that the science knowledge test has those characteristics in the full senior class. Let us say about 10% of the seniors take the advanced physics course, and that, for the sake of the illustration, science knowledge has a strong influence on decisions to take advanced physics ($r = .90$). Two scenarios are useful in examining the relationship of gender balance to D. They are illustrated in Fig. 3.12.

In Scenario A the focus is on proficiency and interest in science. The physics teacher feels strongly that a good understanding of general science is important if a student is to profit from an advanced course in physics. Students with a strong record of interest and accomplishment in science are encouraged and students with weaker records are discouraged from taking the course. Thus, in order to play out this scenario, we assume that all women and men in the senior class with a given score on the science knowledge test are about equally likely to end up in the physics class.

As Fig. 3.12 shows, such a selection process would produce nearly normal distributions of science knowledge scores for women and men. Because the selection process tends to give priority to students with high scores, the mean score difference between women and men is somewhat reduced compared to the class as a whole, but the smaller range of scores results in a D of −.26, about the same as in the total class. The big change is in representation—about twice as many men as women in physics!

In Scenario B the focus is on gender balance as well as proficiency and interest in science. There is a strong and successful effort in the school to

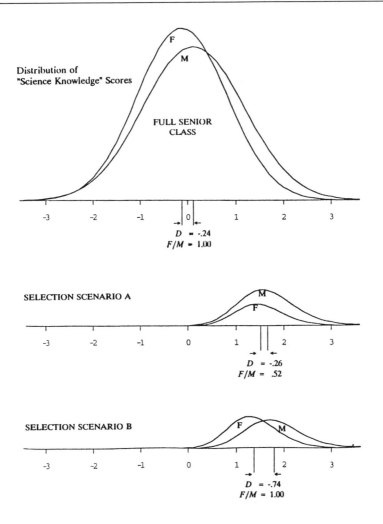

FIG. 3.12. Two scenarios for selecting an advanced physics class—illustration of the trade-off between representation (*F/M*) and mean difference (*D*). Score distributions on A and B are computer generated, based on statistical assumptions stated in the text. Arrows indicate female and male score means.

interest young women in physics. As a result, we assume that equal numbers of females and males sign up for advanced physics, and in that respect, there is no gender difference in the course (F/M = 1.00). However, to get the same number of women and men, it is necessary to assume that more women with somewhat lower scores take the course. Therefore the gender balancing has come at the expense of a larger mean difference in science knowledge scores: $D = -.74$ compared to $-.24$ in the senior class overall. In this example, that 50-point change is due partly (36%) to the fact that there is a somewhat greater difference in the actual female and male score means in the physics class than in the senior class ($-.42$ vs. $-.24$). It is also partly due (64%) to the restricted range of scores in the physics class.

Which scenario is "better?" There is an argument for both if one accepts the propositions that more women should study science and that students with more proficiency and interest in science are likely to get more out of the course. Is it better to have a more equal representation of women and men, or is it better for the women and men to be more comparable in relevant background knowledge and skill?

Regardless of the merits of this particular case, the point is that gender balance in the restricted group has a reciprocal relationship with mean difference on a pertinent proficiency in the restricted group. The F/M ratio in the restricted group is one of the main factors that affects that mean difference. Both gender balance and mean difference are important outcomes of sample restriction and one is a trade-off for the other. We should add a point that is perhaps obvious: If women proficient in science are discouraged from continuing study in that field, neither equal proficiency nor equal representation of women and men is likely in the advanced course.

It is important to appreciate that the effects of sample restriction depend on the relation of the measure of science knowledge to selection for the course and performance in the course. If more women take the course, will their increased representation necessarily result in lower average performance in the course? Certainly not, because in practice, science knowledge may not be critical, either to selecting the course or to making a good physics grade.[19] Later, we learn what has actually happened as more women have taken advanced science courses in high school over the past decade.

Because of these relationships, the relative number of females and males who take an examination can be an important consideration in describing and understanding gender difference and similarity in selected groups, but as we have noted, the nature of the selected group depends partly on the character of the selection, and we ordinarily have little precise information about that process. Table S-6 in the *Supplement* provides detailed data on F/M ratios in the same format as the companion Table 3.2 that was devoted to standard mean differences.

---

[19]Initial differences in relevant science knowledge cannot be disregarded, but there are many ways that students can bring compensatory skills to bear in achieving complex course objectives. See Willingham (1974a, p. 87) for an example.

From even a brief examination of such F/M ratios, it is evident that when able high school or college seniors have options, females and males often choose different courses and tests. Two to three times as many women as men took some tests such as education and French; three to six times as many men as women took some other tests such as computer science and physics. Other tests complete the pattern: Women tend to take more language and men tend to take more mathematics and physical science.

What is the relationship of F/M to D in such selective test data? Individual subject tests offer a comparison. As previously noted, the AP tests and ATP achievement tests are both administered near the end of high school to samples of generally similar selectivity. Of the 15 ATP tests, 13 can be matched reasonably well with AP examinations on the same subject. Average F/M and D values for each of the 13 pairs are plotted in Fig. 3.13.

One might speculate that females or males score better on a particular test because they represent a more select group. For example, females score higher than males on a particular test because only a few very good women students take the test. The opposite is more the case. Each gender tends to take those tests on which they do better. That is no surprise, but what happened to the reciprocal relationships between F/M and D? Figure 3.12 shows how that trade-off applies to results for a particular test if the ratio of females to males varies in different selected samples of high scorers on that

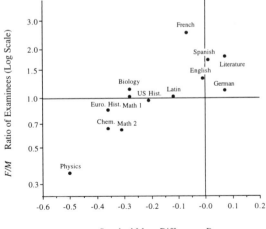

FIG. 3.13. Standard mean difference (D) and female–male ratio (F/M) for examinees taking selective tests in 13 subjects. Each subject here is represented by an average D and F/M for an ATP test and an AP test (2 tests in AP Latin and 3 in AP Physics). All foreign languages refer to composition, not literature. Math 2 is more advanced than Math 1. All data are based on averages for 1992 and 1993.

test. Figure 3.13 shows the opposite pattern (high D associated with high F/M) because the situation is quite different.

Figure 3.13 compares results for different tests that show different patterns of gender difference, independent of F/M. The pattern is strongly influenced by that variation in D and the course-taking habits of students. Presumably, more women take language tests (especially French) because they do relatively better and they like languages more. If a more select group of women was taking language tests, there would likely be a greater mean difference, favoring women. The same principle would likely hold for men taking physical science, but the trade-off is not a certainty. The small sample of women taking physics, for example, are not necessarily the ones most able to do well in physics. More generally, what can be said about the likely effects of sample restriction on gender differences that we observe on selective tests as opposed to tests administered to representative samples?

Effects on Actual Test Data.   The work described in Lewis and Willingham (1995) makes clear that a number of factors determine the effects of sample restriction on gender differences in actual test data. Our general impression is that those effects are complex and may vary enormously, depending on specific conditions. Further work is obviously needed, but a few tentative conclusions are indicated.

Of the three main components that describe the effects of sample restriction, SDR (reflecting differential variability of female and male scores) is particularly important. Differential variability typically works in only one direction—to increase male advantage. Its effect is constant, regardless of the level of gender difference in the original group (including zero) or the F/M ratio in the restricted sample. Because SDR is typically in the region of .90 for several important categories of tests, it can be expected that this factor will often increase D by .10 to .15 even if the proportion selected is not especially high (say, $p = .25$; see Lewis & Willingham, Fig. H in the *Supplement*).

The effect of differential variability is enhanced if selection is more extreme. This means that one would expect to see more negative movement of Ds in subject tests taken by very select as opposed to less select samples. That trend is visible in advanced science and math achievement tests (AP, ATP, GRE) as compared with science and math tests taken by more representative groups of students. It is important to appreciate, however, that most of the effects of extreme selection on Ds are due to range restriction, not to an increase in the difference between actual female and male score means (see Tables F, G, and H of the Lewis & Willingham report in the *Supplement*).

We have commented on the fact that Ds for some selective tests (language especially) are likely affected by large variations in the ratio of females to males in the restricted group of examinees. Lewis and Willingham (1995) raised the more general question of whether the three components of sample restriction can account for the changes in D that occur between representative samples in Grade 12 and selective samples at the same grade (Table 3.1 vs. Table 3.2). The statistical model described by Lewis and Willingham was used to predict what Ds might result—from sample effects alone—if the same tests administered to representative 12th graders had been administered to the more select group who take college admissions tests. Those results were then compared with actual Ds observed on 13 college admissions tests.

Overall, the predictions matched fairly well the gender differences actually observed in tests administered to the more selective college-bound groups. These results indicate that much of the generally small but persistent negative shift in Ds based on selective tests can be accounted for by the statistical effects of sample restriction. One exception was tests of language use for which Ds appear to drop noticeably from representative to select groups (from about .40 to .15), but were not predicted to do so on the basis of sample restriction. The other, rather similar exception, was high school grade average where a noticeable negative shift in Ds among selected groups of students is apparently not due to sample restriction.

Our general impression is that the sample restriction model is quite helpful in understanding gender differences observed on selective tests, although we are not at all certain how to explain the two exceptions. We should emphasize that this was a limited analysis and there is obviously much yet to learn about this complex topic.

An interesting study in Iowa by Hoover and Han (1995) demonstrated empirically the effect of sample restriction on gender difference. They concluded that "a large proportion of the observed gender differences in achievement on tests like the ACT can be explained by selection into the ACT/SAT test taking population (and into the public universities in Iowa) on the basis of high school grades" (p. 6). Their results appear to be quite consistent with the Lewis and Willingham model. Hoover and Han concluded that "current concern about possible gender bias in ACT and SAT might be better focused on reasons for the gender differences in high school grades, in achievement variability, and in high school course-taking behavior." (p. 6). Similarly, a study in Sweden by Makitalo (1994) indicated that gender differences are more likely to favor males on admissions tests because of the effects of self-selection to higher education.

The Graduate Level Cohort

In Table 3.2, data at the graduate level come from five test batteries: Graduate Management Admission Tests (GMAT), Graduate Record Examinations—General (GRE—G), Graduate Record Examinations—Subject Tests (GRE—S), Law School Admission Test (LSAT), and Medical College Admissions Tests (MCAT). These programs account for the great majority of admissions tests used by graduate, law, business, and medical schools. The GRE Subject Tests cover 20 subject areas and are required by some graduate departments. The GRE General and the other three batteries are typically required by all or the great majority of schools or departments within these four types of postgraduate institutions.

Table 3.2 gives the general impression that males score somewhat higher relative to females at the post-BA level, but this is not true in all categories. In fact, generalizable conclusions about gender differences at the undergraduate versus the post-BA level are limited because the tests and the reasons for taking them vary considerably. Often undergraduate and graduate tests within the individual categories are not directly comparable. A more serious problem in comparing test performance of women and men at these two levels is the fact that samples of examinees at the postgraduate level are nonrepresentative in quite different ways.

For example, the several subject tests in the MCAT battery can tell us little about gender differences on such tests at that age level because they are idiosyncratic to highly self-selected medical school applicants. Furthermore, the various subject tests in the GRE Subject Test series cannot be viewed as representative of students who choose to go into particular graduate fields because they are required by only some departments.[20] Because of such noncomparability, it is potentially misleading to assume that a difference in D for, say, history at the undergraduate and graduate level reflects a real shift in the relative performance of women and men in that subject. Similarly, one cannot assume that a change in the F/M ratios for history tests at the two levels faithfully reflects the number of women and men actively pursuing the study of history. Data on enrollment and earned

---

[20]Examinees may sit for a GRE Subject Test for other than the obvious need to meet an admissions requirement. For example, some take the tests in connection with undergraduate program evaluation. In some graduate fields, half or more of the examinees who take a subject test do not take the GRE General. Evidently, a significant number are taking the Subject Tests as a departmental admissions alternative to the GRE General. Such influences on the nature of the samples are impossible to evaluate, although it seems clear that gender difference and similarity on the subject tests are, in part, simply a reflection of which departments require students to take the tests for what reasons.

degrees in chapter 4 is a more dependable source regarding that aspect of gender difference and similarity at the graduate level. Nonetheless, some comparisons can be instructive, if properly qualified.

Graduate Versus Undergraduate Differences. Recognizing that neither undergraduate nor postgraduate cohorts are representative of women and men in general at that age level, it is still interesting to compare relative performance across that transition point. For that purpose, two aggregate samples of students seem sufficiently representative of the two levels to give a useful indication of possible changes from one to the other. Taken together, the samples of students who take the ACT and the SAT account for the great majority of students entering 4-year undergraduate colleges, the primary feeders for postgraduate programs. Institutions and testing programs at the graduate and professional level are more numerous and diverse. The aggregation of graduate, law, business, and medical schools do, however, cover the bulk of such students and many of the more prominent academic fields and professions. The general admissions tests taken by applicants to these various types of institutions at both levels typically include a verbal and a quantitative ability test, or a test that is sufficiently similar to serve the immediate purpose.[21] Table 3.4 summarizes such comparative data for undergraduate and graduate applicants.

Is there any noticeable shift in either gender representation or gender score difference on verbal and quantitative admissions tests at the undergraduate and graduate level? There appears to be very little difference in the number of women and men taking admissions tests at the two levels—slightly more women in each case. On the other hand, there is a substantial difference in the proportion of females among examinees for graduate versus professional schools.

There is evidence of some negative shift in the standard mean difference on the verbal and quantitative measures from the undergraduate to graduate level, particularly in the case of the quantitative tests. The males gain a quarter of a standard deviation in their relative performance on quantitative skills. This is a reliable change because the samples are quite large, but the reason for the change is not clear. The difference could be due to one or

---

[21]At the undergraduate level, we use ACT Reading because, of the four ACT tests, it is the most similar to the other verbal ability tests. At the graduate level we have similarly used MCAT Reading. In order to include law school applicants, we have used the LSAT as a verbal measure, although it could easily be viewed as either a reasoning or a verbal test. The data in Table 3.4 come from Table 3.2 here and Table S-6 in the *Supplement* and are based on the most recently available year, typically 1992. MCAT data for the 1990 edition and sample were used in order to have both a verbal and a quantitative test. The latter is not included in subsequent editions of the test.

TABLE 3.4

Standard Mean Difference (*D*) and Female–Male Ratio (*F/M*) for Examinees Taking Verbal and Quantitative Admissions Tests at the Undergraduate and Graduate Level

	Standard Mean Difference			
	Undergraduate		Graduate	
Admissions Test	*Verbal*	*Quant.*	*Verbal*	*Quant.*
ACT	.00	− .25		
SAT	− .06	− .36		
GMAT			− .12	− .49
GRE-G			− .23	− .63
LSAT			− .09	—
MCAT			− .06	− .36
Weighted average	− .03	− .31	− .16	− .56

	Female–Male Ratio	
	Undergraduate	Graduate
ACT	1.22	
SAT	1.11	
GMAT		.68
GRE-G		1.49
LSAT		.78
MCAT		.74
Weighted average	1.16	1.09

Note. Typically 1992. See footnote 11 in chapter 2.

more of several factors: an effect of greater sample restriction at the postgraduate level, more self-selection to undertake graduate study by women who are more proficient in nonquantitative skills, or differential courses of study at the undergraduate level.

We know that people who go to graduate and professional school are a select sample of undergraduates. Why not apply the model of Lewis and Willingham (1995) to estimate the effect of sample restriction, just as we did at the undergraduate level? The model is not usable here because the situation is different in two important respects. First, to estimate sample effects, we have to assume that there are no construct or cohort differences. There is no way to determine whether there are cohort differences because the only comparable data on verbal and quantitative skills for a representative sample of college students come from tests administered 4 years earlier than the graduate tests. Second, we have in this case almost no basis for estimating the statistical characteristics of sample restriction that the model requires.

Differences by Graduate Field. There is also evident in Table 3.4 a somewhat larger male shift in the scores of students applying to graduate school than is the case for students applying to professional schools. Graduate education is quite heterogeneous. It is possible that performance of females and males on the GRE General is more evenly balanced within individual graduate fields, as appears to be the case in the three professional schools. Furthermore, it probably makes more sense to view relative test performance of women and men within particular graduate fields than across graduate education generally. Table 3.5 shows summary data for 14 graduate fields.

The fields in Table 3.5 are arranged in order of F/M ratio. It is quickly obvious that the number of test takers in these fields varies considerably, as does the relative number of females and males. It is also well-known that test score means vary among graduate fields (Conrad, Trismen, & Miller, 1977; Graduate Record Examinations Board, 1992; Grandy, 1994b).

Two aspects of Table 3.5 are noteworthy. The last line shows F/M and D for the total group of students represented in these particular fields. The next to last line shows corresponding figures, as averages of summary data within the individual fields. The positive shift in the Ds on the next to last line indicates much less gender differences within fields than is true of the graduate group overall. Within fields, about half of the differences on verbal and quantitative measures has gone away, as has all of the difference on analytical measures.

TABLE 3.5
Female–Male Ratio (F/M) and Standard Mean Difference (D) for GRE General Test Scores in 14 Graduate Fields in 1992

Field	N	F/M	Standard Mean Difference, D		
			Verbal	Quantitative	Analytical
Health care	9,896	11.82	−.17	−.35	.05
Social work	5,951	5.41	−.11	−.21	.21
Education	40,746	3.00	−.11	−.37	.02
Psychology	25,393	2.70	−.17	−.35	.03
Social studies	4,732	1.96	−.09	−.35	−.02
English	10,339	1.62	−.23	−.45	−.11
Performing arts	5,001	1.25	−.10	−.30	.01
Biological science	10,296	1.12	−.04	−.29	.10
Political science	9,495	.86	−.09	−.28	−.05
Mathematics	3,223	.80	−.31	−.49	−.06
History	6,606	.62	−.05	−.30	.06
Physical science	4,017	.41	−.17	−.46	−.01
Computer science	5,669	.31	−.33	−.58	−.19
Engineering	17,811	.23	−.01	−.30	.13
Unweighted average of 14 fields	11,370	1.27	−.14	−.36	.01
Total	159,175	1.49	−.27	−.74	−.25

Note. See Table S-7 in the Supplement for test score means and standard errors of D and F/M. The average for F/M is a geometric mean to avoid some slight distortion due to the F/M ratio scale.

This shift means that within fields, women and men are on more of an equal footing regarding test scores than would appear to be the case from looking simply at the total pool of GRE scores. The different result for individual fields results from a tendency for women to enroll somewhat more frequently in fields where scores are lower (at the top of the list) and men to enroll more frequently in fields where scores are higher (at the bottom of the list). Therefore the more balanced pattern of scores within fields results because of, and at the expense of, some degree of gender stratification across fields.

The second interesting aspect of Table 3.5 is the lack of any clear relationship between F/M and D as was noted in Fig. 3.13. The absence of a strong tie between F/M and D is partly because selectivity in different fields is likely to be associated with different combinations of the three GRE General Tests. Another reason may have to do with the nature of selectivity here and in the earlier analysis. The AP and the College Board Achievement Tests are all taken by groups that are highly selected. This circumstance apparently encourages a positive relationship between F/M and D. However, in the graduate pool, the fields vary considerably in selectivity, allowing both males and females to stratify according to interest and academic ability.

GENDER DIFFERENCES
WITHIN ETHNIC GROUPS

As we have emphasized in an earlier discussion, it is never safe to assume that women and men can be adequately described simply by a mean difference. Individual women and men vary far more than do the two groups on virtually any measure that one might choose. Similarly, subgroups of women and men may well vary according to background, interests, and so on. Ethnic identity is only one of many ways in which one might define subgroups within gender, but a careful look at possible ethnic differences in female–male test performance is certainly warranted because such variations can have considerable social and educational significance. In this section we have the limited objective of trying to shed some light on this question: Are there generally comparable patterns of gender difference and similarity in test performance across ethnic groups?

Until now, limited attention has been given to this question. True, there is a substantial literature on test performance of women and men. Similarly, there is a large literature on ethnic differences in test performance, but surprisingly little analysis of gender difference *within* ethnic groups. There is a great deal of data, published or otherwise available. Major testing programs routinely compile such information (Admissions Testing Program,

1992; Advanced Placement Program, 1992; American College Testing Program, 1988; Graduate Record Examinations Board, 1991c). NAEP has perhaps the most extensive data on gender and ethnicity. Due to the volume of data, NAEP reports most often describe assessment results only by gender and ethnicity separately (e.g., see Applebee, Langer, Mullis, Latham, & Gentile, 1994), although data on female and male performance within ethnic group are readily available from NAEP on CD-ROM.

To our knowledge, there has been no systematic review of research literature on this topic in recent years. There have been a limited number of studies of individual tests or particular ethnic groups (e.g., Moore & Smith, 1987; Petersen & Livingston, 1982; Sue & Abe, 1988), and a few studies involving more extensive analyses of multiple sets of test data (e.g., Hyde et al., 1990; Jensen, 1971; Mazzeo et al., 1993). The most typical finding in the studies available has been relatively little variation in gender difference from one ethnic group to another.

The studies one finds in the research literature on this topic are often of limited value to our purpose because gender differences within ethnic groups was only a secondary interest of the researchers. Detailed comparisons of gender differences among ethnic groups are not always possible, either because the data are too sparse to be reliable or simply not available. We have been able, however, to accumulate a substantial amount of useful data that are based on nationally representative samples of 12th-grade students or on large selective testing programs. These analyses always involved Black, Hispanic, and White examinees. Results are presented for subdivisions of the Hispanic group or for other ethnic groups when the data were available in sufficient quantity for analysis.[22]

Representative Test Data

We had in our database test performance results for women and men among White, Black, and Hispanic 12th-grade students from four major national surveys: NAEP, NELS, NALS, and HSB. Table 3.6 shows several apparent variations in gender differences among these three subgroups, but the results were quite inconsistent.

---

[22]We have attempted to designate ethnic groups consistently, although there are several complications. Multiple terms are employed and usage changes. Different programs and publications often use different terms, sometimes inconsistently. When data refer to a specific testing program or are reproduced from a particular publication, we have adopted the terminology of the source. In other instances we have used the following designations for examinee groups: American Indian, Asian American, Black, Hispanic (or Mexican American and Other Hispanic), and White.

TABLE 3.6

Standard Mean Differences (With Standard Errors) Within Representative Groups of White, Black, and Hispanic Examinees at Grade 12

| Test | Standard Mean Difference, D(SE) | | |
	White	Black	Hispanic
NAEP			
Writing (1992)	.57(.03)	.50(.07)	.54(.09)
Reading (1992)	.36(.04)	.33(.07)	.26(.09)
Math (1992)	−.12(.04)	−.12(.09)	.12(.11)*
Science (1990)	−.24(.04)	−.22(.10)	−.26(.11)
History (1988)	−.24(.05)	−.13(.09)	−.04(.12)
Civics (1988)	−.16(.05)	−.23(.11)	.09(.13)[a]
NELS (1992)			
Reading	.28(.03)	.28(.08)	.07(.07)*
Math	−.04(.03)	.07(.08)	−.29(.07)*
Science	−.27(.03)	−.15(.08)	−.50(.08)*
History	−.08(.03)	−.04(.08)	−.28(.07)*
NALS (1992)			
Prose	.12(.06)	.23(.09)	.14(.10)
Document	.06(.06)	.25(.09)[a]	.09(.10)
Quantitative	−.05(.06)	.15(.09)[a]	.03(.10)
HSB (1980)			
Vocabulary	−.05(.02)	−.17(.05)*	−.01(.06)
Reading	.03(.02)	−.09(.05)*	.02(.06)
Math	−.23(.02)	−.24(.06)	−.19(.06)
Picture-number	.22(.02)	−.06(.05)*	.16(.06)
Mosiac comparisons	.31(.02)	.14(.06)*	.24(.06)
3-D visualization	−.25(.02)	−.24(.06)	−.22(.06)

[a]Different from White group, $p = .05$ to $.09$.
*$p < .05$.

For example, two of the surveys showed a somewhat different pattern of gender difference for Black and White students. In one survey (NALS) the performance of women relative to men appeared to be slightly better in the Black group than in the White group. A second survey (HSB) showed the opposite effect, and two surveys indicated comparable gender difference for Black and White students. There was a similar situation among the Hispanic students, but with two different surveys. In one survey (NAEP), Hispanic women did better relative to men in their group than was true of White women. A second survey (NELS) suggested the opposite trend.

Such contradictory results suggest that these small variations in gender differences across ethnic groups are probably due to differences in the survey samples. The ethnic subgroups typically number several hundred women and a like number of men, perhaps not enough to give a stable result in all cases for such disaggregated analyses. That considered, the general impression we get from the results is that gender differences on these types of tests probably do not vary much among ethnic groups in the general population.

Selective Test Data

We report here on gender differences within ethnic groups for three types of tests: undergraduate admissions tests, advanced course placement tests, and graduate admissions tests. It is useful to note several aspects of selective test data that are pertinent to this discussion and different from the data based on nationally representative samples of students.

First, recall that the samples are quite different. Selective program data actually represent the full population of concern, and the samples are typically large.[23] The statistics are therefore fairly stable, although the results may well vary from group to group because the samples are self-selected and are not necessarily representative of such students nationally. Nonetheless, variations in results from one ethnic group to another may be important because these particular samples are important; for example, high school graduates who go to college, students who study science, and so on.

Second, we are concerned here with female–male ratios as well as mean differences. In representative samples the F/M ratio is, by its nature, always very near 1.00 and of little interest, but in selected samples F/M indicates selective representation of women and men. For that reason, we have come to appreciate more fully that in some situations F/M can be viewed, with D, as a complementary outcome measure of interest.

Undergraduate Admissions Tests. The total group of students who take either the ACT or the SAT likely includes the great majority of all high school graduates who go to 4-year colleges each year. Both the ACT Program and the College Board collect information on the ethnic identity of examinees. Response categories for examinees (with some variation in terms used by the programs) include American Indian, Asian American, Black, White, and two or three groupings of Hispanic students. We calculated F/M ratios and Ds for these various groups in each program. The results are reported in detail in Tables S-8 and S-9 in the *Supplement.*

For students taking the SAT, we examined gender differences by ethnic group for 1991 and 1992, as well as 1982. The results were quite similar in 1991 and 1992. There was a slightly different pattern in 1982; we address that in the next section concerning trends over the past decade. Looking at all of the undergraduate admissions test takers for 1992 (ACT and SAT results), the general impression—with one exception—is that there was very

---

[23]ACT based these program statistics on a 10% sample of data on hand, but one would expect these results to vary little from those based on the entire population because the sample is large and one can assume it to be truly representative of students who participate in the testing program.

little variation in the pattern of gender difference and similarity from one ethnic group to another. The F/M ratio of female and male test takers and the standard mean difference, D, in test performance was, for each ethnic group, generally quite similar to results already reported for all women and men.

The exception came with the Black examinees. This was the only ethnic subgroup that showed a pattern of gender difference distinctly different from that of the White group among both the ACT and the SAT examinees. In pooled results for all undergraduate admissions test takers, both F/M and D were more favorable to women among the Black students than was true of the White students. Whereas the F/M ratio was 1.16 among White test takers, it was 1.40 among Black test takers. As we have previously discussed, if a larger proportion of a group elect to take an advanced test, one might expect the average score to be correspondingly somewhat lower because the additional students are likely to be a less select group who will tend to score lower. The Black women's average test score was slightly lower than that of the Black men, but the difference was *smaller* than was the case with the White majority students.[24] That is, among the Black students, more women than men are taking admissions tests, and they are doing relatively better than is true in other groups.

Advanced Placement Tests.   In order to examine gender differences within ethnic groups on selective tests in different subject areas, we went to data from the AP Program of the College Board. As previously noted, these groups are highly self-selected. Because this is a large program, it offers extensive test performance data, even for ethnic groups that are proportionally small. We calculated F/M ratios and Ds for five ethnic groups on data for each of nine AP examinations for which there were typically more than 500 examinees in each ethnic group in 1992. Detailed data are reported in Table S-10 in the *Supplement*. The main results are summarized in Fig. 3.14.

First, note in Fig. 3.14 the very slight differences in average Ds from one ethnic group to another. Even for individual tests, the Ds were fairly consistent across ethnic groups. Generally speaking, the variations in the relative mean performance of females and males on the AP examinations are associated with different tests, not with different ethnic groups. An interesting minor exception was the Asian American group. The average D for Asian American students was little different from that of White stu-

---

[24]Mean differences reported here are average Ds for all six ACT and SAT subtests. F/M ratios were corrected to account for different numbers of female and male high school graduates. D and F/M were weighted according to program volume (see Tables S-8 and S-9 in the *Supplement*). All standard errors are .01 or smaller.

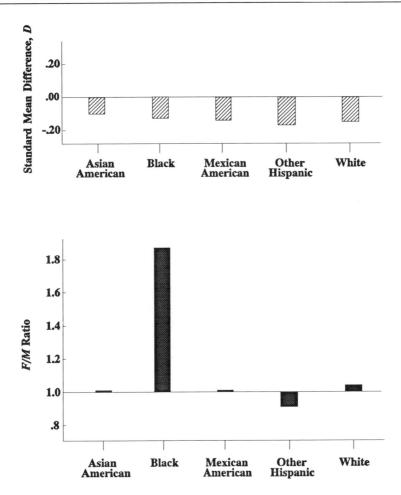

FIG. 3.14. Standard mean difference (*D*) and female to male ratio (*F/M*) on Advanced Placement examinations for five ethnic groups. Average results for nine AP examinations for which there were sufficient data to represent all groups. See Table *S*-10 in the *Supplement* for detail.

dents, but relative to men in their group, the Asian American women did slightly better than the White women on each of the nine tests.

In the lower portion of Fig. 3.14, results regarding the female–male ratio of AP examinees are generally similar, with one prominent exception. Black women were far more likely to take AP examinations than were Black men, by a factor of almost two to one. Despite heavier representation, the Black women maintained the same level of performance relative to men that was true in other groups. Data from the 1993 AP examination results showed an almost identical pattern.

Graduate Admissions Tests. The Graduate Record Examinations Board is the primary source of test data concerning admissions to graduate schools—especially data on gender differences within ethnic group. The GRE General Test is far more useful than the GRE Subject Tests for our present purpose because the former provides a standard measure for a much larger group of students across many areas of graduate study. We examined F/M ratios for seven ethnic groups and corresponding Ds for the three GRE General tests: Verbal, Quantitative, and Analytical.

In 1992 GRE General data, women in two ethnic minority groups performed slightly better in relation to men than was true of White majority women. The average Ds for Black and Asian American examinees were some .15 to .20 more positive than those of the White group. Except for the Black students, the F/M ratios for the minority groups were close to 1.00 in 1992. Thus, in most ethnic groups women were not as heavily represented among GRE General test takers as was true of the White majority students (F/M = 1.27). Currently, these are perhaps the most notable gender differences among ethnic groups at this level. These various patterns, regarding F/M as well as D, were somewhat different 10 years earlier in 1982. Overall there do not appear to be consequential and stable variations in the pattern of gender differences on these measures among ethnic groups in the total pool of graduate applicants (see Table S-11 in the *Supplement*).

There is, of course, more variation when one looks at individual areas of graduate study. The finer level of analysis can be useful because graduate areas of study are quite different, but this focus goes beyond our objectives in this report. The GRE Board has recently provided a great deal of detailed information about GRE General examinees by gender and ethnicity for nine graduate areas over the past decade (Grandy, 1994b; see also GRE, 1991b). We move now to the general question of what changes can be noted in the patterns of difference and similarity in the test performance of women and men over the past 10 years.

TRENDS OVER THE PAST DECADE

In this chapter we have presented a number of analyses of data that describe patterns of gender difference and similarity. This information helps to shed additional light on ways in which variations in test constructs, age cohorts, and selected samples affect the differences we observe in test performance of women and men. Have there been changes over time? Differences among groups of students from year to year is another version of cohort variation.

Understanding the character of trends over time is obviously important because of the social and educational implications. Women's career interests and aspirations have been undergoing change for some time. There have been intensive efforts in recent years to improve educational opportunities for women and to encourage strong programs of study, particularly in mathematics and science. Is there evidence of change in patterns of test choice and/or test performance?

Research literature on this aspect of the topic has tended to focus, perhaps somewhat too narrowly, on the question of whether there is any overall difference in cognitive skills between women and men and the answers have varied. Authors of some major meta-analytic research surveys have concluded that gender differences are declining (Hyde et al., 1990; Hyde & Linn, 1988). That interpretation of the meta-analytic data may be open to some question (see chapter 2), but other investigators have also presented data recently indicating that gender differences are on the decline. For example, Feingold (1988) summarized test performance of females and males on the Differential Aptitude Tests and the PSAT over several decades and entitled his study, "Cognitive gender differences are disappearing" (see also Feingold, 1993a). Linn (1992) recently reviewed several lines of evidence for "the closing gender gap" in verbal, spatial visualization, and mathematical ability.

On the other hand, Cleary (1992) did a major study of gender differences in which one question of interest was whether test performance of women and men had changed significantly over the past quarter century. She concluded, "No consistent trends are evident over time" (p. 76). Had Cleary gone back a few more years to Project TALENT, the major national survey in the early 1960s, she would likely have qualified her conclusion. TALENT data (Table 3.1 in Flanagan et al., 1964) showed Ds of −.60 and −.44 in natural science information and total mathematics at Grade 12. Compare these results with Ds of −.17 and −.11 for science and math, respectively, in our Table 3.1.[25]

---

[25] In the course of an analysis focusing primarily on differential variability of female and male test scores, Hedges and Nowell (1995) recently observed that "average sex differences have been generally small and stable over time" (p. 41). Hedges and Nowell did note some narrowing of gender differences in mathematics and science, although their report did not include any data on Grade 12 students from the early 1960s. Their earliest data were based on Project TALENT students, but only those at age 15 in 1960. Data from Flanagan et al. (1964) show a marked decline in Ds from Grade 9 to Grade 12 in both mathematics (−.07 to −.44) and science (−.41 to −.60). Thus, considering also the 12th-grade TALENT data, the narrowing gender difference in mathematics and science over the past three decades is much more apparent.

Evidence from the National Assessment of Educational Progress is also pertinent. A major purpose of NAEP has been to gauge trends over time. In their summary of NAEP Report Card surveys over 20 years, Mullis et al. (1990) reported:

> In reading, the gender gap favoring females has been narrowing slowly across time. This is primarily due to gains in males' average reading proficiency, especially at age 17, and to the concurrent lack of change in females' reading achievement. In mathematics and in science, little progress has been made in closing the gender gap favoring males. (p. 49)

A subsequent survey involving the NAEP Trend Tests (Mullis, Dossey, Foertsch, et al., 1991) provides evidence against the narrowing gap in reading. That new result indicated no significant difference in the extent of female advantage in reading in 1990 as compared with two decades earlier.

Why is there such inconsistency in results and conclusions on what would seem to be a straightforward factual question? We now better appreciate that there are at least three reasons why one might find contradictory results in comparisons across time. Different tests can give different answers, as can different age cohorts or different types of samples. Halpern (1989) seemed to have captured the spirit of the problem when she commented on the Feingold (1988) analysis with an article entitled, "The disappearance of cognitive gender differences: What you see depends upon where you look."

Comparing current data with the extensive Project TALENT survey in the early 1960s, it does appear that there is now less gender difference in mathematics and science scores at Grade 12 than was true three decades ago. In an effort to shed some additional light on trends in relative test performance of women and men in recent years, we have tried to focus on important aspects of the problem for which available data offer some hope of stable and dependable answers. Thus our search is limited to the test performance of 12th-grade students over the past decade, partly because we have the best data for these years and students. Also, it is probably the group and the period of greatest interest that can add most to what we know. We have focused on large samples and tests that changed very little or not at all over this time period.

Finally, we have looked at multiple sets of data in the hope of seeing useful answers in the pattern of results. The following sections concentrate on three types of data: tests administered to representative national samples of 12th-grade students, admissions tests that are taken by the general population of college-bound students, and the series of subject achievement tests in the AP Program. The latter two types of data involve selected samples in which representation of women and men is an important consideration in evaluating gender difference and similarity. Accordingly, in those samples we regard D and F/M as complementary measures of equal potential importance.

Trends in Representative Samples

We had representative 12th-grade data in both the early 1980s and the early 1990s for two test series: NAEP Trend Tests (NAEPt) and Differential Aptitude Tests (DAT). NAEPt probably provides the best national data available on subgroup test performance over time because the five subject tests have remained essentially constant. Also, the successive surveys have been based on multiple, carefully drawn national samples. The content of the NAEP Report Card series varies somewhat from one survey to another.

The DAT is a useful benchmark because this eight-test battery has been widely used in basically its present form for several decades. DAT results from 1947 through 1980 figured prominently in Feingold's (1988) conclusion that gender differences had "declined precipitously" over the past several decades. DAT results for 1980 and 1990 are based on different editions, which involved some updating of content within the same general test design.

Test data based on NAEPt and DAT over the past decade give the general impression of a small trend favoring women. Five of the 13 tests in these two series (two NAEP and three DAT) showed a statistically significant shift in standard mean difference—all in the direction of higher performance by women relative to men. The average D for all 13 tests in the two series was slightly higher in 1990 (.07) than in 1980 (.00). The details are shown in Table 3.7.

College Admissions Tests

Currently, about three out of five high school seniors take either the ACT with its four subtests or the SAT with its two subtests (see Note 4 of the Lewis & Willingham report in the *Supplement*). SAT examinees also took the Test of Standard Written English (TSWE) in this period. Note that the group taking the SAT overlaps substantially with the group taking the PSAT, which is a shorter version of the SAT. All together, this makes nine tests regularly taken by college-bound students. As far as we are aware, there were no consequential content changes in any of these tests during the 1980s, although both testing programs did systematically screen all test questions that showed any statistical evidence of gender bias. (SAT data were compared for 1982 and 1992; ACT data were compared over 9 years—1980 to 1989—because the ACT tests were changed in 1990.)

TABLE 3.7

Trends in Standard Mean Difference (*D*) Over an 8- to 12-Year Period for Tests Administered to Representative Samples in Grade 11/12

National Assessment	Initial D (SE)	D (SE), 8–12 Years Later	Difference in D
Writing (1984–1992)	.57(.06)	.55(.04)	−.02
Reading (1980–1992)	.18(.02)	.27(.04)	.09*
Mathematics (1982–1992)	−.18(.02)	−.15(.04)	.03
Science (1982–1992)	−.36(.03)	−.23(.04)	.13*
Civics (1976–1988)	−.29(.02)	−.24(.07)	.05
Differential Aptitude Tests	*D (SE) in 1980*	*D (SE) in 1990*	*Difference*
Verbal reasoning	.00(.03)	.21(.04)	.21*
Numerical ability	.01(.03)	.15(.04)	.14*
Abstract reasoning	−.02(.03)	−.03(.04)	−.01
Clerical speed & accuracy	.32(.03)	.31(.04)	−.01
Mechanical reasoning	−.89(.03)	−.84(.04)	.05
Space relations	−.22(03)	−.03(.04)	.19*
Spelling	.50(.03)	.45(.04)	−.05
Language usage	.40(.03)	.46(.04)	.06

*p = < .05.

During the 1980s there were some very small changes in the pattern of mean gender differences for these tests—statistically significant differences because the samples are very large. On the mathematics section of both the ACT and the SAT, the *D* increased by .08. Most of the other changes in *D* were also positive but smaller. There were no significant mean shifts favoring males. The data are shown in Table 3.8. To offer a more detailed picture of the trend, Fig. 3.15 shows *D*s for SAT-V and SAT-M for each year during the period 1982 to 1992, plus two more recent years. Yearly variation in the ratio of female to male examinees is also shown, but note that the scale for *D* and *F/M* are not directly comparable. These graphs illustrate several points about the question at hand, and about the character of yearly changes in score averages for such large testing programs

The SAT Verbal and Math mean scores typically vary slightly from year to year. The standard errors for these mean differences are very small (.002) because the samples are so large. Because each point on the lines is plotted to the nearest .01, every difference that is visible to the eye is a real difference, even if not consequential. There is no obvious correspondence in the yearly fluctuations for SAT-V and SAT-M, or for *F/M* ratio. Fluctuations in one direction in one year are just about as likely as not to reverse themselves in the following year. However, over the decade there is a trend to slightly higher scores for women relative to men—corresponding to about 5 points on the (200 to 800) verbal scale and 10 points on the math scale.

TABLE 3.8
Trends in Standard Mean Difference (*D*) Over a 9- to 10-Year Period for Undergraduate Admissions Tests

Test	Initial D	D, 9–10 Years Later	Difference in D
College Board (1982–1992)			
SAT-Verbal	−.09	−.08	.01*
SAT-Math	−.44	−.36	.08*
PSAT-Verbal	−.11	−.06	.05*
PSAT-Math	−.37	−.33	.04*
TSWE	.14	.16	.02*
ACT (1980–1989)			
English	.19	.18	−.01
Math	−.36	−.28	.08*
Social studies	−.25	−.23	.02*
Natural science	−.39	−.39	.00

Note. Standard errors for *D*s were .002 for CB data; .007 for ACT data. *F/M* for early and later years were: SAT and TSWE, 1.07 and 1.10; PSAT, 1.21 and 1.26; ACT, 1.21 and 1.19. Data span 9 years for the ACT because the test was changed in 1990.

*$p = < .05$.

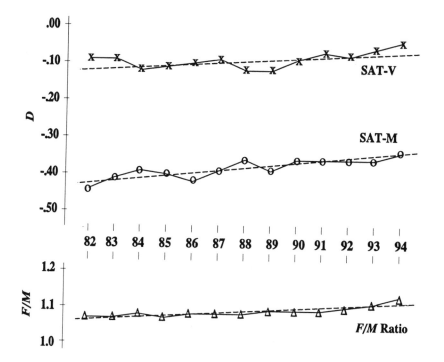

FIG. 3.15. Yearly trends in standard mean difference (*D*) and female–male (*F/M*) ratio among SAT examinees—1982 to 1994.

Why the positive trend in these Ds? One possibility would be that the female group is more select in the later years. The trend line for F/M offers no support for that hypothesis. Relative to men, there are actually somewhat more women in the SAT sample in 1994. The trend line for F/M among SAT examinees went up .05 during the period. (However, in the overall college-bound sample, that trend was offset by a slight reduction in the proportion of women among ACT examinees in 1989 compared to 1980.) Changes in D for the SAT could be due to subtle changes in the test because of the recent practice of deleting items that show any suspicion of possible gender bias. That explanation seems unlikely because it implies that such change in the score pattern for both SAT-V and SAT-M would occur only in the period during which such procedures were introduced (i.e., mostly from 1988 to 1990).[26] Another more likely explanation is that women are getting a better education and doing slightly better on the test despite being somewhat more represented in the sample of examinees.

The nature of the score gains of women on the SAT is further revealed in Fig. 3.16, which shows changes for SAT-V and SAT-M by ethnic group. Five minority groups and two test scores give 10 ways to compare test performance of minority women and men in 1992 with 1982. The ethnic minority women gained relative to the men in their group in 9 instances out of 10. On SAT Math the relative gain of women was quite similar across the various ethnic groups. On SAT Verbal, score gains of women were due only to women's gains in four of the five minority groups.

Advanced Placement Examinations

The various subject tests of the AP Program of the College Board provide a valuable set of data for examining possible changes in the academic achievements of women and men over the past decade. The examinations are keyed to specific syllabi defining quite difficult college-level courses. As we have noted, a select group of high school students take these examinations, and as a group, they do extremely well on a variety of indicators of success in college (Willingham & Morris, 1986). How many women take these examinations and how well they do on them should be good indicators of possible changes in patterns of gender difference in demanding programs of study in secondary school.

---

[26]Another consideration is that items are removed if preliminary statistics suggest that they might be unduly difficult for either females or males. Because there are typically a few of each type among SAT trial items, one would not expect any noticeable change in D due to their removal, and that has been the experience.

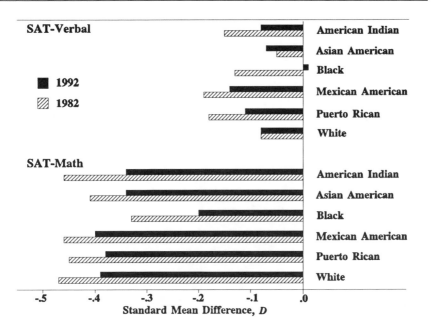

FIG. 3.16. Change in standard mean difference for ethnic groups on the SAT between 1982 and 1992. Detail in Table *S*-9 in the *Supplement*.

There are 29 current AP examinations. Twenty of those were also offered a decade ago. In order to obtain a stable estimate of trends through this period, we have pooled results for 1982 and 1983 for comparison with 1992 and 1993. Where possible, data were combined for examinations in the same area (e.g., French language and French literature), yielding results for 12 subject areas. Figures 3.17 and 3.18 show *F/M* ratios and *D*s a decade apart for the 12 subjects (see Table *S*-12 in the *Supplement* for detailed data). The results seem clear and reasonably consistent.

• There has been a small increase in the proportion of women among AP examinees. There were more than two and a half times as many AP examinations administered in 1992 and 1993 compared with the corresponding 2-year period a decade earlier, and the number of women increased more rapidly than the number of men. As a result, the proportion of women among AP examinees increased from .48 to .52.

• Across the decade the general pattern of test taking remained much the same—women preferring to take some AP examinations, men others. AP data show one notable shift. Increases in the number of women relative to men were concentrated quite consistently in subject areas where women had been underrepresented a decade earlier (see Fig. 3.17). This trend was particularly evident in natural science

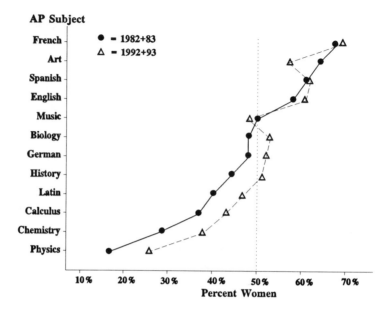

FIG. 3.17. Percentage of women among AP examinees in different subject areas—changes over a decade.

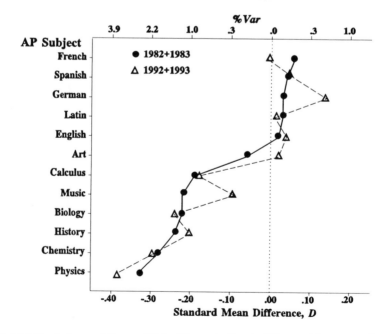

FIG. 3.18. Standard mean difference (*D*) for AP examinations in different subject areas—changes over a decade. %Var = Percentage of score variation associated with gender.

and mathematics, where the number of male AP examinees increased by a factor of 2.6 over the decade, and the corresponding increase for women was 3.4. As a result, the proportion of women in these areas increased from .37 to .43.

• Although relatively more women were taking AP examinations in the 1990s, relative performance of women and men in most subjects was very similar in the early 1980s and the early 1990s (see Fig. 3.18). The overall average D was −.13 in 1982–1983 and −.12 10 years later. Stumpf and Stanley (1996) reported essentially the same pattern of mean differences over this period.[27]

• The overall impact of these trends has been to augment the number of young women who are performing at a high level in mathematics and science. Over this decade the F/M ratio among high school seniors who demonstrated college-level proficiency (an AP grade of 3 or better) increased in both mathematics (.49 to .62) and natural science (.51 to .60).

We have distinguished two important indicators of gender difference and similarity in a selected group: mean performance and female–male ratio. Because restricting a sample to a very select group tends to have reciprocal (i.e., opposite) statistical effects on these two measures, it would not be unreasonable to expect one measure to go down if the other goes up and nothing else in the educational system changes. It is dramatically clear that D and F/M are *not* inevitably linked. Substantial increases in representation of women, in scientific areas in particular, have not come at the expense of any change in relative performance level. This finding seems to be evidence of real improvement in the secondary education of young women over the past decade.

SUMMARY

Our objective has been to shed some light on the ways in which variation in test constructs, samples, and student cohorts may affect observed gender differences. To this end, a large quantity of test data were analyzed—some based on representative national samples of students, some based on annual data from major testing programs. The analyses focused mainly on three measures of gender similarity and difference: D, the standard mean difference in scores of females and males; F/M, the ratio of females to males in a selected group; and SDR, the ratio of female to male standard deviations, which is an index of relative variability of scores. Consistent with our

---

[27]Stumpf and Stanley (1996) also reported data for 14 College Board Achievement Tests that show much the same 10-year trend—an increase in the number of women examinees relative to men in science and mathematics, but little change in relative mean scores. Our analysis emphasizes trend in college-creditable AP scores earned by women and men as a complement to D, because we see the number of high school graduates who are highly proficient in science and math as a sensitive barometer of the quality of training that women and men are receiving in these areas.

purpose, the following summary frequently cites gender differences according to variation in construct, cohort, or sample. But our summary follows our chapter, which was not readily organized in a logical and readable manner according to these three possible sources of variation. Therefore, as an additional aid in thinking about these results, we have outlined the main findings in Table 3.9 according to construct, cohort, and sample variations. The results were described in the following five sections.

A 12th-Grade Profile

At Grade 12, the average D for 74 tests was .02. Based on results for a wide variety of tests and large nationally representative samples of high school seniors, there does not appear to be any overall difference in the average test performance of young women and men. There were differences among

TABLE 3.9

**Gender Difference and Similarity in Test Performance Associated
With Variations in Constructs, Cohorts, and Samples**

Construct Variations
- Averaging across all available tests, there is no apparent difference in the test performance of women and men in general populations of Grade 12 students.
- Women tend to score higher on verbal skills, especially language use and samples of actual writing, although scores of females and males overlap substantially.
- Men tend to score higher in more technical areas like physical science, geopolitics, and some types of math, although scores of females and males overlap substantially.
- In some subjects there was a small but fairly consistent tendency for women to perform relatively better on tests in a free-response test format whereas men scored somewhat better on a multiple-choice format.

Cohort Variations
- By age/grade. There is evidence of two types of gender differentiation. Females and males tend to increase their score advantage somewhat by Grade 12 on those tests on which they already scored higher at Grade 4; by Grade 12 male scores are 10% more variable, on average, than are females scores.
- Over the past decade. There were (a) small gains in the mean scores of women relative to men on some tests, and (b) significant gains in the relative number of women taking Advanced Placement tests in mathematics and science and in the representation of women among high school students who demonstrate college-level proficiency in those subjects.
- By ethnic group. There was no consistent variation in the pattern of gender differences among ethnic groups in representative populations. Black women participated more frequently in some selective testing programs.

Sample Variations
- Most of the shift to somewhat more negative standard mean differences for advanced tests is apparently due to the following three statistical effects of sample restriction.
- Range restriction. Other things equal, a select group of high-scoring examinees will show a more extreme standard mean difference that the total group for statistical reasons, even if the actual mean difference does not change.
- Differential variability. If scores are more variable for one group, as is often the case for males, representation of that group will tend to be increased in a sample selected from either the bottom or the top of the original score distribution.
- Gender balance. If a group is selected in a way that overrepresents females or males, the standard mean difference will tend to move in a direction favoring the other gender.

test constructs; that is, among 15 different categories of tests. Most commonly, however, gender accounted for no more than 1% of the variation in test scores. As reported in previous research, women tended to do well on verbal tests—especially writing, which showed the largest gender difference of any of the academic test categories. Males tended to do well in technical subjects, especially natural science. The largest difference among the 15 categories was in mechanical and electronics tests, where men excelled. In most test categories, men's scores were somewhat more variable. The average standard deviation ratio for the 74 tests administered to representative 12th graders was .91.

Trends From Grade 4 to Grade 12

Test performance of girls and boys showed two patterns of increasing gender differentiation from Grade 4 to Grade 12—one based on mean performance and another based on score variability. The significant change in the mean performance for girls was their gain in language skill and writing from Grade 4 to Grade 8. The gain for boys came later, from Grade 8 to Grade 12, on tests in mathematics, science, and geopolitical subjects (e.g., history and civics). The other test categories showed no significant changes in relative performance across this grade span.

There was a small difference in score variability at Grade 4, but male variability increased through the grades more than did female variability, especially on tests that are most clearly associated with subject knowledge like civics and science. In NEAP data, for example, the ratio of females to males in the top 10% of the class had dropped to about .70 in mathematics and .50 in science by Grade 12. On the other hand, the ratio of females to males among high-scoring 12th graders in writing and reading was 2.6 and 1.6, respectively.

Advanced Tests in Selected Samples

The average D for 55 tests administered to selected samples of students near the end of high school was −.15, compared to an average D of .02 for the 74 tests based on representative samples. There was no clear evidence that this shift was due to the nature of the constructs measured. We obtained a similar result (an average shift in D of −.18) when we compared gender differences for tests in the same category in selected and representative 12th-grade samples.

One gender difference noted among the tests administered to selective samples was the (inconsistent) tendency for females to do relatively better on test questions in a free-response (e.g., essay) format, whereas males tend to do relatively better on the multiple-choice format. The pattern of such differences suggests that they may actually result from the two assessment formats measuring somewhat different constructs on which females and males are differentially proficient in some subject areas. In any event, this interesting possibility does not help to explain the tendency toward higher male scores in selected samples because the selective tests have more, not less free-response material. The shift to somewhat more negative Ds for the advanced tests appears to be due mainly to the statistical effects of sample restriction.

Three types of sample effects were identified. They interact in different ways in different situations. First, range restriction comes as a natural result of selecting a group of high- (or low-) scoring individuals. Range restriction increases the apparent standard mean difference between groups—an arguably spurious statistical effect. It is clear, however, that a second sample effect—differential variability of female and male scores—has an important effect on gender difference for some selective tests, usually an effect favoring males because male scores are often more variable. The third sample effect is the ratio of females to males in the selected group. This F/M ratio is also an important indicator of gender difference and similarity. For a given measure within a given selected sample of high scorers, F/M and D have a trade-off relationship; as one increases the other decreases. However, from one type of test to another, the two tend to be positively related. That is, subject tests that are self-selected by students are more likely to be taken by the gender that scores better.

In general, there appears to be a slightly greater difference favoring males in mean test scores at the graduate as compared with the undergraduate level, but generalizations are hazardous. There are no data on representative samples of college students that would permit a comparison of the pattern of gender difference and similarity at entrance and at graduation. Also, available data shed limited light on this topic because the nature of the tests and the samples taking them vary considerably. The pattern of gender difference and similarity differs somewhat from one graduate field to another, and there is noticeably less difference within fields than is true of the graduate group overall. Although this means that women and men are on more of an equal footing with regard to test scores, that more balanced pattern within fields comes at the expense of gender stratification across fields.

Gender Differences Within Ethnic Groups

Several large sets of data were examined in order to determine whether there are generally comparable patterns of gender difference and similarity across ethnic groups. In representative samples of students, there were some different patterns, but contradictory results for different sets of data lead to the conclusion that gender differences on these types of tests probably do not vary much from one ethnic group to another in the general population. There were some consistent differences in the pattern of gender differences for some selective tests and samples. Among Black students taking undergraduate admissions tests (ACT & SAT), women were more likely to sit for the tests, and more likely to perform well compared to Black men, than was true in other groups. Also, Black women were considerably more likely to take AP examinations than were Black men, but scored just as well.

Trends Over the Past Decade

Previously published data indicate that gender differences in mathematics and science were larger three decades ago than they are currently. Recent reports on trends in gender differences have been inconsistent and difficult to interpret. Several large sets of test data on 12th-grade students were examined in order to evaluate what changes in patterns of gender difference may have occurred from the early 1980s to the early 1990s. This analysis was based on tests that had undergone little if any change during this period. Among tests administered to representative samples, some showed no change in D; some showed a small but significant shift to relatively higher female performance by the end of the decade. There were also small changes favoring women in undergraduate admissions tests, mainly in mathematics, with no attendant change in the proportions of women and men in the selective groups that take such tests.

The most notable change from the early 1980s to the early 1990s has been a consequential shift in the representation of young women in high school taking AP examinations in science and mathematics. This decade saw an increase from .37 to .43 in the proportion of women among students taking these difficult courses and examinations and a corresponding increase in the representation of women among high school graduates who demonstrated high achievement in those areas. This important result clearly demonstrates that the reciprocal relationship between gender representation and mean gender difference that is often observed within a given restricted sample does not hold from one cohort of students to another.

The pattern of results for tests administered to representative samples, for admissions tests, and for AP tests is consistent in this respect. In each of these three categories of tests, some tests showed no change over the decade, whereas others showed a change favoring women either in mean differences or in representation in selected groups. No changes over the decade favored men.

Our analysis has not altered one general impression with which we started. Girls and boys, as well as women and men, are a great deal more similar than they are different. Test score distributions for females and males overlap substantially, especially on general skills in general populations. Gender differences are sometimes more noticeable and potentially more important when one examines specific types of particular constructs (knowledge and skill) in a particular sample of females and males. Chapter 5 considers some of these construct differences in more detail.

4

Grades, Accomplishments, and Correlates

Carol A. Dwyer

Linda M. Johnson

This is the second of two descriptive chapters reporting data on gender differences and similarities in achievement. Although test scores such as those reported in chapter 3 are an important element in our understanding of gender and achievement, there are obviously other aspects of achievement that may have little to do with test performance. Other types of achievement may be difficult to assess, but are often very important in their own right. Furthermore, in order to understand some of the similarities and differences that we see in test scores, we also need to understand some of the other ways in which people differ from one another. The purpose of this chapter is to look at the achievement picture more broadly by examining data on a number of relevant characteristics and attributes. These range from other ways of gauging academic accomplishment (e.g., academic honors, courses taken, grades in school) to differences in attitudes, interests, and activities in and out of school. As in the previous chapter, we have used data from large, nationally representative samples where possible. The next chapter comments on some of the complex and important issues raised by the data in these two descriptive chapters, as well as some of the inconsistencies they show.

Our goal for this chapter involves compiling, summarizing, and demonstrating the gender similarities and differences that occur on important and interesting variables relevant to academic accomplishment other than test scores. We believe that the broad sources of data on which we have drawn, in and of themselves, provide a rich and compelling portrayal of the complex relationships between gender and achievement.

In what follows it should be clear that there are many ways in which individual girls and boys, and men and women can and do differ from one another. There are also ways that males and females as groups tend to differ. When confronted with data on such group and individual differences, conflicting feelings and difficult values issues arise: Do we wish that there were no female and male differences in any achievement characteristics? In just some characteristics? Do we value some realms of achievement more than others?

How does gender relate to the social and economic consequences of academic achievement? The educational literature is replete with data on the negative outcomes of low academic achievement and the positive outcomes of high academic achievement. In the context of test scores, some concerns about both the overrepresentation of males at the bottom of the educational spectrum and the small number of highly qualified women entering mathematics- and science-related fields were raised by Willingham, Cole, Lewis, and Leung in chapter 3 of this volume. In this chapter, we address this issue from the perspective of other indicators of academic achievement. We hope that our readers will find the data in this chapter valuable in their own attempts to resolve the broader values questions implicit in consideration of gender similarities and differences and of high and low academic achievement.

GENDER, GRADES, AND EDUCATIONAL ATTAINMENTS

Data from a wide variety of sources and educational settings show that females in all ethnic groups tend to earn higher grades in school than do males, across different ages and eras, and across different subject matter disciplines. Many researchers in past times and today consider this to be such an obvious fact that they treat it as axiomatic. For example, Tyler (1965) wrote, "all studies of *school* achievement agree that girls consistently make better school records than boys" (p. 241). The phenomenon of boys' academic difficulties has in fact been observed since the first attempts to record such matters. Ayres (1909), reporting on a study conducted between 1906 and 1908, found that a substantial majority of school "laggards" and noncompleters were boys, and characterized the problem as being not "of recent origin" (p. 7). In the era in which Ayres wrote, for every 100 boys starting first grade there were 93 girls; by the eighth grade, only 24 of these boys remained, and 28 girls (Snyder, 1993). Such findings have persisted to this day: Modern reviews of the subject are unanimous in their finding of higher grades for females (Ekstrom, 1994; Pennock-Roman, 1994; Stockard & Wood, 1984).

Beginning in their earliest school years, girls receive higher ratings of school success than boys. With the more global education indicators that are characteristic of the elementary school grades, girls' higher academic achievement relative to boys' is even more apparent than it is with the specific course grades given in the later school years. Global indicators that show girls at an advantage include referrals to special education for learning disabilities—over two thirds of the students in special education classes are boys (U.S. Department of Education, 1988). Even in college, more males than females report learning disabilities (Dey, Astin, Korn, & Riggs, 1992), taking the SAT under nonstandard conditions (College Board, Admissions Testing Program, 1993b), repeating a school year (Snyder, 1993), or being diagnosed as having a serious reading difficulty (Scott, Dwyer, & Lieb-Brilhart, 1985).

As indicated in Fig. 4.1,[1] the NELS second follow-up showed more high school boys than girls reporting educational placements indicative of academic difficulty. These included being in dropout prevention programs, remedial English or mathematics, special education, and programs for the educationally handicapped.

---

[1]*Standard errors*, and in some cases additional information, are reported in the *Supplement* where indicated for the following chapter 4 figures:

	Supplement Table	Supplement Note
Fig. 4.1		S-7
Fig. 4.2	S-13	S-8
Fig. 4.3	S-14	
Fig. 4.4	S-14	
Fig. 4.5	S-13	
Fig. 4.6		S-9
Fig. 4.7		S-10
Fig. 4.8		S-11
Fig. 4.9		S-12
Fig. 4.10		S-13
Fig. 4.11		S-14
Fig. 4.12	S-18	
Fig. 4.13	S-19	
Fig. 4.14	S-19	
Fig. 4.15		S-15
Fig. 4.16		S-16
Fig. 4.18	S-20	
Fig. 4.19		S-17

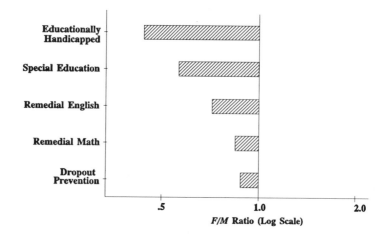

FIG. 4.1. Educational placements indicative of academic difficulty—female to male ratios (*F/M*). Source: NELS Second Follow-up.

Data on school numerical grades and letter grades are more plentiful for high school students, particularly college-bound test takers, than for any other group. In analyses of grades across many subject matter areas, both the College Board (1993b) and the American College Testing Program (ACT, 1993) show that women who take these tests report receiving higher grades in high school than do men. Figure 4.2[2] shows that in both these self-selected samples of college-bound seniors provided by ACT and the SAT, as well as the more representative national samples of high school seniors surveyed by the NELS and the HSB projects, females have consistently higher overall grade point averages (GPAs) than do males. This difference is larger in the nationally representative samples.

Data from Astin (1993), in a comprehensive study of achievement through 4 years of college, concur with the generally accepted finding that women get better grades in college than do men, even after controlling for their better high school grades. Astin concluded that this is part of a general pattern of widening gender differences during college.

Analyses by the National Center for Education Statistics (Owings, McMillen, Burkett, & Pinkerton, 1995) focused on admission criteria used by highly selective colleges. These criteria included a GPA of 3.5 or higher,

---

[2]Where applicable in gender comparisons included here, we have presented both the standard mean differences (*D*) between females and males and %*Var*, the percentage of score variation associated with gender. In doing so, it was our intention to give the reader two views of gender differences and the gender similarities in the data (see chapter 2, p. 22).

total scores of 1100 or higher on the SAT, academic courses taken (four credits in English, three in math, three in science, three in social science, and two in foreign language), highly positive teacher recommendations, and two or more school-related extracurricular activities. Owings et al. reported that more females excelled with respect to grades, with 22.5% of females compared to 15.3% of males achieving GPAs of 3.5 or higher. Males achieved higher SAT scores, and each of the remaining criteria were roughly comparable for males and females, but "the net effect shown was that 6.9% of the college-bound females met all five criteria, compared to 4.7% of the college-bound males" (p. 2).

Grades and Ethnicity

A report based on a sample of 1992 ACT test takers (ACT, 1993) provides a finer grained snapshot of high school students' grades. This report provides data on grades separately by the subject matter studied and by the person's ethnic group. As shown in Fig. 4.3, for this self-selected group of 17- to 19-year-old high school graduates of all ethnicities, women's overall grades are higher than men's (i.e., the value of D is above zero) in all of the ethnic groups analyzed. As shown in Fig. 4.4, the differences favoring women are largest in English (Ds range from .20 to .36). Differences in individual subject matter areas that were close to or slightly below zero were primarily in mathematics (mathematics Ds range from −.09 to .11). In terms of overall GPA, sufficient numbers of Black students took the ACT so that it is clear

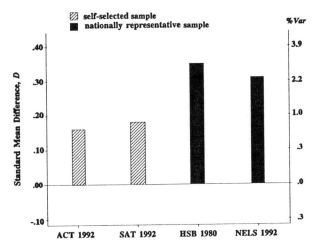

FIG. 4.2. High school GPA for self-selected vs. nationally representative samples of students—standard mean differences (D) and percent of score variation associated with gender (%Var).

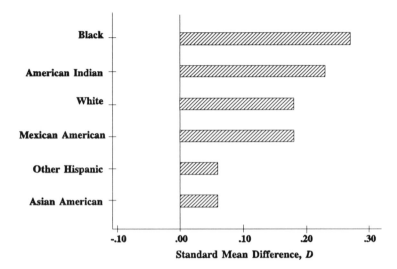

FIG. 4.3. Overall high school GPAs among 1992 ACT test takers by ethnic group—standard mean differences (D).

that the difference in grades favoring females is larger among this group (average over all subjects is .27) than among the White group (average over all subjects is .18). It should be noted, however, that among the different ethnic groups studied, different proportions of men and women choose to take the test, and thus different proportions are included in this survey. This is yet another instance of the difficulty in interpreting data based on self-selected samples—unfortunately, we have no way of knowing how representative the men and women studied are of each of these ethnic groups.

These data on the GPAs of Black students are supported by other studies of Black students' school achievement, where the picture of higher academic achievement among women than among men is generally consistent across a variety of measures of achievement, school settings, and even historical periods (Irvine, 1990; Mickelson, 1989; Nelson-Le Gall, 1992; Pollard, 1993). Mickelson (1984) also reported that gender differences in working-class students' GPAs were almost three times greater than the middle-class differences, with the difference being more pronounced among Black students than among White students.

In these and other studies, across all the ethnic groups, women report receiving the highest of their grades in English and the social sciences, and their lowest grades in mathematics. This pattern is very consistent with many other indicators of subject-matter-related interests among men and women of high school and college age.

Some educators prefer to look at high school class rank instead of, or in addition to, GPAs, but these data are highly consistent with respect to gender. As is the case with grades, college-bound women report having higher class rank than do college-bound men.

Data from groups of people taking tests to enter graduate and professional schools also confirm the general picture of higher grades among females than among males (see Fig. 4.5). As with the data from college entrance tests, however, there are difficulties in interpreting the differences among the testing programs, given the great number of factors that affect why people choose to take these tests or not.

Data on undergraduate GPA reported by GRE test takers in seven ethnic categories show the same pattern of higher grades among women that is seen in high school GPAs, even though the data on college GPAs are based

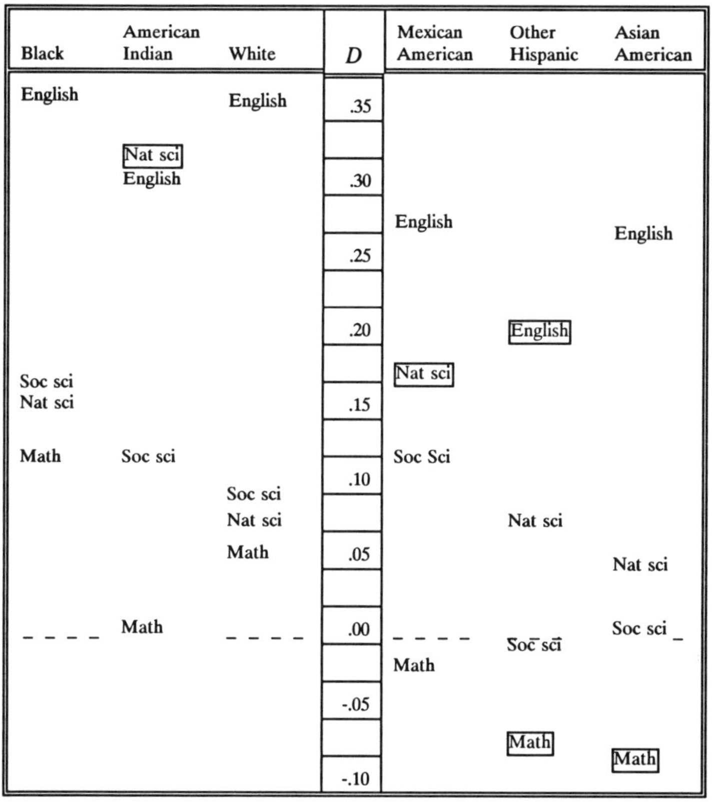

FIG. 4.4. High school GPAs among 1992 ACT test takers by ethnic group and subject matter—standard mean differences (*D*). Boxed items represent departures of .10 or more (plus or minus) from the majority (White) *D*. Source: American College Testing Program (1993).

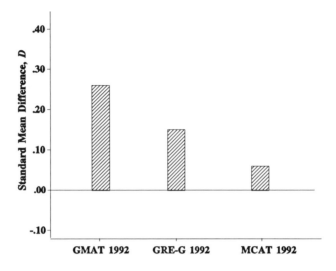

FIG. 4.5. Undergraduate GPA for graduate school admissions test takers—standard mean differences (*D*).

on a more diverse set of courses (see *Supplement* Table S-15). Unlike the ACT sample shown in Fig. 4.3, however, Black GRE test takers did not show a stronger gender difference favoring females than did the White GRE test takers. With respect to the total GRE test taking group 10 years previously, comparable data from 1981–1982 GRE test takers also showed the same pattern of higher female grades, but with generally slightly smaller differences than are seen in 1991–1992.

High School Honors and Advanced Courses

High grades for girls and women are consistent with other indicators of their serious attention to education. More women than men report being enrolled; in their high school's academic or college-preparatory program (F/M = 1.08, SE = .034; NELS88 2nd follow-up). Data from SAT test takers show that women report that they have in general taken high school honors courses more often than have men. Girls reported taking more honors courses than boys in languages, English, art and music, and social science; about the same number in science; and slightly fewer in mathematics (see Fig. 4.6[3]). Note

---

[3]The F/M ratios for all figures and tables in this chapter that are based on data from the College Board Student Descriptive Questionnaire (SDQ) have been corrected for a disproportionate number of females in the database (F/M$_p$* for participation) or (F/M$_a$* for achievement). Total SDQ sample (providing at least one SDQ response) was 1,040,378 (555,568 females and 484,810 males). For other F/M explanations, see footnotes in chapter 2.

that honors or advanced courses may be defined differently in different schools. One common form of such courses is the AP series, in which the number of AP exams taken shows gender differences strongly related to subject matter (see chapter 3 for a discussion of gender and AP test scores).

Educational Plans and Aspirations

Data from SAT test takers (College Board, 1993b) also show that, relative to men, women who are not yet in college, when asked about their plans, more often report definite intentions to pursue advanced placement in college in the areas of foreign languages, English, and the humanities. Men are more likely to report plans in mathematics, the physical sciences, and computer science (see Fig. 4.7). Relative to women's reports of high school honors courses taken, the gender disparity in advanced placement plans is larger. This pattern may reflect an interaction between personal characteristics such as interest and self-esteem, and the differing structural characteristics of colleges and high schools. In college, where alternatives such as area of study are more open to individual choice than they are in high school, men's and women's decisions are more likely to be based on their preferences and a sense of what is feasible for them to accomplish.

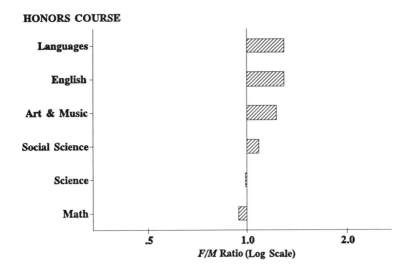

FIG. 4.6. Enrollment in high school honors courses among 1993 SAT test takers—female to male ratios (*F/M*). Honors includes AP accelerated, and honors courses. Source: College Board (1993b).

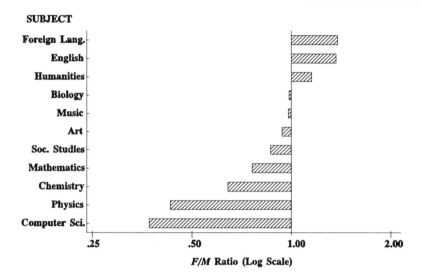

FIG. 4.7. Advanced placement plans in different college subjects among 1993 SAT test takers—female to male ratios (*F/M*). Source: College Board (1993b).

Students taking the SAT are also asked to indicate their long-range degree plans. Women report higher aspirations for future degrees than do men.[4]

These data on those who choose to take the SAT are consistent with data from a nationally representative sample of 10th graders conducted in 1990 as the first follow-up to the 1988 NELS study. Data from this follow-up study show that girls were more likely than boys to say that they plan to go to college right after high school (*F/M* = 1.16), and that they would like to pursue a postgraduate degree (*F/M* = 1.30; Rasinski, Ingels, Rock, Pollack, & Wu, 1993). In a second follow-up to the 1988 NELS study, among a nationally representative sample of 1992 high school seniors, girls were more likely than boys to say that the chances were very good that they would go to college (*F/M* = 1.20). Data on 1992 first-year college students (Dey et al., 1992) indicate that females are slightly more likely than males to say they plan to obtain a master's or higher degree (*F/M* = 1.03).

Meeting Core Academic Requirements

Although women are more likely than men to pursue a rigorous set of courses in high school, and are just as likely as men to meet the academic core requirements of their high schools, according to data on SAT test takers

---

[4]*F/M* for plans for doctoral/related degree = 1.14.

(College Board, 1993b), they are less likely than men to take a fourth year of mathematics or science. It should be noted that, unlike much of the rest of the mathematics and science academic track curriculum, the fourth year of these subjects is optional in many high schools. The fourth year of mathematics is often calculus; the fourth year of science is often physics. Even female students who have been earning high grades in previous mathematics and sciences classes often elect not to take these courses.

A report from the National Science Foundation (Suter, 1993) notes that even though the number of states requiring more than 2 years of mathematics courses for high school graduation increased from 2% in 1980 to 24% in 1990, few students take the most advanced courses offered in schools. The average requirement for mathematics courses is now 2.3 years, up from 1.3 years in 1971 (National Science Foundation, 1990).

Persistence in School

According to the National Center for Education Statistics (NCES), women and men are now equally likely to complete high school (Snyder, 1993). In the past, women were more likely than men to finish high school, but this ceased to be true in the 1970s. Considering all of the U.S. population who are 25 years old or older, the median years of schooling completed is 12.8 for men and 12.7 for women. This 0.1-year difference has held steady for more than 25 years. Before that time, women's median years of schooling was a little higher than men's. These comparisons hold true for both ethnic groups reported by NCES, Blacks and Whites.

Of the students enrolled in any type of college in 1989–1990, the most recent year for which data were available, a slight majority, 54.3%, were women. Women earned 53.2% of the bachelor's degrees conferred that year, 52.6% of the master's degrees, and 37.4% of the doctoral or first professional degrees. Women earned fewer professional degrees than did men: 30.6% of all dental degrees, 34.0% of medical degrees, and 42.2% of law degrees were awarded to women. These figures represent an enormous change from 20 years earlier: In 1969–1970, women earned 8.4% of medical degrees, 5.4% of law degrees, and less than 1% of all dental degrees.

In terms of attainment of qualifications equivalent to high school diplomas and college degrees in the United States, women generally have higher educational achievement levels than their counterparts in other countries, particularly when considering the entire population of women from age 25 through 64 (Alsalam, Ogle, Rogers, & Smith, 1992).

A report on gender and educational attainments in the 24 countries that are members of the Organisation for Economic Co-operation and Development (OECD, 1986) is consistent with the achievement picture in our own country.[5] Among the OECD member nations, girls, in addition to obtaining higher qualifications (e.g., passing grades on external school-leaving examinations; certificates with distinction) in secondary school than boys, are less likely than boys to leave the education system without any qualifications, or to fall seriously behind in their schoolwork. Girls are also more likely than boys to continue their schooling beyond the minimum school-leaving age, and are more likely to be in college-preparatory programs. The number of girls staying in secondary school and continuing to higher education has increased dramatically in many of the OECD nations since the 1970s.

OTHER SUCCESS INDICATORS

Looking only at a college population, Astin (1993) reported that women in his study were actually more likely to complete the bachelor's degree and to graduate with honors. Data from 1992 high school seniors (1988 NELS 2nd follow-up) indicate that the pattern of academic and other honors and awards in high school follows the pattern of girls' and boys' overall interests, with greater incidence of awards and honors to males in the areas of mathematics, science, vocational/technical, and sports (see Fig. 4.8).

Most students, as well as most educators, would agree that success in college extends beyond the grades that one earns there. Willingham (1985) conducted a comprehensive study of the role of personal qualities in college success. In this study, data were gathered on accomplishments in many sectors of academic life: leadership, scholarship, persistence, and distinction in many fields of interest. Figure 4.9 shows that on most of these measures, women's achievements surpass those of men. The differences are large in many areas, much larger than those in more narrowly defined academic indicators of achievement such as grades and test scores, and no doubt represent a combination of proficiency and interest in the area of endeavor. It is striking, if not surprising, that the greatest exceptions to the general finding of greater female accomplishment are in athletic accomplishments, and in acceptance into doctoral and other terminal degree professional programs, although the latter has been changing rapidly in recent years (Snyder, 1993).

---

[5]The 24 countries that are members of the OECD are: Australia, Austria, Belgium, Canada, Denmark, Finland, France, Germany, Greece, Ireland, Italy, Japan, Luxembourg, the Netherlands, New Zealand, Norway, Portugal, Spain, Sweden, Switzerland, Turkey, the United Kingdom, the United States, and Yugoslavia.

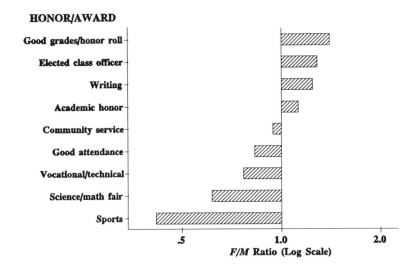

FIG. 4.8. Honors and awards reported by 1992 high school seniors—female to male ratios (*F/M*). Ratio here is the proportion of females (among all particular item respondents) who answer "yes," divided by the like proportion of males (*F/M*ₐ*). Source: NELS Second Follow-up.

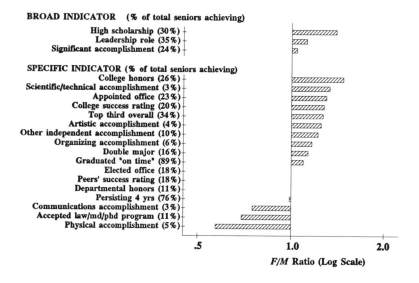

FIG. 4.9. Indicators of success in college—female to male ratios (*F/M*). The first three "broad indicators" represent general areas of achievement, each based on two or more specific indicators. See Note *S*-12 in the *Supplement* for more descriptive information. Source: Willingham (1985). Adapted with permission from *Success in College: The Role of Personal Qualities and Academic Ability*. Copyright © 1985 by The College Entrance Examination Board. All rights reserved.

Academic Competitions

It is clear from many sources of data that boys and girls show distinct preferences for the type of academic challenges that they will undertake. In addition to the broad range of indicators of college success studied by Willingham (1985), there are also a number of national mathematics and science contests, prizes, and competitions that provide some additional insight into the nature of the challenges that are of interest to girls and women, and to boys and men. Although there is little gender-related data available on these competitions, they provide another perspective on how girls and boys choose to participate and how they fare in them. As in other self-selected samples of students, one should not generalize from these participants to the population in general. We have no way of knowing how the students who choose to participate in these competitions differ from those who do not. Academic competitions are also of varying kinds: Some are very closely related to standardized tests, and some are more closely related to schoolwork and later workplace demands. Three competitions in mathematics and science illustrate this range.

"MathCounts" (MathCounts Foundation, 1993) is a national competition for seventh- and eighth-grade students. Although there is an emphasis in the program on coaching at the local level to develop mathematics skills, winning in "MathCounts" is structured in terms of direct competition with other students and teams, and depends heavily on speed in solving discrete problems. Awards are made on the basis of points in various rounds, culminating in a "Countdown Round," which the sponsors describe as a "fast-paced oral competition ... [in which] pairs of mathletes will challenge each other in oral competition" (MathCounts Foundation, 1993, p. 10). Large prizes such as trips and scholarships provide substantial incentive for participation, but among the 224 students in the 1993 competition, only 37 (17%) were girls. Of these, five placed in the top 50 rankings ($F/M = 0.56$). This is an example of a competition that is very closely associated with test scores, and it is one that attracts relatively few girls. Although the girls who do enter may score very near the top (girls placed fifth and eighth in the national rankings in 1993), they are few in number and the individual rankings are heavily dominated by boys.

The Mathematical Olympiads for Elementary Schools (MOES; G. Lenchner, personal communication, November 16, 1993) is a public foundation that conducts an international competition for students who have not yet completed Grade 6. The competition is based on tests developed specifically for this purpose. The MOES sponsors indicate that almost half of the participants are girls, but this is not true of the winners. For example, in 1992–1993, the "pin-winners" (those who scored in the top 10% of the group) included 2,413 girls and 4,744 boys, giving an F/M of 0.51. This is another example of a competition that is almost entirely dependent on performance on tests, and one in which speed of response is intentionally a large factor.

The Westinghouse Science Talent Search (Westinghouse Electric Corporation & Science Service, 1993a, 1993b, 1996), a contest for high school seniors, is one of the most prestigious and lucrative academic competitions in the United States. Entrants work over an extended period of time on a single project, then submit a project report of about 20 pages giving evidence of their research ability in science, mathematics, or engineering. Close work with a teacher or senior researcher is encouraged, provided that the contestant makes clear the extent of the mentor's contribution to the project. The top 40 finalists share over $200,000 in scholarships, with the top 10 receiving scholarships ranging from $10,000 to $40,000. Trips and other awards are also given, providing a strong incentive for participation. Unlike the other competitions just discussed, this is an example of a competition that is not closely tied to a standardized test, although entrants are required to submit college-entrance examination scores as part of their application. Unlike many other competitions, the Westinghouse Science Talent Search rewards sustained effort and "real-life" research skills, including the ability to communicate the research effectively to others. In this sense, it is more closely connected to later scholarly activities than are many other competitions. The top 40 winners in 1992–1993 included 13 females and 27 males. In 1994–1995, of the top six winners, four were females, including the first- and second-prize winners (Adler, 1995). In 1995–1996, the top 40 winners included 15 females and 25 males, a proportion that is very similar to that in other recent years.

Work Habits and Study Skills

Work habits and study skills form a link between accomplishments and interests. Work habits have a strong logical and empirical connection to grades, but they are also indicative of individuals' personalities, interests, and values. Hough (in press), in a meta-analysis of 11 widely used personality inventories, found significant effect sizes favoring women in the category called "dependability" (see *Supplement* Table S-16). High scores on this construct indicate the person's characteristic degree of conscientiousness. The dependable person is disciplined, well-organized, planful, respectful of regulations, and prefers order to disorder.

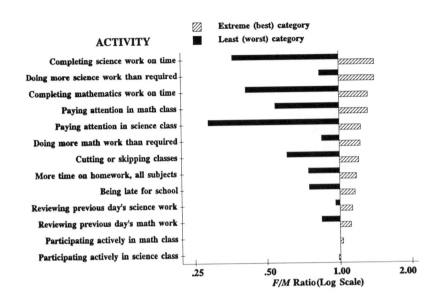

FIG. 4.10. Task-oriented behaviors related to being an effective student reported by 1992 high school seniors—female to male ratios (*F/M*).[6] Source: NELS Second Follow-up.

Data from a follow-up to the 1988 NELS study show that high school senior girls report greater incidence than boys of many task-oriented academic behaviors, even in mathematics and science (see Fig. 4.10[6]).

Figure 4.11 shows that first-year college students also report a similar pattern of positive work-related activities (Dey et al., 1992). Dey et al. also reported that women are more likely than men to report doing 16 or more hours of studying or homework per week (*F/M* = 1.49; *SE* = .039).

A greater number of male than female high school students report seriously dysfunctional school behaviors, according to the 1988 NELS second follow-up. Students were asked how often they were in the following situations:

Cutting or skipping classes.
On in-school suspension.
Being suspended or on probation from school.
In trouble for not following school rules.
Spending time in a juvenile home or detention center.
Being transferred to another school for disciplinary reasons.

---

[6]Ratio is the proportion of females (among all particular item respondents) who answer as indicated, divided by the like proportion of males. The bars in Fig. 4.10 represent the best (extreme) and worst responses for each behavior (e.g., the best response for being late for school is "never" and the worst is "over 15 times"; for paying attention in math class the best response is "always" and the worst is "never").

Although the base rates for these behaviors were small, more males than females responded "more than 15 times" to questions about each of these difficulties (see *Supplement* Table S-17).

VALUES AND INTERESTS

Males' and females' educational and other life choices are shaped in part by avoiding alternatives with characteristics that they dislike, and in part by choosing alternatives with characteristics that they like, although research by Tyler (1961) indicates that dislikes are more salient for females, and likes more salient for males. There are many sources of data about females' and males' values and interests, and likes and dislikes. In this chapter we discuss data from values and interest inventories, which ask representative samples directly about what they think is important in life, and about their likes and dislikes; data from national surveys of students' academic and leisure activities, which give an indication of how students prefer to spend their time; and data on students' choice of fields of study, which provide another perspective on patterns of academic interests of females and males.

Research on Values and Interest Inventories

Research on men's and women's values has a long history. Allport, Vernon, and Lindzey (1970), in an inventory of values held by men and women,

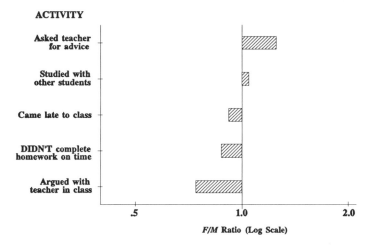

FIG. 4.11. Academic activities engaged in "frequently" by 1992 first-year college students—female to male ratios (*F/M*). Corrected for a disproportionate number of females. Source: Dey, Astin, Korn, and Riggs (1992).

showed that consistent with research dating from the 1930s, men and women have different patterns of dominant values. They identified the following six value orientations:

Theoretical—valuing the abstract, intellectual, and rational.
Economic—valuing practical concerns and activities.
Political—interested primarily in power, competition, and struggle.
Aesthetic—valuing beauty and grace ("diametrically opposed to the theoretical," p. 4).
Social—valuing altruistic and philanthropic ends; concerned with people.
Religious—spiritual life predominates.

As shown in Fig. 4.12, in their norming populations, men were found to be higher on the first three of these orientations and women on the remaining three.

The work of Allport et al. has deeply influenced research on values and interests for many years, and foreshadowed in some respects current research on differences in men's and women's interests. For example, data from instruments used in counseling individuals about career choices are generally consistent with research on values. A very widely used inventory

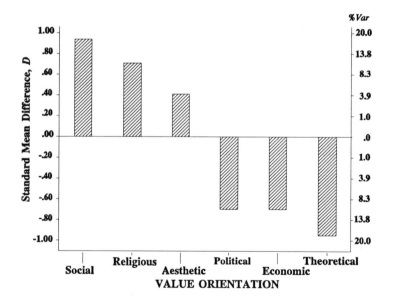

FIG. 4.12. Value orientations in the "*Study of Values*"—standard mean differences (*D*) and percent of score variation associated with gender (*%Var*). Source: Copyright © 1970. From the *Study of Values—A Scale for Measuring the Dominant Interests in Personality* by G. W. Allport, P. E. Vernon, & G. Lindzey. Used with the permission of Houghton Mifflin Company.

of occupational interests, the Strong Interest Inventory, Form T325 of the Strong Vocational Interest Blank®—abbreviated as the Strong or as SII—uses a theoretical framework developed by Holland (1966, 1973) as its organizing structure for scale development and interpretation. Since this chapter was prepared, the 1985 Strong underwent revision. The current version is the 1994 Strong Interest Inventory Form T317 of the Strong Vocational Interest Blanks®. The data presented in this and the following chapter are based on the 1985 form.

Although the work of Allport, Vernon, and Lindzey is not explicitly acknowledged by Holland as a conceptual precursor, the six categories proposed by each show substantial overlap. Holland's contribution has been to develop and clarify the meaning of his six categories in terms of individuals' interests and preferences. In addition, Holland (1973) characterized occupations as belonging to one or more of the following six categories: Realistic, Investigative, Artistic, Social,[7] Enterprising, and Conventional. Drawing on Holland's work, Hansen and Campbell (1985) provided these definitions:

REALISTIC: Persons of this type are robust, rugged, practical, and physically strong; ... usually perceive themselves as mechanically inclined; ... avoid social settings that require verbal and interpersonal skills .... Realistic types prefer such occupations as mechanic, engineer, electrician, fish and wildlife specialist, crane operator, and tool designer.

INVESTIGATIVE: This category includes those with a strong scientific orientation; they usually are task-oriented, introspective, and asocial; ... describe themselves as analytical, curious, independent, and reserved; and especially dislike repetitive activities. Vocational preferences include astronomer, biologist, chemist, technical writer, zoologist, and psychologist.

ARTISTIC: Persons of the artistic type prefer free, unstructured situations with maximum opportunity for self-expression; ... see themselves as expressive, original, intuitive, creative, nonconforming, introspective, and independent. Vocational preferences include artist, author, composer, writer, musician, stage director, and symphony conductor.

SOCIAL: Persons of this type are sociable, responsible, humanistic; like to work in groups, and enjoy being at the center of the group; have good verbal and interpersonal skills; ... Vocational preferences include social worker, ... teacher, guidance counselor, school administrator, recreation leader, and speech therapist.

---

[7]Despite the use of the same terminology, Holland's "social" category differs from that of Allport, Vernon, and Lindzey. Holland's social category emphasizes liking or disliking direct personal interactions with others. Allport, Vernon, and Lindzey's definition of social emphasizes the value placed on being concerned with the needs of others, and feeling a sense of responsibility for their well-being.

ENTERPRISING: Persons of this type have verbal skills suited to selling, dominating, and leading; are strong leaders; have a strong drive to attain organizational goals or economic aims; ... see themselves as aggressive, popular, self-confident, cheerful, and sociable; ... Vocational preferences include business executive, political campaign manager, real estate salesperson, buyer, and retail merchandiser.

CONVENTIONAL: Conventional people prefer well-ordered environments and like systematic verbal and numerical activities; ... avoid ambiguous situations and problems involving interpersonal relationships; describe themselves as conscientious, efficient, obedient, calm, orderly, and practical; ... Vocational preferences include accountant, credit manager, business education teacher, bookkeeper, clerical worker, and quality control expert. (pp. 28–29)[8]

As indicated in Fig. 4.13, data from an SII sample of adult men and women in general (i.e., people employed in a representative sampling of occupations) indicate that women score significantly higher in the Artistic category, and men in the Realistic and Investigative categories. The other three categories show no significant differences between men and women in this sample (Hansen & Campbell, 1985).

Within each of the six General Occupational Theme categories, and based on the same norming group, the SII has also empirically identified 20 more specific Basic Interest scales. Although gender-linked patterns in the Basic Interest Scales are generally similar to those of the General Occupational Themes in which they are nested, there is some variation within themes. As indicated in Fig. 4.14, for example, within the Social General Occupational Theme, the Basic Interest Scales for Social Service and Domestic Activities are higher for women than for men, athletics are higher for men, and religious activities and teaching show no significant gender differences. (As shown in Fig. 4.13, the Social General Occupational Theme as a whole has no gender differences.) Note that the largest gender differences favoring women are in the areas of domestic activities, art, music/dramatics, and writing. The largest gender differences favoring men are in the areas of mechanical activities, military activities, and adventure. In the 1994

---

[8]Reproduced by special permission of the publisher, Consulting Psychologists Press, Inc., Palo Alto, CA 94303 from *Manual for the Strong Interest Inventory™ - Form T325 of the Strong Vocational Interest Blanks®, 4th edition* by J. C. Hansen & D. P. Campbell. Copyright © 1985 by The Board of Trustees of the Leland Stanford Junior University. All rights reserved. Printed under license from Stanford University Press, Stanford, CA 94305. Further reproduction is prohibited without the publisher's written consent. *Strong Interest Inventory* is a trademark and *Strong Vocational Interest Blanks* is a registered trademark of the Stanford University Press.

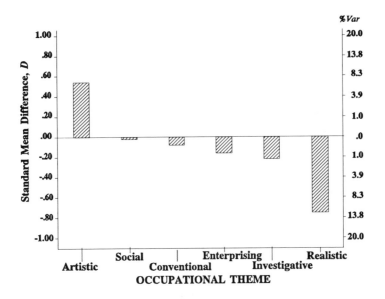

FIG. 4.13. Occupational themes on the *Strong Interest Inventory*—standard mean differences (*D*) and percent of score variation associated with gender. %*Var* = Percent of score variation associated with gender. Modified and reproduced by special permission of the publisher, Consulting Psychologists Press, Inc., Palo Alto, CA 94303 from *Manual for the Strong Interest Inventory™ - Form T325 of the Strong Vocational Interest Blanks®, 4th edition* by J. C. Hansen & D. P. Campbell. Copyright © 1985 by The Board of Trustees of the Leland Stanford Junior University. All rights reserved. Printed under license from Stanford University Press, Stanford, CA 94305. Further reproduction is prohibited without the publisher's written consent. *Strong Interest Inventory* is a trademark and *Strong Vocational Interest Blanks* is a registered trademark of the Stanford University Press.

revision to the Basic Interest Scales of the *Strong*, some new scales were added and some others renamed; for example, Domestic Activities was dropped and Adventure was renamed and moved to the new Personal Style Scales.

At a still more specific level, Hansen and Campbell (1985) reported the SII items showing the largest differences between men and women responding "like." The 10 items showing the largest differences favoring women, starting with the greatest difference, are (in the 1994 revision of the *Strong*, at the item level, some items have been deleted and some new items added):

Decorating a room with flowers.
Sewing.
Costume designer.
Looking at things in a clothing store.
Family pages in newspapers.
Interior decorator.

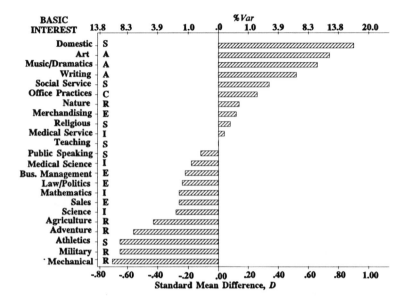

FIG. 4.14. Basic interest scales on the *Strong Interest Inventory*—standard mean differences (*D*) and percent of score variation associated with gender. Letter designations represent these General Occupational Themes: A = Artistic; C = Conventional; E = Enterprising; I = Investigative; R = Realistic; S = Social. %*Var* = Percent of score variation associated with gender. Modified and reproduced by special permission of the publisher, Consulting Psychologists Press, Inc., Palo Alto, CA 94303 from *Manual for the Strong Interest Inventory*™ - *Form T325 of the Strong Vocational Interest Blanks*®, *4th edition* by J. C. Hansen & D. P. Campbell. Copyright © 1985 by The Board of Trustees of the Leland Stanford Junior University. All rights reserved. Printed under license from Stanford University Press, Stanford, CA 94305. Further reproduction is prohibited without the publisher's written consent. *Strong Interest Inventory* is a trademark and *Strong Vocational Interest Blanks* is a registered trademark of the Stanford University Press.

Preparing dinner for guests.
Trying new cooking recipes.
Children's clothes designer.
Home economics.

The 10 items showing the largest differences favoring men are:

Enjoy tinkering with small hand tools.
Sports pages in the newspaper.
Popular mechanics magazines.
Manufacturer.
Operating machinery.
Mechanical engineer.
Boxing.

Repairing electrical wiring.
Military officers.
Building a radio or stereo. (Hansen, & Campbell, 1985, p. 80)

These gender difference patterns for men and women in general in the SII norming group are also very consistent with other SII data on men and women in a variety of specific occupational samples. It is important to remember, however, that many other factors besides interest enter into occupational choice, such as economic pressures, social expectations; and, conversely, within a single occupation, men and women tend to have different patterns of interests. Therefore interest does not necessarily coincide with representation in a given occupation.

Hansen and Campbell (1985) also reported that in the SII's Academic Comfort Scale (not in the 1994 revision), which is intended to indicate an individual's degree of comfort in academic settings rather than to predict their academic achievement, women in almost all of the 101 occupational group samples studied showed more academic interest than the male samples did. Hansen and Campbell (1985) characterized these differences as "sizeable" (differing by more than one half standard deviation) in about 30% of the occupations.

The theme of women's greater interest in people and personal relationships is a strong one in social and psychological research, but different measures of this phenomenon show somewhat different results, and individuals do not, of course, always conform to generalizations about their group. Hough (in press), in a meta-analysis of 11 widely used personality inventories, reported large effect sizes favoring men in a category called "rugged individualism," in which the relatively lower scores earned by women indicate a greater tendency to be sympathetic, helpful, sensitive to criticism, and to interpret events from a personal point of view (see *Supplement* Table S-16).

Numerous studies have concluded that girls and women as a group, relative to boys and men, are more likely to be person oriented rather than thing oriented in their interests and values (Eccles et al., 1983). Connections have been found between these orientations and the academic choices that students make. Dunteman, Wisenbaker, and Taylor (1979), for example, found that being thing oriented predicted interest in mathematics and science at the college level. Fox and Denham (1974) found that among a group of mathematically gifted junior high school students of both sexes, the students as a group were relatively high on economic, political, and theoretical values characteristic of boys and men as a group, and relatively low on the social service values ordinarily associated with the preferences of girls and women.

Direct competition with others is in general more acceptable to men than to women, and academic competition has been found to lower girls' and women's achievement in school (Casserly, 1980; Eccles, 1987; Peterson & Fennema, 1985). Competition has been specifically cited as a reason for women's avoiding certain fields of study such as engineering and science, which are perceived by many women as involving direct personal competition in order to succeed (Holloway, 1993; Wellesley College Center for Research on Women, 1992). Even within such fields, competition continues to be an issue. In some science programs, women have been reported to find problems more interesting to solve if they have a discernable context, social relevance, if the solution produces some benefit, or if the process of solving it is framed as a collaboration rather than a competitive activity (Holloway, 1993).

Leisure and Extracurricular Activities

In a nationally representative study of 1992 high school seniors (1988 NELS 2nd follow-up), girls' and boys' self-reported participation in leisure and extracurricular activities differed along the lines suggested by interest and values research. As shown in Fig. 4.15, relative to boys, girls' participation was stronger in artistic, religious, social, and service activities, based on those responding that they participate "once or twice a week" or "everyday or almost everyday." (In this follow-up, as in the earlier studies in the series, participation in most extracurricular activities was higher among White than among Hispanic, Black, or Asian American girls, probably reflecting a relationship between socioeconomic status and the amount of time available for leisure pursuits.) The finding of girls' greater tendency, relative to boys', to take classes for self-improvement during their leisure time is consistent with the other indicators of girls' and women's strong academic interests and work habits discussed earlier in this chapter.

When participation and leadership in extracurricular clubs and school groups are queried for the same NELS sample of high school seniors, girls and boys differ greatly in their overall participation, with girls' participation higher than boys' in nearly every area (see Fig. 4.16). There are relatively smaller differences in leadership and office holding in these groups, but there is a clear tendency for boys to occupy more of these positions overall.

Choice of Fields of Study

Another type of information that bears on females' and males' interests comes from data on their choice of fields of study. Although the element of course choice is relatively small in high school, as indicated earlier in this

ACTIVITY

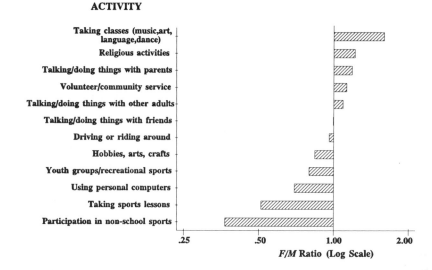

FIG. 4.15. Leisure activities reported by 1992 high school seniors—female to male ratios (*F/M*). *F/M* ratio among those respondents who checked one of the two extreme responses: "Once or twice a week" and "everyday or almost everyday." Source: NELS Second Follow-up.

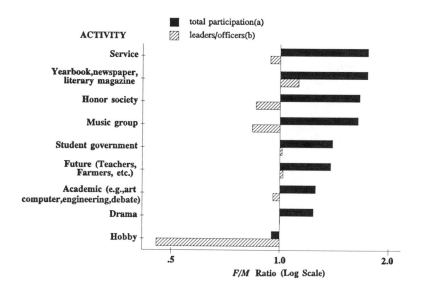

FIG. 4.16. Participation and leadership in school clubs and groups reported by 1992 high school seniors—female to male ratios (*F/M*). Source: NELS Second Follow-up.

chapter, high school girls show a clear tendency to avoid advanced mathematics and science courses. This generalization can be made about choices made about fields of study in college and graduate school as well.

In the early years of high school, most college-bound students usually take at least algebra and geometry. Differences between girls' and boys' participation in these courses is thus largely a reflection of how many girls and boys are taking a college-bound course sequence (see Fig. 4.17). Trigonometry, precalculus, and calculus are taken by progressively smaller groups of both girls and boys. Looking at girls' and boys' participation in these more elective courses, it becomes clear that girls elect to take the more advanced mathematics and science courses less often than do boys (College Board, 1993b). The drop-off in the number of girls electing to take calculus is particularly striking. Similarly, girls' rate of participation in computer mathematics is low relative to boys'.

The same report also shows distinctive patterns of girls' and boys' participation in high school science. In the sciences, girls' participation is highest in biology and strikingly lower in physics. It appears to be a matter of interest and values, rather than lower performance in their previous mathematics and science classes, that motivates girls to choose not to pursue further studies in these subjects. There are indications that even girls identified as very talented in these areas do not choose to continue in them as often as boys of similar ability. Among students above the 90th percentile on the SAT Math, twice as many males as females plan a career in a quantitative field (Grandy, 1994a).

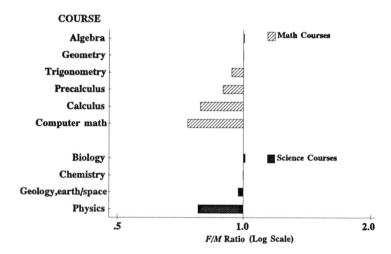

FIG. 4.17. Participation in high school mathematics and science courses reported by 1993 SAT test takers—female to male ratios (*F/M*). Standard errors of these *F/M* ratios are all low (.002 to .004). See footnote 3. Source: College Board (1993b).

This same phenomenon is seen even with girls specifically identified as being highly gifted in mathematics and science. Subotnik and Arnold (1994), in a summary of research on gifted students, reported that women identified as gifted in quantitative areas show less interest than their male peers in pursuing mathematical and science careers. They are also less likely to major in mathematics or science in college. Subotnik and Arnold (1994) noted that these very talented young women have lower academic self-esteem than their male peers, and that even women who were their class valedictorians lowered their academic self-esteem during their under-graduate years, despite "superb performance." According to the American Association of University Women (AAUW) report (Wellesley College Center for Research on Women, 1992), a study of high school seniors in one state found that among students who had taken physics and calculus, far more boys (64%) than girls (18.6%) reported an interest in majoring in science or engineering in college (F/M = 0.29).

The Higher Education Research Institute's (HERI) Cooperative Institu-tional Research Program annual surveys from 1966, 1974, and 1990 provide data on men's and women's intended college majors (Dey, Astin, & Korn, 1991). These data show very consistent profiles for males' and females' choice of undergraduate majors over approximately the past 25 years, although there is an overall tendency for the gender differences (F/Ms) to decrease over the time period covered. Women continue to be more likely than men to major in education, the health professions, and social sciences (see *Supplement* Table S-20 for definitions of these areas). Women are less likely than men to major in fields requiring mathematics and physical science. Thus, after college, they are much less likely to pursue graduate degrees or to seek employment in these areas (see Fig. 4.18[9]). Data from GRE test takers about their intended fields of study in graduate school also show similar patterns of women's preference for majors (see Fig. 4.19), and little change in these preferences from 1982 to 1992 (Grandy, 1994b).

Astin (1993) noted that the college experience does not serve to elimi-nate or even reduce many of the stereotypical differences between women and men. For example, during college, women are more likely than men to

---

[9]All figures in this chapter reporting F/M ratios use a logarithmic scale base 2 except for Figs. 4.18 and 4.19, which use a base 4. For the purpose of Fig. 4.18, English, History/Political Science, Fine Arts, and Humanities (Other) have been combined. Results for 1966 Social Sciences were not comparable to 1974 and 1990 and have not been included. Four categories were excluded from this figure: Undecided, Health Professions, Preprofessional (because data were only available in 1974), and Nontechnical (Other).

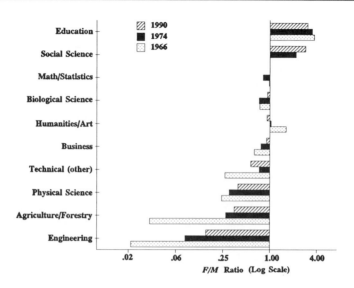

FIG. 4.18. Intended college majors (1966, 1974, and 1990) among first-year college students—female to male ratios (*F/M*). See footnote 9. Source: Dey, Astin, and Korn (1991).

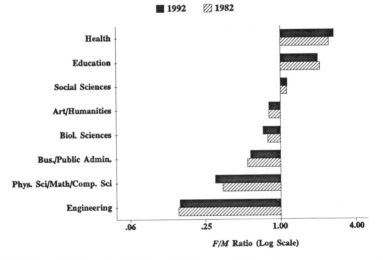

FIG. 4.19. Intended fields of study, 1982 and 1992 among GRE test takers—female to male ratios (*F/M*). See footnote 9. Source: Grandy (1994b).

remain in the fields of education, nursing, and psychology, and more likely than men to drop out of law, medicine, and engineering.

Data from the NCES (Alsalam et al., 1992) show similar patterns on choice of field of study for women of four different ethnic groups for those receiving degrees in 1990 (see *Supplement* Table S-21). In general, women of all ethnic groups at both the bachelor's and doctoral level are more inclined to study humanities or social sciences and education than are White men, and less inclined to study the natural sciences or computer sciences and engineering. The main exception to this generalization is that Asian women are more likely than White men to major in the natural sciences as undergraduates, and slightly more likely to take their doctoral degrees in this area.

Choice of field of study and careers does show some variation in international comparisons. This is particularly striking with respect to physics (and a similar pattern has recently been reported for astronomy). In the United States, according to the American Association of University Professors, women comprised 32% of all college and university faculties in 1992, but only 3% of physics faculties (Raffalli, 1994). Of 20 developed nations studied by the National Research Council of the National Academy of Sciences, the United States tied with South Korea for the fewest women on physics faculties. In France and Italy, women comprise 23% of physics faculty members, and in Hungary nearly 50% (Holloway, 1993; Raffalli, 1994). Considerable international variation exists in mathematics as well. The United Nations (1995) reported that "from a global perspective, gender differences in high-level achievement in mathematics are not constant across ethnic groups, across cultures or historically" (p. 97).

CONCLUSION

This chapter shows that there are many different ways of looking at men's and women's achievements. Judged by many different kinds of criteria, it is clear that men and women at all educational levels have differing patterns of problems, interests, habits, values, attitudes, and achievements.

Using a wide variety of indices including grades, work habits, and other indicators of attitude and effort, relative to boys and men, girls and women tend to have stronger academic records throughout all levels of education, and stronger interests in academic and intellectual endeavor. Girls' grades are higher than boys' overall. Girls as a group earn their highest grades in English and their lowest grades in mathematics.

Males and females have distinct patterns of values and interests in academic and leisure activities as well as in occupational preferences. When they can exercise personal choice, girls and women as a group tend to prefer the arts, humanities, and social sciences as their academic, leisure, and career interests. Relative to males, females choose to avoid mathematics and science whenever they have a choice.

The profile of men's and women's achievements and interests is very consistent across age levels, ethnic groups, and historic cohorts. In addition to the vast range of individual differences among women and among men, however, there are also some indications that even the group picture might be somewhat different under differing life circumstances. Although data on men and women in other nations and in specific ethnic groups in the United States are sparse, they shed some interesting light on how these overall patterns of gender, interests, and achievement can, on closer inspection, be seen to vary. For example, available data from our own country indicate that gender differences favoring girls in grades tend to be greater among Black students than among White students. As another example, girls and women in many other cultures do not seem to share U.S. girls' and women's aversions to mathematics and science.

5

Understanding Gender Differences and Fair Assessment in Context

Nancy S. Cole

This chapter frames the results in chapters 3 and 4 for consideration of fair assessment that follows in the remainder of the book. It builds on key results in those chapters on grades and tests, different types of skills, multiple-choice and alternative assessment approaches, and different interests and experiences. For each of these results, this chapter examines the tested constructs in order to better understand gender differences and related fairness issues to come in subsequent chapters. The final section of the chapter examines the context of testing in which fairness requirements coexist with requirements for usefulness and practicality. The reader will find this chapter key to moving from data about gender similarities and differences to the implications of such data for fair assessment because, as we will see in subsequent chapters, understanding fairness issues often requires understanding constructs.

The preceding chapters presented information on various aspects of academic performance, including data on a wide array of tests, grades, and other measures. Some of these data show differences between females and males; others do not. Some of the results are familiar; some are a bit surprising. What do they mean? Are they fair? How do we judge?

In succeeding chapters, we turn to the issues of fairness in assessment—to how one might reasonably judge aspects of fairness. The purpose of this chapter is to provide a bridge between the results of the first chapters and the considerations of fairness that follow in subsequent chapters. There are two aspects to this bridge.

First, four results raised in the preceding chapters require an analysis of what constructs are being tested if we are to understand the gender differences or issues of fair assessment. We consider four notable results:

- Different gender effects for grades and tests.
- Different gender results that arise from various tests of the same name.
- Different gender effects in multiple-choice tests and some alternatives.
- Gender differences in characteristics and activities other than tests.

Examination of these results in terms of underlying constructs sets part of the context for issues of fairness. Yet fairness issues do not follow directly and simply from the earlier data, even when constructs are properly identified. Fairness issues arise within a broader context. In the final section of the chapter, we provide a brief introduction to that broader context of testing in which fairness issues are weighed along with the usefulness and practicality of tests. The competing purposes and values that affect fairness and how they can be reasonably weighed remain an important theme throughout considerations of fairness that follow.

GRADES AND TESTS

One of the most notable results in chapters 2, 3, and 4 is the difference in findings for grades and for tests. Tests show a variety of gender differences—for some tests there are differences favoring females, for some tests differences favor males, and for some tests there is little difference. With large representative national samples of 12th-grade students and the wide variety of tests in common use, the data showed essentially no overall difference favoring either gender group. Grades also showed some variation in the degree of gender difference by subject, but females outperformed males fairly uniformly.

Are the test results "right" or "fair" indicating variation between females and males but no overall average difference in academic skills? Or are the grades "right" or "fair" in showing females with stronger academic skills than males? Or is the notion of right–wrong, fair–unfair not as simple as it seems? Are there differences between the constructs exemplified by grades and tests that help account for these different results and help us understand what is possibly "right" or "fair" about either result? We believe understanding test–grade differences requires a close look at the types of knowledge and skill that are likely to be represented in grades and tests.

Common Views of Grades and Tests

Students, parents, and educators rely heavily on both grades and tests as primary sources of information about academic performance, for judging student educational progress, and to anticipate or predict possible future academic success. Students regularly receive grades from their teachers based on schoolwork and classroom tests. These grades are periodically summarized by teachers on report cards for students and parents. By contrast, standardized tests are not prepared by the student's own teachers but by other educators through some external agent such as a state agency, a test publisher, or an agent of colleges and universities for college admissions and placement.

Both grades and tests are viewed as important by most parents, students, and educators. They expect both measures to be good indicators of learning and academic success, and they expect both grades and test scores to be fair and dependable. As a consequence, it can be confusing if the two sources do not agree.

Consider how grades and tests relate to each other statistically. Table 5.1 gives the grade and test combinations earned by 5,680 females and 5,862 males in the NELS (Rock, Pollack, Owings, & Hafner, 1990). Students on the main diagonal (the boxed cells from lower left to upper right) have very similar score levels for tests and grades; they are the students for whom tests and grades closely agree. Students off the main diagonal have varying degrees of discrepancy between tests and grades with the greater discrepancies indicated by those cells farthest from the main diagonal.

TABLE 5.1
Numbers of Females and Males at Grade–Test Score Levels

High School GPA	Composite Test Scores[a]			
	Low	Med. Low	Med. High	High
High				
F	14	108	513	607
M	12	51	226	573
Med. High				
F	152	589	832	265
M	106	327	632	461
Med. Low				
F	511	837	452	63
M	421	801	708	200
Low				
F	401	268	66	5
M	575	507	216	45

Note. Data on 12th graders tested in 1992 in the National Education Longitudinal Study.

[a]High school GPA and test score composites are divided into categories in which High indicates scores higher than one standard deviation above the mean; Med.High indicates scores between the mean and one standard deviation above it; Med.Low and Low indicate the corresponding scores below the mean.

As expected, grades and tests most often yield similar results. When they differ, people seem to think they understand test–grade differences for an individual student when grades are lower than test scores. Such differences are indicated in Table 5.1 by the cells below the diagonal—to the lower right. This difference is interpreted to mean that a student has the skills needed to perform better (as shown by the test), but is not using those skills consistently (as shown by the grade). Such an interpretation assumes that grades and tests involve the same academic skills, and the difference is due to whether or not the student is motivated to use those skills.

The data in the earlier chapters indicate that this type of difference (tests higher than grades) is more typical of males than females. This can be seen by the greater number of males than females in the cells below the diagonal (to the lower right) in Table 5.1. Figure 5.1 uses the same data as Table 5.1 but in finer grained test and grade categories (eight rather than four) and reports results for the ratio of numbers of females to males in each cell. In Fig. 5.1, the pattern just cited—test scores higher than grades being more typical of males than females—is shown by a smaller F/M ratio in cells below the diagonal. In the most extreme cells below the diagonal (the six shaded

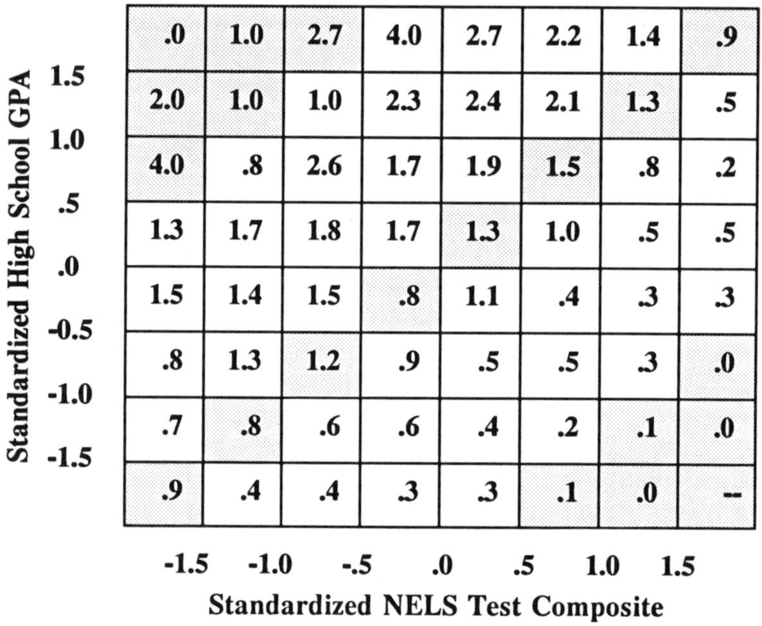

	-1.5	-1.0	-.5	.0	.5	1.0	1.5	
1.5	.0	1.0	2.7	4.0	2.7	2.2	1.4	.9
1.0	2.0	1.0	1.0	2.3	2.4	2.1	1.3	.5
.5	4.0	.8	2.6	1.7	1.9	1.5	.8	.2
.0	1.3	1.7	1.8	1.7	1.3	1.0	.5	.5
-0.5	1.5	1.4	1.5	.8	1.1	.4	.3	.3
-1.0	.8	1.3	1.2	.9	.5	.5	.3	.0
-1.5	.7	.8	.6	.6	.4	.2	.1	.0
	.9	.4	.4	.3	.3	.1	.0	--

Standardized High School GPA (vertical axis)

Standardized NELS Test Composite (horizontal axis: -1.5 -1.0 -.5 .0 .5 1.0 1.5)

FIG. 5-1. Female/male ratios at different score levels in the joint distribution of NELS test composite and high school GPA. Data on 12th graders tested in 1992 in the NELS. Both standardized scores have a mean of zero and standard deviation of 1.0.

cells), the average F/M ratio is 0.1 (there are only 6 females and 63 males). Similarly, the F/M ratios in all cells below the diagonal except one are below 1.0, indicating more males than females.

Interpretations for the reverse test–grade difference (scoring lower on tests than on school grades) do not come as easily. People tend to be puzzled by a student who achieves higher grades when particular skills required (as shown by the test) are apparently weaker. The explanation of this discrepancy, even if the word *overachiever* is applied, is less compelling than for the reverse discrepancy. One reaction is to question one of the two measures. Either the tests must be inaccurate or biased or the grades must be putting too much weight on the wrong things. According to these interpretations, tests and grades should measure the same construct, and this anomalous result implies that one or the other must be flawed. The results in chapters 3 and 4 and in Table 5.1 and Fig. 5.1 indicate that females tend, more often than males, to show this second discrepant pattern (grades higher than test scores). In the most extreme cases in Fig. 5.1 (the six shaded cells to the upper left), there are twice as many females as males (42 females and only 20 males). Across the board, the ratios are above 1.0 for all but three cells above the diagonal. To better interpret these different patterns, we believe one must consider the wide variety of skills (constructs) involved in coursework and grades as opposed to the more limited and precisely specified set of skills (constructs) underlying a test score.

The Constructs Measured by Grades and Tests

As indicated by the names of subjects (math, language, history) they both carry, there is undoubtedly much in common to grades and tests. Tests are designed with substantial input from educators about the major areas of knowledge and skill taught in classes at particular age levels, so one could expect that both tests and grades share skills and knowledge in common. The uncountable studies demonstrating the positive correlation of grades and tests confirm this expectation. People who score high on one have a strong tendency to score high on the other, without regard to gender. As Table 5.1 shows, it is far more common to find that individual students' grades and test scores reflect comparable levels of accomplishment than to find the discrepancies just noted.

In spite of this strong commonality, grades and tests do differ in some important ways—ways that could be overlooked by focusing only on the common knowledge and skills they address. To understand better the gender results on grades and tests, we need to look at the differences as well as the similarities.

The formal literature on the bases for grading and concerns about the nature and use of grades extends back several centuries (Cureton, 1971; Starch & Elliott, 1912). Characterizations of school grades have varied greatly in the literature. At best, a grade is a comprehensive and defensible professional judgment of the student's achievement in relation to a well-defined body of knowledge or skill made by the person most familiar with a student's work and the subject matter. At worst, Dressel is reported to have called a grade "an inadequate report of an inaccurate judgment by a biased and variable judge of the extent to which a student has attained an undefined level of mastery of an unknown proportion of indefinite material" (Chickering, 1983, p. 12).

Grades take different forms in different settings. Particularly after the junior high school years, grades usually take the form of numbers or letters that can be summed or otherwise statistically manipulated to create GPAs. In earlier years, grades more often take the form of evaluative ratings such as "making progress" or narrative reports ("Tommy is a joy to work with and has begun to experience some success with his reading"). In these early grades, many teachers believe it is appropriate to evaluate children on the basis of effort or improvement as well as on results and they often report using grades as a means of motivating and rewarding students.

At higher levels, the uses of grades are not so explicit. Milton, Pollio, and Eison (1986) found that individuals on college faculties implement one of three different standards with grades, differences likely common before college as well. They may give grades with reference to some absolute norm or abstract idea of perfection; they may use performance relative to peers as their standard; or they may rely on information about individual change or progress.

A grade comes from a particular course, taught over many months, following a particular curriculum, in a particular school, by a particular teacher. Throughout the levels of schooling, grades are often based on several different types of work (homework, projects, classroom tests, participation in class, etc.) accumulated over a long period of time, and typically without a clear agreement among teachers as to a common standard for assigning a particular grade to a particular student.

Grades are criticized as well as relied on. Grades are criticized for unreliability (different teachers grading the same student work differently), for grade inflation (unwarranted increases in average grades), for not conveying clearly what students have learned, for being too heavily normative (restricting numbers of grades at various levels), and for promoting unhealthy competition among students (Willis, 1993). Grades are also counted on more heavily than any other factor in identifying outstanding students for awards during school or for admission to the next level of education. They are likely the foremost factor that parents count on in judging the learning progress of their children.

Some different factors enter into achievement as defined by standardized test scores (Geisinger, 1982; Milton et al., 1986; Smith & Dobbin, 1960). Tests are based on specific and limited samples of student work. That work usually involves answers to a particular set of questions based on content specifications defining the body of knowledge included and the relative weight given to each part. Typically students receive the same or similar questions. The answers are typically obtained in a specific and quite limited period of time (a few hours at the most). There are explicit rules for judging individual answers and rules for converting responses on single questions to total scores. Note that although classroom tests contribute to grades, those tests have diverse characteristics that typically differ from the characteristics of standardized tests noted here. Thus, our references to tests are to standardized tests. Teacher-made classroom tests, we believe, are best thought of as one of the diverse types of exercises and activities on which grades are based.

Tests are subject to many of the same types of criticisms and concerns as grades. Tests are criticized for focusing learning too narrowly, for promoting unhealthy competition, for giving results only normatively—as relative position among peers, not in terms of what students have learned and not learned. Tests are likely the second most relied-on source of information about academic success.

Reconsidering Results on Grades and Tests

Grades and tests are alike in addressing similar skills and knowledge but unlike in that grades are commonly reported to address additional skills, knowledge, and perhaps other characteristics and behavior. Thus, it is not surprising that grades and tests tell us some consistent and some different things about academic performance of females and males. It may be that test-taking skills are another difference between grades and test scores—a possibility that is examined in the next chapter.

Results on both test scores and grades show gender differences in academic performance by subject field, and both give basically similar orderings of performance for each gender. However, the two measures differ in that females generally score higher than males on academic performance according to grades, but, according to tests, which gender scores higher depends on the subject. Both these consistent and inconsistent results are apparent in Fig. 5.2, which presents results from chapter 3 on test performance alongside data from chapter 4 on grades.

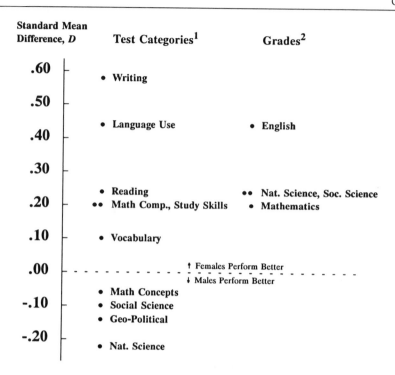

FIG. 5.2. Tests and grades in nationally representative samples of high school seniors.
[1]Results for 10 categories of tests in Grade 12 from Fig. 3.2.
[2]Results from NELS 1992 seniors for whom transcript information was available (78%).

Females perform better in writing, language usage, and English than they do in mathematics and sciences, whether indicated by test scores or by grades. By both measures, males perform better in mathematics and sciences than they do in language skills. Both results illustrate the consistency from the two measures with respect to different subject fields. However, gender differences on test performance vary widely by subject, but grades show much less variability and are higher for females across major subject areas in many samples.

It is quite clear that grades tap a broader array of skills than tests. Is there evidence of differences between females and males on the additional skills and characteristics grades tap that could account for grade–test differences? If females displayed more of the skills and characteristics involved uniquely in grades (but not in tests), then the different levels of results for grades and tests such as those in Fig. 5.2 would be expected and understandable.

To consider this possibility, we turn to data from chapter 4 on gender differences in various nontest aspects of academic performance. The results compiled in Fig. 5.3 give a picture of females more often than males doing the types of things that may be rewarded in better school grades. Females show more task-oriented behaviors such as completing, attending to, and reviewing schoolwork. They seek teacher advice and study with other students more often. They devote more leisure time to taking out-of-school classes and substantially less to sports. One might characterize these as "studenting" activities involving attentive and sustained work.

In addition, results on honors and awards (Fig. 4.8) and school participation (Fig. 4.16) indicate that females participate most in activities involving language skills and the arts, consistent with the subject patterns shown in both test and grade results in Fig. 5.2.

Results of differences on "studenting" activities make it considerably less surprising that females outperform males on grades. Grade–test differences

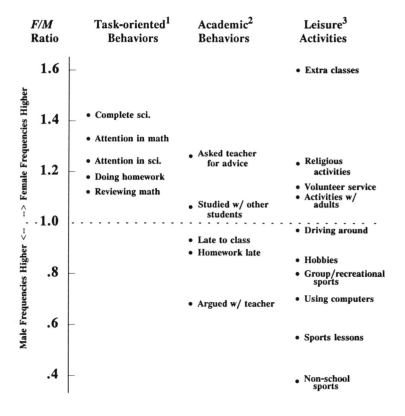

FIG. 5.3. Grade-related behaviors and activities.
[1] Selected entries from Fig. 4.10 (based on NELS).
[2] Taken from Fig. 4.11 (based on HERI).
[3] Selected entries from Fig. 4.15 (based on NELS).

could be accentuated further by the possibility that language skills are prominent in grades even beyond the forms of language on tests. The issue remains whether the level of activity differences and the possible role of language skill differences in grades are sufficient to explain why females perform better than males in grades in all major subjects, overriding the strong subject effects shown on tests and in subject-related differential activities.

Discussions of male–female differences in the public press tend to focus on test performance differences in science and mathematics. In this isolated context, the issue of gender differences is often cast as an issue of female deficiency in performance. The data in Figs. 5.1 and 5.2 are good reminders that this deficiency model is sorely inadequate. In representative samples, females outperform males in mathematics and science grades and on various tested subjects. The issue might instead be cast as questions about male deficits in school grades and in language-related skills. On balance, neither deficit model provides the best approach to understanding this complex set of results.

How Construct Analysis Helps Understanding

Key results in grades and on tests are understood differently when the constructs are carefully analyzed:

1. Grades and tests do have similarities as the public commonly assumes. They are alike in measuring a similar set of key subject skills and knowledge by design. Although aspects of the tasks used to assess these common skills and knowledge can differ from grades to tests, the data show strong correlations between them, affirming the similarity of aspects of the construct.

2. Contrary to some belief and practice, tests and grades differ in several ways as well. Grades involve not only the skills and knowledge represented in tests, but also (a) additional skills and knowledge (e.g., perhaps communicating about the subject or levels of understanding or synthesis beyond those typically tested), and (b) behaviors such as attention to prolonged or complex activities requiring sustained effort and concentration that improve effectiveness in school classes (and hence may improve grades more than test scores). This latter category includes behaviors that might be characterized as effective "studenting."

3. Based on the understanding of differences between the constructs described in Point 2, it is somewhat less surprising that average grades of females are consistently higher than those of males regardless of subject. Females show higher levels of participation than males in "studenting" activities, consistent with factors that differentiate grades from tests. Females also show superiority over males in language skills that may differentiate grades from tests. However, little is known about gender differences in other subject-related skills that grades may differentially tap.

4. For each gender group, grades and tests both show a similar ordering of subjects. Subjects on which females have higher grades are also the tests on which they have higher scores. Similarly, males have the highest test scores and highest grades in the same subjects. In addition, the ranks of school subjects seem to mirror ranks of out-of-school activities for both females and males. Such participation could be an important factor differentially influencing grades and tests.

Looking Ahead to Fairness Issues. Understanding construct issues is necessary for understanding fairness issues in future chapters, especially in chapter 7, in which we consider fairness in test design and use. For example, the differences in the construct being measured by grades and tests are important in our examination of gender differences in particular school subjects, especially mathematics. There the issue is to understand the fairness implications of females scoring relatively higher than males in mathematics grades in school as compared to tests.

Tests are often used to anticipate or predict future grades, a practice that likely further confuses differentiation of the test and grade constructs in the public mind. As argued here, tests are not surrogates of grades. If there is a pattern of gender difference on grades and tests, is there not likely to be a pattern of differences also in predicting grades from test scores? We also pursue that question in chapter 7.

TYPES OF SKILLS

In chapter 3, tests of similar types were often clustered together to understand general overall trends. Although this practice is appropriate and useful for examining overall trends, it could lead readers to the mistaken conclusion that tests clustered by similar names in fact test the same construct.

A close look at Table 3.1 indicates the possibly surprising result that all tests of a particular name do not show an identical gender difference. Some language areas show larger gender differences than others and some mathematics tests show larger gender differences than other math tests. Recognizing the differences in types of skills (constructs) measured by apparently similar tests is necessary in order to understand the gender differences they produce or to make progress on fairness issues.

Differences in Skills

In considering the constructs often represented in grades, we noted that school subjects involve a wide variety of skills. Educators commonly seek to instill many different skills in students. Much discussion of educational goals and assessment involves identifying the most important skills to emphasize in instruction and testing. Just as different teachers make different decisions about what to include in their own courses, different tests reflect different decisions about what skills to test. As a result, tests that carry the same name may include different skills and such resulting construct differences can impact gender differences.

The wide array of skills and knowledge in a subject may all have similar value as learning outcomes so that the choice among them for inclusion on tests may be based primarily on covering the subject. In such cases, two tests may span the same domain but the particular skills tested may differ. If either set of skills is differentially strong for males or females, one of the tests might show larger gender differences than the other. One has to examine the skills tested (the constructs of the tests) to make sense of such puzzling differences.

Differences in Language Skills

Language tests provide a good example of the possibilities for assessing different constructs in the same general area of proficiency. However, these differences in school-level language tests are often more visible than is sometimes the case because instruction in school addresses different subskills more explicitly and language tests are often labeled with the name of the subskill. For example, in Table 3.1, four major categories of verbal and language tests are separately examined—writing, language use, reading, and vocabulary/reasoning.

As can also be seen in that table, standard mean gender differences vary widely across the four categories from an average of .57 (12th-grade females scoring considerably higher than 12th-grade males) for writing, to .43 for language use, to .20 for reading, to .06 for vocabulary/reasoning. Even within category, there is some variation in the gender differences shown, most notably in reading. This result suggests construct variation (skills or knowledge) within the set of reading tests given to 12th graders.

Within the language skills category, it appears that educators and the public largely treat each of these different subskills as of similar importance and value, each deserving attention in instruction and in measures of learning outcomes.

Differences in Skill Levels

Not all skill distinctions involve equally valued outcomes. Some distinctions clearly involve constructs of different value. When skills are associated with different levels of expertise, some tests may concentrate on lower level skills and some on higher level skills. Skill level distinctions involve a dimension from lower to higher skills. Higher skill levels are not just more skills but more important and more complex skills. For example, in early reading a lower level skill is decoding single words; a higher level skill is understanding the meaning of a sentence or paragraph. For differences in skill levels of this type, there is no doubt that higher level outcomes are preferred to lower level ones.

There has been a long history of attention to skill levels and most subjects reflect some notion of a skill hierarchy. For many years tests and instructional processes were designed and analyzed using the well-known Bloom taxonomy (Bloom, 1956), which involves six levels—from knowledge (the lowest) to comprehension, application, analysis, synthesis, and finally the highest level, evaluation.

Many fields acknowledge a distinction between at least two levels under the labels *knowledge* and *application* in which applying knowledge to new situations and new problems is deemed a higher level than just knowing facts or information alone. Many current discussions of this topic include reference to the difference between basic skills and so-called higher order skills. It is sometimes noted that in a future of technology and rapid change, citizens will need higher order skills to a greater extent than in the past. Much discussion of national educational standards concerns the need to instruct students in such higher order as well as basic skills (NCTM, 1989; Ravitch, 1995).

Much cognitive science research of recent decades has attended to level distinctions as well, but frequently from a somewhat different perspective. Here the attention has often been to the different cognitive structures and approaches to problems of novices and experts (Chi, Glaser, & Farr, 1988; Dreyfus & Dreyfus, 1986). Higher order from this perspective means the types of understandings and approaches experts with much experience and practice in a field bring to a problem and how those differ from the understandings and approaches of beginners in the field. The distinctions derived from this line of research refer more to different ways knowledge is organized by experts as compared to novices than to a simple progression of skills from low to high. Expertise is, of course, more highly valued than are novice skills.

An important aspect of cognitive approaches is the attention given to the time devoted to and required in mastering higher skill levels. Such time includes formal study as well as various types of related incidental learning and practice. The importance of time and practice is helpful in understanding why leisure activities and interests can have a critical mediating effect in determining levels of accomplishment. Fennema and Peterson (1985) noted, for example, "the learning of mathematics, particularly the skills required to perform high-level tasks, does not occur quickly and at one time. Rather the skills are developed over a period of years by participating many times in the activities necessary for performing high-level tasks" (p. 31).

Skill and skill level distinctions become especially important when associated with gender differences. Understanding the underlying skill levels may be critical to understanding the nature of gender differences and effective ways to address fairness issues in testing.

Skill Level Differences in Mathematics

Mathematics requires particular attention because skill level distinctions are common and are often hidden from casual public view. Reports of mathematics performance differences on tests between males and females are frequent and well-known. However, there is still more to be learned about these differences from better understanding some of the different constructs, particularly different skill level constructs, involved in mathematics tests.

Snow and Ennis (1996) studied a nationally representative sample of more than 6,000 eighth graders from the NELS (Rock et al., 1990) and compared performance of males and females on two subscores. One subscore was created to reflect basic mathematics facts and computational skill; the other, to reflect a higher order inferential reasoning skill. Results on the two subscores were then compared for males and females across all total test score levels. The results summarized in Fig. 5.4 indicate that lower scoring females tend to outperform lower scoring males on basic facts and computation although at higher score levels these subscores did not differ. By contrast, males at all score levels tended to outperform females on inferential reasoning subscores.

This analysis shows how the nature of gender differences can be masked or distorted by looking at total score alone and paying no attention to construct components. If a test involved primarily the skills included on the first subscore, we might conclude the gender differences were minimal. If the construct focus of a test were, however, on inferential skills, gender differences would be clearly apparent. We might have even called the first test "fair" and the second "biased" without attention to critical construct differences between them.

Another study by this group of researchers indicates that males gain more on inferential reasoning in high school than do females (Kupermintz et al., 1995). This work further illustrates the enhanced fairness and usefulness of assessment that distinguishes underlying constructs and thereby helps to clarify educational implications.

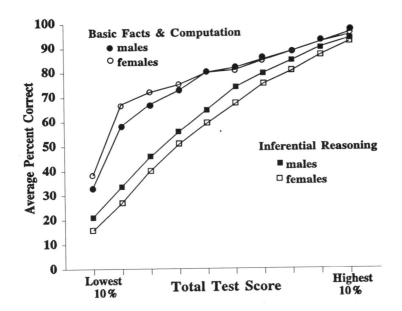

FIG. 5.4. Female–male performance in two mathematics skills across the total test score range. Adapted with permission from Snow, R., & Ennis, M. (1996). Correlates of high mathematical ability in a national sample of eighth graders. In C. Benbow & D. Lubinski (Eds.), *Intellectual talent: Psychometric and social issues* (pp. 301–327). Baltimore: Johns Hopkins University Press.

D. Rock (personal communication, January 5, 1995) analyzed results for high school seniors on mathematical, reading, and science skills in terms of levels of proficiency in the subject. Each proficiency level was measured by a separate subset of test questions judged to reflect a different skill level. The results are suggestive of small but possible variation by skill level within subject, particularly in mathematics, with males performing slightly better on more complex math questions (see Table S-22 in the *Supplement* to this volume).

Doolittle and Cleary (1987) classified questions from the ACT Mathematics test into six content categories. Males significantly outperformed females on the geometry category and on arithmetic and algebraic reasoning questions involving word problems. Females performed significantly better than males on intermediate algebra and arithmetic and algebraic operations. The authors hypothesized that the geometry results support notions that male examinees "tend to have developed certain spatial skills to a greater degree" and the other categories suggest "that males have developed relatively stronger mathematics reasoning skills (measured partially by arithmetic and algebraic reasoning items) and that females have developed relatively stronger algorithmic or computational skills" (p. 164).

In looking only at overall results in a subject, one might easily miss a pattern such as that in mathematics in the studies noted here. Such results have complex implications for how to fairly design mathematics tests as well as for the design of instructional programs to improve the mathematics performance of young women, indicating again the importance of understanding the constructs measured.

How Construct Analysis Helps Understanding

Differences in types of skills or constructs are important from several perspectives:

1. Many types of skills are taught in subject fields but rarely are all of those skills assessed on tests. Tests represent particular samples of all possible skills for inclusion. When the samples of skills are very different for two similarly named tests and the differences in the two sets of skills relate to gender differences, one test may show gender differences and the other may not. It is critical to understand the actual constructs being measured at a level of detail below the test name to understand such contrasting results.

2. When different skills are involved, a critical component skill may be an essential part of learning that should not be ignored in tests or instruction. However, if there are gender differences in learning such higher level skills, their inclusion on tests will likely result in gender differences in test scores. In this section we saw two examples: writing as a critical language skill that tends to favor females, and inferential reasoning as a critical mathematical skill that tends to favor males.

Looking Ahead to Fairness Issues.   Because the degree of gender difference in test performance is often affected by the types of skills measured within the test, differences in performance by females and males often stimulate one or both of the following desires: (a) to use a different test or change the test so no differences are exhibited or (b) to improve the educational experience for the lower scoring group. In either case, it is important to understand construct differences to decide what should be measured and for what purposes.

Such differences raise the critical issue of the bases for including some skills rather than other skills on tests. This is an issue of test design. In chapter 7, in which we address fairness issues in test design, understanding skill constructs and the gender differences in them proves essential.

MULTIPLE CHOICE AND ALTERNATIVE APPROACHES

Table 3.3 presented data on the AP Program showing that the standard differences for free-response or essay portions (average D of $-.06$) are less than for the multiple-choice portions (average D of $-.20$). Does this mean that gender differences are an artifact of multiple-choice approaches and that we need only switch to alternative approaches to eliminate gender differences? The answer to this question depends largely on construct issues.

Differences and Similarities in Testing Approaches

Most standardized educational testing in this country has used multiple-choice approaches. Such testing has been widely used largely because multiple-choice tests produce a great deal of information about academic skills and knowledge at very low cost.

In recent years, there has been increasing concern that multiple-choice testing may have drawbacks not realized in the past. One concern is that such tests may be too limited in the skills they tap—that measures are needed that more "authentically" represent real-world skills and the context for application of skills. This concern is accentuated by the additional consideration that the form of the test may have unforeseen consequences for the educational enterprise, perhaps misrepresenting to students, teachers, and parents what knowledge and skills are most important to teach and to learn.

Alternative testing approaches or free-response formats have been developed and many are being used experimentally in several educational contexts (Baker, O'Neil, & Linn, 1993; Bennett & Ward, 1993). Most are not new as testing approaches. What is new is the effort to use them on a large scale in the United States. Major examples of free-response alternative formats are:

- *Constructed response formats*: Formats requiring the test taker to supply the answer rather than select from multiple answer options; types range from tasks requiring simple numerical answers to tasks requiring extended oral or written responses such as an essay; usually requires human judges to score.
- *Simulation formats*: Formats that simulate some realistic task and/or performance; task simulations seek to provide realistic context for the task; performance simulations seek to elicit realistic performance in response to tasks; performance simulations often require human judges.
- *Performance formats*: Formats involving actual samples of work or skill performance produced in a real world, as opposed to special testing, context and typically observed or judged by human judges.
- *Portfolio formats*: Formats based on collections of any of these types produced over time and scored by human judges.

As alternative testing formats become increasingly available, all the questions now asked about multiple-choice questions will need to be asked about these new formats. Some examples are:

- What constructs do they measure?
- How do they differ from multiple-choice tests, from grades, and from other types of measures?
- How are they affected by prior activities, interests, and experiences?
- What are their implications for understanding gender differences?
- What are their systemic effects on education?
- What do they cost and is the cost worth what they add?

Our ultimate preference among available measures will depend on answers to these and similar questions, and no single test type is likely to be "best" by all relevant criteria.

With this background we turn back to the question that motivates this and later sections: Are there gender differences that are due only to artifacts of the format used in the testing? If so, does this require only switching to a new format that does not create such "artificial" gender differences?

Gender Differences and Test Format

As noted, efforts to use alternative formats in large-scale testing of students are, for the most part, very new in the United States. Although some of the alternative formats described here are under development and experimentation, the only free-response format that has received substantial use is the constructed response format and its most common form is the essay. Likely the greatest use of the free-response format in large-scale standardized testing is through the AP Program of the College Board. As described in chapter 3, most AP examinations include both multiple-choice and free-response parts, with the two parts typically receiving equal weight in the examination score.

The AP data in chapter 3 showed some overall gender differences between the multiple-choice and the free-response formats (primarily essays or written problem solutions). Gender differences on the multiple-choice sections of some 27 AP examinations showed an average D of $-.20$ (the results favored males by this standard difference). By contrast, the free-response portions of the same 27 examinations produced little if any gender difference ($D = -.06$). Such results seem to suggest the possibility that a consistent format effect may exist. However, for this to be a format effect per se, the effect should be consistent across subjects except for small chance fluctuations.

On closer examination it is apparent that the differences between the two formats vary considerably across subject fields. As shown in Table 3.3, for 11 AP examinations, males and females perform quite similarly on the multiple-choice and free-response sections, reflecting no gender-related format difference.

For the remaining 16 examinations, females perform relatively better on the free-response sections, but the degree of advantage ranges from a small relative advantage (a difference of .11 between free-response and multiple-choice standard differences) to a larger relative advantage of .39. For some reason the gender-related format difference on these 16 exams varies in size across examination subjects.

Because the free-response and multiple-choice differences on AP tests vary so much by subject, they cannot be explained simply by differences in the two formats. The obvious alternative to consider is whether this effect is due to differences in constructs associated with the two formats.

How Construct Analysis Helps Understanding

Understanding construct differences is important to understanding format differences and their relation to gender concerns. The following construct considerations help to understand the possibilities and limitations of alternative test formats.

1. Gender differences on multiple-choice and presently used free-response formats are not uniform in direction or size. Thus, we cannot expect that alternate test formats will automatically reduce or eliminate gender differences. In fact, we can learn about the likely impact of alternate test formats on gender differences by examining the constructs involved.

2. Different formats are often used precisely because of the desire to measure different constructs—constructs not readily measured in multiple-choice forms. When different constructs are associated with different formats, the impact on gender differences depends on the nature of the different constructs and the associated gender differences.

3. The free-response format often involves writing as in the AP data noted here. Writing raises issues of critical importance on two counts. First, gender differences in writing suggest that tests involving the ability to write clearly and coherently may favor females, depending on the extent to which writing skill is part of the construct tested. Second, written answers may involve additional types of skills. For example, written answers often call for analysis or synthesis of information. If there are gender differences on these skills, tests involving them will show gender differences.

Looking Ahead to Fairness Issues.   Test format is an issue of considerable importance to questions of fairness in testing. If, in tests measuring the same construct, some formats consistently favor one group, a fairness issue is clearly raised. In chapter 7, we consider in more depth the AP Test case discussed here and other data to determine whether, across apparently similar constructs, a format effect produces gender differences.

Even when format effects per se are not indicated, formats may be associated with constructs that show gender differences. It is equally critical to recognize and understand these gender-linked constructs as it is to identify gender-linked formats. We also examine this issue in more depth in chapter 7.

Finally, the association of writing with free-response test formats raises some important issues of gender differences and fairness. There are gender differences (favoring females) in writing skills from early school years onward. Writing is important as a valued skill with a broad role in all of education and much of employment as well. It is also important because writing seems the best way we have at present to get at some types of valued skills such as analysis, synthesis, and integration. Appreciating the role of writing in assessment is likely as vital to understanding gender differences and fairness as is comprehending the more often cited differences in mathematics. In chapter 7 and again in chapter 8, we confront the writing issue and its implications for fairness in assessment.

IMPACT OF INTERESTS AND EXPERIENCES

Results from chapter 3 indicate that gender differences vary widely by school subject. As summarized in Fig. 5.2, females outperform males on tests of writing, language use, and reading; males outperform females on tests of science. In addition, Fig. 3.2 indicates that these differences increase over the school years, becoming wider from Grades 4 to 8 and wider still from Grades 8 to 12. Females start better in writing and language use in Grade 4 and increase their advantage by Grade 8, holding it to Grade 12. Males start with fewer advantages at Grades 4 and 8 but begin to improve, relative to females, by Grade 12 in mathematical concepts, geopolitical areas, and natural sciences.

Such results raise questions about why these diverging patterns of proficiency occur. Don't females and males take similar sets of courses throughout the school years? Why do gender differences in language and science increase through the years? Do these results indicate that something is wrong? If something is wrong, is it with the tests or with education, and what should we do about it? As in previous sections of this chapter, we seek to understand these questions in terms of constructs and to understand implications of the results in chapters 3 and 4 for how we approach issues of fairness in assessment in subsequent chapters.

Course-Taking Patterns

As a nation, the United States has clearly committed to substantial commonality in courses for all students throughout the school years. Students take the same courses in the early grades and it is not until junior high school that a few options appear. In high school, there are requirements for high school graduation that involve required years of English, mathematics, history and social studies, and science (Coley & Goertz, 1990), substantially limiting opportunity for highly differential course-taking patterns until the late high school years.

Some diverging patterns of course taking in high school appear after course requirements are completed. As indicated in chapter 4, females take fewer mathematics and science courses beyond those typically required for high school graduation or college admissions. They take more high school honors courses than males in languages, English, art, music, and social science.

As greater choice opens, the course-taking patterns of females and males diverge further. They choose different patterns of AP courses late in high school (Fig. 3.17) and express different plans for advanced coursework in college (Fig. 4.7). In particular, more female than male students take AP courses in foreign languages, English, and humanities, whereas more males than females take advanced courses in computer science, physics, chemistry, and mathematics.

Their selections of major field in college diverge, with females majoring more often than males in education and social science and males majoring more often in engineering, agriculture and forestry, and physical science (Fig. 4.18). These patterns continue into graduate study as well, with females choosing to study health fields and education more often than males and males choosing engineering, physical science, mathematics, computer science, and business more often (Fig. 4.19).

Such patterns demonstrate that divergence occurs, but their timing (in high school and beyond) is too late to "cause" performance divergence at Grades 4 and 8. The later divergence in fields of study could be a result of the earlier divergence in performance, or other factors might affect both the early divergence in performance and the later divergence in field of study. For example, it is not certain that girls and boys are treated the same in mathematics classes in early grades. Based on their studies, Fennema and Peterson (1985) suggested that at that age boys are developing more autonomy, which is important in developing high-level skills in mathematics.

Patterns of Interests and Values

An obvious possibility in understanding divergent patterns for females and males involves gender differences in interests, values, and experiences. If there are gender differences in these areas that are consistent with the existing performance differentials, then one might reasonably expect that at least part of the early appearing performance differential may result from differences in what people like to do and how they spend their time.

Certainly there are numerous reports of different play activities of young girls and boys from early ages (Millar, 1968). Further, the activities summarized in Fig. 5.3 indicate patterns of activities and experiences that are different for females and males. It is important to note that many of these activities involve substantial time commitments, indicating a substantial difference in the out-of-class time females and males spend on activities related to aspects of academic performance.

We have formal measures of interests and values only in students of high school age or older, typically in the form of vocational interests and broad value dimensions. Results for vocational interests and values from chapter 4 are summarized in Fig. 5.5.

We find young women scoring higher than young men on domestic, artistic, writing, social service, and office service vocational interests and young men scoring higher than young women on business, law, politics, mathematics, science, agriculture, athletics, and mechanical interests. Value orientations differ as well, with high scores for females on social, religious, and aesthetic values and high scores for males on political, economic, and theoretical values.

Although the data reported here are not tracked through the school years, there can be little doubt that such gender variations in interests and activities exist well before high school. The fact is that females and males report enjoying different activities and acting on those interests outside the classes in which they are required to participate.

Interest Patterns and Tests

It is clear that gender differences in interests and experiences exist. It is also likely that such differences affect academic achievement in subjects. The interest and value pattern differences found are generally consistent with patterns of performance differences; areas in which interest differences exist are generally the same as those in which performance differentials exist. Thus, it appears that interests and experiences are likely contributing factors both to performance differences that develop through the school years and to patterns in subject field selection in high school, college, and careers.

Such differences raise a related issue for testing. Interest patterns likely affect what is actually learned and hence are associated with valid performance differences on tests. Could interest differences also affect

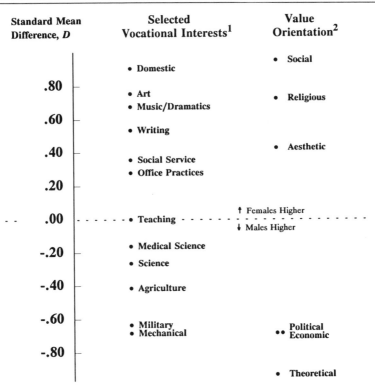

FIG. 5.5. Vocational interests and values.
[1]Selected scales from the results reported in Fig. 4.14 (see footnote 8 in chapter 4; based on the 1985 version of *Strong Interest Inventory*, Hansen & Campbell, 1985).
[2]Results from Fig. 4.12 (based on Allport, Vernon, & Lindzey; Copyright © 1970. From the *Study of Values-A Scale For Measuring The Dominant Interests in Personality* by G. W. Allport, P. E. Vernon, and G. Lindzey. Used with the permission of Houghton Mifflin Company.

test scores in inappropriate ways, exaggerating gender differences? This could happen if test content related to interests in ways that went beyond connections required by the construct.

It has long been recognized that different interest patterns can affect test performance in these additional, non-construct-driven ways. Measures of reading and writing skill are thought to be affected somewhat by the individual's knowledge of and interest in the content involved (Carlton & Harris, 1992). For this reason, it is common on general reading tests to have multiple reading passages that span a wide array of interest areas, for example, from arts and humanities to science. It is similarly common for general writing tests to present a choice of topics or to present a single topic general enough to allow examinees to bring their own experiences and interests to bear.

In these two cases, such reading and writing tests are measuring whether a person can display a general skill when not impeded by lack of interest or experience with a particular topic. In such cases, it is important not to have the test performance impeded by differences in interest or experience that are not relevant to the skill.

By contrast, other constructs necessarily involve material of certain types leaving little choice or option for the test maker. If the construct is technical reading skills (i.e., reading in science or technical fields) then the construct demands that the reading topics involve technical material, even if those taking the test differ in interest in such material. If the interest-related aspect is part of the construct, then interest differentials cannot and should not be avoided regardless of gender differences.

When the construct definition leaves open possibilities for test material on which interest and experience may vary, the interests and experiences may introduce construct-irrelevant error in tests if not controlled in some way. For example, within the aforementioned technical and science reading test, a passage might involve either electronics or biology (two aspects of technical and science fields in which there are gender differences in interests). A test using only electronics passages would likely favor males more than one using only biology passages. To control for this, a balance of reading passages would typically be sought.

In these examples, one must understand the construct to judge how to make reasonable decisions about the appropriate impact of possible differences in interests and experiences. Again, understanding the construct is essential both to interpreting differences and to acting on them in creating fair tests.

How Construct Analysis Helps Understanding

Gender differences in performance by subject field, in interest patterns, and in experiences seem to have important interacting effects.

1. Gender differences by subject field diverge through the school years in spite of the fact that students study basically the same subjects until well into high school. Gender differences in choice of courses and field of study appear in high school and later when such choices are available to students.

2. There are gender differences in patterns of vocational interests, experiences, and values that are quite consistent with performance differences. Such interest and experience differences could be a part of the explanation for the diverging performance patterns that exist.

3. Interest and experience pattern differentials surely impact test performance. Some such impact is an appropriate and expected part of the construct being measured. Other potential impacts of such different patterns are not relevant to the construct and must be controlled (eliminated or balanced). We must understand the constructs to understand which types of interest and experience differentials must be controlled in testing.

Looking Ahead to Fairness Issues. The impact of differential interests and experiences on key educational constructs is critical to understanding gender differences and fairness issues. Many of the gender differences identified in chapters 2 and 3 parallel differences in interests and experiences in chapter 4. This similarity suggests that interests and experiences may be powerful explanatory variables for differences in learning that seem to occur. The existence of such explanatory variables rightly affects approaches to test fairness questions, although it does not eliminate the questions.

The choice of material for use in test exercises involves issues of interest and experiences. When constructs do not call for particular types of material, the fairness issue concerns appropriate choice of material and how to balance for interests within the latitude the construct allows. We examine this issue further in chapter 6.

Beyond the material selected to examine a particular construct, the choice of constructs to measure is a critical test design issue that can have serious implications for gender differences in test performance. In chapter 7 we explore construct choice issues more closely, often in the context of interest and experience differences.

THE CONTEXT OF TEST FAIRNESS[1]

In chapter 1 we characterized test fairness as a systemic problem—a variety of issues that must be considered within the context in which tests are developed and used. Individual fairness issues tend to be mainly connected with particular steps in the assessment process, although the steps are interrelated in various ways. We described those connections with the assessment process in chapter 1 in order to provide a framework for thinking about test fairness and also to identify fairness issues more directly with the decisions that are made in developing and using a test. This chapter helps us to understand another aspect of the broader context.

---

[1]This section draws on several years of conversations between the author and Warren W. Willingham, making specific attribution of ideas impossible. Thus this section should most properly be considered a joint effort.

Each section in this chapter has examined possible implications of observed gender differences in light of variations in the constructs that a test measures. From that discussion, it is clear that variations in the tested construct can result in different patterns of performance by women and men that may raise fairness issues. Construct variations can also have quite different educational implications and pose quite different practical issues in assessment. So this chapter provides another perspective on the systemic character of test fairness. It is important to identify and debate all aspects of a test that may bear on its fairness. Eventually, however, one must decide whether the development and use of the test is justified. Three criteria tend to determine the answer to the question of justification:

- How useful the test is in serving its intended function.
- How fair the test is for individuals and groups of examinees.
- How well the test meets practical constraints.

These three criteria are more complicated than they may appear, and they overlap in various ways. The first two—usefulness and fairness—comprise much of what we normally construe as test validity. Note, however, that a test can be apparently useful and fair, but measure something a bit different from what was actually intended. A risk in that case might be some unforeseen consequence of using the test. For that reason, validity is always the overarching standard of test quality. Usefulness, fairness, and practicality are best viewed as social criteria, employed ultimately by test users. It will be helpful to bear in mind several important aspects of these criteria as we move into the discussion of assessment issues in the following two chapters.

Usefulness.   We develop educational tests in order to serve some worthwhile social function. First and foremost, use of the test is justified by its usefulness in serving that function. In thinking about test function, it is important to include not only the immediate purpose to which the scores are put, but also other possible effects of using the test. Some effects may work backward in time to influence—beneficially or not—the teachers and learners who anticipate the coming test. Other effects may work forward in time to influence what types of talent tend to be rewarded and developed over time. A test may not serve the useful function intended if we do not understand adequately what construct the test measures. Two alternate tests are not likely to measure precisely the same construct or to stack up exactly the same on these several interpretations of usefulness. More important for our purposes here, the test that appears to be the most useful overall from an educational standpoint will not necessarily be the test that has the most desirable features with respect to fairness.

Fairness.   As we argued in chapter 1, test fairness depends fundamentally on comparability. However, issues of fairness for individual examinees are sometimes different than for subgroups of examinees (Willingham, in press). For example, the most useful test for all high school physics students would include a careful sampling of all knowledge and skills typically included in the course, but that would not be the fairest test in schools that had no physics laboratory. On the other hand, reducing test content to what is available in every school threatens the usefulness and fairness of the test for students generally. As another example, the relative amount of mathematics and writing in a testing program is likely to be viewed quite differently by women and language minority students. In yet another example, an experimental test may be more useful than any other test available for predicting success in a particular program of study, but the test would pose a fairness issue if it proved susceptible to cheating or to coaching tricks. In chapter 7 we see a number of instances in which the interests of two subgroups or the interests of a subgroup and those of individual examinees may be in conflict.

Practicality.   Many assessment alternatives are impractical, either because they are not feasible technically or they prove to be unacceptable in actual operation. For some types of test material, it may not be technically possible to produce the multiple test versions that a testing program would need each year, or to ensure that scores for the different versions are sufficiently comparable, or to maintain test security when that is important. For examinees and test users, failures in practicality are for more prosaic reasons: The test takes too much time, it is too complicated, or it costs too much. Tests must meet acceptable standards of practicality if they are to compete with procedures that are less burdensome, even though less useful and fair. Problems of practicality are partly problems of will—the will of test developers to make effective assessments more practical, and the willingness of users to put higher priority on good assessment in relation to practicality issues.

When we develop, evaluate, and justify a test, we necessarily do so with these three criteria in mind. No test is likely to be perfect with respect to usefulness, fairness, or practicality, but it must meet an acceptable standard on each of these criteria, and fairness deserves a very high standard. The following two chapters give a good sense of what is involved in reaching for a high standard of fairness. As we move on to consider those fairness issues, it is also good to recall, however, that a fair test will not likely have an opportunity to serve a constructive purpose unless it is also useful and practical.

6

Fairness Issues in Test Development and Administration

Brent Bridgeman

Alicia Schmitt

Chapter 1 described four major stages in the creation of a valid and equitable assessment system: design, development, administration, and use. Chapter 6 focuses on fairness issues related to the two steps in the middle of this process. We start here because these steps are closely related and have been at the center of much of the debate over fairness in testing. Furthermore, the complex issues of design and use (and the importance of these issues), addressed in the next chapter, are more easily understood with a grounding in the relatively straight-forward equity issues related to development and administration. Chapter 7 takes up even more complex issues concerning fairness in test design and use.

Once decisions have been made regarding what will be measured (e.g., developed verbal abilities relevant to success in college) and generally how it will be measured (e.g., multiple-choice tests or essays), attention must be paid to the procedures for test development and administration. These procedures may have an impact on the fairness of the assessment for individuals and for groups. In general, the goal with respect to fairness is to make the assessment as comparable as possible for all examinees. For a valid and equitable assessment, this comparability must be at the level of the underlying constructs—the essence of what the assessment is intended to measure. Comparability in the most obvious external features of an examination is no guarantee of comparability at the deeper level, just as lack of comparability in surface features is not necessarily evidence of unfairness in assessing the construct of interest.

Concern that test construction and administration practices could im-pact on gender differences is certainly not new. For example, Dwyer's (1979) review covered many of the same issues that we address here. However, much more data is now available, and over the past 15 years a number of techniques were developed for statistically assessing the extent to which test questions function differently for men and women. In addition, the increas-ing importance of performance assessments has raised new comparability and equity issues. In this chapter, issues related to the content, context, and structure of test questions are discussed first. Next, we discuss fairness issues related to standardized testing conditions, focusing especially on test ad-ministration and scoring practices that might contribute to gender differ-ences. In the final section, we consider fairness issues that are especially pertinent for performance assessments.

FAIRNESS IN TEST QUESTIONS

Established professional standards specify review processes and empirical procedures as ways to strive for fair tests. In this chapter, these two proce-dures, used at the test development stage to help ensure that test questions are fair to different groups, are respectively referred to as *test sensitivity review* and *differential item functioning*. Through these two procedures the fairness of test questions with specific content, context, and structure is evaluated at different stages of the test development process. Test sensitivity review is a judgmental process used to evaluate sensitive material before it is admin-istered. Differential item functioning is a data-based process used to identify items with performance differences by comparable groups after items are pretested.

Test Sensitivity Review

Guidelines for the development and evaluation of fair tests have been offered by the American Psychological Association (APA) since 1954 and by APA with the American Educational Research Association (AERA) and the National Council on Measurement in Education (NCME) since 1955. The 1985 *Standards for Educational and Psychological Testing (Standards)* are the most recently revised guidelines. In 1988, the *Code of Fair Testing Practices in Education (Code)* was also issued; in addition to APA, AERA, and NCME, the American Association for Counseling and Develop-ment/Association for Measurement and Evaluation in Counseling and Development, and the American Speech-Language-Hearing Association contributed to the development of this code. The *Standards* and *Code* declare the major obligations of professionals who develop or use educational tests. Specifically, standard 3.5 of the *Standards* states:

> When selecting the type and content of items for tests and inventories, test developers should consider the content and type in relation to cultural backgrounds and prior experiences of the variety of ethnic, cultural, age, and gender groups represented in the intended population of test takers. (*Conditional*). (American Educational Research Association, American Psychological Association, & National Council on Measurement in Education [AERA/APA/NCME], 1985, p. 26)

Although this standard has been designated as *conditional*, in that its importance for test construction and evaluation varies depending on how feasible its implementation is, it is considered *primary* for tests that are likely to affect a large number of test takers.

The corresponding code for test developers from the *Code* is "test developers should strive to make tests that are as fair as possible for test takers of different races, gender, ethnic backgrounds, or handicapping conditions" (*Code of Fair Testing Practices in Education* [*Code*], 1988, p. 3). Standard 3.5 of the *Standards* specifies, "when the relevance of such [cultural background] factors is in doubt, test developers might establish a review process using expert judges both to select item material and to eliminate material likely to be inappropriate or offensive for groups in the test-taking population" (AERA et al., 1985, p. 26). Similarly, Point 14 of the *Code* recommends that test developers should "review and revise test questions and related materials to avoid potentially insensitive content or language" (*Code*, 1988, p. 3).

Testing and publishing organizations have adopted these review guidelines. For example, Educational Testing Service (ETS) in the *ETS Sensitivity Review Process Guidelines and Procedures* (1986) set guidelines so that its tests and publications reflect the multicultural and multiethnic nature of its clientele. These guidelines specify the following criteria: (a) no use of stereotyping language, (b) no use of inflammatory or highly controversial material (e.g., abortion, euthanasia), (c) no use of language that is inappropriate in tone (e.g., patronizing, insulting, elitist, inflammatory), (d) no racial or ethnic group should be represented to the exclusion of others, (e) no gender group should be represented to the exclusion of the other, and (f) no use of inappropriate underlying assumptions (e.g., ethnocentric, elitist, and/or gender-based beliefs and language). The CTB/McGraw-Hill Book Company has very similar editorial practices. Their review process has set procedures to ensure balanced representation of gender, ethnic, and other minority groups and use of unbiased language that is free of stereotypical references (G. Dudney, personal communication, March 30, 1994).

As part of a sensitivity review process, trained reviewers evaluate materials following the set guidelines. Material questioned by the reviewers may be edited or screened out. In addition, balanced representation of gender and ethnic groups is a goal. For example, appropriate balance of gender and ethnic representation in standardized tests such as the SAT is part of their design. According to Cruise and Kimmel (1990), there is mixed evidence on "whether a more balanced use of gender-linked language or the use of more reading passages about women will have an impact on the relative performance levels on the test [SAT-Verbal] of women and men" (p. 12). (See Donlon, Ekstrom, Lockheed, & Harris, 1977, and Schau & Scott 1984.) Cruise and Kimmel (1990) further noted that "there are important social reasons for seeking a more balanced selection of language and reading passages" (p. 12). Thus, balance is important whether or not it has a demonstrable impact on test scores. Through a judgmental review process, testing organizations try to ensure that they develop publications and tests that are free from potentially offensive language.

An example of the subtle biases in reading passages that sensitivity reviewers are trained to detect was given by Ramsey (1993):

> When prospective reviewers are able to see the ethnocentrism at the heart of the next statement, they are on their way to becoming able sensitivity reviewers:
>
>> The 3,000 Innuvialuit, what Eskimos of Canada's western Arctic prefer that they themselves be called, live in the treeless tundra around the Bering Sea.
>
> The underlying assumption here, of course, is that the real name of these people is "Eskimos" even though they call themselves something else. The practice of putting one's own group in a passage if unsure of its acceptability works very well here. When, say, a White reviewer puts his or her group in this sentence and has it read, "The 3,000 Anglos, what the gringos of the United States prefer that they themselves be called, live in the … ," it is easy to see why this apparently innocuous sentence is at odds with all the [sensitivity] *Guidelines* stand for. (p. 383)

Differential Item Functioning

Differential item functioning (DIF) procedures were developed as empirical ways to determine if the item performance of comparable subgroups is different. DIF focuses on differences in performance between groups that are matched with respect to the ability, knowledge, or skill of interest. The total score on the test being analyzed is used as the matching criterion in order to identify any individual item that functions differently; that is, an item that is differentially difficult for a subgroup of examinees who are equally capable of answering questions of this general type. DIF does not address the question of whether the general type of skill or knowledge is a fair choice to measure and use in a given situation. Such questions are taken up in the following chapter.

In accordance with professional guidelines, empirical evaluation of the differential performance of subgroups on test items has been incorporated by testing organizations as part of their test development process. For example, ETS and CTB McGraw-Hill use statistical analyses to determine the differential item performance of ethnic and gender groups. DIF procedures are used in addition to sensitivity review procedures to further reduce bias and improve the quality of tests.

One of the DIF methods used at ETS is the Standardization Procedure (Dorans & Kulick 1983, 1986). With this procedure an item is said to exhibit DIF when the probability of correctly answering the item is lower or higher for examinees from one group than for equally able examinees from the comparison group. The Standardization method compares proportions correct for the keyed response (or distractor of interest; Dorans, Schmitt, & Bleistein, 1992) at each level of the matching variable for a reference and focal group. The standardization index of differential standardized differences (DSTD) quantifies DIF in the p (proportion correct) metric. The index ranges from -1 to $+1$, or from -100% to 100%. Negative values of DSTD indicate that the item disadvantages the focal group, whereas positive values indicate that the item favors the focal group. For practical purposes, values between $-.05$ (-5%) and $+.05$ ($+5\%$) are considered negligible; values outside the $-.10$ and $+.10$ (or the 10%) range are considered sizable. For operational purposes, a $|DSTD| \geq .10$ is a recommended cutoff; for exploratory research purposes, a less reliable cutoff of $|DSTD| \geq .05$ is often used.

Another method used at ETS is the Mantel–Haenszel (MH) method (Mantel & Haenszel, 1959), which was adapted by Holland and Thayer (1988). Both methods were extensively described by Dorans and Holland (1993). At ETS, categorization of DIF items is based on the standard ETS DIF operational item screening classifications (N. Petersen, personal communication, September 14, 1988). These classifications are:

1. "A" items have a MH delta DIF value that is *not* significantly different from 0 (at the .05 level) or an absolute value less than 1.00.

2. "B" items have a MH delta DIF value that is significantly different from 0 (at the .05 level) *and* either an absolute value of at least 1.00 but less than 1.50 *or* an absolute value of at least 1.00 but not significantly greater than 1.00 (at the .05 level).
3. "C" items have an absolute MH delta DIF value of at least 1.50 *and* significantly greater than 1.00 (at the .05 level).

DIF on test items can be done at different points in the test development process: at assembly (using pretest data), before score reporting, and after score reporting. Most testing organizations have opted, within constraints, to evaluate for DIF at the pretest stage. In addition, information about factors that have been identified to be related to DIF (through accumulation of operational DIF analyses or special DIF studies) can be used to set test construction specifications. Most research on identifying factors related to DIF has been done with paper-and-pencil multiple-choice items. Recently, some work has also been done with essays (Mazzeo, Schmitt, & Bleistein, 1993; Pomplun, Wright, Oleka, & Sudlow, 1992) and student-produced responses to math items (Lawrence, Lyu, & Feigenbaum, 1995; Schmitt & Crone, 1991). In addition, exploratory DIF studies have been done with data from computer-delivered tests (Haynie & Way, 1994; Way, 1994).

Findings from exploratory DIF studies indicate that some item content, format, and structure factors seem to be related to the differential item performance of a gender group. The content factors are human relationships or aesthetics/philosophy content, science-related content, specialized terminology (e.g., science, industrial arts, military), and special interest terminology. In math tests, there seems to be some indication that math items with algebra or geometry content are related to DIF. In addition, specific types of math word problems have also been related to DIF. Format characteristics related to DIF that have been examined are vertical versus wraparound presentation of multiple-choice alternatives and the use of visual material such as graphs, charts, or diagrams. Item position within a test has also been explored as a possible factor associated with DIF.

Test questions that are associated with passages whose content is of more interest to a particular gender group are sometimes found to be easier for that group (Wood, 1978). Performance on antonyms and analogy items classified as having human relationships or aesthetics or philosophy content have been found to be differentially easier for women than for comparable men (Carlton & Harris, 1992; O'Neill, Wild, & McPeek, 1989). Performance on reading comprehension items associated with passages with science-related content have been found to be differentially more difficult for women than for comparable men (Doolittle & Welch, 1989; Lawrence &

Curley, 1989; Lawrence, Curley, & McHale, 1988; McPeek & Wild, 1992; Scheuneman & Gerritz, 1990; Wendler & Carlton, 1987). Content-related gender DIF was also evident on the computer-adaptive licensing examination for nurses; questions in the health promotion and maintenance area differentially favored female examinees (Haynie & Way, 1994). Science achievement test items have also been found to be related to gender DIF. CTB McGraw-Hill science test items have been reported to have a greater number of items that are differentially more difficult for females (*Comprehensive Tests of Basic Skills Technical Report*, 1991). Women have been found to perform differentially better on algebra items, whereas men perform differentially better on geometry items (Carlton & Harris, 1992; Doolittle, 1989; Schmitt & Crone, 1991; Wild & McPeek, 1986). Math word problems have been found to be differentially easier for men, whereas more abstract pure math items have been found to be differentially easier for women (Carlton & Harris, 1992; Doolittle & Cleary, 1987; Harris & Carlton, 1993; O'Neill et al., 1989). Math problems presented in typical textbook style or solvable by using school-taught strategies have been found to be differentially easier for women (Gallagher & De Lisi, 1994; Harris & Carlton, 1993). Neither the presentation of multiple-choice alternatives (vertical vs. wraparound), the use of visual material such as graphs, charts, or diagrams, nor item position within the test have been found to be consistently related to DIF for gender groups (DeMauro & Olson, 1989; Dorans, Schmitt, & Curley, 1996; O'Neill, McPeek, & Wild, 1993; O'Neill, Wild, & McPeek, 1995).

Although most DIF studies have been of multiple-choice assessments, DIF has also been studied in constructed-response questions. Within the essay format on AP examinations, differential DIF may be associated with topics that are of special interest to one gender group (Mazzeo et al., 1993). For example, on the Biology examination, they noted a slight tendency for topics on organismal biology to favor males relative to topics on population biology, although they also noted that topic variability within a content area may be greater than the variability across topic areas. For White examinees on the English Language and Composition examination, some topics seemed to favor males, whereas others favored females. For example, White women performed worse than White men on a topic that asked them to compare the styles of two passages written by Native Americans about the harshness of the American prairie ($D = -.13$); White women performed better than White men on a question that required an evaluation of the assertion that human nature wants patterns, standards, and structure in behavior ($D = .18$). Nonessay constructed-response questions may also be evaluated for possible differential gender effects. On the mathematics section of the SAT, 10 questions require students to grid a numerical answer on an answer sheet. Initial findings suggested that this question type may be more difficult for women than traditional multiple-choice questions (Schmitt & Crone, 1991). However, more recent data from much larger samples indicate virtually no gender DIF for the grid questions (Lawrence et al., 1995).

Most of the factors found to be related to DIF are based on studies evaluating operational test forms that were constructed before routine statistical DIF screening procedures were implemented. Because of the exploratory nature of most of this research, the number of operational items having the studied factors are restricted to a small number of naturally occurring cases. Consequently, many of the reported findings from these exploratory studies need further empirical corroboration. To date, only a limited number of empirical DIF studies, where the number of items representing the factor of interest is expanded, have been conducted. Examples of such studies are Curley and Schmitt (1993), Dorans et al. (1996), Jackson (1992), Scheuneman (1987), and Schmitt, Curley, Bleistein, and Dorans (1988). The following results refer to findings from two of these studies in which gender DIF was evaluated.

Curley and Schmitt (1993) performed an empirical investigation to corroborate several factors found to be related to DIF. Most of the factors studied dealt with specialized terminology. In this study, verbal items with initial high DIF were retested and reevaluated after making revisions to the items.

The first item in Fig. 6.1 is an example from the Curley and Schmitt (1993) study showing that after the technical or specialized science terminology was revised, the differential difficulty for females was reduced.

The VORTEX:WATER item had DIF statistics that indicated that this item was differentially more difficult for females; when the stem of this item was changed to WHIRLPOOL:WATER the item was no longer considered to have DIF. The only change made was to replace the technical (specialized) science term of VORTEX for the more common term of WHIRLPOOL. It is of interest to note that the difficulty (P) for the total group was also reduced.

O'Neill and McPeek (1993) speculated on possible reasons that female examinees tend to find science items differentially more difficult:

> The science results for both the vocabulary items and the reading comprehension items may well reflect differences in attitudes about science for men and women. Differences in the proportions of men and women taking courses in science and planning careers in science have been widely documented (e.g., Ramist & Arbeiter, 1986). It may be that there are differences between the

Statistics	Item Text	Statistics	Item Text
DIF Category C % Correct 35 Biserial R .45 DSTD:	**VORTEX:WATER::**	DIF Category A % Correct 76 Biserial R .37 DTSD:	**WHIRLPOOL:WATER::**
1 2 -19 3 -1 14	(A) volcano:crust (B) river:delta (C) tornado:air * (D) geyser:steam (E) earthquake:fault (OMITS)	1 1 -6 3 1 0	(A) volcano:crust (B) river:delta (C) tornado:air * (D) geyser:steam (E) earthquake:fault (OMITS)
DIF Category C % Correct 55 Biserial R .45 DSTD:	**RIVET:METAL::**	DIF Category A % Correct 85 Biserial R .43 DSTD:	**PIN:CLOTH::**
3 1 5 -28 3 16	(A) needle:thimble (B) cork:bottle (C) nail:hammer (D) staple:paper * (E) rope:swing (OMITS)	0 -1 0 2 -1 0	(A) needle:thimble (B) cork:bottle (C) nail:hammer (D) staple:paper * (E) rope:swing (OMITS)

FIG. 6.1. Effect of revision of scientific terminology.

groups in their interest in science topics, their confidence in their abilities to understand scientific subject matter, and their comfort level with science passages. (p. 259)

The second pair of items in Fig. 6.1 presents the effect of revising the industrial arts terminology of an item with negative DIF for females (Curley & Schmitt, 1993). The specialized industrial arts word RIVET may be less well-known by female examinees, thus making the item differentially more difficult for them. When the complete stem of the item was changed to: PIN:CLOTH and all the distractors were kept the same, the negative DIF was eliminated, but the item became easier for the total group (proportion correct went from .55 to .85).

After revisions, both items in Fig. 6.1 became easier. Such changes in item difficulty make it hard to tease out the interrelationship between changes of terminology, item difficulty, and DIF (Linn, R. 1993c).

Examples of two item pairs showing the effect of military terminology on DIF are presented in Fig. 6.2 (Curley & Schmitt, 1993). Items with terminology considered traditionally stereotypical, such as words depicting conflict or military terms, have been found to be related to gender DIF (Rosser, 1989; Wendler & Carlton, 1987).

Statistics	Item Text	Statistics	Item Text
DIF Category C % Correct 78 Biserial R .47 DSTD: -21 4 4 5 3 6	CONVOY:SHIPS:: (A) flock:birds * (B) ferry:passengers (C) barn:horses (D) dealership:cars (E) highway:trucks (OMITS)	DIF Category A % Correct 73 Biserial R .60 DSTD: 4 0 -2 0 -1 -1	TROUPE:DANCERS:: (A) flock:birds * (B) ferry:passengers (C) barn:horses (D) dealership:cars (E) highway:trucks (OMITS)
DIF Category C % Correct 76 Biserial R .33 DSTD: 1 5 3 1 -19 9	DETONATE:EXPLOSION:: (A) collide:momentum (B) decipher:code (C) energize:stimulant (D) strike:ore (E) ignite:fire * (OMITS)	DIF Category A % Correct 72 Biserial R .44 DSTD: 0 1 1 0 -3 0	PROVOKE:REACTION:: (A) collide:momentum (B) decipher:code (C) energize:stimulant (D) strike:ore (E) ignite:fire * (OMITS)

FIG. 6.2. Effect of revision of military terminology on DIF.

As can be seen, the first item of each pair is differentially more difficult for female examinees. When the stem of these items is changed so that the analogical association no longer consists of words with military connotation, the negative DIF for female examinees is basically eliminated. Only in the first example could the revised item stem be considered to have traditionally stereotypical positive terms for female examinees. As with the previously presented examples, all the items with negative DIF have terminology that is more specialized and that may be more familiar to male examinees because of their interest level.

Jackson (1992) did an empirical evaluation of factors related to gender DIF on math percent items. She systematically varied and repretested math items with item characteristics that seemed to have consistently shown negative DIF for female examinees. Her main finding was that items that test percents greater than 100% "can be problematic for females [examinees] unless they are straightforward routine type problems" (p. 11). An example of a pair of items showing this finding is shown in Fig. 6.3.

As the figure shows, the second version of the pair of items was changed from 5% to 80% in order to have "a more common percent greater than 100%" (Jackson, 1992, p. 10) as the correct answer. Both versions of this item are solved in the same way, but the first item of the pair was differentially harder for female examinees, whereas the second version had no DIF. Similarly, percent increase questions were found to be differentially harder for female examinees when the answer was a nonroutine percent greater than 100%. When abstract questions with nonroutine answers greater than 100% were rewritten to have a concrete setting they were differentially less difficult for female examinees. Nevertheless, questions rewritten to have less technical scientific settings did not have less DIF for female examinees (Jackson, 1992).

In both of these experimental studies the number of items representing the factors of interest was very small. Because of this, although results are of interest, they should be considered somewhat tentative. Furthermore, demonstrating that DIF can be reduced by avoiding certain question content does not necessarily mean that such content necessarily should be avoided. If dealing with nonroutine percents greater than 100% is a needed skill, such items should not be eliminated just because they show DIF. On the other hand, if dealing with concrete situations is as important (or more important) than dealing with abstract questions, DIF results can identify potential unfairness in a test that contains a disproportionate number of abstract questions. Similarly, including military terminology in a verbal analogies test was probably not done because knowledge of such terminology was deemed to be a needed skill, and DIF results can legitimately be used to eliminate such questions. Thus, the difficulty of an item should come only from an assessment of the construct that the item is designed to measure and not from a construct (such as knowledge of military terms) that is irrelevant to the basic function of the question.

Methods for dealing with construct-irrelevant characteristics of test questions need to be established and followed. Part of the problem is that

Statistics	Item Text	Statistics	Item Text
DIF Category C Delta 17.3 Biserial R .74 DSTD: 6 1 -3 -3 -5 5	If x is 5 percent of y, then y is what percent of x? (A) 20% (B) 95% (C) 200% (D) 950% (E) 2,000% * (OMITS)	DIF Category A Delta 17.0 Biserial R .75 DSTD: 1 4 1 -9 0 2	If x is 80 percent of y, then y is what percent of x? (A) 12.5% (B) 20% (C) 25% (D) 120% (E) 125% * (OMITS)

FIG. 6.3. Examples of percent problems with and without gender DIF.

establishing with certainty which factors are sources of systematic construct-irrelevant variance, or bias, is not a simple task. In an effort to reduce the influence of these unintended factors, test publishers may produce guidelines that proscribe the use of certain questions or types of questions. At ETS, a "Supplementary DIF Policy" was developed based on results indicating "that items with certain characteristics tend inordinately to show negative DIF for focal group members" (ETS, 1994, p. 1). These procedures identify characteristics that need to be avoided in all subject matter and skills tests (e.g., use of military terminology or a sports context). However, they also specify that exceptions are permitted because "the characteristics to be avoided are not yet well-defined, and not all items with those characteristics show elevated values of DIF" (p. 1). Exceptions to the guidelines are permitted if items are needed for valid measurement of the intended construct or if the items are known to have acceptable levels of DIF.

DIF results can be used to establish guidelines so that those characteristics of items that have been associated with differential performance by subgroups are considered when assembling tests. Use of such guidelines in conjunction with DIF information can be beneficial to prevent the use of construct-irrelevant characteristics in the construction of test questions (Hambleton & Jones, 1994).

Comparability Across Different Test Forms

Even if test questions were carefully reviewed and statistically screened, unfairness could still result if some students had to take a more difficult set of questions than other students. Strict adherence to detailed content specifications tends to make different sets of test questions (or test forms) roughly comparable. However, it is generally not possible to construct different test forms that are exactly equal in difficulty. Test publishers use statistical equating procedures to make the necessary adjustments so that students are neither advantaged nor disadvantaged by the particular test form they happen to take (Angoff, 1971b; Cook & Petersen, 1987). If equating is successful, students should not care which test form they receive. Correlational techniques, such as factor analysis, can be used to show that two test forms seem to be assessing the same underlying construct. From the perspective of gender fairness, the gender difference on one form should be the same as on the alternate form. As Dwyer (1979) suggested, subtle content differences between forms may have only a small impact on within-gender analyses but could bias comparisons across gender. For example, suppose one form of a reading test had a science passage and another form had a philosophy passage. With a sample of only males, the two forms might appear to be equatable. However, the gender difference could be larger on the former than on the latter, suggesting that the forms are not equivalent for studying gender differences. Thus, when test forms are statistically equated, possible differential impact of the equating on various subgroups should be evaluated.

FAIRNESS IN TEST ADMINISTRATION

Sensitivity reviews, DIF procedures, and test form equating can help to assure that the questions in a test form do not unfairly discriminate against any individual or group. However, even if the test questions were totally fair, other aspects of the testing situation still might lead to test scores that did not fairly reflect the knowledge and abilities of certain individuals or groups of individuals.

One of the important reasons for standardizing test administration procedures is to guard against the unfairness that could be created if testing conditions varied too much for different examinees. Most people would probably agree that it would not be fair to test one group in a cold, dark room with a set of 200 hard questions that must be answered in 1 hour if another group was given 20 easy questions to be answered in 2 hours in a warm, bright room. The easy solution is to ensure that all examinees receive exactly the same questions under exactly the same conditions: easy, but wrong. Consider the following directions for test administrators for a mythical international test of mathematics skills:

> Please make sure that testing is the same for all students. Directions should not be tailored for specific groups; regardless of the native language in your country, all directions must be read only in French. Students must not use any artificial aids; please confiscate all eyeglasses before beginning testing. Students who try to use their left hands should be reminded that this is a standardized test and such deviations will not be tolerated.

Clearly, total standardization of all procedures is as inappropriate as is a total lack of standardization. The accommodations that are made for examinees with disabilities (e.g., braille examinations for blind students) are a prime example of relaxation of standardization in the interest of fairness and better measurement of the construct of interest (Willingham, 1988; Willingham et al., 1988). The regulations that implement Section 504 of the Rehabilitation Act of 1973 indicate that admissions test results for people with disabilities must "accurately reflect the applicant's aptitude or achievement level or whatever other factor the test purports to measure, rather than reflecting the applicant's impaired sensory, manual or speaking skills (except where those skills are the factors that the test purports to measure)" (Department of Health, Education, and Welfare, 1977, p. 22683, Sect. 84.42). Thus, examinations for disabled and nondisabled individuals should be as comparable as possible in measuring the underlying construct even though this might make them quite different in external appearance. Standardization at the task level is nonsensical—the blind student cannot read standard text and sighted students do not know braille, but with the appropriate testing mode, reading comprehension skills can be assessed in both groups. Although the issues are complex, research suggests that nonstandard versions of the SAT and GRE administered to examinees with disabilities are generally comparable to standard tests in the following respects: reliability, factor structure, DIF, prediction of academic performance, admissions decisions, test content, and satisfaction with testing accommodations (Willingham et al., 1988). However, results also suggested that extended time limits, although sometimes necessary, tended to limit comparability. Specifically, examinees with disabilities "were more likely than others to finish the tests; some items near the end of the tests were relatively easier for some groups of handicapped students; and in some instances, college performance was overpredicted by those test scores based on considerably extended testing time" (p. xiii). Strict comparability between scores of tests administered under different conditions is an elusive goal, but comparability of scores when needed accommodations are not made is impossible.

The complexities of balancing competing fairness demands can be illustrated by the problem of establishing a policy for calculator use on the mathematics section of the SAT. Several years ago, when calculator use was largely restricted to a relative handful of wealthy students, the clearly equitable solution was to ban calculator use on the SAT for all students. But in recent years, calculator use has became commonplace, although not universal, in both rich and poor school districts. By 1991, 98% of the students in Grade 12 indicated that they or their families owned a calculator (Mullis, Dossey, Owen, & Phillips, 1991). Furthermore, mathematics teachers encouraged calculator use in the classroom and in testing situations (National Council of Teachers of Mathematics, 1989). Is it then fair to assess these students, who have been taught to rely on calculators for routine calculations, with tests that forbid calculator use? However, if calculators are allowed, is that fair to the few students who attend schools where calculator use is discouraged? Studies showing that allowing students to use calculators on the SAT does not seem to provide an advantage for a particular ethnic group or gender may provide some comfort (e.g., Bridgeman, Harvey, & Braswell, 1995), but there is probably no policy that would be equally beneficial to all individuals or to groups defined in nontraditional ways (such as the group that routinely used calculators for all classroom tests vs. the group that was never permitted to use calculators on tests).

The key problem, then, is to identify which standard test administration conditions tend to enhance fair assessment and which threaten it, realizing that, at times, no totally equitable solution is possible. In the following sections, we focus on a variety of standard testing conditions and the impact of these conditions on issues of fairness generally and on gender fairness specifically.

Time Limits

Time limits serve at least two important functions in standardized testing. First, they are an administrative convenience or even an administrative necessity. Testing must be scheduled in particular time slots to accommodate school schedules or to define the working conditions for test proctors. Even teachers who are not at all interested in assessing speed of performance may be interested in getting home before midnight. Second, speed of performance may be related to the construct the test is trying to measure. In pure speed tests, such as clerical coding speed, the task is presumed to be so easy that the only differences among people are related to differences in speed. In pure power tests, scores are totally independent of speed and allowing more time would not lead to an increase in scores. Many tests fall somewhere between. In some cases, the addition of a speed component is presumed to enhance the assessment of a particular construct, for example mathematical insight. The problem in Fig. 6.4 (taken from the SAT) can be quickly answered by the student who has developed the insight to see that it is merely necessary to compare 6/2 with 12/4.

The less insightful student can still get the correct answer (C) by carrying out all the indicated multiplication and division. Assuming that there were many items of this type on a test, the insightful student and the student who carefully, but inefficiently, completes all the calculations would get very different scores with a strict time limit; with no time limit they would get identical scores. Thus, the time limit may be essential to ensure that the test is assessing the intended insightful reasoning construct. On the other hand,

SUMMARY DIRECTIONS FOR COMPARISON QUESTIONS

Answer: **A**   if the quantity in Column A is greater;
            B   if the quantity in Column B is greater;
            C   if the two quantities are equal;
            D   if the relationship cannot be determined from the information given.

Column A   Column B

$\dfrac{6 \times 6 \times 6 \times 6}{2 \times 2 \times 2 \times 2}$ $\dfrac{12 \times 12 \times 12 \times 12}{4 \times 4 \times 4 \times 4}$

FIG. 6.4. Sample quantitative comparison question.

if the test were designed to determine only whether students could find the correct answer, the strict time limit would unfairly penalize the students who slowly and carefully calculated the correct response. The same question administered under the same conditions might be a fair assessment in one context but unfair in another.

If the time limit were related to the construct of interest, a finding of differential performance by gender groups under timed and untimed conditions would be of interest but would not necessarily indicate that the timed test was unfair; the two groups might truly differ on the construct being assessed. However, if a time limit were imposed primarily for administrative convenience, and one gender group performed relatively better under timed than under untimed conditions, there would be a clear concern regarding the fairness of the time limit.

Methods for Assessing the Impact of Time Limits.   Some procedures for estimating the impact of time limits on scores (often referred to as *speededness*) look at data from a single test administered under a single timing condition. Although many methods have been suggested for evaluating speededness from a single test administration (Rindler, 1979), the ETS guidelines (Swineford, 1974) are probably the most widely used. These guidelines suggest that virtually all students should respond to at least 75% of the questions, and at least 80% of the students should reach the last question. Such indices, when evaluated separately by gender, may be used to provide tentative evidence on whether a test is differentially speeded for men and women. For example, Wheeler and Harris (1981) examined the speededness of a high-school-level physics achievement test that had a female–male D of −.67. They found that a slightly higher percentage of men than women completed the test (54.3% vs. 48.0%) but that the percentage completing 75% of the test was nearly identical in both gender groups (98.9% vs. 98.7%) and the number of items reached by 80% of the examinees was 71 out of 75 for both men and women. Thus, the test appeared to be speeded for both men and women, but speededness differences alone could not explain much of the mean difference between genders.

A somewhat more sophisticated approach uses DIF methodology to control overall score level before looking for evidence of differential performance on the questions that were not answered at the end of a test section. Schmitt, Dorans, Crone, and Maneckshana (1991), using DIF methodology that matched on both speeded and unspeeded criterion scores, found that neither matching criterion provided evidence for gender-related differential speededness on either the verbal or mathematical portions of the SAT. Similarly, Lawrence (1993), using a variety of internal criteria that took overall mean differences into account, found no gender-related differential speededness on either the SAT or GMAT. However, for the reasons given in the following, these results should be considered as providing only very tentative evidence.

Speededness estimates from a single test administration (whether using the Swineford guidelines or DIF methods) are based on a number of highly questionable assumptions. The first assumption is that questions not answered at the end of the section were not reached because the candidate ran out of time. However, on a test with a correction for guessing, test takers may choose to omit the difficult questions at the end of a section; there is no way to distinguish these intentionally omitted responses from responses that the test taker did not have time to consider. The problem is even worse on tests with no correction for guessing because test-wise candidates will randomly mark the remaining questions when they are running out of time; all questions would be answered, and the guidelines would suggest that the time limit was not a problem.

Another critical assumption is that questions are attempted in the order presented. However, candidates may skip questions that appear to be time consuming and plan to return to them later. Indeed, *Taking the SAT I Reasoning Test: The Official Guide to the SAT I* (College Board, 1995) recommends omitting questions and returning to them if time permits. If time were called just as the candidate answered the last question (but before returning to any of the skipped questions), the test would be considered as unspeeded by the usual criteria. Even if all questions were attempted within the time limit, there is no way of knowing how much higher the score might have been if more time were allowed or if scores would have been differentially higher for a particular population subgroup. Therefore, speededness indices that are derived from a single test administration, whether based on the Swineford criteria or DIF methods, are useful for demonstrating the presence of speed effects, but cannot be used as evidence for the absence of speed effects.

Experimental studies in which testing time is varied avoid the problems inherent in trying to estimate the effects of timing from a test administered under only one timing condition. Experimental studies have generally failed to indicate that strict time limits systematically favor either gender; that is, there are no (or inconsistent) time limit by gender interactions.

Klein (1981) studied speededness effects on both the multiple-choice and essay portions of the California Bar Examination. For the multiple-choice study, 60 questions were divided in half into Set A and Set B. A random half of the 2,904 applicants took Set A in 55 minutes followed by Set B in 90 minutes, while the other half took Set B in 55 minutes followed by Set A in 90 minutes. Means and standard deviations by gender were not reported, but it was noted that there were no statistically significant correlations between score change with extra time and gender. Note, however, that the relatively speeded condition (30 questions in 55 minutes or 1.8 minutes per question) would be considered relatively unspeeded in other contexts; by way of comparison, the 1993 SAT Verbal allowed .7 minutes per question. Another indication that the 55-minute time limit was not very severe was that mean scores increased by less than 1 point when 35 extra minutes were provided.

The essay portion of Klein's study used the same design, with applicants given 55 minutes to write on one topic and 90 minutes for another topic with the same counterbalancing as used for the multiple-choice tests. For the essays, the extra time did permit significant score gains (about .65 in standard deviation units), but once again gains were not correlated with gender.

Results are much more easily interpretable when means and standard deviations, by gender, are provided. Familiar gender D values can then be reported for both relatively speeded and relatively unspeeded conditions. In one of the best designed and most comprehensive studies of this type, 20- and 30-minute versions of both the verbal and quantitative sections of the GRE General Test were administered at 550 testing centers throughout the United States (Wild & Durso, 1979). The additional 10 minutes produced small score gains in the ethnic and gender groups studied, but there were no differential score gains across groups; the additional time was equally beneficial to all subgroups.

Data from another study (Bridgeman, 1992) with GRE quantitative (GRE-Q) questions (albeit in an experimental open-ended format), suggest that women might perform relatively better on the more speeded version of the test.[1] This outcome may at first appear to be unreasonable given that men, on average, take more quantitative courses in college and are more likely to be in quantitative majors such as engineering and the physical sciences (Wah & Robinson, 1990), and thus may be expected to be faster on quantitative questions. However, even if men were slightly faster, they would not necessarily be at an advantage on the more speeded test. This paradox is related to the way questions are arranged on most standardized tests. The most difficult questions are typically concentrated at the end of the test. If students run out of time, they will not be able to attempt to answer these difficult questions. To the extent that students with a stronger mathematics background should have a greater chance of answering these questions correctly (if they have time to consider them fully), it is not unreasonable to expect that the longer time limit could favor students with better preparation. Results for the Wild and Durso (1979) and Bridgeman (1992) studies, expressed in D units, are presented in Table 6.1.

Although it has been suggested that women may be at a disadvantage on the SAT Math because they use time-intensive algorithmic strategies (Linn, 1992) or less efficient time-allocation strategies (Becker, 1990), large-sample experimental studies varying timing on the SAT were not found. Two small studies using SAT questions administered under experimental conditions had inconsistent and nonsignificant results (Dreyden & Gallagher, 1989; Evans, 1980). A large-scale experimental study of the type conducted by Wild and Durso (1979) is clearly needed. Although their findings may be generalizable, there are sufficient differences between the GRE and SAT tests and populations that their work should be replicated in the SAT population, using the question types on the new SAT I: Reasoning Tests (e.g., long reading passages and open-ended math questions).

Time Limits on Essay Examinations.   Effects of time limits are not limited to multiple-choice or short-answer examinations. Time pressures on essay examinations could interfere with prewriting organizational activities, with the actual writing, and with the opportunity to check and revise what was written. If the test contained more than one question, scores could also

---

[1]Bridgeman (1992) reported a nonsignificant gender by form (more vs. less speeded) interaction in a gender by ethnicity by form analysis of covariance (with GRE score from an operational administration as the covariate). Because many students reported gender but did not report ethnicity, the sample size for Table 6.1 (which did not require ethnic classification) was larger than the sample size in the original analysis by 987 students, and a small but statistically significant gender by form interaction emerged. Although this difference is probably still too small to be of any practical importance, it is of theoretical interest because it is in the opposite direction from the general expectation, with women scoring relatively higher on the more speeded form.

TABLE 6.1
Speeded Versus Less Speeded Administrations of GRE Questions

Study/Group		F	M	D
Wild and Durso (1979)				
26 GRE-Verbal questions				
Speeded	N	5,154	4,980	
(20 Minutes)	Mean	11.22	12.64	−.25
	SD	5.84	5.63	
Less speeded	N	4,868	4,864	
(30 minutes)	Mean	12.30	13.64	−.23
	SD	5.90	5.52	
14 GRE-Quantitative questions				
Speeded	N	5,166	4,944	
(20 minutes)	Mean	6.03	8.11	−.63
	SD	3.15	3.42	
Less speeded	N	4,895	4,939	
(30 minutes)	Mean	6.65	8.92	−.65
	SD	3.40	3.58	
Bridgeman (1992)				
14 GRE-Q questions in open-ended format				
Speeded[a]	N	1,425	1,103	
	Mean	4.98	6.43	−.39
	SD	3.96	3.45	
Less speeded	N	1,438	1,050	
	Mean	5.12	7.01	−.57
	SD	3.14	3.51	

Note. Standard error of Ds is .02 for Wild and Durso and .04 for Bridgeman. Standard error of the difference between Ds are .03 and .06, respectively.

[a]Speeded test was 10 multiple-choice and 14 open-ended questions; less speeded test was 5 multiple-choice and 14 open-ended questions. Score for both tests based on the 14 open-ended questions that were common to both forms. Time limit for both tests was 30 minutes.

be affected by the failure to allocate time appropriately across the various questions. Except for the Klein (1981) study of the essays on the California Bar Examination mentioned earlier, published studies comparing men and women with different essay timings were not located. However, unpublished data from the field trials for the SAT II: Writing Subject Test (SAT-W) are relevant (D. Wright, personal communication November, 1994). High school juniors who reported that they were college bound were asked to write an essay intended to measure general ability in written expression that did not assume any specific subject matter knowledge. Some subjects were given 15 minutes, others 20 minutes, and a third group was allowed 30 minutes to write the essay. All essays were independently scored by two raters who did not know which essays were produced under the various timing conditions. As indicated in Table 6.2, score differences (favoring women) were the largest in the most speeded condition.

Time Limits on Computerized Examinations.   Time limits on computer-delivered tests pose a whole new set of fairness issues that must be addressed as such examinations become more common. Although expenses related to renting computer time at a testing center must be considered, time limits for administrative convenience are generally less important for computer-delivered tests because of the individualized nature of the testing. However, time limits that are related to valid measurement of the construct of interest may be more problematic with computerized assessments. In some computer-delivered examinations the computer is used merely to administer a standard test in which the examinee may mark questions and return to them for later consideration; although this experience is somewhat different from taking a paper-and-pencil test, time management strategies should be fairly similar. However, some computer-delivered tests are also adaptive. In a typical computer-adaptive test, the computer selects the next question based on the response to the current question; each question must be answered in order, and skipping questions or returning to reconsider previous questions is not permitted. Thus, the time management problem is quite different for this type of examination. When faced with a problem that does not have an answer that is immediately apparent (and that would have been initially skipped in a paper-and-pencil administration), the examinee must decide whether to guess or to take the time to figure out the correct answer. If the examinee answers too quickly, time left over at the end of the examination is wasted because the examinee cannot return to previously answered questions.

An additional time management problem is created by the branching nature of the test in which able students get progressively harder questions. Such an able examinee may be working at an appropriate rate on the initial questions but fail to appreciate adequately how much extra time will be required as the questions become significantly more difficult. Research is

TABLE 6.2

Speeded Versus Less Speeded Administrations of Essay Tests for High School Juniors

Group		F	M	D
Very speeded	N	1,126	952	
(Two 15-minute essays)	Mean	11.73	10.13	.49
	SD	3.18	3.38	
Speeded	N	2,397	1,937	
(One 20-minute essay)	Mean	6.34	5.67	.34
	SD	1.93	2.04	
Less speeded	N	1,185	980	
(One 30-minute essay)	Mean	7.08	6.55	.26
	SD	1.90	2.11	

Note. Standard errors of Ds range from .03 to .04; standard error of difference between Ds range from .05 to .06.

needed to determine whether the ability to make such choices differs by gender or by any other subgroup classification. Computer-adaptive and paper-and-pencil tests differ on more than just timing considerations; a more comprehensive look at gender differences on computer-adaptive tests is presented later in this chapter.

Conclusions.   Failure to find consistent gender by timing interactions in the studies reviewed here should not discourage attempts to find such interactions with other tests or at other grade levels. Nevertheless, these results do suggest that, at least on academic reasoning tests, time limits do not appear to be an important consideration in explaining gender differences in test scores. However, these results are limited by two important considerations. First, the failure to find gender-related differences in group means does not preclude the possibility that the scores of specific individuals from either gender might be significantly affected by time limits. Second, even with the extended time limits studied, some students may have felt some time pressure. The results reviewed are relevant to substantial timing differences on typical standardized test tasks, but they may not generalize to the complex, ambiguous, multistep tasks that some authors (e.g., Linn, 1992) have recommended. Time allocation for such tasks is measured in hours or days, not minutes and seconds.

Guessing and Omitting

On multiple-choice tests, students who do not recognize the correct answer may guess from among the alternatives provided. Sometimes such guessing could have an impact on test scores and gender differences. Data from low-stakes national examinations in mathematics and science suggest that when "I don't know" is provided as an option, females are more likely to select it than are males (Hudson, 1986). However, most high-stakes examinations do not include "I don't know" as an explicit option, and willingness to guess must be inferred from patterns of omitting questions. If the test score is based on the total number of correct answers with no penalty for incorrect answers, students should always guess when uncertain. However, all students do not follow this optimal strategy, and women may be more likely to omit questions than men. Research on the GRE General Test administered in October 1984 indicated that the majority of both men and women omitted no more than a single question on the 140-question examination (Grandy, 1987). Nevertheless, a nontrivial minority omitted enough questions to have some impact on their scores; over 10% of the 57,656 examinees omitted more than 10 questions. For each of the three test sections (verbal, quantitative, and analytical), the group of students omitting more than five questions was at least 60% female, although women were just 52% of the total examinee population. Although these individuals could have raised their scores with random guesses, the impact of these gains on the overall gender differences for the examinee population would be nil (as indicated in Grandy's Tables 19–21). Similarly, a study of ninth graders and university applicants in Israel found that women were slightly less likely to guess even when there was no penalty for guessing, but that "although gender differences in guessing tendencies are robust they account for only a small fraction of the observed gender difference on multiple-choice tests" (Ben-Shakhar & Sinai, 1991, p. 23).

A reluctance to guess is clearly harmful on tests that are scored simply by counting the number of correct answers, but the impact of such reluctance on tests that include a correction for guessing is much less clear. Although most classroom tests and elementary and secondary achievement tests do not include a correction for guessing, many national admissions tests do. Among tests with a correction for guessing are the PSAT/NMSQT, the SAT I: Reasoning Tests, SAT II: Subject Tests, GMAT, and GRE Subject Tests (but not the GRE General Test). They are scored by a formula that exacts more of a penalty for a wrong answer than for an omission. Specifically, they are scored by the formula $R - (W/(k-1))$ where R is the number of questions answered with the right answer, W is the number of questions answered with the wrong answer, and k is the number of response options for each multiple-choice question. Thus, on average, students who guess randomly on the questions they cannot answer will receive the same score as students who omit such questions.

Although sometimes erroneously referred to as a penalty for guessing, note that the random guessers do just as well as the persons who omit those questions for which they have no knowledge of the correct answer. Indeed, the correction can be a penalty for not guessing (Slakter, 1968b). If the examinee is not certain of the correct answer, but has some knowledge of the question, an informed guess is better than leaving the question blank. The problem is that a misinformed guess is worse. Response options are often written to be attractive to the misinformed examinee. Lord (1980) observed that low-ability examinees frequently are drawn to attractive, but wrong, answer choices; their scores on a series of difficult questions are often worse than random guesses.

One comprehensive study of guessing on the SAT (Angoff, 1989) concluded that high-ability students may gain by guessing (because their guesses are informed by correct, although incomplete, partial information), whereas low-ability students may be hurt by guessing because their guesses are based on incorrect partial information. Angoff noted that this relationship was quite weak and that in general, students who were more willing to guess got about the same scores as students who were less willing to guess (after the correction formula was applied). A previous study by Angoff and Schrader (1984) reached the same conclusion for the three tests studied (SAT Verbal, a College Board Chemistry achievement test, and the GMAT). Studies with other tests (Cross & Frary, 1977; Slakter, 1968a) have suggested that students would get slightly higher scores if they guessed on the items they omitted. Contradictory findings are not too surprising given the possible differences in propensity to guess in different populations and differences among tests in the attractiveness of incorrect answer choices. Even when found, however, gains from encouraging guessing generally appear to be quite modest. In the Cross and Frary study, average scores on a 20-question test increased by less than .25 of a point when examinees were asked to answer previously omitted questions.

If guessing were more beneficial than omitting, and if women were less likely to guess than men, then scoring with a correction formula might exaggerate gender differences. As we have already seen, the evidence for the first part of this proposition is equivocal. Evidence of a general tendency for women to avoid guessing on tests with a guessing correction is similarly unconvincing. Slakter (1967) developed a measure of risk taking on objective examinations that asked students to judge whether the two words in a given pair had the same or opposite meanings. In half of the word pairs one of the words was meaningless, so that any attempt to provide an answer for that pair would have to be a guess. Students were told that there was a penalty for incorrect responses. No gender differences in this type of risk taking on objective tests were found in college students. In a subsequent study in Grades 5 to 11 in two school systems, with over 1,000 students in each system, gender differences were extremely small (Slakter, Koehler, Hampton, & Grennell, 1971). Gender differences failed to reach statistical significance, at the .05 level, in one system and accounted for only 1% of the variance in the other. There was a tendency for students in the higher grades to take fewer risks, but grade level and gender did not interact.

Experimental studies of score differences related to guessing instructions (e.g., Angoff & Schrader, 1984; Cross & Frary, 1977; Slakter, 1968a) have typically not included gender as a variable. Nevertheless, several data sets provide relevant information. A study of omitting patterns on SAT questions, using DIF methodology that matched men and women on total scores, found that men were slightly more likely to omit verbal questions and women were slightly more likely to omit mathematics questions (Schmitt et al., 1991). For both the verbal and mathematical sections, mean gender differences across all questions in the proportion of omissions were only .01; that is, on a typical verbal question, the proportion of men omitting the question exceeded the proportion of women (with equal total test scores) omitting that question by .01 and on a typical mathematics question the proportion of women omitting it exceeded the proportion of men by .01.

Most questions on the SAT I and the PSAT/NMSQT are scored with the usual guessing correction formula and students are instructed accordingly. However, one group of mathematics questions is not multiple-choice and therefore does not have a correction for guessing. For these questions, the student enters a number on a numerical grid rather than picking from among five answer choices. In terms of content coverage and cognitive demands these grid-in questions are very similar to their multiple-choice counterparts. Although grid-in questions differ from standard multiple-choice questions in more ways than just not having a guessing correction, gender differences on the grid-in questions should be substantially reduced if reluctance to guess were a major contributor to gender differences in the multiple-choice format. Schmitt (1995) analyzed gender differences for the two question formats on the 1993 and 1994 PSAT/NMSQT. Each year two forms were administered, a Tuesday form and a Saturday form. The Ds were corrected for the reliability differences between the short grid-in section and the longer multiple-choice section. As shown in Table 6.3, gender differences were very similar across formats. The largest difference in Ds (in the 1994 Tuesday form) was only .10 and was in the opposite direction of what would be predicted if a reluctance to guess were depressing women's scores; on all other forms the gender difference was virtually identical in the two formats.

Perhaps the clearest evidence for the impact of guessing instructions on gender differences in test scores comes from the GRE General Test, which switched from a formula score (and correction for guessing instructions) in the 1980–1981 test year to a score that counted only the number right in the 1981–1982 test year. Unlike some experimental studies, students were clearly motivated to produce their best possible scores in both test years. As shown in Table 6.4, gender differences were essentially identical with or without correction for guessing instructions and scoring rules.

It is worth repeating that the failure to find gender-related group differences should not in any way lessen vigilance for possible harmful effects on individuals. Persons of either gender who are unwilling to make informed guesses will certainly be at a disadvantage on tests with no correction for guessing and may hurt their chances for success on formula-scored tests.

TABLE 6.3
Multiple-Choice Versus Grid-in Scores on PSAT/NMSQT

Test/Item Format		F	M	D
1993 Tuesday form				
Multiple-choice	N	231,760	179,540	
	Mean	15.1	17.6	−.30
	SD	8.6	9.4	
Grid-in	Mean	4.0	4.6	−.29
	SD	2.5	2.7	
1993 Saturday form				
Multiple-choice	N	177,701	138,847	
	Mean	17.7	20.4	−.35
	SD	8.2	8.6	
Grid-in	Mean	4.0	4.7	−.36
	SD	2.3	2.4	
1994 Tuesday form				
Multiple-choice	N	105,708	81,561	
	Mean	15.6	18.4	−.32
	SD	9.1	10.0	
Grid-in	Mean	3.4	4.3	−.42
	SD	2.3	2.6	
1994 Saturday form				
Multiple-choice	N	103,357	79,574	
	Mean	18.2	21.0	−.35
	SD	8.5	9.0	
Grid-in	Mean	4.7	5.5	−.34
	SD	2.5	2.6	

Note. D is corrected for the reliability difference between multiple-choice and grid-in questions; see Schmitt (1995) for correction formulas.

Answer Changing

Some students believe that their first impression on a multiple-choice question is likely to be correct and that they should not change their initial responses. This belief may be strengthened because students agonize over responses that were changed from right to wrong, whereas answers changed from wrong to right are easily overlooked. Despite the folklore to the contrary, the research evidence is quite strong that answer changing is much more likely to raise scores than lower them (Mueller & Wasser, 1977). In the six studies reviewed by Mueller and Wasser that addressed gender differences in score gains related to changing answers, four found none, one reported males gained more than females, and one reported the opposite. However, in both of the latter two studies, the gender group with the highest mean performance gained the most as a result of answer changing. Thus, they concluded that "when test performance is controlled, there appears to be no sex difference in net gain resultant from changing answers" (p. 12). A more recent study (Schwarz, McMorris, & DeMers, 1991) also found essentially no relationship (correlations less than .10) between gender and both percentage of answers changed and gain resulting from answer changing. However, their sample was limited to 104 students in graduate measurement classes. Thus, additional research would be useful, but there is no reason to expect that practically significant gender differences would emerge.

Other Aspects of Test-Wiseness and Coaching

Test-wiseness refers to the student's ability to use various strategies and clues, unrelated to what the test is designed to measure, to obtain a high score. Besides the topics considered already (using time wisely and adopting an efficient guessing strategy), other aspects of test-wiseness include such strategies as choosing neither of two options that imply the correctness of each other, using information provided in one question to answer other questions, being aware of idiosyncrasies of the test constructor such as adding more qualifiers to the correct answer or tending not to put the correct answer in the first or last positions, recognizing grammatical inconsistencies in certain answer choices, and using specific determiners (such as always, only, and never) in answer choices to eliminate unlikely answers (Millman, Bishop, & Ebel, 1965). Although aspects of test-wiseness received considerable attention in the 1960s and 1970s, possible gender differences were

TABLE 6.4
Formula Score Versus Rights Scores on GRE-Verbal and GRE-Quantitative

Test/Group		F	M	D
GRE-Verbal				
Formula Score				
(Test year 1980–1981)	N	109,125	92,717	
	Mean	486	483	.02
	SD	117	128	
Rights Scores				
(Test year 1981–1982)	N	95,943	83,012	
	Mean	483	478	.04
	SD	119	126	
GRE-Quantitative				
Formula Score				
(Test year 1980–1981)	N	109,125	92,717	
	Mean	484	563	−.62
	SD	121	132	
Rights Score				
(Test year 1981–1982)	N	95,943	83,012	
	Mean	488	569	−.64
	SD	124	131	

Note. Data for 1980–1981 test year are from Goodison (1982); data for 1981–1982 test year are from Goodison (1983). Standard errors are less than .01.

largely ignored (Sarnacki, 1979). One relatively large-scale study did consider gender differences in a sample of 1,070 students in Grades 5 through 11 (Slakter, Koehler, & Hampton, 1970). Their measure assessed four aspects of test-wiseness, assuming that the test-wise examinee should be able to: "1. select the option which resembles an aspect of the stem ..., 2. eliminate options which are known to be incorrect and to choose from among the remaining options ..., 3. eliminate similar options; i.e., options which imply the correctness of each other ..., 4. eliminate those options which include specific determiners" (p. 119). They found that test-wiseness increased with grade level but that there were no significant gender differences or gender by grade interactions. Note that, except for eliminating options known to be incorrect, these strategies would not be useful on carefully constructed tests.

Responsible test publishers try to develop tests that are relatively immune from test-wiseness effects either by revising the tests themselves or by disseminating information on useful test-taking strategies to all test takers. At the same time, coaching schools try to teach test-taking strategies that will give their students an edge. Although anecdotes of huge score gains as the result of coaching abound, a summary of the rigorous research studies suggests gains of less than 25 points for the mathematical sections of the SAT with even smaller gains for the verbal score (Powers, 1993). Unfortunately, Powers' review did not address possible gender differences in gains from coaching.

Stroud (1980), in a reanalysis of data from a Federal Trade Commission (FTC) study of commercial coaching schools, found trivial gender differences (accounting for less than 5% of the variance in the small coaching gains). However, as discussed by Messick (1980), the confounding of coaching effects with self-selection of students into the coached group makes the FTC study difficult to interpret. Smyth's (1990) study of coached and uncoached students from 14 independent secondary schools found that coached boys gained slightly more than coached girls, suggesting that gender differences might increase if all students were coached, but again self-selection of students into the coached group makes interpretation problematic. Because coaching schools are continually trying to find effective coaching strategies, and test publishers are striving to minimize the utility of each new test-taking trick, the question of possible coaching effects needs to be frequently revisited.

Test Anxiety

The relationship of test anxiety to test performance has created considerable interest and controversy since Sarason and Mandler (1952) began publishing in this area. Although some anxieties may facilitate test performance by increasing motivation (Alpert & Haber, 1960), attention has focused primarily on debilitating anxiety, and the term *test anxiety* is usually reserved for this presumably harmful type of anxiety. As clearly shown in a meta-analysis of 562 studies, the relationship of test anxiety to poor test performance is not in doubt (Hembree, 1988). However, merely noting a relationship provides no information on causal direction. Reasonable arguments can be made supporting either the notion that anxiety causes poor performance or the opposite. If students are preoccupied with worry and self-criticism during a test, they are not focusing their limited cognitive resources on the task at hand and their performance would be expected to suffer (Wine, 1971). On the other hand, students with poor study habits and limited knowledge in a subject area may develop test anxiety simply because of their inferior test performance (Tobias, 1985). These positions are not necessarily in conflict as both causal influences could exist together; indeed, they could work in tandem in a downward spiral of anxiety, causing poorer performance, causing still higher anxiety.

Hembree (1988) argued that the experimental studies summarized in his meta-analysis, showing increased test performance as a result of treatment programs that lower test anxiety, reinforce the view that anxiety causes poor test performance. In 38 studies that treated test anxiety with systematic desensitization techniques, test scores of the treated students were about .32 standard deviation units above scores of students in the control groups. As long as at least some of the causal connection is from high anxiety to low test scores, test makers and users should be aware that anxiety may be depressing test scores.

Gender differences in self-reported test anxiety also are well-documented. Hembree's (1988) meta-analysis of 73 studies in Grades 5 through 10 (13,244 students) noted a mean effect size (D) of .43, indicating that females reported significantly higher test anxiety than males. Note that in this age range average school grades and test scores of females are higher than averages for males in most academic areas (see chapters 3 and 4), thus the girls' higher anxiety is presumably not caused by objectively inferior performance. If girls' higher anxiety causes any test score decrement, then the girls' superiority in this age range may be even greater than it appears. For Grades 11, 12, and college undergraduates the mean D for test anxiety (across 39 studies) was .27, with differences for the more select sample of undergraduates about the same size as for the high school juniors and seniors. An additional caveat is needed when interpreting presumed emotional states based on self-reports. Although females report higher anxiety, it may simply be more socially acceptable for them to do so. Males may be equally or more test anxious, but may be less willing to admit it, even on an anonymous questionnaire.

Although these results suggest that differences in test anxiety levels might be responsible for some of the gender difference observed in test scores, the impact of these differences is difficult to quantify. A comparison of gender differences on the same test in high- and low-anxiety testing situations provides the necessary data. Such comparisons are especially useful because they do not rely on questionable self-reports of anxiety states.

As part of a study of new quantitative question formats for the GRE General Test, Bridgeman (1992) included a check on whether scores in a low-anxiety experimental situation were comparable to scores on the operational test. At some test centers, a 30-question quantitative test section was administered as part of a regular administration; students knew that one section would not count but they had no way of telling which section was the experimental section. At other test centers, the same section was clearly identified as experimental with both written and oral instructions. The experimental nature of the task was reinforced by having test takers hand in their regular answer sheets before answer sheets for the special experiment were handed out. Students at these centers were informed that the scores on the experimental section would not be reported to any institution. Sample sizes were reasonably large; 902 males and 1,245 females took the test section under operational (high-anxiety) conditions, and 1,080 males and 1,494 females took it under experimental (low-anxiety) conditions. Gender differences were virtually the same under both conditions with Ds of $-.57$ and $-.52$ in high- and low-anxiety conditions, respectively. With a standard error of the difference of .06, these Ds were not significantly different from each other.

Because scores on the PSAT/NMSQT are not reported to colleges for admissions purposes, it is arguably a high-anxiety test only for the relatively few students who hope to qualify for scholarships. A study that matched PSAT/NMSQT scores for 469,555 students with their SAT scores obtained a few months later found that gender differences were virtually identical on both tests (Lehman & Lawrence, 1992). Data from a subsequent study permit a comparison of PSAT/NMSQT scores to scores on a similar test that was not used for either admissions or scholarship purposes. As part of the field trials for the new SAT I (Feryok & Wright, 1993), sections of existing SATs, as well as new experimental sections, were administered to large samples of high school juniors who reported that they were college bound. Students knew that scores on this experimental test would not be reported to any colleges or scholarship agencies, although their high schools would receive score reports. In one subsample of 1,938 men and 2,949 women from this field trial, students' scores from the 50 mathematics questions in a regular administration of the PSAT/NMSQT were matched with their scores on a 30-question SAT Math section administered under the experimental conditions. The gender differences on the operational PSAT/NMSQT mathematics section, in D units, was $-.33$, and on the experimental SAT Math section it was $-.38$.

Anxiety levels are not necessarily related to an objective analysis of risk, as evidenced by the nervous flyer who will not be persuaded by statistics on airline safety. Therefore, although we found that gender differences were about as large on high-stakes admissions tests as on low-stakes experimental tests that should elicit less anxiety, we cannot rule out the possibility that differential anxiety levels have some impact on gender differences in test scores. However, the results do suggest that changes in score reporting procedures that may reduce test anxiety (such as giving the examinee the option of either discarding the score on a given test or including it in a permanent record) probably would not have a noticeable impact on gender differences in test scores. However, the potential impact of anxiety-reducing changes in score reporting procedures for highly anxious persons of either gender should still be considered.

Computer-Based Tests

Computer administration of tests may reduce some equity concerns while raising some new equity issues. New question formats that computer delivery permits will have to be evaluated for possible differential performance just as new paper-and-pencil formats must be evaluated. Even when the computer is used to administer four- or five-option multiple-choice questions that are developed to essentially the same specifications as an established paper-and-pencil test, possible impacts of the different delivery modes should be considered.

The most complete data on a paper-and-pencil (P&P) and computer adaptive test (CAT) that use the same question types are from the GRE program, which offers tests in both administration modes. Scores on the P&P and CAT versions of the test are intended to be interchangeable, and the comparability of scores in the two formats was extensively studied (Schaeffer, Reese, Steffen, McKinley, & Mills, 1993; Schaeffer, Steffen, Golub-Smith, Mills, & Durso, 1995). It is important to note that computer skills are not needed for the CAT; selecting multiple-choice answers is straightforward and no typing is required. Nevertheless, the modes differ on more than just the use of the computer to administer the items. Specifically, for the GRE General Test in 1995:

- In the P&P test, the examinee may have to answer some questions that are very easy or very hard for her or his ability level; in the CAT, items are selected to be at the appropriate difficulty level for the examinee.
- In the P&P test examinees may skip questions for later consideration or change answers on later review; in the CAT questions must be answered in order and cannot be changed once the next question is presented.
- Section time limits (in terms of seconds per item) for the CAT are more generous than for the P&P test, and unanswered questions at the end of a section that are considered wrong in the P&P scoring are ignored in the CAT scoring (i.e., CAT scores are based only on attempted items as long as 80% of the items are attempted, and if fewer than 80% are attempted no score is reported).
- Reading passages in the CAT must be read from the video screen and scrolling is required to present the entire passage.

Given these substantial differences in testing modes, the possibility that testing mode could differentially impact men and women was explored (Bridgeman & Schaeffer, 1995). Data for all the comparisons came from operational administrations of the P&P or CAT GRE tests. Although comparisons between old and new testing formats are sometimes confounded if scores on the old format count whereas scores on the new format are for experimental purposes only, examinees in these comparisons were equally motivated to perform in both formats.

A comparison was made between all men and women who had taken the GRE in P&P format during the 1993–1994 test year (i.e., October 1993 through June 1994); these differences were contrasted with differences for men and women who had taken the CAT from March 1994 through February 1995. Both samples were limited to U.S. citizens who indicated that their best language was English and who were taking the GRE for graduate admissions or fellowship consideration. Results are summarized in Table 6.5.

Gender differences were virtually identical in the two testing modes. Because examinees were free to choose the testing format that they preferred, those who were especially apprehensive about computerized testing could avoid that format. If all students were forced to take the test on computer, it is possible that different patterns of subgroup performance could emerge. However, note that the majority of examinees in both groups were women; the percentage of women in the P&P group was only slightly larger than the percentage of women in the CAT group. It is also possible that individuals of either gender may have certain characteristics that would

TABLE 6.5
Scores for Paper-and-Pencil (P&P) and Computer-Adaptive Test (CAT) Samples

	Women	Men	
Sample/Score	M (SD)	M (SD)	D
P&P-Verbal	479 (108)	511 (112)	−.29
CAT-Verbal	484 (106)	514 (110)	−.28
P&P-Quantitative	495 (120)	575 (131)	−.64
CAT-Quantitative	503 (124)	587 (133)	−.65
P&P-Analytical	534 (122)	562 (125)	−.23
CAT-Analytical	547 (137)	583 (140)	−.26

Note. P&P sample size is 148,268 women and 85,624 men (63% women); CAT sample size is 17,015 women and 12,588 men (58% women).

give them more of an advantage on one format than the other. In particular, individuals who are slow and careful may be relatively advantaged on the CAT, which allows almost twice as much time per question as the P&P examination. However, this advantage may not be as large as it appears for high-scoring examinees because the branching nature of the test presents them with a higher proportion of difficult (and presumably time-consuming) questions than would a standard linear test.

Because gender differences on the CAT GRE appear to be quite similar to differences on the P&P GRE, the preliminary data suggest that a shift to CAT testing should neither lessen nor increase gender differences. It remains unclear whether the various features of CAT testing (e.g., more generous time limits, no chance to change answers) are each individually immune from gender effects or whether a possible advantage on one feature is counterbalanced by a disadvantage on another feature. As more data accumulate, similar analyses can be conducted with ethnic and linguistic minority groups. Finally, it should be noted that both the P&P and CAT tests studied here used essentially equivalent multiple-choice questions and the basic task of the student was the same in both modes. As computer-delivered tests with more open-ended answer formats are introduced, the issue of possible gender differences with these new formats must be revisited. As indicated in chapter 5, studies of multiple-choice and essay formats have suggested that differential gender effects may be found when the task demands differ across question formats (Breland, Danos, Kahn, Kubota, & Bonner, 1994; Bridgeman & Lewis, 1994; Mazzeo et al., 1993).

ESSAYS AND PERFORMANCE ASSESSMENTS

Although some of the fairness issues in test design and administration discussed here apply to assessment techniques that go beyond multiple-choice tests (e.g., the need to determine the impact of time limits on essay examinations), other issues are unique to essays and other performance assessments. Such assessments are intended to reflect good instructional activities, be more engaging for students, and better reflect criterion performances that are important outside the classroom (Linn & Burton, 1994). Performance tasks can include oral presentations, debates, exhibitions, collections of student-produced materials (portfolios), videotapes of performances, experiments, and results of scientific or other inquiries (Archbald & Newmann, 1988). Despite their obvious strengths, performance assessments also create new challenges to developing fair assessments. Problems of rater biases, content balance, choice of assessment task, and score unreliability all take on increased importance with performance assessments.

Rater Biases

Although gender biases could intrude on several aspects of multiple-choice testing from question selection through various administration practices, the scoring process is gender blind; the scoring machine cannot tell if the answer sheet being processed is from a male or a female. However, on essay tests and other performance evaluations, the gender of the examinee may be known (or guessed) by the scorer. Subjective evaluations could then be influenced by gender-related biases or expectations. One experimental paradigm compares scores on essays (or other written products) when the rater thinks the essay was written by a male with the score on the same essay when the rater thinks it was written by a female. For example, Finn (1972) found a gender-related scoring effect among urban fifth-grade teachers (but not among suburban teachers). The teachers were asked to rate two essays and were given false information about the achievement level, race, and gender of the authors. The urban teachers assigned the lowest ratings to essays that they thought were written by White female students. Finn argued that these low ratings are related to high expectations for the writing of White females that were not realized in the average quality essays that the teachers were asked to rate. He noted, "Among the comments the teachers wrote on the essay sheets, the most common for this group of authors, was of the sort 'a student with these characteristics can certainly do better work than this'" (p. 406). Although such findings are provocative, a meta-analysis of 119 studies related to gender bias in ratings suggests that the male advantage is negligible with a D of $-.07$ (Swim, Borgida, Maruyama, & Myers, 1989).

Classroom essay tests are subject to biases based on teacher expectations, but, in national testing programs, essays are typically read by raters who have no information on the gender (or any other background characteristic) of the essay's author. Nevertheless, biases could appear if graders guess the gender of the author or respond to some aspect of the essay that is related to gender but unrelated to what the essay is supposed to assess. Such an extraneous factor is handwriting, and women generally have clearer hand-writing than men. In a study of 300 essays in U.S. History (150 each by males and females) and 300 essays in European History from the AP program, ratings of handwriting indicated Ds of .92 and .37 for the U.S. and European History samples, respectively (Breland, Danos, Kahn, Kubota, & Sudlow, 1991). However, handwriting was a very poor predictor of overall essay scores. Furthermore, a historical content score based on carefully controlled counts of main points, supporting evidence, and factual errors was far superior as a predictor of essay scores. This historical content score showed the same lack of gender difference as the holistic scores originally assigned to the essays, although men scored significantly higher on the multiple-choice portion of the examination.

In other contexts and with less experienced raters, handwriting might have more of an impact on scores. In one common experimental design, the same essays are rewritten in good and poor handwriting. Using such a design with 16+ English Language papers in England, Briggs (1980) found a significant handwriting effect. The raters were experienced English teach-ers, but they had no previous experience with large-scale essay assessments. Hughes, Keeling, and Tuck (1983) found a similar effect for essays written by children aged 11 to 12 years old and evaluated by undergraduates taking a course in research methods. An additional feature of their study presented fabricated achievement data to the scorers along with the essays. This information was intended to create high or low expectancies for the essay performance. Essays allegedly written by high-achieving students received higher scores than essays allegedly written by low-achieving students, but there was no interaction between handwriting quality and expectation. Chase (1986) used essentially the same design, but also included contrived information on the gender and race of the essay author. Raters were 80 in-service teachers. Overall, handwriting did not have a significant impact on the scores; indeed, none of the main effects was significant. The four-way interaction (handwriting × race × gender × expectation) was significant: "Poor handwriting conveyed the advantage to Black females and White males from whom the reader expected little, and to Black males and White females from whom the reader expected much" (p. 39).

The importance of expectations in assigning ratings was further demon-strated in a study comparing scores of essays typed on a word processor and handwritten versions of the same essays (Powers, Fowles, Farnum, & Ram-sey, 1994). Their results indicated that the handwritten versions received higher scores. Apparently, expectations are higher for essays written on word processors, and minor errors that might be overlooked in a handwritten essay stand out on the printed page. Making raters aware of the problem may reduce it, although a second study reported in the same article found that handwritten essays still received higher scores even when raters were aware of the biases found in the first study. Scoring would be fairer if all essays were written on the word processor, but this might disadvantage students who did not know how to use a word processor. Requiring all students to write essays by hand would be unfair to students who routinely rely on a word processor for writing. In a few years, it may be reasonable to expect all students to have word processing skills, but meanwhile there is no completely satisfactory answer to this dilemma.

Content Balance

As already noted, groups and individuals may perform better in some content domains than others (e.g., women perform relatively better on analogy questions with aesthetics or philosophy content and men perform relatively better on reading passages with science-related content). In a multiple-choice examination with a large number of questions, such relative strengths and weaknesses can be balanced, and inadvertently including a question that is differentially difficult for a particular group would have only a minimal impact on the total test score. However, a performance assess-ment frequently contains only one or two extended tasks. Balance may be much more difficult to achieve on such examinations. Furthermore, the consequences of inadvertently including a single biased question may be much more severe if that question represents half of the test. Thus, perform-ance assessments may require increased vigilance for content imbalances or questions that are differentially difficult for a particular group.

The content balance problem can be clearly seen in data from essays that are used in the AP program.[2] For analysis, we selected the 1993 and 1994 examinations in U.S. History and Biology. These examinations each test a large number of students and have F/M ratios close to 1.0 (see Table S-10 in the *Supplement*). For the U.S. History examinations, gender differences for the multiple-choice questions (MC), for the document-based question

---

[2]Thanks to Rick Morgan for providing these data.

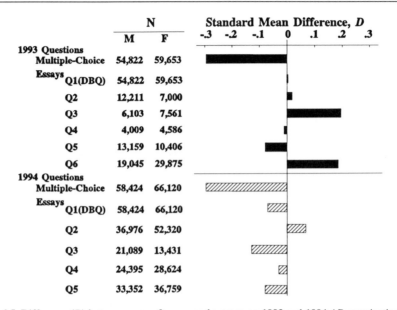

	N		Standard Mean Difference, D							
	M	F	-.3	-.2	-.1	0	.1	.2	.3	
1993 Questions										
Multiple-Choice	54,822	59,653								
Essays Q1(DBQ)	54,822	59,653								
Q2	12,211	7,000								
Q3	6,103	7,561								
Q4	4,009	4,586								
Q5	13,159	10,406								
Q6	19,045	29,875								
1994 Questions										
Multiple-Choice	58,424	66,120								
Essays Q1(DBQ)	58,424	66,120								
Q2	36,976	52,320								
Q3	21,089	13,431								
Q4	24,395	28,624								
Q5	33,352	36,759								

FIG. 6.5. Difference (D) between means for men and women on 1993 and 1994 AP examinations in U.S. History.

(DBQ, which requires interpreting documents and integrating them into an essay), and for the other essay questions (Q2–Q6 in 1993 and Q2–Q5 in 1994) are presented in Fig. 6.5. All students responded to the DBQ, but chose just one (in 1993) or two (in 1994) topics to answer for the other essays. Although gender differences on the MC questions were virtually identical in both years, conclusions about the size (or even direction) of the gender difference in the essays was dependent on the particular essay selected for analysis. For the DBQ, there was either no difference ($D = .00$ in 1993) or a slight difference favoring men ($D = -.07$ in 1994; standard error was less than .01). The general impression from the small set of essays that happened to be administered in 1993 is that women generally do at least as well as men and sometimes substantially better. Exactly the opposite conclusion can be drawn from the five essay topics that were selected by test developers for the examination in 1994. Looking at only a single year, or worse still at a single topic, can thus provide a distorted picture of performance across the (hypothetical) domain of potential topics.

Because students were permitted to choose among several essay topics (except on the DBQ), interpretation of the size of a gender difference on a given topic is somewhat problematic. For example, if all students were forced to write on the topic for Q3 in 1993, the gender difference could be larger or smaller than that observed. (More on the problem of student choice of topic is presented in a subsequent section.) However, there was no choice on the Biology examination; all students responded to all four topics. As shown in Fig. 6.6, two topics from the 1993 examination showed noticeable gender differences (Ds of −.14 and −.21; standard error = .01) whereas the other two topics showed a negligible gender difference (Ds less than −.03). Suppose the entire test consisted of only two essays (which would not be unusual for a performance assessment). If the test consisted of only Topics 1 and 2, we might conclude that sizable and consequential gender differences existed, but if Topics 3 and 4 were used instead, we might conclude that gender differences were trivial. Achieving an appropriate content balance is a difficult, if not impossible, task when an entire content domain must be represented in two or three questions. Nevertheless, such a balance is essential if reliable scores are needed to make inferences about individuals or groups.

Reliability

In the current context, reliability refers to the generalizability of scores across raters and tasks. Carefully defined scoring rubrics and intensive training can generally bring rater reliability within reasonable bounds, but generalizations across tasks in performance assessments can be problematic (Dunbar, Koretz, & Hoover, 1991; Linn & Burton, 1994; Shavelson, Baxter,

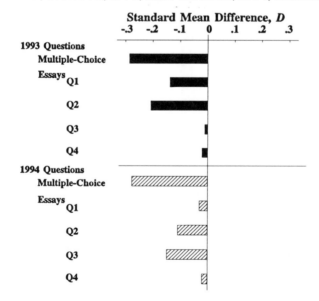

FIG. 6.6. Difference (D) between means for men and women on 1993 and 1994 AP examinations in Biology. All students answered all questions. For 1993, male N = 22,015; female N = 24,984. For 1994, male N = 24,169; female N = 28,763.

& Gao, 1993). Shavelson et al. (1993) studied three science tasks for fifth- and sixth-grade students. One task asked students to determine which of three paper towels holds and absorbs the most water; the second task asked students to determine the electric circuit components (batteries, bulbs, and wires) in each of six black boxes; the third task involved determining sow bugs' preferences for various environments. Rater agreement was fairly high, but students who performed well on one task did not necessarily perform well on the other tasks. The authors concluded that 23 similar tasks would be needed for a reasonable degree of confidence in rankings of students based on such tasks (i.e., for a relative G coefficient of .80). R. Linn, (1993a) investigated the performance-based tasks on AP examinations. He determined how many hours of testing time would be required to achieve a generalizability coefficient of .90 or higher if the entire examination were composed exclusively of such tasks. Although generalizability was very good for some examinations (Physics C: Electricity and Magnetism would require only 1 hour and 15 minutes to reach the specified level), other examinations would require as much as 13 hours (European History). Eight of the 21 subjects would require at least 6 hours of testing time if they were composed exclusively of performance-based tasks of the type that are currently used.

One consequence of the low reliability for many performance tasks is that gender differences spuriously may appear to be reduced on tests composed of such tasks relative to multiple-choice assessments. If reliability is sufficiently low, all group differences will necessarily disappear. (If scores were assigned to all individuals in each group by a random number generator, the average scores in all groups would be essentially identical. Unreliability can act as such a random number generator to swamp any true group differences that might exist.) Thus, it is important not to equate a reduction in mean group differences with an increase in fairness. Indeed, the same unreliability that reduces group differences also reduces fairness from the individual's point of view. To the extent that unreliability introduces random noise into test scores, true differences among individuals become harder to detect and students are unfairly ranked more on luck than on their standing on the construct that the test is supposed to measure. Despite the potential for performance assessments to artificially minimize group differences, some research suggests that differences between majority and underserved minority groups may actually be greater for performance assessments than for traditional tests (Linn, Baker, & Dunbar, 1991).

It may be tempting to avoid the unreliability inherent in performance assessments by assessing only constructs that can be measured highly reliably with multiple-choice or short-answer examinations. However, this may introduce a serious threat to test validity—construct underrepresentation (Messick, 1989). A test cannot be valid if it misses or seriously underrepresents some important component of the focal construct. For example, a history test composed exclusively of multiple-choice questions almost certainly will be more reliable (in terms of form-to-form consistency) than a history test (with the same total testing time) that also includes two or three essay questions. However, the former test cannot assess the organizational and persuasive skills that are assessed with the essays. As we have already seen, this construct underrepresentation affects not only the validity of the assessment, but also gender equity if the underrepresented construct is one in which a particular gender group (women in the case of essay-writing skills) tends to excel. Highly reliable assessment of the wrong construct is not preferable to less reliable assessment of the right construct. Nevertheless, unreliability can be as serious a threat to test validity as construct underrepresentation, so it is worth considerable effort to make performance assessments as reliable as possible.

Choice of Assessment Task

A common assumption in virtually all multiple-choice assessments is that all examinees will respond to exactly the same questions or to different questions that have been equated by rigorous statistical procedures. It should be a matter of indifference to the examinees which set of equivalent questions they have to answer. However, such equating may not be possible with authentic performance tasks, and indifference to which set of tasks is assigned may not even be a desirable goal. One characteristic of authentic performance tasks is that they should be interesting and engaging to the students. If males and females were engaged by different types of activities (as suggested in chapter 4), then complete standardization of tasks may be incompatible with assessment of optimal performance. For example, some students may be most engaged by a mathematics activity that is put in a sports context. These students may be predominantly males. Should they be denied the opportunity to work in this high-interest area simply because it is not equally attractive to both genders? However, if students are allowed to work in the areas that most interest them, it may be impossible to equate performances across tasks.

Suppose a nationwide history examination were designed to see how well students could organize evidence and present valid arguments about an area that they had studied in depth. Some classes may have spent much of their time on causes of the Civil War whereas others spent more time on causes of the Great Depression. A single question on causes of the Civil War may at first seem to be fair (exactly the same demand is made on all students), but it clearly discriminates against the students whose classes emphasized causes of the Great Depression. As long as knowledge of these specific events was not being tested (but rather the ability to present reasoned arguments), it would seem to be fairer to allow the examinee to choose the event that they know best. However, this introduces a difficult scoring problem as the raters try to determine whether this essay on the Civil War is equivalent to that essay on the Great Depression. Wainer and Thissen (1994) summarized the problems of allowing, and not allowing, examinee choice in educational testing. They began with a quote from Kierkegaard that aptly describes the dilemma: "If you allow choice, you will regret it; if you don't allow choice, you will regret it; whether you allow choice or not, you will regret both" (p. 159).

Although allowing choice may be beneficial or harmful to individuals who make good or poor choices, it is unclear what impact choice may have on group gender differences. Five examinations in the AP program allow examinee choice on some free-response questions (primarily essays) while also having a set of mandatory questions that must be answered by all students. Pomplun, Morgan, and Nellikunnel (1992) showed that examinees with the same level of performance on the mandatory parts of the examination often got quite different scores on the free-response questions that they happened to select; some examinees seemed to benefit from choosing a topic with relatively high average scores, but other examinees were apparently disadvantaged by their choice of question on which scores were relatively low. If men disproportionally chose questions that tended to yield high scores and women chose the lower scoring questions, this choice behavior could contribute to gender differences in total scores. Indeed, Wainer and Thissen (1994) provided an example from one form of an AP history examination where this appeared to happen. However, this gender difference does not appear to be a generalizable phenomenon. Morgan, Pomplun, and Nellikunnel (1993), in a study of three different AP examinations, found that no gender or ethnic subgroup was consistently hurt by making bad choices.

CONCLUSION

Comprehensive sensitivity reviews and statistical monitoring procedures, such as DIF, are necessary to assure that test questions are as fair as possible. Test administration procedures should be evaluated to make certain that they do not place an unfair burden on any group or individual. However, although these test development and administration procedures are potentially important, the studies reviewed in this chapter suggest that they play a relatively minor role in explaining observed gender differences in national testing programs. Tinkering with the phrasing of questions, time limits, or the correction for guessing is unlikely to have a major impact on the size of gender differences on cognitive assessments. Although we still have much to learn, especially about performance assessments, the key to understanding gender differences is probably at the level of the underlying constructs, not the surface features of test administration. The construct-irrelevant variance that could be introduced through insensitive question-writing procedures or unfair test administration practices should certainly be monitored and minimized, but other factors appear to be involved in producing the real and substantial gender differences that were apparent in chapters 3 and 4. Choice of construct may play a vital role in understanding these differences; this issue is explored in the following chapter.

7

Fairness Issues in Test Design and Use

In order to better understand fairness issues and to better connect such issues with decisions in the assessment process that can affect examinees, we have distinguished four stages in assessment: design, development, administration, and use. The previous chapter focused on fairness issues in development and administration, the second and third stages, which are closely connected. This chapter is concerned with design and use, which are also closely connected. Following some comments on the nature of fairness in test design and use, this chapter takes up eight topics that have important fairness implications: (a) choice of construct, (b) gender differences on free-response measures, (c) the multiple-choice format, (d) writing, (e) mathematics, (f) grade prediction, (g) selective admissions, and (h) fair test use in context.

The four successive stages of assessment (Fig. 1.1) are clearly related in the sense that each follows and depends on the one just previous. For example, the development of a test (Stage 2) is based on test specifications created in test design (Stage 1). On the other hand, the four stages do not follow in simple progression. For example, test development requires frequent cycling back, particularly in the early stages of test creation. In the process of developing and administering a test, one accumulates evidence in field trials as to its usefulness, fairness, and practicality, and that evidence suggests ways to improve the original design specifications.

Test design (Stage 1) and test use (Stage 4) are related for obvious reasons. Tests are intended to serve a purpose. Their design must be appropriate to that intended use. Furthermore, test design must take account of the fact that using a test may well have consequences beyond the immediate purpose served, and the nature of those consequences may well be influenced by the test's design. Finally, the use to which a test is put should be consistent with its design. All of this means that decisions we make about test design and test use are often interdependent, as are our judgments about the fairness of those decisions.

Some fairness issues appear in more than one stage. For example, three important topics—test speededness, computer-based testing, and statistical procedures to enhance fairness[1]—were discussed in the previous chapter because they involve fairness issues in test development and administration. We do not address these topics again in this chapter, but it is important to note their connection to test design. Decisions may be reached at the design stage as to approximately how much time is available to administer a given test, how it is to be administered, and what general level of reliability is desirable, given the intended use.

For example, a decision to administer a test by computer is likely to be based on such considerations as the types of assessment that are possible on computer, what advantages might accrue to examinees and score users, how well computer delivery is likely to meet fairness criteria in actual practice, and so on. These and other fairness issues are addressed in the course of test development when decisions are made about specific characteristics of a computer-based test and how it is delivered electronically. However, some consequences regarding the nature of the eventual test are not easily reversed once the initial decision is made to use either the computer or paper and pencil.

Throughout this book we have viewed test fairness as an important aspect of test validity. Validity is the all-encompassing technical standard for judging the quality of the assessment process. Validity includes, for example, the accuracy with which a test measures what it purports to measure, how well it serves its intended function, other consequences of test use, and comparability of the assessment process for different examinees. We see fairness reflected in various aspects of comparable measurement, and anything that reduces fairness tends also to reduce validity.

At the end of chapter 5, Cole described three social criteria for building tests and justifying their use: usefulness, fairness, and practicality. The usefulness of the test comes first because we develop tests in order to serve some socially useful function. Consequently, we consider fair design and use in relation to the function a test is intended to serve. Usefulness must be viewed broadly because the social justification of testing requires that function include both the intended purpose of the test and any important systemic effects that may follow from its use.

---

[1]The main statistical characteristics that are specified in test design are the test reliability (which is determined largely by the number and types of items and affects speededness that we discuss elsewhere) and item parameters that affect the shape of the distribution. The latter could differentially affect the relative score positions of high-scoring and very high-scoring women, depending on whether the test had a long or a short tail at the top.

The second criterion is whether the function can be served fairly. In making that judgment we have to balance the interests of different groups of examinees, and we have to balance the interests of individuals as well as groups. As we will see, it may be difficult to achieve such balance, partly because the interests are sometimes contradictory, and partly because different values may suggest different solutions.

The third criterion is whether a test can meet essential requirements of practicality. Cole gives examples of practical constraints in several categories—technical limitations, cost or other burden to examinees, acceptability to users, and so on. This chapter gives only passing attention to such practical constraints because we feel that, in principle, aspects of test design and use that bear on fairness should be judged independently of such constraints insofar as possible. Several important features of fair test design and use that were discussed in chapter 1 need some elaboration.

Test Design

What constitutes fair test design? In chapter 1 we answered that question as follows: A fair test design should provide examinees comparable opportunity, insofar as possible, to demonstrate knowledge and skills they have acquired that are relevant to the purpose of the test. An important qualification is that tests are ordinarily intended to serve a limited educational function along with other information. Consequently, a judgment as to whether examinees have comparable opportunity to demonstrate relevant knowledge and skill must rightly be based on all the measures ordinarily used in making a particular decision about examinees; for example, whether to admit an applicant.

This view of fair test design is based on consideration of the main threats to fairness at this stage of test creation. The most important choices in test design concern what knowledge and skills to measure and how to measure them. There are two distinguishable phases in test design. It is first necessary to establish the purpose of the test, what constructs will be useful in serving that purpose, and what assessment format to use. Next comes more detailed decisions regarding the particular types of questions, scoring methods, statistical characteristics, and so on—all reflected in a set of test specifications.

Different writers have suggested different schemas to describe the various constructs that a test might measure.[2] For our purposes, Fig. 7.1 usefully

---

[2]Perhaps the best known is Guilford's "structure of intellect" (Guilford & Hoepfner, 1971). Another is Guttman's (1969) facet theory. More recent examples are offered by Gardner (1983) and Sternberg (1985). Our three-facet schema in Fig. 7.1 comes closest to the Campbell and Fiske (1959) trait-method unit where trait subsumes knowledge and skills, and method corresponds to format, as we have broadly interpreted it.

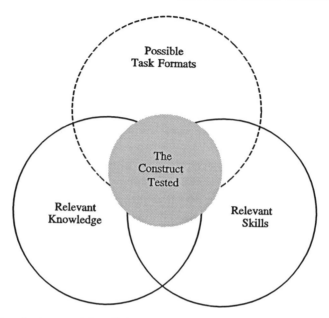

FIG. 7.1. Three-facet representation of a test construct.

represents three important facets of a test construct: knowledge, skills, and the format of the assessment task. These three overlap, as indicated, and they will vary in their importance from one construct to another. Format is one of the facets because the assessment method may affect the nature of the knowledge and skills that are measured. Format is subsidiary because, strictly speaking, we are interested only in the knowledge and skills. Nonetheless, assessment format may be critical either in the limitations it imposes or the opportunities it creates in measuring different constructs. (Baker et al., 1993; Bennett & Ward, 1993).

In educational assessment it is traditional to refer to particular knowledge and skills in describing a construct or specifying the content of a test, even though the two are tightly related and may be difficult to distinguish. For our purposes, it is sufficient to note simply the joint role of knowledge and skill. Adding task format is also helpful in clarifying the important role of format in test reform and the possible implications for test fairness. We interpret format broadly to include all aspects of the assessment task, its delivery to the examinee, and the mode of response required.

Note especially in Fig. 7.1 that the shaded center refers to the construct tested—the knowledge and skills actually represented on the test. These are not necessarily all the knowledge and skills that the test developer intends to include, nor all of the relevant knowledge and skills that could be represented. Also, it is important to remember that the tested construct may include—perhaps invisible to the naked eye—knowledge, skills, or other factors that may not have been intended and may not be relevant to the purpose of the test. Several such factors—for example, speededness and irrelevant knowledge requirements—were considered in the previous chapter.

What are the main threats to fairness when, in the course of designing a test, choices are made regarding what to measure and how to measure? The threats to fairness are the same as the threats to validity: *construct under-representation* and *irrelevant difficulty* (Messick, 1989, 1994d). Construct underrepresentation means measuring some aspects of the construct, but not others. Irrelevant difficulty refers to aspects of the task that are not germane to the intended construct. In both cases, the potential fairness problem arises from the fact that different examinees (and perhaps women and men) may score differently even though they are equally proficient on the intended construct; that is, the test may not provide comparable opportunities to score well.

It is almost never possible, for practical reasons, to measure all relevant aspects of the construct—whether it is something relatively narrow like computation skill, or something far broader like knowledge of history, teaching skill, or promise for graduate study. If it is a narrow construct, like computation, it is feasible that the test can sample most types of knowledge and skill that are relevant; that is, the center circle in Fig. 7.1 can cover most of the larger circles. On the other hand, a test can measure only limited aspects of a broad construct like promise for graduate study. By measuring only some aspects, we necessarily underrepresent the knowledge and skills that are left out. Therefore, to some extent we necessarily overestimate or underestimate the competence of individuals or groups who would have done better (or poorer) on what was not included.

The use of alternate assessment formats is one way to make tests more realistic and better connected to instructional objectives by measuring a broader range of important knowledge and skills or to actually change the conception of what knowledge and skills are important; that is, to change the construct and its educational relevance (Resnick & Resnick, 1992; Shepard, 1992). Thus, choice of format is often one aspect of choosing the construct. For example, proficiency in history is not the same construct in multiple-choice (MC) and essay format, and the relative performance of women and men is not the same on the two formats (Breland et al., 1991). As we will see, however, changing the assessment format does not necessarily change the construct that is measured.

Note also that choice of format can raise fairness questions because some formats may be differentially difficult (or easy) for some examinees or for women and men generally. If it is something about the format, per se, that is differentially difficult, then we are not talking about construct underrepresentation, but about the second general threat to fairness in test design: difficulty in the test or its administration that is irrelevant to what is being measured. As Messick (1989) noted, the difficulty may be quite relevant to the specific assessment task presented to the examinee, but not relevant to the construct of interest. Suppose, for example, that an unusual calculator, familiar to more men than women, was specified for use with a test. In that case, women might tend to receive lower scores than deserved because the test was more difficult for reasons irrelevant to the skill and knowledge that the test was intended to measure.

What types of evidence bear on fair design? In the main, evidence that bears on the two major threats to comparability that were already noted: construct underrepresentation and irrelevant difficulty. Underrepresentation can mean limited choice of relevant constructs (e.g., reading but not mathematics) or limited aspects of a construct (e.g., math knowledge but not math reasoning). We look for evidence of excess weight on some knowledge and skills or omission of others *and* evidence that the pattern of performance for individuals or women and men is not the same on those different knowledge and skills. In the second case, we look for evidence of irrelevant difficulty associated with any specific feature of the assessment process that is not pertinent to what is being measured.

Test Use

What constitutes fair test use? In chapter 1 we answered that question as follows: Fair test use should result in comparable treatment of examinees by avoiding adverse impact due to incorrect inferences or inappropriate actions based on scores and other information normally used with scores. By comparable treatment, we mean applying equivalent standards so that test use is comparably valid for all individuals and groups. There are, of course, specific indicators of validity, but only the test user can decide when test use is comparably valid in light of institutional and social values that apply to the particular situation. Therefore, in any discussion of fair test use, it is essential to consider the purpose of the test, the context of its use, other measures involved, and the consequences of use. Comparable treatment also has these basic features: appropriate consideration of all relevant information concerning the individual's characteristics and competencies, and use of the same decision process for all.

In recent years there has been considerable criticism of testing practices (Taylor, 1995) and a number of efforts to strengthen guidelines for test use. Professional guidelines for test use attend to a wide variety of topics concerning adequate training of persons who use tests, proper use of tests for different purposes, and correct practices in particular situations or with specific types of test materials (AERA/APA/NCME, 1985; Association for Measurement and Evaluation in Counseling and Development, 1992; *Code*, 1988; College Board, 1988; Educational Testing Service, 1987; Eyde et al., 1993; NCME Ad Hoc Committee, 1995). We focus here on the two major forms of test use: interpretations and actions. The main concern is with those aspects of test use that can pose systematic threats to fairness for individuals and groups, especially women and men.

Interpretations involve inferences about the meaning of scores. Such interpretations can take different forms. Teachers, administrators, and examinees themselves use scores to form impressions of proficiency—impressions that can unfairly mislead if they go beyond interpretations that are warranted, or if they are based on an incomplete view of proficiency. Traditionally, test bias or the fairness of test interpretations has been evaluated by examining the relationship between test scores and a particular criterion for different groups of examinees. The idea is to see whether the same interpretations hold.

Selection decisions, scholarship awards, course credit, graduation—all represent *actions* that are based partly on scores. Actions introduce additional threats to fairness because scores may not be used as intended or in accordance with interpretations. The decision process may be inconsistent, or be based on arbitrary standards, or place unwarranted weight on a particular score, or ignore critical information.

What types of evidence and considerations bear on fairness in test use? How does one decide whether treatment is comparable? The easier part of this question concerns evidence. The previous paragraphs suggest various types of information that bear on the fairness of test use: whether scores underestimate performance of one group or another, whether scores are used consistently and evenhandedly, whether pertinent information is overlooked, and so on. We examine such evidence in this chapter.

However, as we will see, more difficult issues often turn on other considerations. As discussed at the end of chapter 5, an essential balance must be struck among three major requirements: The test must be useful, it must be as fair as possible to all parties, and it must be viable from a practical standpoint. Willingham (in press) also discussed usefulness, fairness, and practicality, referring to these three considerations as the social matrix of test justification. A form of test use that seems fair to one group may appear just the opposite to another. A test alternative that seems fairer than the original test from some perspectives may be less effective in serving the original intended purpose. Another test alternative that seems fairer in some respect may pose unmanageable threats to test security or seriously limit reliability—problems that may pose different but equally serious fairness issues.

In discussing fairness issues in design and test use, we have focused our attention mainly on high-stakes tests used typically at ages 17 to 22, especially college admissions tests. There are several reasons for this emphasis. Selective tests at this age have important consequences for students. Therefore, their use is inherently relevant to fairness questions—more than would normally be the case with tests used, for example, in connection with instruction, school accountability, or counseling. Another reason that we refer frequently to admissions tests is because much of the available data and research is based on these tests. Comparable fairness issues arise, however, with other high-stakes tests used for selective purposes; for example, grade placement at younger ages, school-leaving examinations for older students, or scholarship awards.

Test fairness, like test validity, is an extraordinarily broad subject. It is not possible here to address all aspects of test design and use that might deserve discussion. In the following sections, we take up eight topics that we believe have a particularly important bearing on gender fairness or have received much attention in recent years. All eight concern both design and use, although the emphasis varies.

The first three topics mainly involve issues in test design. We start with a discussion of possible effects of the *choice of construct* on relative performance of women and men, then consider the effects of format choice by examining in some detail patterns of *gender differences on free-response measures*, followed by an examination of the more specific question as to whether *the multiple-choice format* is a source of irrelevant test difficulty. The next two topics are almost equally concerned with design and use. These sections consider possible fairness implications in the assessment of two critical types of knowledge and skill: *writing* and *mathematics*. The final three topics focus mainly on test use: *grade prediction*, *selective admissions*, and *fair test use in context*.

CHOICE OF CONSTRUCT

The first question to decide in designing a test is, "Broadly speaking, what should the test measure?" That question immediately leads to other questions: What is the function of the test? What constructs are relevant to that function? There is no disagreement on this point: Validity in relation to function is the primary characteristic that justifies the use of any test (Cronbach, 1980; Linn, 1994; Messick, 1989). However, one must ordinarily choose among relevant constructs because it is not possible to measure all. The threat to comparability and fairness comes from underrepresenting the relevant constructs; that is, choosing to measure some things and not others—possibly to the advantage of some examinees and to the disadvantage of others. Our purpose here is to consider how the process of making such design decisions may affect the fairness of a test for individual examinees, and specifically for women and men. As we have noted, the assessment format can have an important bearing on the construct tested. We focus here mainly on knowledge and skills and take up format choice in the following section.

It is clear from the data presented in chapters 3 and 4 that there are consequential mean gender differences in some categories of knowledge and skill. In general populations of high school seniors, for example, women often score better on tests in writing, language use, and reading (median positive Ds from .20 to .55; less positive in select populations). Men tend to score better on tests in natural science, geopolitics, and math reasoning (median negative values of D in the low 20s; more negative in select populations). The choice of constructs that are considered relevant to the purpose of a test can obviously have an important effect on the resulting scores of women and men. Two areas—writing and mathematics—are sufficiently important to warrant later discussion in separate sections.

This section introduces construct choice as a basic consideration in building a valid and fair test and provides an illustration of the potential effects of such choice on test performance differences of women and men. These are extraordinarily broad issues. With limited space, only the most critical considerations can be addressed. We start at the beginning: What function is the test intended to serve?

The Functional Basis for Construct Choice

Educational assessment serves various functions; for example, (a) to assign and promote in lower grades, (b) to guide learning and instruction, (c) to place students in remedial and advanced courses in high school and college, (d) to certify school-leaving requirements, (e) to encourage educational accountability, and (f) to facilitate undergraduate and graduate admissions. The knowledge and skill that would be appropriate for tests serving these functions may vary considerably.

As we have said, two steps are normally necessary in deciding what goes into a test. The first is to select the general types of knowledge and skill that are most relevant to the purpose of the test and the best format for assessing that knowledge and skill. The second is to develop detailed specifications of content. Both steps determine the nature of the construct tested. In some cases it is obvious what general types of knowledge and skill are appropriate. For example, a test intended for placing students in the more advanced of two courses in a sequence should focus on prerequisite knowledge and skills; that is, material covered in the first course. Here the principal design task is to develop detailed test specifications that match the course (College Board, 1994b). Developing tests whereby students fulfill requirements for high school graduation or admission to college illustrate a different situation. In these cases there are arguable options as to what general types of knowledge and skills might be included.

On the basis of what validity considerations does one decide which constructs to use when the function of the test suggests multiple possibilities? There are two broad considerations: One is evidence as to whether a test so designed is likely to serve well its immediate intended purpose; another is the broader systemic consequences of using the test (Cole & Moss, 1989; Messick, 1975, 1994b; Resnick & Resnick, 1992). From both vantage points, the choice must satisfy the criteria of usefulness, fairness, and practicality.

Immediate Purpose.   Consider an admissions test. The immediate purpose of an admissions test is typically viewed as helping admissions officers predict which applicants will do well academically. To be sure, the scores are only part of the admissions decision. Other available information about applicants is also used in predicting academic performance or in serving other institutional objectives. Deciding what to measure in the test is not at all the same as deciding what information is relevant to admissions decisions. We examine that important distinction in a later discussion of test use. Meanwhile, in deciding how to design the test, one might first review a range of constructs that seem to be relevant and appropriate to the task. Figure 7.2 illustrates the types of information about student performance that are typically available at age 18 and a range of assessment possibilities.

The left column in this illustration reflects the fact that young people learn throughout their lives in a variety of situations, not just the classroom. The next two columns make an important distinction regarding specificity versus generality. Column 2 lists measures of particular types of achievement and competence and Column 3 includes tested abilities that apply more generally to a variety of situations and activities.

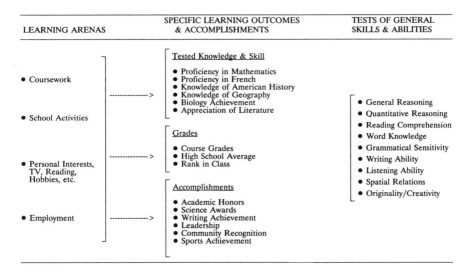

FIG. 7.2. An illustration of possibilities for educational assessment at age 18.

In the middle column, grades and accomplishments are the student's most obvious track record. Such information is highly relevant to an overall assessment of learning and achievement at that age, but the information is not always reliable and comparable from student to student or school to school. Tested knowledge and skill of specific learning outcomes is often considered essential for some purposes like awarding advanced placement credit for a course and sometimes as a diploma requirement.

Some selective institutions also use tests of this type for admissions requirements, but more commonly, tests of general skills and abilities such as those in the last column of Fig. 7.2 are used to supplement the student's grade record. Most of those listed have been frequently represented in admissions tests. For example, reading comprehension and word knowledge are often used together in a test of verbal reasoning or verbal comprehension. These general skills and abilities have been commonly identified in factorial studies. All are represented in Carroll's (1993) Structure of Cognitive Abilities.[3] The specific achievements in the second column and the general abilities in the third column are often closely related, although the former represent knowledge structures in a particular subject, whereas the latter are better viewed as more widely applicable cognitive process structures (Cole, 1984; Messick, 1984).

---

[3]The names here are generally similar but not exactly the same as those used by Carroll (1993). For example, he uses *lexical knowledge*, whereas we use the more common *word knowledge*.

Most college courses call for either verbal proficiency (e.g., literature, history, languages), or numeric proficiency (e.g., engineering, science, business), or, more likely, developed abilities in both areas. As shown by Ramist, Lewis, and McCamley (1990), these two abilities correlate well with grades in a wide range of courses. This finding is so prevalent that a verbal test and a quantitative test of some type are the constructs most commonly included in admissions testing programs.[4]

There is some variety of constructs, of course, within the verbal and quantitative domains. An important decision is whether to measure skills that are more directly related to the student's specific prior coursework (e.g., knowledge of algebra or English grammar) or skills like quantitative reasoning, reading comprehension, and writing that are applicable to a broader range of academic work. The choice among such constructs may have some effect on the predictive characteristics of the test, but the broader systemic consequences of using one type of construct or another may be more subtle and more profound. Such construct choices also raise a fairness issue because they may well make a consequential difference in the mean scores of women and men. The same principle holds in evaluating any alternate constructs that may be otherwise more or less equally valid.

Despite much research over many years, the effort to find other measures that would improve college grade prediction has been largely unsuccessful. For example, in a longitudinal study of success in college, Willingham (1985) examined more than 100 different types of information in college application folders and found that the most useful additional measures improved the prediction of 4-year scholarship to only .61 from the correlation of .57 based on high school rank and the verbal and math scores on the SAT. Other measures are tried, of course; two cases are interesting and useful to mention.

On several occasions in earlier years the College Board offered a writing sample in its Admissions Testing Program. Those early efforts often foundered, partly because the writing sample did not demonstrably improve grade prediction, and partly for practical reasons—the test was costly and difficult to administer, and evidently not often used by colleges (French, 1966). The College Board now has a writing test (SAT II: Writing) in much more extensive use than was the case 30 years ago. Today the rationale for requiring such a test is more likely to stress the obvious relevance and

---

[4]Programs using a mathematics test and a verbal test (either reasoning or English skills) include SAT Reasoning, American College Test, GMAT, and GRE General Test. The MCAT included both types of constructs until 1991 when Writing was added and Quantitative was dropped as a separate measure.

importance of writing in academic work. What about abilities that are altogether different? The College Board offered a Spatial Relations test for many years, from the 1930s to 1958. The test was used mainly by engineering schools, but was eventually dropped because it failed to provide enough uniquely useful predictive information to a sufficient number of institutions (Angoff, 1971a).

These two cases show interesting differences and similarities. Writing and spatial relations are clearly different with respect to the relative mean performance of women and men (see Table 3.1; and, in the *Supplement,* Table S-1.) In fact, these two tests stand almost at opposite poles in providing women and men an opportunity to show their strengths. That difference is obvious now, but was apparently not given much weight decades ago when decisions to offer or drop these two tests were debated. As for similarity, both tests made marginal contributions to verbal and math scores in predicting freshman grade average, yet they represented developed skills that were highly relevant for some, perhaps many students.

Systemic Consequences.   We referred earlier to two validity considerations in justifying the choice of constructs in test design: One was evidence that the construct serves the immediate purpose of the test and another was the systemic consequences of using the test. The preceding discussion emphasizing prediction has dealt mainly with the immediate purpose. Systemic consequences include future educational and social effects as well as effects that work backward to influence examinees, teachers, and others who are in some way concerned with or affected by the testing process. It is useful to think of such influence as the "washback effect," as it has been called in language assessment literature (Alderson & Wall, 1993; Messick, 1996).

The future effects of using a particular type of test may be quite separate from and just as important as its immediate use; for example, in selecting students or deciding who has reached a standard of proficiency. Longer term considerations sometimes receive scant attention because there is no easy way of evaluating such effects. There may be no good criteria (Guion, 1974) or the criteria normally available may reflect short-term or overly narrow concerns. For example, Willingham (1974b) outlined several aspects of performance in graduate school, widely considered to be very important (e.g., teaching skill, independent research, professional contributions), but seldom represented formally in evaluating either student performance or admission measures. The short- versus long-term consequence of using different mathematics constructs in college admissions tests provides an example. The criterion of immediate interest tends to favor a short-term evaluation as to what type of math test might best predict freshman grades. The long-term consideration that is likely to be more critical to an academic discipline and a professional field is whether a generally applicable mathematical proficiency is being encouraged and developed. We return to this problem later.

The possibility of cognitive differences being manifested in different ways by different examinees is another way of thinking about alternate constructs that may have important systemic consequences. For example, Linn (1992) suggested that women do relatively better in scientific reasoning that involves "integrated understanding" based on complex realistic problems rather than on discrete skills and knowledge that depend more on prior interest and familiarity. Similarly, Gordon (in press) suggested that fair tests need to reflect the diversity of a pluralistic society and should provide examinees with optional assessments that reflect the experiences and perspectives of the individual. Both writers argue the superior validity of these approaches on educational grounds as well as fairness. Such ideas deserve serious exploration. As always, validity is the ultimate criterion against which alternate measures need to be evaluated. Any assessment that plays an important role in education must be seen as useful, fair, and practical.

The systemic consequence of greatest concern in recent years is the backward-working influence of tests. The assessment reform movement is principally dedicated to enhancing the beneficial influence of all tests on student learning, teaching, and educational practice in general (Resnick & Resnick, 1992; Shepard, 1992). A critical question is whether admissions tests should lean toward measures of common, standards-based outcomes of secondary education or more general measures of developed ability that are less likely to raise fairness issues related to curriculum variations from school to school (i.e., the types of tests listed in Columns 2 and 3, respectively, of Fig. 7.2). For some tests the washback effect may be a principal purpose of the assessment. Baker (1994) recently described, for example, the development of an end-of-course performance test to measure "deep understanding" of American history that would have a demonstrable beneficial effect on teaching and learning in the classroom.

The assessment reform movement has focused special attention on the need for more realistic free-response assessment formats. The following section examines what we know of the female–male performance differentials that may be associated with different types of free-response assessments. But first, we conclude the present discussion with an empirical illustration of how much effect the choice of different knowledge and skill can have on the relative test performance of women and men.

Effects of Construct Choice on Gender Difference

Imagine this situation. A school board has decided to develop a new school-leaving examination to ensure that all graduates meet minimum standards. The board easily agrees on the first essential; namely, that the content of the test must be relevant to the community's views as to the most important educational outcomes for the school. This illustration will serve its purpose by focusing only on the immediate issue as to what broad areas of knowledge and skill ought to be represented. Other questions will be debated, of course, on how to ensure that the specific design and use of the test will promote effective teaching and learning.

The board agrees that including a pair of tests will provide some balance, but still contain costs. Further, the board feels that for a student to be denied graduation, the student would have to score below an acceptable level of proficiency on *both* tests. It is understood that students will have to meet the other usual graduation requirements as to course credits, grade average, attendance, and so on. After some discussion, four alternate designs are proposed, each based on a different rationale and a different pair of tests. Each design has supporters, who argue as follows.

Design 1: Mathematics and Science. Like it or not, our future well-being is dependent on continued growth and development through technology. In order for the community and the country to compete, it is essential that students attain a minimum level of competence in math and science.

Design 2: History and Science. Yes, technology is essential to our future, but another critical need is to avoid destroying our environment or ourselves. It is essential to profit from past mistakes and to learn how to live together. History and science is a better combination.

Design 3: Reading and Mathematics. Many students forget most of the facts they learn in high school. The main objective is to be sure they develop a love for reading and appreciation of numbers—both important intellectual skills in dealing with complex issues.

Design 4: Reading and Writing. The reality is that most people make practically no use of math, and they do not read or write very well. Almost all jobs and essential adult responsibilities still require reading and writing. If there is a minimum educational requirement, those two skills define it.

One of these arguments, we assume, will carry the day. The four designs are based on quite different constructs that typically show somewhat different patterns of performance by female and male 12th graders. What differential effect might we expect these designs to have on the gender balance among those students *not* granted a diploma? The answer would depend, of course, on the particular tests that were developed and the detailed curriculum-based specifications that would justify the immediate use intended. But we can get some idea of how many women and men might meet such graduation standards by examining data from national assessments that included tests of this general character. In order to make comparable comparisons of the four designs, we assume arbitrarily that the minimum educational standard set for each test has the effect of identifying the lowest 10% of all seniors on that particular test. The issue is not how many fail but the relative failure rate of women and men. Results are shown in Table 7.1.

The first three lines of the table show three statistical characteristics that largely determine how many females and males will fail, that is, fall in the bottom 10% on both tests. These are: D, the mean gender difference; SDR, the differential variability of female and male scores; and r, the correlation between the scores of the two tests. The key number is "F/M Failing," the ratio of females to males among the failures.

Design 1, based on math and science, identifies almost a third more women failures than men. Moving from Design 1 to Design 4 identifies a progressively larger proportion of male failures. The change is due first to relatively more score variability for males in Design 2 compared to Design 1. Greater male variability places more males at the bottom. Then there is a shift in Designs 3 and 4 to tests on which females tend to score higher. In Design 4 the F/M ratio indicates three times as many men failing as women. Design 4 identifies fewer failures overall than do the other designs because the writing and reading tests are less highly correlated than the other pairs, so fewer students score low on both tests.[5]

The illustration makes a simple but important point about test design. Different construct choices, each based on plausible rationales, can have quite different outcomes for particular groups of examinees. Is each outcome correct and fair, given the rationale? Perhaps, but if the school board had an advance opportunity to examine such different results, it would surely engage in serious discussion as to which outcome seems most comparable to other known facts about the performance of young women and men in secondary school, and how different types of school-leaving examinations might differentially affect their behavior and learning in high school or in the years immediately following. Again, validity and fairness issues arise

---

[5]In Table 7.1, the reading–writing data came from 1992 NAEP; the other data came from 1992 NELS. Because NAEP is designed for group assessment, the correlation of .42 between reading and writing is lower than would be expected, but this fact should not greatly affect the proportion of females and males in the lower tail.

TABLE 7.1

Four Hypothetical Secondary School Leaving Requirements—Effects on the Ratio of Females and Males (F/M) Failing to Graduate

	Graduation Requirements Based on			
	1. Math & Science	2. History & Science	3. Reading & Math	4. Reading & Writing
Test characteristics				
Mean D	−.17	−.21	.09	.43
Mean SDR	.95	.93	.93	.96
r between measures	.77	.76	.71	.42
Outcome effects				
% Failing	4.9	5.0	4.8	3.2
F/M Failing	1.31	1.04	.78	.34

Note. In each of the four cases, "failures" were those students who scored in the bottom 10% on both proficiencies.

partly from what we put in the test and partly from what we choose not to measure—either because it is impossible to do so or because, for practical reasons, we cannot include everything we might like to measure.

These questions properly arise at the point of test design, but answers depend heavily on intended use and the consequences of use. Are these mainly measurement decisions? Hardly. They largely turn on educational philosophy, social and political attitudes, and personal values. On the other hand, it is certainly a measurement responsibility to engage these issues with users in order to understand and evaluate such implications of test design. Careful consideration of fairness issues in the design of *The Praxis Series: Professional Assessments for Beginning Teachers*™ is a good example of this principle (Dwyer, 1993; Dwyer & Ramsey, 1995).

Summary: Topic 1

Choosing what constructs to measure is the first important decision in the assessment process. This section considers the implications of that decision for gender fairness in light of different patterns of performance by women and men on tests measuring different knowledge and skills as was illustrated in chapter 3.

Several important aspects of construct choice were discussed. Validity in relation to function is the overarching technical criterion of quality that justifies the use of any test, but tests can have systemic effects that go beyond their immediate purpose. Typically, tests are intended to measure only part of the constructs of interest, and to be used with other measures. It is on the basis of all such measures used in making an educational decision that one judges how adequately the relevant knowledge and skills are represented. Choosing test constructs involves not only selecting the general types of knowledge and skills that are most relevant, but also developing detailed content specifications.

All of these aspects of construct choice may have fairness implications if they result in women and men scoring differently without valid reasons. A hypothetical situation involving alternate school-leaving examinations was used to illustrate differential outcomes of testing that are possible for women and men even when each of the alternate choices of constructs seems plausible from an educational perspective.

Deciding how constructs are to be assessed is also a measurement issue with broader potential consequences. If the assessment format can change the nature of the construct being measured, then construct choice can be partly a matter of format choice. We move now to that aspect of test design and examine the potential effects of format choice on gender differences in the following two sections. Topic 2 examines gender differences and construct differences that might be associated with different free-response formats; Topic 3 examines possible gender differences and construct differences on MC and FR versions of tests that differ only with respect to the format.

GENDER DIFFERENCES
ON FREE-RESPONSE MEASURES

We have suggested that fairness in test design is mainly a question of whether examinees have comparable opportunity to demonstrate knowledge and skills that are relevant to the purpose of the test. Choice of format can affect that opportunity for two reasons. One reason is that a particular format may cause a test to be more difficult for some examinees in irrelevant ways. Another important consideration is that knowledge and skill, as we have emphasized, are not independent of format. Indeed, a major reason for the burgeoning interest in alternate assessment formats in recent years is the reasonable assumption that additional formats may be essential in order to broaden the nature and complexity of constructs we are presently measuring.

Here our interest is the influence of format on gender fairness. To that end, we examine available data in an effort to shed some additional light on when and why women and men perform differently on free-response formats. This will involve comparing mean scores of women and men on many different sets of free-response data. In all cases we use performance on MC tests in the same subject as a baseline. Throughout this section, the search is for gender-based format effects. In all cases, *format effect* means simply that the average score of females, relative to males, varies across formats. On a history test, for example, we estimate a format effect by comparing D, the standard mean difference for women and men, on the two sections of the test that are based on FR and MC questions.

$$\text{Format effect} = D_{FR} - D_{MC}$$

Thus, a positive format effect means only that women scored better, relative to men, on the FR test than on the MC test, and a negative format effect means that women did relatively better on the MC test. Format effect says nothing about which group tends to score higher in history.

Throughout we are looking for patterns in the results that may help us better understand why women and men sometimes score differently, and whether format effects are more likely due to aspects of the assessment that are relevant or irrelevant to what we are trying to measure. Often, the effort to explain gender differences across test formats involves reflecting and seeking evidence as to how different free-response formats may act to change the construct being measured.

The data reported in chapter 3 (especially Table 3.3) appear to strengthen the assumption that test format plays a role in observed gender differences, but also suggest that the situation is complex, due to the unusual pattern of results from subject to subject. In science and geopolitical subjects, women tended to score relatively better on the FR than on the MC portions of AP examinations. In mathematics and language-related subjects, there tended to be no such format effect.

In chapter 5, Cole gets into this issue, speculating to the extent that the data permitted on possible reasons for the pattern of format-related gender differences across subjects and on possible assessment implications. Here we broaden the question to the gender fairness of alternate forms of assessment generally, and undertake more detailed analyses on a broader range of available data. Later we address a closely related but more specific question: Is the multiple choice format, per se, more difficult for women than for men?

There has been little systematic analysis of gender differences on different FR formats, probably because widespread interest in alternate assessment formats is relatively recent. Various writers have used one of two expressions: FR (free-response) or CR (constructed response). We use FR and CR interchangeably here as terms of convenience to cover a variety of assessment alternatives to multiple-choice tests that require the examinee to pick the best answer from several possible responses provided. Study of the topic is complicated by several problems. Free-response assessment has multiple meanings, manifested in a bewildering variety of assessment techniques. Furthermore, fairness in FR assessment can raise quite different issues, depending on the character and the purpose of the assessment. Finally, data that would be useful in addressing the topic are in short supply. Some comment on the variety and purpose of FR assessment will help to frame the data analyses and discussion that follow.

Variety in Free-Response Assessment

There have been several strands in the development of FR alternatives to the now familiar multiple-choice test. Some have deep roots, especially as represented in the work of John Dewey (1902) and the progressive educators early in this century. Nontraditional educators in more recent years (Chickering, 1969; Cross, Valley, & Associates, 1974; Keeton & Associates, 1976) have championed an educational reform in that same tradition, with emphasis on assessment practices that serve primarily to empower students and to help them realize their personal learning goals. Assessment to this end comes in various formats; for example, products, performances, work records, portfolios, evidence of personal or interpersonal development, and so on. In this tradition, the validity of the assessment process is often based more on detailed standards and procedures for individualized expert judgment of competence (Whitaker, 1989) than on the technical aspects of educational measurement that are normally required to produce scores sufficiently comparable for purposes of public accountability.

Assessment reform is a related movement over the past two or three decades that has encouraged alternative assessment formats and placed special emphasis on certain key features: developed competence rather than aptitude for learning (McClelland, 1973), demonstration of competence in actual performance (Alverno College Faculty, 1994), criterion standards rather than normative standards (Glaser, 1963), and, more recently, cognitive analysis of proficiency (Gardner, 1983; Mislevy, 1993, 1995; Sternberg, 1985; Tyler & White, 1979). A principal goal of assessment reform has been the improvement of instruction and learning outcomes. Free-response formats have been manifested especially in criterion-referenced tasks, simulations, portfolios, and performance standards.

A more recent but closely related development is the standards movement, which has swept the country because of concern for the improvement of education (Goals 2000, 1994) and the hope that improved, performance-based assessment will provide the needed lever (Baker et al., 1993). Principal goals are improved learning and improved accountability through improved assessment. These objectives are partly reflected in an aphorism congenial to many educators, "You get what you assess …. You do not get what you do not assess" (Resnick & Resnick, 1992, p. 59). Similarly, the goal is to produce tests worth teaching to, and tests on which hard work by students and teachers yields results befitting the effort.

Federal, state, and private agencies have been extremely active—defining educational and assessment goals (Advisory Committee on Testing in Chapter 1, 1993), funding major research and development programs such as the Center for Research on Evaluation, Standards, and Student Testing (1995) and organizing innovative state assessment programs. Among the earliest and best known of these state programs was Vermont's portfolio assessment, which has illustrated both the promise and the problems of alternate assessment formats (Koretz, Stecher, & Deibert, 1992; Koretz, Stecher, Klein, & McCaffrey, 1994).

Performance assessment has been the centerpiece of these developments. This new assessment has been referred to variously as alternative, authentic, and performance based. It refers to exercises that require examinees to demonstrate what they know and can do in applied and contextualized FR exercises. There are many varieties of such exercises: complex problems requiring detailed steps or explanations, others calling for brief written answers, single words or numbers, graph constructions, multiple-document problems, artwork, lengthy essays—even experiments with equipment (for examples, see Baker, Aschbacher, Niemi, & Sato, 1992; Barton & Coley, 1993). The common attributes or elements of well-developed performance-based assessment were characterized by Baker et al. (1993, p. 1211) as follows:

1. Uses open-ended tasks.
2. Focuses on higher order or complex skills.
3. Employs context sensitive strategies.
4. Often uses complex problems requiring several types of performance and significant student time.
5. Consists of either individual or group performance.
6. May involve a significant degree of student choice.

Baker et al. (1993) described these attributes as deriving from two major sources: research-based concepts of cognitive psychology and the ideals of teaching practice. Some writers argue that performance assessment should be based on criterion-relevant, authentic tasks (J. Frederiksen & Collins, 1989; N. Frederiksen, 1984; Wiggins, 1989, 1993); others recommend that a more theoretically based construct will prove more generalizable and more educationally useful (Messick, 1992). There is also debate on the desirability and the effectiveness of different ways of linking tests to the educational process (e.g., Cizek, 1993a, 1993b; Shepard, 1991, 1993).

However, in discussing the move to performance-based assessment, Baker et al. (1993) also emphasized, "What is driving all this activity is a rapidly changing policy context that promises to raise the achievement of American students to internationally competitive standards" (p. 1210). Regardless of the conceptual foundation, a principal goal of current assessment reform in practice is to somehow achieve a closer match between the curriculum, the actual learning experiences of students, and the demands of assessment exercises.

A final major strand in the development of FR assessment is measurement technology. Technology is not intended as an answer to assessment reform. Technology certainly cannot alone deliver assessment reform objectives, although it can help. Measurement specialists are motivated to utilize new technologies because of two considerations. First, FR exercises are difficult and expensive to score. This characteristic necessarily imposes limits on the application of FR questions in major testing programs. Technology provides the most likely means of designing and delivering some alternate types of assessment that would otherwise be impractical or too costly in large programs. An equally important consideration is the need for objective measurement procedures to ensure standards of technical quality—in the face of new demands for flexible, customized assessment. It is only through high technical quality that test producers can deliver the level of score comparability that examinees and test users expect in large, high-stakes testing programs.

Three types of technical development show particular promise for expanding the range of alternate assessment formats. One is the development of new varieties of "constructed-response" tests items, especially types of FR exercises that can be presented to examinees and scored automatically by computer (Bennett & Ward, 1993). Another is the development of "natural language" computer software programs that are capable of recognizing and scoring the variety and the degrees of correctness of FR answers to complex questions (Kaplan & Burstein, 1994). Finally, there is considerable promise in new computer-based simulations of complex performance tasks that can be administered and evaluated electronically as reliably as would be possible by expert judges, although in much greater detail (Bejar & Braun, 1994). The common objective in all of these developments is to carry out complex assessments in ways that are practical and also maintain high measurement standards of validity.

Fairness Issues

The first point we wanted to make is now obvious: There is enormous diversity in FR assessment—diversity in both the character and the intended purpose of the assessment. One promise of performance-based and other forms of FR exercises for fairer tests lies in their potential—through this rich diversity—for making more realistic tests that are more directly connected with learning outcomes in a diverse society. This potential gain in fairness touches all examinees.

Our second point follows naturally from the first. In the face of this diversity in assessment alternatives, it is no surprise to detect a wide range of potential test fairness issues. For example, depending on the purpose of the assessment, the primary fairness concern may be whether the assessment serves the learning interest of a particular individual, or whether two assessments yield comparable results, or whether an assessment program matches an instructional program, or whether an assessment program that matches an instructional program in theory will actually represent fair opportunity in practice for a given group of examinees in a particular school. These different fairness issues have not gone unnoticed. Some writers have emphasized systemic threats to test equity. Darling-Hammond (1994) argued, for example, that equitable performance assessments depend as much on how they are used in school reform as how well they are designed. Similarly, Madaus (1994) cautioned that testing programs have many ways to misfire and, over time, create inequity inadvertently.

Some writers have discussed in depth the traditional measurement standards for test fairness that alternate forms of assessment must address, as well as new concerns to which this broadened character and mission of assessment give rise (Linn, 1994; Linn, Baker, & Dunbar, 1991; Linn & Burton, 1994; Messick, 1994a; Rothman, 1994; Shavelson, Baxter, & Gao, 1993). Others have discussed at a very practical level the problems posed by performance assessment despite its attractions (Breland, 1996; Mehrens, 1992; Swanson, Norman, & Linn, 1995). Some of those issues pertaining to test development and administration were discussed in chapter 6. In this section we focus on fairness aspects of FR assessment that pertain to test design—mainly because there is yet only limited experience and data that bear on fairness in the use of alternate forms of assessment.

In test design, we have differentiated two main threats to fairness. One threat is the inclusion of elements, such as a particular test format, in which performance depends partly on skills not actually relevant to the construct being assessed. Another is the failure to represent important knowledge and skills pertinent to the purpose of the test. Different performance tasks in the same subject area will often, if not typically, demand different knowledge and skills; indeed, that is a principal rationale and benefit in broadening the range of assessment alternatives. The fairness problem arises from the fact that different individuals or groups have different interests and learning experiences and may therefore score somewhat differently, depending on which assessment tasks are chosen from among the numerous reasonable alternatives.

In constructing an individual test form, test developers must choose particular FR exercises. Exercises will necessarily vary somewhat in content, and individual examinees will be differentially advantaged. The potential fairness problems posed by those content variations were discussed in the previous chapter. The effect can be large if only a few exercises are included in a given assessment (Linn & Burton, 1994; Shavelson et al., 1993). However, before choosing any individual exercises, a general test design has to be established. Should the testing program include FR exercises, and, if so, what type—short answer, essay, lab experiment, listening or speaking task, or detailed problem solution? What effect might such choice of format have on the construct measured and on the relative performance of women and men?

We have now come, full circle, to the objective stated at the outset of this section. Can additional analysis of available data improve our understanding of gender difference and similarity on different types of FR assessment? Will that lead to a better appreciation of the fairness implications of decisions in test design? To this end we need to control, as much as possible, differences in results that may be due to variation in other factors—especially cohorts and samples. Accordingly, in searching for useful data, we have concentrated our attention on broadly representative groups of students near the end of secondary school.

As we know from chapter 3, some subjects and skill areas show significant differences in mean score level for women and men. Consequently we have looked for test data where there is available both FR and MC data for the same samples of women and men on the same general subject or skill. By comparing gender difference for FR and MC tests on the same examinees and the same subject matter, we focus more sharply on the possible effects of format. The challenge is to understand how a different format has changed the construct tested in ways that tend to favor either women or men. Within these guidelines, we were able to collect a considerable amount of pertinent data for further analysis. The following sections compare results for FR and MC tests in three statewide programs, several national assessments, three foreign countries, and the AP program.

Three State Assessment Programs

Through most of two presidential administrations, educational reform has been fueled and guided, in considerable part, by the idea that the health of the schools and the country can be enhanced if clearer standards of pupil achievement are articulated, assessed, and accounted. Federal initiatives have encouraged these connections and their implementation (Goals 2000, 1994; National Council on Education Standards and Testing [NCES], 1992). Meanwhile, considerable grass-roots interest and efforts have resulted in a number of newly designed state assessment programs. These various programs have typically placed at least some emphasis on performance assessment and have attempted to link that assessment deliberately with curriculum and instructional goals (Barton & Coley, 1993; Linn, Kiplinger, Chapman, & LeMahieu, 1991).

State assessment programs vary a great deal, and at this writing relatively few meet the particular needs of this analysis. Some programs are limited and not very informative; others are still in a developmental stage; in still others data are restricted to small nonrepresentative samples. Some of the more interesting programs do not include needed information, such as a MC comparative baseline or gender identification. We were able to obtain three pertinent sets of data from Georgia, Kansas, and Kentucky. Table 7.2 summarizes mean gender differences on the MC and the FR portions of the several subjects included in each assessment program.

Values for the standard mean difference, D, between the test performance of females and males for the MC tests (first column) show a pattern generally similar to that evident in the 12th-grade national data in chapter 3 (Table 3.1).[6] The average gender difference for the 12 MC tests was near zero. Gender differences for the FR assessments tended to favor the women. This format effect is much like that reported for the AP examinations in chapter 3. The last column shows that the health test in Georgia was the sole instance among these 12 assessments in which the women did not do at least slightly better on the FR than on the MC portion. Why health is an exception is not clear, and information regarding the content of the assessment was limited (Bunch, 1993). Some data on social studies tests in chapter 3 suggested that women tend to have more factual knowledge about health than do men. If so, such a difference might show up more readily on a MC test.

---

[6]Test sections based on FR items are often considerably less reliable than those based on MC items, but the analysis of Mazzeo et al. (1993) suggests relatively little effect of lower reliability on D.

TABLE 7.2

**Standard Gender Differences on Multiple-Choice and Free-Response Tests
at the High School Level in Three State Assessment Programs**

Assessment		MC	FR	FR–MC
		\multicolumn{3}{c}{Standard Mean Difference, D^a}		
Georgia	English	.33	.44	.11
Grade 11	Social studies	.02	.09	.07
	Math	.08	.10	.02
	Science	−.03	.07	.10
	Health	.33	.17	−.16
Kansas	Reading	.10	.32	.22
Grade 12	Math	−.22	.14	.36
	Science[b]	−.19	.19	.38
Kentucky	Reading	.06	.30	.24
Grade 12	Social studies	.02	.14	.12
	Math	−.02	.04	.06
	Science	−.11	.07	.18

[a]Positive values of FR–MC indicate that females, compared to males, do relatively better on free-response than on multiple-choice questions. Standard errors of D for MC and FR ranged from .01 to .02, except for Georgia where standard errors were .03 to .04.

[b]Average result for two forms.

Note. Data were provided by Georgia State Assessment Program, Kansas State Assessment Program, and Kentucky Instructional Results Information System.

A more interesting question is whether there is any test format effect across states that might be associated with a different approach to FR assessment. Some clues may lie in the numbers in the last column in Table 7.2 (FR –MC) for those subjects in which there are similar tests in the three states; that is, math, science, and reading (or English). The relative perform‐ ance of females and males in those subjects was generally similar on the MC and FR portions of the Georgia assessment. The Kentucky assessment showed slightly more format effect favoring females on FR exercises than was true in Georgia. There was a notably larger format effect in the same direction on the math and science assessments in Kansas. Is there something about the test design in these latter two state assessments that might account for the different format effect?

The math FR exercises in Kansas and Kentucky look generally similar. In both cases there is emphasis on application of math principles in context, and the test instructions direct examinees to demonstrate understanding, show applications, and so on (Kansas State Board of Education, 1993; Kentucky Department of Education, 1995). A possible underlying differ‐ ence is the form of the desired response from the examinee. Released items from the two state programs appear to place somewhat more stress on the use of graphics in the Kentucky assessment (e.g., "Make a table or graph.")

> In Sylvia's math class the grading is as shown:
>
> | If Average Score is: | Then Grade is: |
> |---|---|
> | 90 or higher | A |
> | 80-89 | B |
> | 70-79 | C |
> | 60-69 | D |
> | Less than 60 | F |
>
> Sylvia's test scores on the first four 100-point tests given in class were 84%, 91%, 90% and 88%. On the last 100-point examination given before class grades are assigned, Sylvia received a 94.
>
> **(A)** Based on all test scores, what class grade would you assign Sylvia?
>
> **(B)** Give your reasons for the grade you assigned. Discuss or show why you chose to give Sylvia this grade.

FIG. 7.3. Illustrative item from the Kansas Mathematics Assessment. Reprinted with permission of the Center for Educational Testing and Evaluation, University of Kansas, Lawrence, Kansas.

and more emphasis on narrative explanation in the Kansas assessment (e.g., "Give your reasons ... Discuss."). Figure 7.3 illustrates such a narrative feature in a mathematics item from a recent Kansas assessment.

This item is context rich and has more than one possible answer, depending on how one views the relevance of the mean grade versus the median grade, or perhaps extra weight on the final test. The item not only calls for some understanding of math principles as they might apply to a concrete situation; it also calls for some ability to articulate the reasoning. Such qualities might account for the higher performance of females on the FR compared to the MC portion of the Kansas mathematics assessment—a result not typical in mathematics. On the other hand, it seems wiser to regard such results as illustrative rather than the basis for conclusions about format effects. As we saw in the previous chapter, a pattern of gender difference or similarity can be strongly influenced by the character of the particular FR exercises when only a few exercises can be chosen for a given test.

National Assessments

In the past few years NAEP has released data on three assessments that included substantial portions of FR exercises as well as an MC section. These

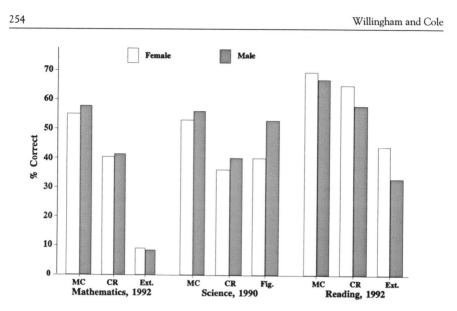

FIG. 7.4. Average "percentage correct" for female and male 12th-grade students on different question formats in NAEP Assessments in mathematics, science, and reading. Formats: MC—multiple choice; CR—constructed response; Ext.—extended response; FIG.—figural response. Standard errors for percentage correct in MC sections was about 0.5; other sections, less than 1.0.

were the 1992 Mathematics Assessment (Dossey, Mullis, & Jones, 1993), the 1992 Reading Assessment (Langer et al., 1995), and the 1990 Science Assessment (Jones, Mullis, Raizen, Weiss, & Weston, 1992). The average performance level for 12th-grade females and males on different question formats within each of these assessments is shown in Fig. 7.4.

The format labels in this figure are those used in the NAEP reports, where *constructed response* (CR) is the term of choice rather than free response. That label was not used in an entirely consistent manner, however, in the various subject assessments. In the mathematics assessment, CR typically meant a number or one-word answer; in reading, CR usually meant two or three sentences; and in science, some of both, but generally quite brief answers. In mathematics, an extended response could be a list of steps or two or three sentences; in reading, an extended response was perhaps several times that many sentences. These distinctions may be important if, as these data suggest, the amount of writing makes a difference. Questions in a figural format involved a qualitatively different response. As Fig. 7.5 illustrates, such items required the examinee to draw an arrow, a line, or some such mark on a figure.

Instead of the standard mean difference, *D*, that we have typically used, results in Fig. 7.4 are reported in the "average % correct" that was used by NAEP. As an additional framework for interpreting the magnitude of the

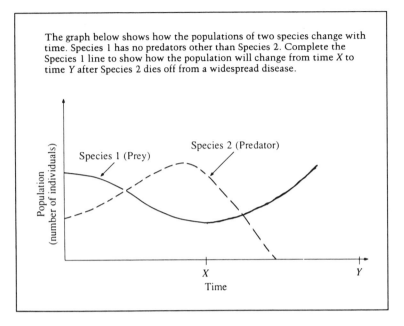

The graph below shows how the populations of two species change with time. Species 1 has no predators other than Species 2. Complete the Species 1 line to show how the population will change from time X to time Y after Species 2 dies off from a widespread disease.

FIG. 7.5. Illustration of a figural response item from the NAEP 1990 Science Assessment. Source: Jones et al. (1992), p. 42. Used with permission.

differences in Fig. 7.4, it is useful to recall that the standard mean gender differences reported earlier (Table 3.1) for these particular NAEP assessments in mathematics, science, and reading were –.11, –.24, and .26, respectively. Three aspects of the results in Fig. 7.4 are noteworthy.

In mathematics and science, where the constructed response was typically limited to a very short answer, the use of CR versus MC format made no difference in the pattern of female and male performance. In the reading assessment, where FR meant writing, a more extensive FR was associated with a larger differential in the percentage of correct responses favoring females (i.e., +5 percentage points for CR, +9% percentage points for Extended Response compared to MC). When free response meant a figural response (in science), there was a 10% gender differential in the opposite direction. In this case males had relatively *more* correct responses on CR than on MC items.

NELS Performance Assessment. A special School Effects Study was undertaken in conjunction with the 1988 NELS. The school study included performance assessments in science and mathematics (Pollack & Rock, in press). Both MC and CR measures were administered in 247 schools. Each CR section included four questions with multiple parts that were scored analytically. That is, examinees were given a specific number of points for different elements of correctness in their responses.

The standard mean difference, D, for the MC and CR sections were $-.20$ and $-.21$ in mathematics; $-.21$ and $-.38$ in science.[7] As we have found in most other sets of data, there was no evidence of a format effect in mathematics. The data do show a format effect in science, but opposite to that observed in the state assessment data and in the AP results reported in chapter 3. As was the case with the figural response items in the NAEP Science Assessment, mean scores on this NELS Science Assessment also favored males somewhat more on the CR section than the MC section. Of the four CR exercises in science, the largest gender difference ($D = -.53$) occurred on a question that required drawing diagrams of solar and lunar eclipses and explaining why the earth shadow of the latter is larger than that of the former. On these two national assessments—NAEP and NELS—where CR test material in science favored males, both involved figural response tasks. The common element in this format effect appears to be spatial and/or mechanical skills, areas in which males tend to do well (see discussion in chapter 2 and Table 3.1).

Such a connection was also demonstrated in an analysis of the original NELS Science Test, which consisted of 27 MC items (Hamilton et al., 1995). These authors found that performance of 10th graders on the MC science items could be described on the basis of three factors: basic knowledge and reasoning, quantitative science, and spatial-mechanical reasoning. The spatial-mechanical factor was based on "items that require comprehension of maps, diagrams of physical systems, and reasoning about them" (p. 561). Gender was the best predictor of performance on the spatial-mechanical factor (a correlation of .48) but it showed little relation to performance on the other two factors (.02 and .07, respectively).

In their review of gender differences in spatial ability, Linn and Petersen (1986) did not find consistent evidence of a direct connection between spatial skills and science achievement. These recent data suggest, however, that over-or underrepresentation of spatial-mechanical material should be carefully reviewed as a possible fairness issue in the design of science tests—in either MC or FR format.

---

[7]The Ns for females and males were 1,091 and 1,141, respectively. In the CR math section, three exercises involved figures of the type often found on MC math tests, although none called for a figural response nor appeared to require any visualization.

International Findings

As the United States has experimented with alternate forms of assessment and gradually introduced more FR material into testing programs, other countries have tended to move in the opposite direction. Historically, educational systems in other countries have relied almost exclusively on essays and other FR forms of examination questions. The introduction of some MC testing over the past 20 years has raised test format as a fairness issue and also provided an additional data source of interest. We focus here on data from three countries where it was possible to obtain test data for females and males on both MC and FR tests in the same subject.

A change in the General Certificate of Education (GCE) examinations in England in the late 1970s attracted considerable attention. It was during that period that a MC section was introduced in most of the exams; it was also during that period that the relative level of performance for women and men shifted (Murphy, 1980; Wood, 1978). Since 1951 there have been roughly the same number of women and men taking the more common "O level" exams. The proportion of women taking the less common and more demanding "A level" increased from 31% in 1951 to 43% in 1977. In every year during that period, save 1977, a higher proportion of women passed at both levels. Murphy (1980) accounted for the higher mean scores of women as follows:

> It has been argued in the past that the superior female pass rate at "O" level has been achieved because of the greater maturity of girls at this age .... The higher female pass rate at "A" level has sometimes been explained by there being a smaller and more select group of girls who stay on at school to do "A" levels. This suggestion can be supported by the fact that there has been some evidence of a narrowing of the difference between the pass rates of male and female candidates as their entry statistics have come more in line with each other. (p. 173)

Murphy went on to argue that the relatively sudden change in pass rates in the late 1970s must have come about due to the introduction of the MC portion on which males score relatively better than on the older FR exam. He illustrated such an effect with the Geography exam on which, in previous years, women and men typically had comparable pass rates. Relative to women, men gained 10% in pass rate from 1976 to 1977 when the MC portion was introduced. In 1977 the standard mean difference between female and male scores on the FR and MC portions of this examination were −.05 and −.51, respectively.

In a subsequent report, Murphy (1982) examined gender differences on 16 GCE examinations for which scores were available on MC and FR portions on which there was "a large degree of overlap in the educational skills and abilities tested" (p. 214). Standard mean differences for examinations listed under the "England" heading in Table 7.3 are based on those data. The general pattern of the results is similar to that described in chapter 3, where the performance of females and males was compared on MC and FR sections of AP examinations. Overall, males did somewhat better than females on the MC portions, and considering all of the exams together, there was no gender difference on the FR portions.

TABLE 7.3

Standard Gender Differences on Multiple-Choice (MC) and Free-Response (FR) Examinations in England, Ireland, and Queensland, Australia

| Country/Exam | Subject | D | | |
		MC	FR	FR-MC
England				
English language O	L	−.17	.27	.44
Economic history O	G	−.34	.06	.40
Geography O	G	−.44	−.08	.36
Physics O	S	−.27	−.01	.26
Economics A	G	−.15	.05	.20
Mathematics O (Modern)	M	−.31	−.13	.18
Economics O	G	−.33	−.16	.17
Religious studies O	—	.13	.30	.17
German O	L	−.02	.12	.14
English literature O	L	.11	.23	.12
Chemistry O	S	−.25	−.13	.12
Commerce O	—	−.26	−.15	.11
Mathematics O (General A)	M	−.18	−.18	.00
Statistics O	M	−.25	−.26	−.01
French O	L	.16	.12	−.04
Mathematics O (General B)	M	−.18	−.22	−.04
Mean		−.17	−.01	.16
Ireland				
Math	M	−.55	−.33	.22
English	L	−.01	.10	.11
Irish	L	.05	.15	.10
Mean		−.17	−.03	.14
Queensland				
Analyze, assess, conclude	—	−.06	.02	.08
Structure, sequence	—	−.02	−.10	−.08
Apply techniques, procedures	—	−.32	−.43	−.11
Comprehend, collect	—	−.05	−.19	−.14
Mean		−.11	−.18	−.06

Note. Standard errors for MC and FR standard differences are approximately .01 to .04 for England, .05 for Ireland, and .01 for Queensland. Data from Queensland represent average results for 1993 and 1994. The "England" data quoted are extracted from Murphy (1982) with permission.

This set of data also shows much the same pattern of format effects, subject by subject, as was noted in the AP data. With the exception of English Language, the examinations in Language (L) and Mathematics (M) tended to show little format effect; those in Geopolitics (G) and Science (S) were more likely to show relatively stronger male performance on the MC sections. Murphy (1982) proposed that the underlying explanation may be "the candidate's ability to use language" (p. 218). His reasoning was that language skill is more common in women and less needed in objective tests, but is not as likely to come differentially into play on some tests like mathematics. He noted that the test results for modern math do not quite fit that pattern, but did not comment on the results for English Language. This latter examination would presumably require language skills in both the MC and the FR test sections and would not be expected to show a format effect. The fact that it did is the main exception among the 16 GCE exams to the format-by-subject pattern that we previously observed in chapter 3.

In 1988 substantial changes in assessment occurred again in England and Wales with the introduction of the General Certificate of Secondary Education (GCSE). The GCSE includes a central examination that emphasizes criterion-referenced standards and another component based on course-work (i.e., assessment by teachers throughout the course). In their informative account of these shifts in assessment practices and test fairness debates in the United Kingdom, Gipps and Murphy (1994) described a substantial improvement in the proportion of women earning grades of A to C in English, math, and science—greater than males for the first time in 1992. On the other hand, they reported a different trend at the advanced level of the new exams where "male candidates achieved higher average grades overall and were much more likely to achieve the maximum points score used for university entrance than girls" (p. 256). Stobart, Elwood, and Quinlan (1992) described these results for individual examinations, although the findings are difficult to interpret due to changes in the examinations and the inclusion of varying proportions of teacher marks.

Table 7.3 also shows mean gender differences by MC and FR format for representative samples of secondary school students from Ireland (Bolger & Kellaghan, 1990) and Queensland (data were provided by the Board of Senior Secondary School Studies—Queensland, Australia). The Irish data show a small format effect similar to that seen in the English data—a tendency toward higher male performance on MC tests. Among the data presented here, those from Queensland are unique in one respect. The assessment is intended to evaluate the "core skills" emphasized in the curriculum, and the results are so reported, rather than according to traditional subject areas. The results show little if any format effect in the relative performance of females and males, although there was a noticeable gender difference favoring the women ($D = .36$) on an essay performance test taken by these same 12th graders. A possible explanation might be the predominant use of relatively brief free responses: "choosing a key; writing one word, a sentence, a paragraph; producing a diagram, sketch; performing a calculation" (Board of Senior Secondary School Studies, 1995). Another study (Bell & Hay, 1987) similarly showed much the same pattern of gender differences for each of three formats of the Year 12 English Language examination in Western Australia.

Advanced Placement

We first noted the differential gender difference on MC and FR formats in the analysis of AP results in Table 3.3 in chapter 3. The tendency of women to score somewhat better on AP examination questions in a FR than in a MC format comes as less of a surprise than the apparent connection of that difference with subject matter. In the 1993 AP data, gender difference varied by format mainly on tests in scientific and geopolitical subjects. We have speculated about possible reasons for that association between format effect and subject matter in the AP results, and now come back to it for a closer look.

One question that comes to mind is how stable such patterns are, so we repeated the analysis with AP data from 1994. Figure 7.6 presents two types of results for the 27 AP examinations.[8] The upper panel shows the mean difference, D, for the 27 FR sections in 1993 plotted against the D for the corresponding 27 FR sections in 1994. It is clear that the degree of gender

---

[8]Patterns of gender differences on 27 AP examinations were plotted on Fig. 7.6 as follows:

A—Math: Calculus BC	O—Macroeconomics
B—Math: Calculus AB	P—Music Theory
C—Computer Science AB	Q—Psychology
D—Computer Science A	R—History of Art
E—Physics C-Mechanics	S—Engl. Lang. & Comp.
F—Physics B	T—Engl. Lit. & Comp.
G—Physics C-Elect. & Mag.	U—French Language
H—Chemistry	V—French Literature
I—Biology	W—Spanish Language
J—U.S. History	X—Spanish Literature
K—European History	Y—German Language
L—Gov. & Politics, U.S.	Z—Latin: Virgil
M—Gov. & Politics, Comparative	Σ—Latin: Catullus-Horace
N—Microeconomics	

difference on the FR section is quite consistent from one year to the next. Figure 7.6 shows that all but 3 of the 27 examinations (G, P, and Σ) are in the band where D differs by no more than .10 from 1993 to 1994. The correlation between the 1993 Ds and the 1994 Ds for the 27 FR test sections plotted in the figure was .92. The corresponding correlation for the MC sections of these tests was similarly high.[9]

This high degree of consistency in the D values for both the MC section and the FR section suggests that we are very likely to find a similar pattern in the difference between the two (i.e., the format effect) in 1994 data as was observed in 1993 data in chapter 3. Such is the case, as we see in the bottom panel of Fig. 7.6. This plot shows the format effect for the 27 exams in 1994; that is, the gender difference on the FR versus the MC sections.

Earlier, for working purposes, we defined a consequential format effect as a difference in the D value of .10 or more. According to this rule of thumb, any test lying outside the diagonal band showed a format effect. The pattern seen here for 1994 is quite similar to the pattern for 1993 data in Table 3.3. All of the history and government exams and all of the exams in natural science show a D for the FR section that is at least .15 larger than the D for the corresponding MC section. None of the other exams show such a difference. The other two examinations in a so-called geopolitical subject (O and N, both Economics) straddle the line separating exams that do and do not show a .10 format effect. As was the case in 1993, the exams in mathematics and language largely show no format effect. Only two (Z and T) lie outside the band, and barely so.

It is worth pausing to reflect on what that consistent pattern from 1993 to 1994 does and does not mean. The external AP Development Committees in the various subject areas make few changes in the general specifications for the format of individual AP examinations from one year to the next.[10] That being the case, a stable pattern of gender differences on the MC and FR sections means that the test development staff construct items and exercises in a consistent manner from year to year, at least with respect to gender. It does not mean that the pattern shown in the lower panel of

---

[9]For comparison, the same correlation for the 27 MC sections was .97. This apparently somewhat more stable pattern of gender difference for the MC section from year to year is probably due to the higher reliability of the MC section. The average reliability of the 27 MC and FR sections in 1994 were .88 and .73, respectively. The FR estimate refers to score reliability; that is, it reflects both rating and task differences. Lower reliability as well as somewhat more yearly fluctuation of gender difference would be expected on the basis of the limited number of FR exercises (see Linn & Burton, 1994, and illustrative data in Figs. 6.5 and 6.6). The average reliability of the composite of MC and FR was .89. These averages are based on reliabilities reported by Morgan (1995).

[10]AP test specifications are described in a series of "Scoring Guides" (see, e.g., College Board, 1994b).

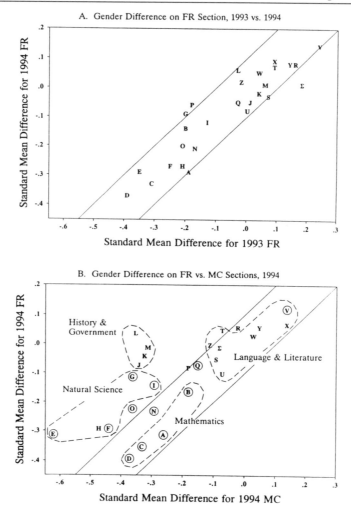

FIG. 7.6. Consistencies and inconsistencies in the pattern of standard gender differences on multiple choice (MC) and free response (FR) sections of 27 AP examinations. The 27 AP examinations are identified in footnote 9. Circled letters indicate tests that were scored analytically; others were scored holistically.

Fig. 7.6 would hold if the examinations were designed differently. We have just observed a similar pattern in the English GCE examinations, but we have also seen clear evidence in the state and national assessment data in mathematics and science that different types of FR exercises in a subject can yield different format effects.

What explains the outliers in the bottom panel of Fig. 7.6—the fact that some subjects lie within the band indicating no format effect, and others lie outside? There are several possibilities to consider. Is there a different pattern of gender differences across the two formats because the constructs are different? Or the tasks are different? Or the scoring is different? To some extent, we can examine these possibilities.

Construct Differences. We hypothesized earlier that there could be a format effect (FR–MC) in the pattern of mean gender differences if the constructs being measured were somewhat different in the two formats. One indication of whether the constructs are different is the level of the correlation between scores based on test material presented in the two formats. Morgan (1994, 1995) reported these correlations, each corrected for the fact that the FR and MC scores are not perfectly reliable. Average correlations in 1994 for the four subject clusters in Fig. 7.6 were:

History & Government	.85
Language & Literature	.85
Mathematics	.98
Natural Science	.96

Indeed, the relationship between the two exam sections is different in the four subject areas. These correlations suggest that in the mathematics and science examinations, the FR and MC sections measure quite similar constructs, but they measure somewhat different constructs—presumably complementary aspects of the prescribed syllabus—in history and government and in language and literature. The correlations corresponding to those just given were almost identical in 1993.

These correlations do not, however, fit the pattern that might be expected if construct differences alone accounted for the presence of a format effect in some subjects and not in others. The examinations in history and government as well as those in language and literature are measuring somewhat different constructs in the MC and FR sections, but the former group of tests shows a format effect and the latter group does not. Furthermore, the examinations in mathematics and natural science are both apparently measuring quite similar constructs in the MC and FR sections, yet the latter group of tests shows a format effect and the other does not.

There is further evidence to consider regarding the first two subject areas where the two formats are measuring different constructs. A format effect would come about only if the MC and FR formats measure different constructs *and* women and men score differently on the aspects that were different. Language tests measure quite different constructs—reading, writing, listening, and speaking—that cut across formats. We see in Lines 7 and

8 of Table 7.4, however, that there is no consistent gender difference on any of these skills in the highly selected AP population.

In history it is a different story. Breland et al. (1991) did a detailed study of the effect of format on gender differences in two AP History examinations. They reported that quality of writing largely accounted for the different pattern of female and male performance on the MC and FR sections. In this situation, it is unclear to what extent quality of writing is separable from proficiency in History. Our interpretation is that women did relatively better on the FR than on the MC portions of AP U.S. History partly because of superior writing and partly because the women better displayed their knowledge of history in the essay format.[11] That interpretation argues that, in this instance, writing is relevant to the construct being measured.

A notable subsidiary finding was that handwriting and neatness played no role in accounting for the women performing relatively better on the FR section than on the MC section. Such construct-irrelevant factors have long been suspected as a bias in ratings of essays that favors women, and some writers (Bolger & Kellaghan, 1990; Murphy, 1982) have cited laboratory simulation studies (Briggs, 1980; Hughes et al., 1983) as possible evidence of such a connection. The contrary finding of Breland et al. (1991) is an important result because it is based on papers rated in an actual testing program.

Task Differences. Free-response tasks may vary widely as to content or subject matter, but we are here more concerned with the nature of the response; that is, the character of the performance. Complexity, authenticity, and realism are, of course, aspects of the FR assessment exercise that attract considerable interest, although we have no data and no practical approach to studying such dimensions that are within the reasonable scope of our study. However, there are several characteristics of interest that can be examined—length in particular.

In the AP free-response assessments, length means more time and usually more writing. On seven AP exams the FR section was based largely on brief responses—short explanations, a series of steps, and so on. On 18 exams, the FR section was based largely on a smaller number of longer essays. In both types of material, slightly less than half of the exams showed a format effect. Table 7.4 offers additional comparisons for FR material *within* exami-

---

[11]Breland et al. (1991) based their interpretation of writing as the primary explanation of the gender–format interaction on the results reported in their Table 16. The differential format effect of .25 ($p = .03$) was reduced to .09 ($p = .44$) and to .04 by adding first writing and then FR content as predictors. But if FR content had been added first, the format effect would have been reduced to .14 and then .04—a result suggesting that the content of the FR responses also played some role in accounting for the gender by format interaction.

TABLE 7.4

**Standard Gender Difference for Different Task Formats
Within the Same Advanced Placement Examination**

Type of Exercise	1993		1994	
	MC	FR	MC	FR
1. Variable Length Essays				
History of art	.01(.030)		−00.(.029)	
5'-10' essays(7)		.26(.031)		.14(.029)
30' essays(2)		.02(.030)		.02(.029)
U.S. Government	−.35(.012)		−33.(.011)	
15' optional essays(2)		.04(.012)		.04(.011)
45' optional essay		−.06(.012)		.05(.011)
Comparative govt.	−.25(.028)		−29.(.028)	
30' optional essay		.07(.028)		−.03(.028)
45' optional essay		.05(.028)		.03(.028)
2. Short Answer vs. Essay				
French language	−.01(.020)		−05.(.020)	
Short answer		.01(.020)		−.06(.020)
40' essay		.04(.020)		−.11(.020)
German language	.13(.038)		07.(.038)	
Short answer		.06(.038)		.06(.038)
40' essay		.13(.038)		.06(.038)
Spanish language	.03(.012)		.05(.011)	
Short answer		.04(.012)		.07(.011)
40' essay		.06(.012)		.07(.011)
3. Doc-based ques. vs. Essay				
U.S. history	−.31(.006)		−.32(.006)	
DBQ		.00(.006)		−.07(.006)
Optional essay		.01(.006)		.02(.006)
European history	−.35(.012)		−.30(.011)	
DBQ		.09(.011)		.05(.011)
Optional essay		−.02(.011)		.08(.011)
4. Musical skills	−.24(.045)		−.16(.043)	
Harmonic dictation		−.14(.045)		−.09(.043)
Melodic dictation		−.10(.045)		−.02(.044)
Composition		−.15(.045)		−.04(.043)
5. Scientific skills				
Chemistry	−.35(.012)		−.44(.011)	
Problem solving		−.12(.012)		−.18(.011)
Balancing equations		−.09(.012)		−.11(.011)
Short essay		−.26(.012)		−.33(.011)
Items above that offer:				
Option		−.20(.012)		−.28(.011)
No option		−.18(.011)		−.23(.011)
6. Content vs. Language				
French Literature	.13(.055)		.16(.057)	
Content		.25(.055)		.17(.058)
Language		.10(.056)		.01(.058)
7. Writing vs. Speaking				
French language	−.01(.020)		−.05(.020)	
Essay		.04(.020)		−.11(.020)
Speaking		−.03(.020)		−.05(.020)

Type of Exercise	1993		1994	
	MC	FR	MC	FR
7. Writing vs. Speaking (cont.)				
German language	.13(.038)		.07(.038)	
Essay		.13(.038)		.06(.038)
Speaking		.13(.038)		.08(.038)
Spanish language	.03(.012)		.05(.011)	
Essay		.06(.012)		.07(.011)
Speaking		.01(.012)		.03(.011)
8. Reading—Listening[a]				
French language				
Reading	.01(.020)		−.01(.020)	
Listening	−.03(.020)		−.08(.020)	
German language				
Reading	.12(.038)		.06(.038)	
Listening	.15(.038)		.10(.038)	
Spanish language				
Reading	.02(.012)		.12(.011)	
Listening	.00(.012)		.00(.011)	

Note. Standard errors of Ds for MC and FR sections are shown in parentheses. Standard errors for differences in Ds between FR sections will be somewhat reduced due to section intercorrelations.

[a]Multiple-choice questions based on different sensory input.

nations. On numbered Lines 1 through 8, the table contrasts gender differences for eight different types of format variations. Lines 1 and 2 compare D values for FR material of different length. Except for the small puzzle in History of Art, where women did better on short than on long essays, gender difference does not appear to vary with length of exercise.

Giving examinees some choice or option as to which exercise they undertake is an aspect of the task that some have felt contributes to assessment authenticity and fairness (Baker et al., 1993). Five of the AP examinations (both history, both government, and chemistry) allow examinee choice on at least half of the FR material. All five of these exams showed a format effect in 1993 and 1994. Is this coincidence or is choice a factor in the format effect based on gender? The data in Table 7.4 suggest coincidence. Three of the five exams allow a comparison of gender difference on choice versus no-choice material within the examination (Lines 3 and 5 of Table 7.4). In none of the three instances did choice appear to be associated with gender difference.

Scoring Differences. If males tend to do relatively better on MC tests where discrete items are scored right or wrong and females tend to do relatively better on essays that are usually scored holistically, does the nature of the scoring help to explain gender differences on FR material? Holistic scoring implies an overall judgment, taking predetermined features into account. Analytic scoring normally means awarding a designated number of points when different aspects of correctness are included in the answer, when certain facts or exceptions are noted, when the solution process is appropriate, and so on. The analytic score is then the sum of the points.

The dominant mode of scoring was analytic on 12 AP exams and holistic on 13 exams. In both scoring modes, slightly less than half of the exams showed a format effect; in other words, there was no evidence of any simple relationship between scoring method and format effect. The role of scoring method is a bit more puzzling if we examine again the lower panel of Fig. 7.6, where the circled exams had analytically scored FR sections. They are largely the exams in mathematics and natural science. In these subject areas the examinations are heavily problem oriented and they are analytically scored—yet there is a format effect in science and not in mathematics.

Observe also that we get a format effect in science, even though in both science and mathematics the MC and FR sections are apparently measuring very nearly the same constructs. Earlier we estimated the correlation between "true" scores in the two science formats to be .96! Even though that estimate is probably a bit high, one lesson here is that group differences are apparently quite possible even though two formats measure very similar knowledge and skills.[12] Given that possibility, the format effect is not hard to understand in the case of biology and chemistry, both of which call for a significant amount of discussing and explaining in the FR sections. But what of physics, which calls mostly for short answers on the FR section?

The difference in physics may lie partly in the nature of the analytic scoring. The AP scoring guides for mathematics suggest that the main emphasis is on using the correct procedure to get the right answer. In the physics exams, scoring guides appear to place more frequent emphasis on the quality of the answer—quality in the sense of recognizing multiple correct answers, alternate solutions, underlying principles, significant applications, and so on. (College Board, 1994b, 1994c). This distinction between math and physics in FR scoring is not clear cut, but effective writing may be more of an advantage in the case of physics.

---

[12]Within some of the natural science AP examinations, the different FR exercises varied in character. Because the reliability estimates were based on one form rather than parallel forms, the reliabilities were likely a bit low. Thus, the estimate of average true score correlation between FR and MC formats reported here (.96) is probably somewhat high (R. Morgan, personal communication, January, 1996). By partitioning the between- and within-group variance, it can be shown (with our thanks to Charles Lewis) that when $r_{xy} = .96$ and $D_y = .00$, the limits of D_x are $\pm.58$. D_x approaches those limits only when the correlation of r_{xy} is due solely to between-group variance on variable x; for example, when a construct is identical in the two formats except for additional factors perfectly correlated with gender.

Another possibility may be content differences associated with different skill requirements in the MC and FR sections of the science examinations. By its nature, science often engages spatial-mechanical principles. Such material may be more frequently found on the MC sections than on the FR sections. Or, the format effect may come simply from differences in linguistic versus spatial processing. Lohman (1994) argued that many individuals tend to be more fluent in either linguistic or spatial symbols—women more often the former, men more often the latter. The two skills may well come differentially into play in the FR and MC sections. These impressions serve best to suggest the need for further careful analysis that might better explain such patterns of female and male performance—and provide further information useful in designing examinations that match the AP coursework as accurately as possible.

Summary: Topic 2

This section started with a brief discussion of the several strands of educational and assessment reform that have led to the recent strong interest in alternate forms of FR assessment. This movement has been motivated by the promise of more beneficial effects of assessment on individuals and on the educational system. Whether such alternate assessments are fair to women and men depends first on how well validity is served, but this section is more narrowly focused.

The objective was to shed additional light on differences and similarities in the performance of women and men on different types of FR exercises in order to understand possible fairness implications for test design. To this end, format effects were examined for various types of tests that provided both FR and MC data: three statewide programs, several national assessments, three foreign countries, and the AP program. A format effect was defined as a discrepancy in the gender difference on a FR test compared to the gender difference on a MC test in the same subject for the same sample of students. The data suggested several tentative impressions.

- Women were more likely than men to do better on FR formats compared to MC formats, but that was not a consistent effect.
- Format effects tended to vary across subjects. Consequential format effects were seldom found in mathematics or in language and literature. Format effects did occur in science and geopolitics, evidently because these subjects are more likely to engage skills in different formats that favor one gender or the other.

- When there was a FR format effect favoring women, writing appeared often to play a role. It is not clear when and to what extent this effect may be due to superior composition and discourse, to greater skill or fluency in articulating the correct answer, or to a higher level or more integrated understanding of the correct answer to the question posed.
- Figural FR material was often associated with a format effect favoring males, probably because such material frequently involves mechanical or spatial skills on which males tend to score well.
- Apparently, format effects can be quite stable if the design of the FR exercise remains the same, but format effects can readily change—for reasons that are sometimes not clear—if the nature of the test is changed or if a test contains only a few FR questions.

These results suggest that an obvious current need in test design is development of a better understanding of what effects format has on the nature of the construct (i.e., the actual knowledge and skills measured) and when variations associated with alternate formats are relevant or irrelevant to the construct intended to be measured. It is important not to over- or underrepresent either linguistic (writing) skills, on which women tend to excel, or spatial (visualization) skills, on which men tend to excel. We move now to a third topic on test design, and ask whether performance differences may be associated with choice of the MC format itself, aside from what is being assessed.

THE MULTIPLE-CHOICE FORMAT

The previous section examined differences in test performance of females and males that are associated with variations in FR format. Here we focus on a closely related question: Are there gender differences and fairness issues that result from the MC format alone? This question requires some disaggregation of issues. But first note that in this section we typically use CR (constructed response) rather than FR (free response), a term less frequently used by the original authors in the studies cited. This choice is mostly to avoid confusing shifts in terminology in this section but also reflects the more limited type of free response (e.g., brief answer rather than essay) that is involved in the MC versus CR format issue discussed here.

Does the distinction between MC and CR, and the worry that often focuses on the multiple-choice test, refer to the MC *format* itself, or to the types of *constructs* typically tapped by MC questions, or to possible *systemic* educational effects of heavy emphasis on this format? It is clearly all three, but the nature of the problem and the possible implications depend on which aspect of the MC–CR distinction one is talking about. Shortly we return to these three aspects of the MC concern, but this section deals mainly with format, the first aspect.

Format Effects

Asking the examinee to select the correct answer from among several alternatives causes one to wonder about possible sources of score difference that are unrelated to the construct that is being assessed: test-taking strategies, the tendency to guess and the examinee's effectiveness in doing so, the extent to which coaching may enhance individual differences in test wiseness, and so on. Some critics have worried that the MC format may be unfair because it is an artificial situation in which some students have special ability to "test well." These issues have been debated for many years (see, e.g., Goslin, 1967; Haney, 1981; Hoffman, 1962) and discussed more recently as a possible source of gender bias (Gipps & Murphy, 1994; Linn, 1992; Rosser, 1989). For example, Gipps and Murphy (1994) cited research suggesting that boys are more anxious about FR questions, whereas girls "express their dislike of multiple-choice items because you don't have to think" (p. 215). This concern is about the form of the test item, not its substance. The question is whether the specific format of MC tests influences the relative test performance of women and men—indeed, of examinees generally.

In chapter 6, Bridgeman and Schmitt reviewed research literature that examines possible gender differences in test wiseness, guessing habits, and other aspects of test taking often associated with the MC format. In this chapter we approach the MC format question from the standpoint of actual test performance. The issue is whether the knowledge and skill required to answer a question are different if examinees are allowed to choose among alternate answers (MC) rather than come up with their own answer (CR). The contrast is between the MC question and a test format often used in the classroom: The teacher poses a question or problem, the student supplies a brief answer.

More specifically, in this section we compare tests based on discrete open-ended questions to which the examinee supplies a brief answer scored right or wrong with tests based on stem-equivalent questions in MC format. For our purposes, stem-equivalent means the same or a highly similar question stem, or MC and CR versions of questions drawn from comparable pools of items. We located 12 studies of paired tests involving such stem-equivalent items. Results of the studies are summarized in Table 7.5.

TABLE 7.5

**12 Studies Examining Gender Difference and/or Construct Difference
for Stem-Equivalent Tests in Both Multiple Choice (MC)
and Constructed Response (CR) Format**

Study	Test	MC/CR Construct Difference?	MC/CR Gender Difference?
1. Dossey et al. (1993)	Math	—	No
2. Beller and Gafni (1995, 1996a)	Math	—	No
3. Traub and Fisher (1977)	Verbal comp.	Yes	—
4. Traub and Fisher (1977)	Math reasoning	No	—
5. van den Bergh (1990)	Reading comp.	No	—
6. Ward et al. (1987)	Reading comp.	No	—
7. Ward (1982)	Verbal comp.	No	—
8. Ackerman and Smith (1988)	Writing skills	Minor	—
9. Bridgeman and Rock (1993)	GRE Analytical	No	No
10. Bridgeman (1993)	GRE Quantitative	—	No
11. Lawrence et al. (1995)	Math	No	No
12. Katz et al. (1996)	Math	No	—

12 Studies of the MC Format

The comparison of MC and CR formats must rely largely on studies that were designed specifically to address the format question. There are, however, two pertinent sets of data based on national assessments that are useful to examine first (Studies 1 and 2 in Table 7.5). In the previous section we reported a good deal of normative data on the performance of women and men on a variety of tests including both a MC section and a section on which the examinee supplied the answer. In almost all cases those data are not suitable for the issue at hand because the open-ended questions were deliberately aimed at different skills than the questions in MC format. In one data set—the 1992 NAEP Mathematics Assessment—the MC and "Regular CR" questions were quite similar except for the format difference. Results are shown in Fig. 7.7.

This assessment included both MC and CR questions in each of five math content areas (Dossey et al., 1993). In the great majority of cases the required response to the regular CR questions was simply a number, a word, or a mark of some sort. Responses were scored correct or incorrect. In Fig. 7.7 the percentages of correct answers for females and males shows much the same pattern on each of the five pairs of MC and CR sections. There is little if any evidence of any format effect associated with gender.

Another recent analysis of gender difference by test format (Study 2 in Table 7.5) holds special interest because it involved national mathematics assessments in seven countries. Beller and Gafni (1995, 1996a) compared

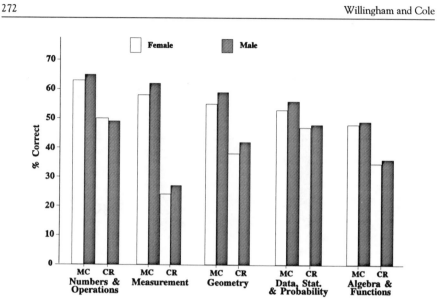

FIG. 7.7. Average "percentage correct" for female and male 12th-grade students on multiple choice (MC) and regular constructed response (CR) questions in five areas of mathematics in the 1992 NAEP National Assessment. Source: Dossey, Mullis, & Jones (1993), pp. 174, 178.

female and male performance, specifically attempting to control for task differences. They looked for evidence of a format effect among items measuring the same content and cognitive skills in both MC and CR format. Beller and Gafni (1996a) concluded that, "The results of the study suggest that item format per se cannot account for gender differences in test performance" (p. 18)[13]

The remaining 10 studies in Table 7.5 were designed specifically to compare the MC and CR format with questions that were otherwise comparable. In most cases researchers comparing MC and CR test formats have a broader concern than whether particular subgroups score differently on the two formats. The interest is typically whether tests in different formats are measuring the same construct, as evidenced for example, by all examinees falling in the same rank order on the two formats, except for

---

[13]Beller and Gafni (1995) originally reported that the gender difference favoring boys on the IAEP math tests was *greater on CR items* than on MC items. The difference was small but generally consistent. For example, on items measuring procedural knowledge in mathematics, where both MC and CR items were frequently represented, a format effect favoring males on CR items was found in all seven countries at age 9 as well as age 13. A later study (Beller & Gafni, 1996a) reported that item effect size was consistently correlated with item difficulty in these data (i.e., males doing better on more difficult items) and that the FR items were more difficult compared to the MC items. They concluded that their original finding was an artifact of this relationship.

errors of measurement. So, as indicated in Table 7.5, 7 of the 10 studies to follow do not actually compare females and males, but rather use various statistical techniques in order to determine whether tests in MC and CR format are measuring the same construct. Measuring the same construct means, by definition, that examinees fall in the same rank order on the two sets of scores (except for errors of measurement). If the rank order of all examinees is exactly the same from one format to another, a mean score difference for any two groups will necessarily be the same across formats. As we noted in the previous section, however, it is important to bear in mind that even a small difference in the two constructs can leave room for nontrivial subgroup differences on the two formats.

First, a word about the origin of Studies 3 through 8 is in order. Hogan (1981) reviewed a number of studies over a 60-year period and concluded that measures in MC and FR format are equivalent or nearly so. Traub and MacRury (1990) discounted much of the research prior to 1970 because of methodological weaknesses in earlier work. Using a broader range of FR material—including essays, for example—these later authors were inclined to conclude that MC and FR tests measure somewhat different characteristics.

In a subsequent analysis, Traub (1993) reviewed those studies that met rigorous standards; for example, including multiple tests in both MC and CR format. He noted that MC and CR tests may measure different constructs in some domains and not others. Four of the studies reviewed by Traub compared MC tests with essay tests, in which case he found some construct differences associated with format.[14] We focus on the remaining six studies (from five articles) that compared tests in MC and CR formats using stem-equivalent questions as already defined.

Only one of these six studies showed any consequential construct difference across MC and CR formats—Study 3 in Table 7.5, involving a verbal comprehension test using synonyms (Traub & Fisher, 1977). In the same article, Traub and Fisher reported no format difference on a mathematical reasoning test (Study 4 on Table 7.5). They found a small factor reflecting FR performance on both the verbal and math tests, although they noted that this result was weakened by the fact that whatever was different about

---

[14]Of the four studies involving essays—examined by Traub (1993) but not considered here—two showed clear format differences (Quellmalz, Capell, & Chou, 1982; Werts, Breland, Grandy, & Rock, 1980); two others involving essays in computer programming showed unsubstantial or no differences (Bennett et al., 1990; Bennett, Rock, & Wang, 1991). The study by Ackerman and Smith (1988) was based on a complex design including MC, CR, and essay formats, making the MC–CR comparison difficult to evaluate. Traub (1993) noted that the MC and CR method factors in that study were minor and not well-defined.

the MC and CR formats was *not* related to several "marker" measures that were included in the analysis. These were measures that might be expected to account for any tendency of some examinees to do better on one format or the other (e.g., the examinee's recall memory, or willingness to guess).

Traub and Fisher's positive finding on the verbal tests is offset by three other studies (Studies 5–7 in our Table 7.5) that showed essentially no format difference for verbal comprehension tests. Two of these studies involved reading comprehension (van den Bergh, 1990; Ward, Dupree, & Carlson, 1987). The third (Ward, 1982) found no consequential format differences on three types of verbal comprehension tests: Antonyms, Sentence Completion, and Analogies. For each test, the MC format was compared with three types of open-ended format, and Ward concluded, "There was no evidence whatsoever for a general factor associated with the use of a free-response format" (p. 9).

The final MC–CR comparison taken from the Traub review (Study 8 in Table 7.5) was a study of writing skill by Ackerman and Smith (1988). These authors compared six such skills tests in MC and CR format. Traub (1993) found format factors common to the MC and CR tests but concluded that the factors were of minor importance.

Since Traub's review, four additional studies pertinent to this topic (9–12 in Table 7.5) have been carried out at ETS. The studies were stimulated by the interest of major testing programs in introducing more diversity in item formats, and the need to better understand the effects of format variation. In one study based on the analytical section of the GRE General Test (Bridgeman & Rock, 1993), it was possible to compare the current MC analytical reasoning item type with an open-ended version. Relative to the men, women scored slightly higher on the open-ended items than on the MC items, but "the difference was neither practically nor statistically significant" (p. 9). Based on their statistical analyses, the authors concluded that the open-ended items in this particular test were not measuring anything different from the MC items.

In another study of the quantitative section of the GRE General, Bridgeman (1993) compared the current MC test with open-ended versions in which students either typed in their answers in a computer administration or gridded in their answers on an answer sheet. His conclusions speak to several aspects of the MC versus CR testing format.

> Both formats ranked the relative abilities of students in the same order; gender and ethnic differences were neither lessened nor exaggerated; and correlations with other test scores and college grades were about the same. For a fixed number of items, the open-ended test may be slightly more reliable because of the elimination of random guessing. But for a fixed length of time,

> the reliabilities would be virtually identical because the open-ended test [takes more time and, therefore] contains fewer items. (p. 25)

In March 1994 the College Board introduced open-ended questions in SAT-Mathematical Reasoning with an answer sheet on which examinees grid in their responses. Lawrence et al. (1995) analyzed these items to see whether they exhibited differential item functioning (DIF) compared to the MC items in the test. Like the Bridgeman (1993) analysis of GRE Quantitative grid-in items, they reported negligible format differences by gender. African American students showed more DIF on the CR items, a difference the authors felt could likely be attributed to the fact that grid-in items are more reliable and provide a clearer picture of group differences. They cited Linn (1993c), who demonstrated that more reliable items better represent the construct and are therefore more likely to show DIF.

A rather different study of MC and CR format differences yielded findings of particular interest. Katz, Friedman, Bennett, and Berger (1996) did a protocol analysis of students' solution procedures while they worked on MC and CR versions of the types of math problems that occur on the SAT. The question stems in the corresponding MC and CR items were either the same or isomorphic variations of the same problem. Half of the subjects had a time limit; the others were told to take as much time as they needed.

The difficulty of individual items varied for MC and CR versions, but overall the results were consistent with those of Bridgeman (1993) on the GRE Quantitative items—no difference in what was measured in the MC and CR formats. Variation in the amount of time examinees were allowed to answer questions did not affect that result. Differences in students' approach to individual items in the two formats appeared to result more from the way items and their answer alternatives were expressed than from format effects or cognitive factors. Results on the entire test were similar for the two formats because examinees solved CR and MC items using similar methods. For example, the investigators were surprised to find that examinees used "backward" solution strategies (i.e., trying out possible answers) on CR items as often as they did with MC items. The possibility of working backwards has long been viewed as a "flaw" peculiar to MC items. The authors reported that examinees appear to be adept at estimating plausible answers to CR items and then checking to see whether the answer works. They ended their report concluding:

> Whereas there may be good reasons for using constructed-response items in large-scale testing programs, from a cognitive perspective, multiple-choice questions of the sort studied here should provide measurement that is generally

comparable to stem-equivalent constructed-response items. Simply removing the options from an MC item will likely not result in better measurement of mathematical skill nor new skills being assessed. (Katz et al., 1996, p. 1)

These Findings and the Larger Context

This section has addressed a limited although important question: Does the MC format itself have any consequential effect on the rank order of examinees, or more specifically, on gender difference? We have reviewed the results of 12 studies involving stem-equivalent items in CR and MC format: two analyses of national assessment data, six studies reviewed by Traub (1993), and four recent ETS studies.

Nine of these 12 studies tested the comparability of the constructs measured in the two formats (Column 3 in Table 7.5). In seven studies the MC and CR constructs were judged to be essentially the same; in one (Traub & Fisher, 1977) the test construct was different in MC and CR formats; in another (Ackerman & Smith, 1988) the format factor was considered by Traub to be of minor importance. Although subgroups would not differ across formats if the constructs are the same (i.e., because the rank order of individuals would then be the same), it is useful to recall again an important point from the discussion of AP Physics results in the previous section. Women and men can perform differently on two tests, even if the two tests measure very nearly the same thing. If a gender format difference is observed or suspected, one needs to look for reasons why the score pattern might differ by format, and whether there is independent evidence that females and males do differ in that respect.

Five of these 12 studies examined gender differences across MC and CR formats (Column 4 in Table 7.5). None showed a format effect. We believe that the findings from these 12 studies considerably weaken the argument that MC format, per se, is a significant source of gender difference in test results. Apparently, test wiseness, guessing habits, and other aspects of test taking connected with the presence of answer options make less difference in the examinee's total score than is often assumed. However, these results pertain only to the first concern—format effects. It is worth noting two related concerns regarding MC tests.

Construct Effects

The typical MC item on most standardized tests tends to be discrete. If it measures a general cognitive skill like math reasoning, it is also likely to be decontextualized; that is, not dependent on knowledge of the particular subject or context. Some have argued that such items are less realistic, less connected with instructional objectives, and less likely to measure constructs that call on higher level cognitive processes. (See, e.g., Frederiksen, 1984, and Wiggins, 1989, who raised this issue generally, and M. Linn, 1992, who discussed it as a possible source of gender bias.) On the other hand, a MC test can cover the content of an instructional domain more thoroughly and more fairly because it contains many items.

Systemic Effects

The first and second concerns about multiple-choice tests—format effects and construct effects—lead to a third concern regarding possible negative effects on instruction and student learning; that is, adverse systemic consequences. Negative effects can take the form of excessive class drill on the specific type of material found on tests at the expense of broader educational objectives, or students spending time on trying to outsmart the test developers instead of their studies (see, e.g., Shepard, 1990; Smith, 1991).

Both of these concerns about the MC format bear on what knowledge and skill is being assessed. But we know from the previous section that choice of format is pertinent to this concern because diverse formats broaden the range of measurement and lessen the likelihood that important constructs will be underrepresented in the test. We found that the pattern of gender difference and similarity does often vary with different types of questions. Women tend often to score somewhat higher on a written FR section than on a corresponding MC section, although the opposite effect occurs with figural FR material.

The fact that the mere presence or absence of answer alternatives is not likely to change either what is measured or the pattern of female and male performance does not mean that format is unimportant. There may be important arguments for alternative formats to broaden the range of constructs that can be assessed or to mitigate possible negative effects on instruction and learning that overreliance on MC testing could have.

It is fitting to close this discussion with two illustrations of how apparently small changes in the nature of the test question can have important effects on what is measured. When comparing items that are not stem-equivalent, it is often easy to see differences between the tasks—like defining a word versus writing an essay—and to understand why individuals and groups might differ in their mastery of the two tasks. It is less obvious, however, that tasks generally similar in appearance may not actually be the same.

Hellekant (1994) recently demonstrated a consistent and noticeable gender difference each year on two "cloze" items presumably measuring the same skills in Sweden's test of English for secondary school students. In a subtest where grammar, vocabulary, and so on were tested in context, some items used incomplete sentences with MC alternatives; others used CR blanks in paragraphs. Women did better on the CR version every year. Although the MC and CR versions look like similar tasks, there is independent evidence that they are not. As Carroll (1993) noted, "cloze tests (*unless* they are in some kind of multiple-choice format) involve not only receptive skills but also productive skills, in that the subject has to supply words suggested by their contexts" (p. 167, italics added).

A similar example is found in a study of creativity in scientific problem solving. Frederiksen and Ward (1978) developed an experimental CR "formulating hypothesis" test that showed particular promise in predicting success in graduate study, but using judges to score the item type made it too expensive to use in an admissions testing program. In a subsequent effort to develop a more practical machine-scorable item type, a MC version proved not to measure the same productive skill reflected in the CR version. Also, the MC version no longer added useful information to current tests and undergraduate grades in predicting graduate success as had the original CR experimental test (Ward, Frederiksen, & Carlson, 1980).

As Frederiksen (1984) later suggested, where there is an MC format effect, it seems to be unidirectional. Turning a MC question into a parallel CR question by removing the MC alternatives apparently has little if any effect on what is measured. It does not follow, however, that one can force a more complex FR question into a generally similar MC format and measure the same thing. In both of the instances just cited, the original CR test question called for productive skills, a form of fluency that MC tests apparently cannot measure.

This distinction brings us back to the construct and what we see as the principal implication of these studies of the MC format. The MC format has obvious strengths, although it places limits on what constructs can be measured. However, the MC format itself—the presence or absence of response alternatives—is probably not the important issue. More consequential is the question of what desirable constructs are best measured with discrete questions that converge to specific correct answers as opposed to questions that are more open to interpretation and diversity of response. Using the CR rather than the MC format may change the tested construct by incorporating additional skill requirements (e.g., writing, spatial, idea production). These can be either weakly or strongly related to the intended construct. It seems clear that what is measured is more important than how it is measured, although the two are obviously connected. Efforts to ensure valid and fair tests are better directed to understanding as well as possible what constructs a test is measuring and the effects of its use.

Summary: Topic 3

A fairness concern that is often raised regarding MC tests is whether this format may unfairly advantage some students because it rewards skills and characteristics of examinees that are unrelated to what the test is intended to measure (e.g., test-taking strategy, tendency to guess). This section compared performance on FR tests to which examinees supply a brief answer scored right or wrong with a test based on equivalent test items in MC format. The question is whether students perform differently when all save format is the same.

Research findings were reviewed from studies that were either designed to determine whether different constructs were being measured in such FR and MC versions of otherwise equivalent tests or whether the relative score levels of women and men were different on the two versions. Thirteen of 14 such comparisons showed no important difference between the two formats. These results suggest that the MC format itself does not have a consequential effect on performance and is not likely to present a significant fairness problem. The findings do not address other arguments for and against MC and alternate assessment formats, but do suggest that what is measured is the priority concern, rather than how it is measured.

The following two topics concern two subject areas—writing and mathematics—that are important from an academic standpoint and also from the perspective of gender fairness. These are rather different skills that tend to represent differential strengths of women and men. Whether these skills are included in testing programs and how they are measured can have important fairness implications because of the educational considerations for examinees generally, as well as possible impact on the test performance level of women relative to men. Both writing and mathematics engage issues in test design as well as test use.

WRITING

From midcentury until recently, students have seldom been required to write in large-scale testing programs in this country, despite the fact that writing is often considered a critical skill in academic work and in adult life as well.

Of all the test results reported in chapter 3 on national samples of students at Grade 12, writing showed the largest gender difference favoring women. These characteristics of writing—its academic relevance, its underrepresentation in testing programs, and a consequential pattern of gender difference—clearly indicate that a design decision on whether or not to include writing is, among other considerations, a fairness issue. In the earlier section on FR measures, we discussed the potential importance of writing in the assessment of other constructs. Here we are concerned with the assessment of writing as writing.

Testing students on their writing has important educational benefits, and there have been advances in this area of assessment (Breland, 1996; White, 1994). Nevertheless, assessing the student's ability to write well is no easy task, from either a measurement or a practical standpoint. What are the implications of including writing in a testing program? How much difference would that make in the overall pattern of female and male scores? Does a valid writing assessment have to include actual writing? Previous experience and research gives us some insight on such issues. We take up the last question first because, as always, the validity of the construct is the primary consideration in assessment.

Assessing Writing

In his encyclopedic review of factor analytic studies of human cognitive abilities, Carroll (1993) described four classes of language skills. The four were distinguished on the basis of receptive versus productive skills in both oral and written language. For example, oral language includes:

- Listening as a receptive skill.
- Speaking as a productive skill.

Similarly, written language includes:

- Reading as a receptive skill.
- Writing as a productive skill.

All four of these skills receive attention in second-language instruction and assessment (TOEFL Program, 1992a, 1992b),[15] but in the main, instructional programs and testing programs for native speakers of English tend to

---

[15]Test of English as a Foreign Language (TOEFL) includes both listening and reading along with other aspects of written language usage. Related examinations sponsored by the TOEFL Program assess speaking and writing proficiency (TOEFL, 1992a, 1992b).

concentrate on the written word. As Carroll noted, it is often difficult to draw a clear line between language and other domains, such as verbal reasoning, because language permeates other abilities. The nature of the language construct depends on the specific test questions. Different forms of vocabulary knowledge, such as analogy items, are often linked with reading comprehension to measure verbal reasoning. Writing—a productive skill—is related to these written receptive skills, but distinguishable in both the cognitive and the statistical sense.

Since the advent of objective test items, numerous types of discrete items have been developed to measure such writing skills as grammar, usage, sentence structure, and so on. (See examples under "VERBAL-Language Use" in Table 3.1.) A more complex objective assessment like, for example, the so-called "interlinear exercise" includes some production because it requires examinees to edit expository prose (Godshalk, Swineford, & Coffman, 1966). All such tests are sometimes referred to as *indirect measures,* as distinct from direct measures based on actual samples of the examinees' writing.

In the long-standing debate over the merits of direct and indirect measures of writing skill, there is little disagreement that direct measures are more authentic, or that indirect measures are more reliable per unit of testing time. The difficulty in obtaining consistent expert judgments as to the quality of student writing is neither recently discovered (Starch & Elliott, 1912) nor yet resolved (Cherry & Meyer, 1993). Disagreement turns rather on whether the direct and indirect scores are consequentially different, and on how one evaluates the educational effects of using one type of measure or the other. Doubt that they are different has probably resulted from the relatively high correlation between direct and indirect scores, and of course, the substantial difference in their cost.[16]

Research over the past three decades has demonstrated, beyond much doubt, that there are important differences between direct and indirect measures of writing skill (Ackerman & Smith, 1988; Breland et al., 1987; Breland & Jones, 1982; French, 1966; Godshalk et al., 1966; Miller & Welch, 1993). Other studies have demonstrated that women and men perform somewhat differently on direct and indirect measures, which is another indication that the constructs cannot be exactly the same (Breland & Griswold, 1982; Dunbar, 1987; Table 3.1 in chapter 3).

How much difference is there between the direct and indirect measures that are typically used? The best evidence comes from two major statistical studies

---

[16]Godshalk et al. (1966) estimated the correlation between indirect measures of writing skill and a highly reliable essay criterion to be in the range of .64 to .71. Breland et al. (1987) estimated the same correlation at .63 to .72.

(Breland et al., 1987; Godshalk et al., 1966). Breland et al. found (see their Table 9.1) that a twice-read 20-minute essay correlated .61 with a highly reliable criterion based on several types of writing. An indirect measure of writing correlated .62 with the same criterion. Using the direct and indirect measures together yielded a correlation with the writing criterion some .11 higher than with either type of measure alone. Approximately the same validity improvement could be obtained by using two essays, but at the expense of lower reliability and probably greater cost to the student.[17] As Breland et al. (1987) concluded, "the results of this study—as well as those by Godshalk et al.—show that the best estimates of students' writing abilities are obtained through tests that combine essay assessments and multiple-choice assessments" (p. 61).

How does the writing construct differ when based on direct versus indirect assessment? In a study of "schools of thought" among essay graders, Diederich (1974) concluded that at least some essay graders were rewarding form, ideas, and flavor—qualities that were largely unrelated to the students' performance on an indirect MC test of writing skills. Using a different approach, Breland and Jones (1982) got similar results. They examined 20 characteristics of essays and found that discourse quality—especially organization and noteworthy ideas—best accounted for overall holistic scores. Essay length was also a very strong predictor of holistic score. The authors considered length (number of words written) to be an indicator of verbal fluency, a necessary ability in order to demonstrate discourse quality. A recent replication of this latter study produced very similar findings, all of which is a bit surprising, considering the brevity of these essays—normally 20 minutes (Breland, Bonner, & Kubota, 1996). The later study added some interesting results on gender differences. Among those essay characteristics that were useful in predicting the total holistic rating, the best predictors were number of words written and, to a lesser degree, several discourse characteristics. These were also the predictors that showed the greatest gender difference—favoring females.

Implications for Use

If direct measures of writing proficiency differ from indirect measures primarily because the former reflect fluency and discourse quality whereas

---

[17]In a personal communication, Breland noted that from Tables F.5, F.13, and F.17 in Breland et al. (1987), the average predictive validity of two essays, as well as essay plus TSWE, are both estimated to be about .54 against course grade and instructors' judgments of writing skill. Their Table 5.4 shows the reliability of two essays in different modes to be .68. This study did not estimate the reliability of essay plus TSWE, but the retest reliability of a similar composite, SAT-Writing, has been estimated to be .84. (Thanks to Carolyn Crone.)

the latter do not, it would probably come as no surprise to those who teach writing and study its nature as a productive exercise (Camp, 1993). Such a distinction can have important implications for the design of writing assessments, depending especially on the purpose of the test. Consider the experience of the College Board some years ago in its early and persistent effort to represent writing in the college admissions process, largely on grounds that it is a critical communication skill. French (1966) addressed a group of educators with this wry account:

> Fifteen years ago, a written composition was an integral part of the Board's achievement test in English. The psychometricians then proved that a verbal aptitude test could predict English grades or ratings on writing ability better than a test which actually required the students to write. The College Board then dropped the English composition from its program. Shouts of horror arose, and a committee was formed. This resulted in a new, ingeniously garnished two-hour essay test called the General Composition Test .... The psychometricians, of course, swung into action ... The College Board then dropped the General Composition Test .... Shouts of horror arose ... (p. 587)

Subsequently, the Board offered a Writing Sample, which students produced in the test center. Ungraded copies were sent to a number of colleges that required it. Initial assessments of the value of the program were guardedly optimistic on grounds that the test would beneficially affect writing instruction in the secondary schools (Valentine, 1962). Later evaluations proved discouraging. Colleges reported that finding graders was a major problem, grading tended to be unreliable, and the Writing Sample had low validity as an admission criterion (Ekstrom, 1964). Apparently the Writing Sample was motivated in large part by broad educational (systemic) considerations, but evaluated on short-term utility and practical concerns. It was discontinued in 1968 in favor of the largely MC English Composition Test.

Is there a fairness issue here? Possibly, if some students work hard to develop writing skills that are relevant to the purpose of the composition test but are not represented on the test. There could also be a gender connection if women are more likely to do well on the underrepresented skills. The purpose of the test is a key question. If the purpose is simply to predict freshman grade average, recent work confirms that an essay is not likely to add useful information (Bridgeman, 1991).

If, on the other hand, the purpose is to improve placement of students in college English courses, the results of Breland et al. (1987) clearly suggest that adding an essay to a MC test of writing skills will likely improve prediction of writing performance in those courses. Subsequent placement studies indicate that a writing composite measure (skills tests plus essay) is definitely superior to SAT-Verbal for placement purposes, and is also a better choice because it reduces underprediction of women's grades (Bridgeman, Hale, Lewis, Pollack, & Wang, 1992)

Furthermore, if the purpose of a writing assessment is to evaluate writing more fully or to beneficially influence writing instruction and its development, then the fluency and discourse skills represented in an essay are highly relevant, whether they add to short-term prediction or not. In this case it is important to be sure that the test measures those skills well and its use is justified on that basis. Requiring an essay may well be a move in the right direction, but as Messick (1992) argued, direct assessment provides no relief from the responsibility to marshall evidence that the test does measure the constructs intended and does further desirable educational objectives (see also Powers, Fowles, & Willard, 1994, for an example). Otherwise the extra burden of direct assessment may prove difficult to sustain. The account of the Writing Sample also illustrates the danger of underestimating practical concerns in designing an assessment program.

In recent years direct assessment of writing proficiency has become much more common (Breland, 1996). Several national admissions testing programs have recently added a writing sample—either required (MCAT, GMAT) or optional (College Board). The GRE Board is planning to do so. "Writing across the curriculum" is another movement that suggests growing acknowledgment of writing as a critical cognitive skill in most academic subjects (Gray, 1988; Jones & Comprone, 1993). Barton and Coley (1994) reported that 38 states use some sort of writing sample for some students.

What effect would a direct writing measure have on the overall score level of women and men in a testing program where actual writing was judged sufficiently relevant to the purpose of the test to warrant its inclusion? We saw earlier in this chapter (Table 7.1) the large impact that a writing requirement can have on how many males fail to graduate high school. Might an essay requirement have a similar effect on gender balance among more proficient students? Also, there is the interest of language minority students to be considered. Might an essay test have opposite effects on women and second-language students? Figure 7.8 shows illustrative data that are relevant to both questions.[18]

---

[18]Until recently he New Jersey Basic Skills Placement Test was administered to the entering freshmen of all publi and many private colleges in the state. Data in Fig. 7.8 are based on 6,013 language minority students, 32,628 women, and 26,953 men in 1992. Verbal Skills is an equally weighted composite of reading and sentence sense; Math Skills is a composite of math computation and algebra.

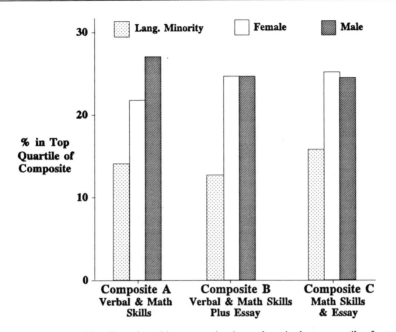

FIG. 7.8. Percentage of female, male and language minority students in the top quartile of composite scores based on different combinations of verbal skills, math skills and essay. Source: Statewide data from the New Jersey College Basic Skills Placement Test (see footnote 18).

The New Jersey College Basic Skills Placement Test was administered each year to entering freshmen. It included two MC tests measuring verbal skills, two MC tests measuring math skills, and an essay test. Figure 7.8 shows what percentage of language minority students, women, and men in this group of some 60,000 freshmen would "qualify" in the top quarter of the total group based on three different composite scores. Using only the MC skills tests, more men than women qualify (Composite A). Adding the essay test balances the percentage of women and men, and reduces slightly the percentage of language minority students (Composite B). Substituting the essay for the verbal skills tests also balances the women and men in the top quartile, but increases somewhat the percentage of language minority students (Composite C compared to Composite A). These results might vary, of course, in other samples or with different tests.

A recent study of the new writing component of the GMAT produced a similar result: an increase in the proportion of women who are likely to be eligible for admission and little effect on ethnic minority groups (Bridgeman & McHale, 1996). Data based on the California Bar Examination also illustrate the effect on gender difference when an essay is added to the multiple-choice Multistate Bar Examination (MBE). Assuming the same proportion of students pass, the *F/M* ratio among those who passed the MBE was .83; the *F/M* ratio among those passing a combination of MBE and essay was 1.08 (Klein & Bolus, 1984).

Summary: Topic 4

Writing is widely regarded as a key cognitive skill in academic work as well as adult life. Research supports the common view that direct measures, like essays, and indirect measures, like MC tests of writing skills represent somewhat different constructs with somewhat different strengths. Choosing one or both rests on their validity for the intended use and on practical considerations. Indirect MC measures are more reliable and can economically cover important skills, such as word usage and editing, that are not necessarily represented in drafting an essay. Strong validity arguments can be made for the use of direct measures of writing when the purpose of assessment puts value on measuring fully the writing construct, as in instructional assessment, or when using the test may have important systemic consequences such as washback on the educational system.

Women tend to score better than men on both direct and indirect measures of writing skill. Due to this gender difference and to the educational relevance of writing, underrepresentation of writing is a reasonable fairness concern in test design and use. It was observed that including writing tended to balance the number of women and men who scored at a high level in testing programs in which there were otherwise more men scoring high. The following topic, mathematics, is another key academic skill that can be measured with somewhat different constructs, depending on intended use. In this instance, however, the gender difference tends to go in the opposite direction from writing.

MATHEMATICS

In the previous section we discussed the implications of the superior performance that women often show on some verbal tasks, notably writing. In mathematics we have a similar although mirror-image situation. Men tend to perform better on some mathematics tests, especially high-stakes tests taken by selected populations of students. These tests can have an important bearing on aspiration and entry into important careers. An added complexity is the tendency of women to make better grades in math courses than scores on math tests. In designing mathematics tests, are we measuring the right knowledge and skills? To address this question, we need to review what we know from previous research and analyses reported in earlier chapters about three topics: difference and similarity in female and male performance on math tests, factors that appear to play some role in the differential development of math proficiency, and how test performance compares to class performance in mathematics.

Principal Features of Gender Differences on Mathematics Tests

One of the most consistent findings over the past three decades has been the generally similar achievement of girls and boys in mathematics in the early grades (Cleary, 1992; Dossey et al., 1988; Flanagan et al., 1964). The main exception is the somewhat superior computational facility of girls at that age. It has also been widely and consistently reported that boys tend to gain in math scores relative to girls as they move through school (Aiken, 1986–1987; Armstrong, 1985; Cleary, 1992; Dossey et al., 1988; Ekstrom et al., 1988; Hilton & Berglund, 1974; Hyde et al., 1990; Maccoby & Jacklin, 1974; Wise, 1985).

Based on current data, however, we estimated the change in mean test scores in mathematics, other than computation, to be only about one tenth of a standard deviation from Grade 4 to Grade 12 (see Fig. 3.2). Three decades ago the relative math gain by males in high school was apparently much larger. Data from Project TALENT, the massive national assessment of high school students in 1960, indicated that gender difference on a mathematics total score (a composite of introductory math, math information, and math reasoning) changed from a standard mean difference of $-.07$ at Grade 9 to $-.44$ at Grade 12 (Flanagan et al., 1964). The largest difference was between Grades 10 and 11 ($D = -.15$ and $-.33$, respectively).

NAEP assessments in 1978, 1982, and 1986 indicate that the greater gain by males in high school is due mostly to their tendency to improve more than do females at the advanced level, often typified by skill in problem solving and reasoning (Dossey et al., 1988; see also Armstrong, 1985; Cleary, 1992; Hyde et al., 1990). The most recent NAEP assessments in 1990 and 1992 (Mullis, Dossey, Owen, & Phillips, 1993) also show that it is at the higher levels of proficiency that males tend to gain more than females by Grade 12.

This pattern of somewhat greater male gain on math reasoning seems part of a more general picture of gender-differentiated math skills in representative populations that has been documented in many reports:

females tending to score higher on computation, little difference on general knowledge of mathematics, and males tending to score higher on problem solving and reasoning, which are emphasized more at higher levels of training (Armstrong, 1985; Benbow, 1988b; Cleary 1992; Doolittle, 1989; Doolittle & Cleary, 1987; Dossey et al., 1988; Friedman, 1989; Gallagher, 1990; Hyde et al., 1990; Linn, 1986; Snow & Ennis, 1996; see chapter 5 for discussion and illustrations of this point).

The tendency of males to score higher than females on problem solving and reasoning is compounded by the fact that men's scores on mathematics tests are typically more variable than are women's scores. In representative 12th-grade samples, we found the average ratio of female to male standard deviations on math tests to be .93 (Fig. 3.1). Data recently compiled by Hedges and Nowell (1995) yield the same estimate.[19] Items that measure problem solving and reasoning are likely to be among the more difficult questions, whereas computation items are likely to be easier. In that case the gender differential in proficiency on these skills that is often observed would tend to result in differential variability. So it is not entirely clear whether a gender difference in problem solving results in some gender difference in high-level math proficiency or the other way around, but the critical result is greater representation of males among the students who score high on advanced math tests.

Based on several national assessments, we estimated in chapter 3 (Fig. 3.9) that the ratio of females to males among the 10% of students most proficient in math declines from about .90 at Grade 8 to about .70 at Grade 12. Independently, and using somewhat different tests and procedures, Hedges and Nowell (1995) also estimated recently the relative number of females and males among the top 10% of math scores nationally (with an age range of 13 to 22, but mostly about 17). The average F/M ratio based on their data was .63,[20] slightly lower than our estimate but in the same range. Such gender ratios among students highly proficient in math, or sometimes more extreme ones, have been reported with some consistency over the past two decades in the results of national talent searches at age 12 to 13 (Benbow, 1988b) and mathematics contests among youngsters in grade school (Stanley, 1993) and college (American Association for the Advancement of Science, 1989).

---

[19]This estimate of SDR = .93 is based on the six math tests in Table 2 and the most recent NAEP survey data in Table 3 of Hedges and Nowell (1995).
[20]Hedges and Nowell (1995) used data from five surveys: Project Talent, NLS-72, National Longitudinal Study of Youth (based on ASVAB), HSB, and NELS. They estimated F/M ratios from means and standard deviations, assuming normal distributions.

As we saw in chapter 3, there was a consequential gain from the early 1980s to the early 1990s in the representation of women among 12th graders who become quite proficient in math. Nevertheless, NAEP assessments still indicate that about half again more males than females are scoring in the top 10% on math tests among all high school seniors nationally (Fig. 3.8). It is not surprising (predictable in fact, as was described by Lewis and Willingham, 1995, and in chapter 3) that the mean gender difference on math tests tends to get larger in more select groups of students. In representative national samples, we found the mean D on Grade 12 mathematics tests to be −.11, but more negative on undergraduate and graduate admissions tests in mathematics ($D = -.35$ and −.59, respectively; see Tables 3.1 and 3.2).

Factors in the Development of Math Proficiency

As we explained in chapter 1, the etiology of gender difference and similarity is, itself, a very broad topic with an enormous literature. We have given considerable attention to describing the nature of such differences in the hope that it will be helpful in advancing our understanding of fair assessment practice. Beyond that descriptive effort, explaining the development of gender differences in math performance is beyond our reasonable scope. (See Wilder, 1997, for a summary of relevant literature.) Nonetheless, it is useful to comment briefly on what we know about factors that may influence differently the development of mathematical proficiency in girls and boys.

Our objective in the following paragraphs is to remind the reader of a few broad research trends and views of this topic from the sociological, educational, and biological perspectives. The benefit, we think, is some added perspective on the nature of gender difference and similarity in mathematics performance, and when gender differences in mathematics are more likely to be real or artifactual.

The evidence bearing on this complex topic is routinely correlational, circumstantial, and nondefinitive. That is true of the sociological, the educational, and the biological data. Such is normally the case with all important issues concerning human endeavor because we are not able to use invasive research techniques or to assign girls and boys randomly to different life experiences. Having said that, we note that some data are a lot more persuasive than other data, and there is reasonably good evidence that social, educational, and biological factors all interact and play some role, direct or indirect, in observed gender differences generally, and probably in math performance as well. This view seems generally shared as a reasonable working assumption (Benbow, 1988b; Cleary, 1992; Halpern, 1992; Neisser (Chair), et al., 1996; Wilder & Powell, 1989).

Benbow (1988b, 1990) postulated a possible role for biological factors in accounting for gender differences in mathematical ability, although she characterized her efforts as partly speculative and resulting in part from an inability to account for differences on the basis of social variables alone. She noted the correlation of mathematical precocity with physiological characteristics such as left-handedness and myopia, and cited prenatal testosterone level and brain lateralization as possible causal mechanisms. Reviewing research on this topic, Wilder (1997) judged the direct evidence for biological links to mathematical ability as weak at best. Furthermore, social and educational factors are far more likely to have assessment implications.

Social influences on gender difference in mathematics proficiency are assumed to operate mainly in socialization and development of young children, in gender differentiation in adolescence, and in sex-role stereotyping (Baker & Jones, 1992; Eccles & Jacobs, 1986; Fennema & Peterson, 1985). In this view differential socialization is manifested in the channeling expectations of peers and mentors, in social constraints, and in prejudicial treatment (Wellesley College Center for Research on Women, 1992). Math is thereby often perceived as a male domain. Confidence of girls and women in their ability to achieve in mathematics and its relevance to their future tends to slide downward in adolescence, and options to engage in math-related activity are less often elected (Dossey et al., 1988, Dwyer, 1974; Fennema & Sherman, 1978; Hilton & Berglund, 1974; Linn & Hyde, 1989; Sherman, 1978).

Aside from such external influences, the social view of emerging gender differentiation in math proficiency in high school assumes two important mediating influences. One is a different pattern of values and interests that influence females and males in somewhat different directions, and colors their views of mathematics as a desirable activity. Another is the different pattern of experiences of girls and boys, which, it can reasonably be assumed, eventually begins to influence what proficiencies are developed to greater or lesser degree. Such differences in interests, values, and experiences are documented in chapter 4.

Like social influences, educational effects are complex. It is possible that girls profit less from formal schooling in mathematics than do boys (Sadker & Sadker, 1994; Wellesley College, 1992). That argument seems somewhat undercut by girls' tendency to do as well or better on tests of math knowledge and to earn equal or better grades in math courses. It is possible, however, that girls and boys are learning different things, as manifested in their somewhat different profile of math proficiency that we discussed previously.

Recent work at Stanford University suggests such learning differences (Kupermintz et al., 1995). These investigators developed knowledge and reasoning subscores for the NELS Mathematics Test and examined female and male gains from Grade 8 to Grade 10. Improvement in math knowledge over this period showed no gender difference, but there was a gender difference favoring males in the gain on math reasoning. Linn and Hyde (1989) suggested that women may be more likely to approach math problems with algorithmic procedures that they learned in school, whereas men may be more inclined to use an intuitive approach when that is more efficient. These assumptions tend to be supported by Gallagher's (1990, 1992) studies of solution strategies used by women and men.

When young women make lower average scores on math tests, one explanation is commonly related to differences in the amount of math coursework in high school. Some evidence for that association lies in the demonstration that people with higher scores have taken more coursework (Burton et al., 1988; Laing, Engen, & Maxey, 1987; Morgan, 1989; Noble & McNabb, 1989). This type of evidence is weakened by the fact that people who have taken more courses are likely to have been stronger in math at the outset. The case is stronger if there is indication that, not only do boys take more math, but among groups of girls and boys similar at the outset, those who take more math gain more in math proficiency. There are several lines of such evidence.

Using Project TALENT data from the early 1960s, Wise (1985) found that gender difference in math interest and in math course taking accounted for gender differences in math achievement that emerged during the high school years. The effect of gender was always indirect, operating through other variables such as girls' lesser interest in math-related careers. Using data from ETSs Growth Study in the same period, Pallas and Alexander (1983) also reported a significant effect of coursework on gender differences, although their design was criticized on technical grounds by Benbow and Stanley (1983).

Using HSB data from the early 1980s, Jones (1987) found that senior year achievement on mathematics tests was highly dependent on number of courses taken in mathematics and that female and male students profited similarly from taking additional math. Jones concluded that adoption of policies that would lessen gender differences in math course enrollment should lessen differences in math proficiency among high school seniors. Using data from the recent NELS survey, Kupermintz et al. (1995) also reported positive effects of advanced coursework on senior year proficiency in mathematics, independent of gender. The positive effects of coursework were stronger on the acquisition of math knowledge than on gains in math reasoning.

On the other hand, Benbow (1988b) argued that differential coursework does not account for all gender differences. Benbow and Stanley (1980, 1983) pointed out sizable gender differences in math reasoning by age 12 to 13, well before there are consequential gender differences in the selection of math courses. In six Study of Mathematically Precocious Youth (SMPY) talent searches starting in 1972 they found about twice as many males as females scoring above 500 on SAT Math. That ratio has tended to hold in subsequent, more broadly based talent searches (Stanley, 1993).

This result may not be as inconsistent as it initially appears. The SMPY talent search in those years focused typically on the top 3% of seventh and eighth graders. Results of most analyses that are based on representative national samples have suggested that *mean* gender differences in math proficiency emerge during, not prior, to the high school years (Cleary, 1992; Dossey et al., 1988; Hyde et al., 1990; see also Fig. 3.2). It is possible that the gender differences in math reasoning observed in very able youngsters are a reflection of the differential variability of test scores that tends to develop earlier and push relatively more males toward the top and bottom of many test score distributions (see chapter 3; also Hedges & Nowell, 1995).[21] Differential learning out of school likely plays a role because boys and girls at that age are studying much the same topics in school.

Grade–Score Gender Difference in Test Use

In recent years various writers have noted the tendency for girls to make better grades in mathematics courses whereas boys tend to do relatively better on mathematics tests (Benbow & Stanley, 1982; Bridgeman & Wendler, 1989, 1991; Linn, 1992; Pallas & Alexander, 1983; Wainer & Steinberg, 1992). Kimball (1989) reviewed studies that, more often than not, showed such a grade–score gender difference and discussed differential experience and learning preferences as possible explanations.

The clearest picture of the relative performance of females and males on math tests and on math course grades comes from the normative data provided by national surveys and major testing programs. These data have

---

[21]The most recent NAEP Math Assessments (shown in Fig. 3.3) showed significant gender differences in variability (*Supplement* Table S-3). The same trend is evidenced in other subjects and tests, although the trend in NAEP Math was not statistically significant. Standard deviations were not reported in earlier assessments. Benbow and Stanley (1980) cited Fennema (1974) as evidence of gender difference in math reasoning in junior high school, but Project TALENT data on very large national samples showed little mean gender difference in arithmetic reasoning early in high school ($D = -.10$ at Grade 9, $-.29$ at Grade 12; Flanagan et al., 1964).

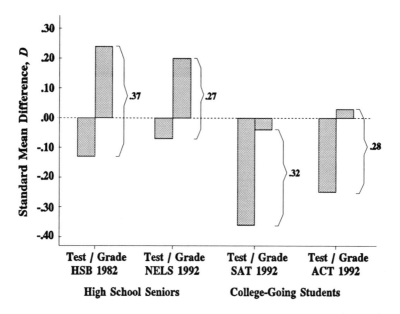

FIG. 7.9. Standard mean differences on mathematics course grades and scores on four mathematics tests. Sources: See footnote 22.

consistently shown the grade–score gender difference for many years. For example, normative data from 1972 show a gender difference of –.30 on ACT Math but a D of .18 on high school math grades for the same group (American College Testing Program [ACT], 1972). A few years earlier the grade–score gender difference was –.48 versus .18 (ACT, 1966).

Data from the College Board have given a similar picture. A compilation of yearly results for college-bound seniors who took the SAT showed almost no difference in the average high school math grades of women and men for each of the years 1973 through 1983. In the same period that large cohort of students was showing a gender difference in SAT Math scores consistently in the range of –.37 to –.45 favoring males (College Board, 1984).

Figure 7.9 illustrates the grade–score gender difference with recent data on the college-going cohort and two representative samples of high school seniors.[22] All four samples, involving different tests, show the same general pattern of grade–score gender difference. The pattern is illustrated here as

---

[22]Test data in Fig. 7.9 are the same as indicated in chapter 3 except for HSB, which was based on the 1980 sophomore sample, retested in 1982 (Rock et al., 1986). NELS and HSB grade data came from the original grade transcript tapes. Math grade means for the SAT group were reported in the 1992 *Profile of SAT and Achievement Test Takers* (College Board, 1992b), and the standard deviations were provided by the program. Math grade data for the ACT group are reported in Table S-14.

the difference between the value of D for course grade and the value of D for test score (i.e., the distance between the ends of each pair of bars). These differences were: HSB, .37; NELS, .27; SAT, .32; and ACT, .28. The pattern appears to be generally consistent across samples and tests, although the data cited earlier suggest that the grade–score gender difference is probably smaller now than was true two to three decades ago.

Is this grade–score gender difference unique to mathematics? Not at all. The four test batteries represented in Fig. 7.9 include 10 other tests or subtests that offer a comparison of grades and scores earned by the same group of students—in each case a large sample representing either high school students nationally or the two admissions testing programs that account for the great bulk of students attending 4-year colleges. The average grade–score gender difference was .31 for English grades (six tests, four reading and two English usage), .31 for Math grades (same four tests shown in Fig. 7.9), .34 for Social Science grades (two tests), and .43 for Science grades (two tests).[23]

These grade–test differentials may be a bit high in mathematics and science because women are not as likely to take the most difficult final course in those two areas (see Fig. 4.17). Nonetheless, the grade–score gender difference is clearly not associated with a particular subject or a particular test. One would certainly expect variations depending on what specific aspect of course or test performance was involved, but the generality of the grade–score difference evidently results from dissimilar characteristics that commonly differentiate course grades and test scores and get reflected in differential female and male performance. Cole discussed grade–score dissimilarities in chapter 5.

Grade–score gender differences are also manifested in the tendency for women's college GPA to be underpredicted by test scores alone (ACT, 1973; Linn, 1973, 1978). We take up that topic in a subsequent section. One factor that can come into play in explaining prediction differences stems from gender differences in course selection and variation in grading standards from course to course (Elliott & Strenta, 1988; McCornack & McLeod, 1988). Noncomparability of instructor's grades has motivated researchers to work at the level of individual courses or class sections. Several ETS studies of mathematics scores and grades have proven particularly interesting (ETS, 1992).

Bridgeman and Wendler (1989, 1991) studied the relationship of SAT Math scores to grades in freshman mathematics courses in 10 colleges. They

---

[23]The detailed results are shown in *Supplement* Table S-23.

found a grade–score difference in college courses much like the high school pattern just described. In the Bridgeman–Wendler study, women often earned slightly higher average grades than men in college mathematics courses despite the fact that the men tended to have higher test scores. The median gender difference in 23 courses was 28 points favoring males on the SAT scale (in algebra, precalculus, and calculus; Tables 3 to 6 in the Bridgeman–Wendler study, 1989, 1991).

Because of this grade–score gender difference, women's grades in freshman mathematics courses were underpredicted when predictions were based on test scores alone. Bridgeman and Wendler (1989) reported, however, that, "combining SAT-M scores with high school GPA not only raised validity coefficients but also tended to eliminate any underprediction of women's course grades" (p. 24). On that basis they concluded that the admissions test could serve a useful purpose in placement, but should be used with evidence of previous performance in math courses.

Bridgeman and Wendler noted that SAT Math alone was not a strong predictor of math grades. At four institutions that had a local math placement test, the local test had a higher correlation with freshman course grade than did SAT Math. This would be expected if the content of the local placement tests emphasizes the specific math knowledge and skill required in freshman math courses (Willingham, 1974a). The median estimated correlation with course grade in an unselected group was .52 for the local placement test and .34 for SAT Math.

Bridgeman and Wendler (1991) also pointed to the content of the tests in accounting for the pattern of gender differences, which were smaller on the placement test than on the admissions test. Whereas SAT Math emphasizes mathematical reasoning and does not depend on specific coursework, scores on math placement tests as well as grades in initial college math courses are more likely to reflect specific knowledge and computational skills. They referred to Doolittle and Cleary (1987), and other studies previously cited, that have documented the different patterns of gender difference and similarity on these different aspects of math proficiency.

Concurrent with the study just described, another group of ETS researchers examined gender differences in course grade predictions in a number of subjects for a much larger set of data based on freshmen from 45 institutions (Ramist, Lewis, & McCamley-Jenkins, 1994). These investigators reported a different pattern of results for initial math courses and other courses in the curriculum in which application of mathematical reasoning is likely to be important. Using high school average and SAT scores, they found that women's grades in freshman math courses (remedial, precalculus, regular math, and calculus) were *underpredicted* by .05 of a letter grade. On the other hand, averaging across 10 types of more advanced math and scientific courses, women's grades were *overpredicted* by .03.[24]

Wainer and Steinberg (1991) dramatized the grade–score gender difference with an interesting analysis. They asked this question: "If two individuals of different sexes in the same kind of course get the same grade, what was the observed difference in their SAT scores?" (p. 2) Using the Bridgeman–Wendler database, Wainer and Steinberg sorted females and males into 25 cells: five grade levels in each of five types of math courses. In all courses students who made higher grades had higher scores. In fact, that was more true of women than of men. But in each cell (i.e., same grade, same course) women had lower scores than men—on average, 35 points lower.

Subsequently, Wainer and Steinberg (1992) repeated the analysis pooling data from the 51 colleges included in the Bridgeman–Wendler and the Ramist et al. studies. They got essentially the same result: Women scored 33 points lower on the SAT Math than did men who earned the same course grade. The conclusion is the same whether based on the Bridgeman–Wendler or the Wainer–Steinberg analysis: Do not use admissions test scores alone to predict grades in college math courses. Recent research based on ACT scores is not as extensive but reached the same conclusion (Noble, 1991; Noble & Sawyer, 1987).

Bridgeman and Lewis (1996) analyzed the Ramist et al. data yet again to rectify what they saw as an incomplete picture in the Wainer–Steinberg analysis; namely, what happens when you include high school grades in the analysis, and when you look at different courses of the same type (e.g., calculus for liberal arts majors, calculus for engineers)? Their findings are reproduced in Table 7.6.

The first column in the table shows results comparable to and quite similar to those of Wainer–Steinberg. The second column shows that the test score gender difference was 8 to 14 points smaller when computed

---

[24]Table 17 of Ramist et al. (1994) listed 10 types of courses that involved advanced mathematics and science:

Advanced biological sciences
Advanced math
Advanced physical sciences/engineering
Computer science
Economics
Lab or major physical sciences/engineering
Lab/major biological sciences
Nonlab and nonmajor biological sciences
Nonlab physical sciences/engineering
Technical/vocational

TABLE 7.6

Gender Difference at Each Grade Level on SAT-M, Standardized High School GPA, and Standardized Composite Scores Computed Across and Within Calculus Courses

| | Mean Score for Females Minus Mean for Males | | | | | |
| | SAT-M | | STD HSGPA | | STD Composite | |
Grade	Across	Within	Across	Within	Across	Within
A	–35	–21	17	23	–11	2
B	–38	–28	21	24	–10	–2
C	–37	–29	20	21	–11	–5
D	–42	–33	30	31	–7	–1
F	–44	–35	30	29	–8	–4

Source: Bridgeman and Lewis (1996). Adapted and reproduced by permission of Educational Testing Service, the copyright owner. All signs were changed to conform with usage in this volume. Standardized (STD) scores are adjusted to the mean and standard deviation of SAT-M. The composite is based on the weighting of SAT-M and high school GPA that produced the best prediction of calculus grade.

within individual calculus courses, rather than across all calculus courses undifferentiated. On this basis the authors concluded that about one quarter of the gender difference observed in their data and by Wainer–Steinberg was an artifact of women and men selecting calculus courses with somewhat different grading standards.

The next two columns show almost mirror-image results when the same analysis was carried out with high school GPA. The high school GPA of women was *higher* than that of men who made the same calculus grade in college. By similar logic one might question whether the high school GPA is fair to males. The last two columns show that the two effects cancel one another out when the two predictors are used together in a composite, in accordance with professional recommendations and standards (AERA et al., 1985; Anastasi, 1990; Gardner, 1982). The authors characterize what differences remain as "minuscule" because all results are reported here on the same type of 200 to 800 scale as SAT Math.

Bridgeman and Lewis were also able to carry out the same analysis on precalculus courses where the findings were similar except that there was little difference in the results within and across courses. Again, this study ends with the same conclusion: Use previous grades along with test scores to ensure that course grade predictions are as fair and valid as possible for both females and males. On the basis of the various findings reviewed here, what can we say regarding assessment implications, especially test design?

Test Design Connections

There is wide agreement that negative signals to young women tend to reinforce negative attitudes about mathematics and take a toll on the development of high-level mathematical skills. Extensive programs to encourage young women to study mathematics (Chipman et al., 1985; Klein, 1985) are apparently paying off in larger enrollments of women in advanced courses and higher test scores relative to men than was true a generation ago. Nonetheless, remaining differences at advanced levels of proficiency can have consequential impact on possibilities of study and success for women in some important fields.

Differential performance of females and males on math course grades versus math tests is part of a larger and seemingly consistent picture. On different tests in the same subject, and in different subjects, women tend to make better grades and men tend to make better test scores. Predicted performance in math courses shows very little gender difference if both prior grades and test scores are used together. That fact aside, the gender difference between grades and test scores could be reduced by putting more math knowledge and algorithmic skills in tests rather than reasoning and problem solving. Would that be a wise thing to do? This brings us back to the question posed at the outset of this discussion: Are we measuring the right knowledge and skills?

The answer hangs critically on the function of the test and its validity in serving that function. Some mathematics tests are intended to serve the specific ongoing efforts of teachers and learners in a particular program and must be designed accordingly. In that sense, instructional assessment differs from the summative tests that we have discussed in this volume. For that reason we set aside instructional assessment, and, instead, consider these three educational functions: to place students in courses, to select applicants, and to certify educational outcomes.

Should a test that is used to place students in the proper math course contain specific math knowledge, algorithmic skills, and so on, that are required for success in the higher of two optional courses? Certainly, if that is the primary purpose of the test. Keying test content to course content will make a more valid test and will likely minimize any grade–score differences for women or other subgroups. If the test is also used for other purposes or may be seen by students and teachers as an important representation of broader educational objectives, then test design issues shift accordingly. In that instance there is a stronger case for ensuring the validity and fairness of placement decisions with additional information (grades in prior math courses) and focusing test design decisions on the broader function of the test.

Designing a test to select students for an advanced educational program or scholarship assumes the broader function. In addition to serving the immediate selection purpose, there must be some assurance that the long-term interests of institutions and society are served by the types of skills that are advanced by being represented on the test. In that regard, mathematical reasoning necessary to solve complex problems is a cognitive skill broadly applicable to academic work and career demands in many fields. In comparison, knowledge of specific mathematical conventions and their computational applications are narrowly important at particular educational junctures, but in adult life and careers, these skills are increasingly taken over by electronic tools.

In that spirit the National Council of Teachers of Mathematics (NCTM) appointed a commission to "create a coherent vision of what it means to be mathematically literate both in a world that relies on calculators and computers to carry out mathematical procedures and in a world where mathematics is rapidly growing and is extensively applied in diverse fields" (NCTM, 1989, p. 1). The Commission's report placed heavy emphasis on problem solving and learning to reason mathematically. Further, the Commission advised that demonstration of good reasoning should be rewarded even more than the ability to find correct answers (Commission on Standards for School Mathematics, 1989). On the other hand, it can be argued that quantitative reasoning is not consistently necessary throughout the college curriculum. How much weight a mathematics test should have in relation to other measures is a legitimate question we examine in a later section.

The washback effect of using one type of math test or another is an additional complexity. Math items that are decontextualized and discrete are good for measuring reasoning and good for avoiding coaching tricks. Adding contextual material to math items may be educationally advantageous but can easily pose fairness problems by influencing test performance for irrelevant reasons. Furthermore, admissions tests were not designed to influence students and instruction directly, but currently they often do so. Unplanned washback effects raise new questions. Should somewhat more specific objectives of math courses be more deliberately represented? Would a move in that direction better balance the representation of math skills on which women and men tend to do well?

Various types of tests are intended to certify the outcomes of instruction in mathematics; for example, national or state assessments, program evaluations, and examinations like AP tests that serve as a basis for exempting course requirements and awarding credit. Tests that serve this function present little design ambiguity. The course syllabus and the educational objectives are paramount. For that reason, the NCTM Standards are emphasized in the design of the 1996 NAEP Mathematics Assessment (National Assessment Governing Board, U. S. Department of Education [NAGB], 1995). Here the main fairness issue in design is the same as the main validity issue; that is, whether the constructs relevant to instructional objectives are adequately represented. In the case of admissions tests, the question of how directly test design should follow curriculum objectives is more complex and debatable.

Summary: Topic 5

Test data indicate little gender difference in math performance at the early grades and some relative gain by males in high school—a difference that has lessened in recent years. By Grade 12, young women and men differ mainly on mathematical reasoning. Women are underrepresented in the most advanced math courses in high school, and research does confirm that math coursework makes a difference in math test performance. Gender differences on advanced tests are also a reflection of somewhat more variability in the scores of men. Among the most gifted students, gender differences in math reasoning appear early.

A number of investigators have noted the tendency for women to make better math grades relative to men, and men to make relatively better scores on math tests. This discrepancy was found to be consistent for different math tests and different large samples. Because of this discrepancy, women's grades in college freshman math courses may be underpredicted if predictions are based on test scores alone. An important implication of these studies is that mathematics tests designed for admissions should be used for math course placement only with evidence of prior grades.

Whereas validity arguments favor knowledge and computation for a freshman mathematics course placement test, mathematicians have emphasized reasoning and problem solving as a preferred basis for national standards of advanced literacy in mathematics. Validity arguments also favor these higher level skills for admissions tests because such skills are applicable to a wider range of advanced coursework and career demands.

Similar questions as addressed here regarding prediction of women's grades in math courses arise with respect to the freshman GPA. This related issue has received much research attention over the years because it bears on the fair use of admissions tests. Predicting freshman GPA also engages other technical questions about the comparability of grades from student to student—all of which is discussed in the next section.

GRADE PREDICTION

Do admissions tests lead to an underestimation of women's overall academic performance in college (Wellesley College, 1992)? In thinking about using tests to predict freshman GPA, it is important to keep in mind a distinction. Prediction involves an interpretation of the meaning of scores and their possible implications.[25] Interpreting scores in relation to actual college performance helps to ensure that the use of scores is comparable. Prediction has an obvious and important bearing on selection, but it is not the same as deciding who is to be admitted (Cole, 1981). We get to that more complex topic in the next section. Meanwhile, in order to appreciate the implications of prediction for women and men, we must first examine briefly the nature of prediction and what seems to affect it.

Predicting Freshman GPA

For many years prediction research, in the form of the institutional validity study, has been a principal source of validity evidence for college admissions tests and information guiding their proper use at individual institutions. Technical manuals for the major testing programs describe that work (ACT, 1988; Donlon, 1984), and a recent book, *Predicting College Grades* (Willingham, Lewis, Morgan, & Ramist, 1990), reports new prediction research on a number of related topics.

College prediction studies are normally based on freshman GPA, a choice dictated by several considerations. The freshman GPA has a more common meaning from student to student than does an upper division average. Also, performance in the freshman year has a heavy bearing on whether students stay in school and what major they choose. Finally, researchers and institutions are reluctant to wait 4 or more years for criterion data on seniors. Validity coefficients based on 4 years of study tend to be quite similar to those based on the freshman year (Willingham, 1985; Wilson, 1983), but as we later argue, there is much value in more intensive, longer range studies.

---

[25]Note that this distinction between interpretation and use is not quite the same as that found in Messick's (1989) four-faceted description of construct validity. In his distinction, interpretation refers to the meaning of the construct, not to implications of use. For our purposes, we bow to the widespread usage of "interpretation" in practice as expectancies or implications stemming from demonstrated criterion relationships. Also, in selective admissions it is important to differentiate predictive relationships from actual use of scores in decision making, which may be quite different because score use is often subjective rather than algorithmically determined. In any event, the distinction is frequently important because central issues in score use concern the ways in which score use does or should differ systematically from established prediction equations or expectancy tables. See Kane (1992) for a similar treatment of score interpretation.

Figure 7.10 illustrates schematically what the relationship between a composite predictor (test score and high school average) and the freshman GPA might typically look like.

The diagonal dashed lines—one for females, one for males—show the positive relationship between the predictor and freshman GPA; that is, that the average freshman GPA earned (2.5 overall) increases with increasing predictor scores. The vertical bars at selected predictor scores show how much actual GPAs vary above and below the mean GPA that is typical for students at that predictor level. For example, freshmen who are one standard deviation above the class average on the predictor will tend to earn nearly a B average, but 5% will earn close to an A average and 5% can be expected to achieve a C average or lower.

Why is there so much variation in the college GPAs of students who entered with comparable test scores and school records? With an individual student in mind, parents and teachers often have little difficulty in coming up with likely explanations: The student was especially diligent or distracted in college, or had a particularly strong or weak high school program, or grew

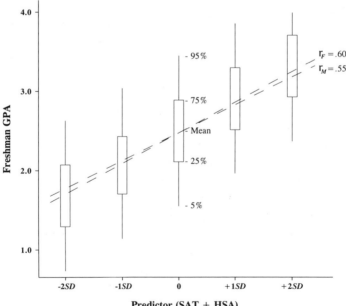

FIG. 7.10. Illustration of freshman GPA prediction—increasing mean freshman GPA with increasing predictor scores, variation about those means, and differential validity for females and males. The five "box and whisker" plots illustrate the standard error of estimate (*SE*) for the total group; that is, the variation of actual GPAs above and below the mean predicted or estimated GPA. Due to differential validity (.60 vs. .55), the male *SE* is 4% greater than the female *SE*.

up in an environment that nourished or deprived intellectual development, or undertook an unusually demanding or relatively easy course of study in college, or had other responsibilities, or received special help in college, or the predictors used may have over- or underestimated what that student could do in the near term.

Whereas it often seems easy to understand prediction errors for particular individuals, it may be more difficult to account for or to accept the idea that, for some combination of reasons, a group of students may perform somewhat differently than expected on average. In either event—with individuals or with groups—if the correlation is anything less than perfect, predictions that are differentially accurate are arguably, to that extent, differentially fair. Our case in point, of course, is women and men, and the question is whether one gender (and necessarily the other) is differentially represented among those students who do better or poorer than predicted in Fig. 7.10.

Cleary (1968) is usually credited with first defining test bias or unfairness in terms of two types of prediction errors; that is, the two ways in which a subgroup may be unevenly represented above and below the common regression line.[26] First, the regression line for the subgroup may be steeper or more shallow, indicating that the test is a more or less effective predictor for that group than for the total group. For example, if the line is steeper, members of the subgroup with high scores will tend to have their GPAs underpredicted, and there will be opposite errors for students with correspondingly low scores. Second, the regression line for the subgroup may be parallel to that of the total group but higher or lower, indicating that GPAs for the subgroup will tend to be over- or underpredicted at all score levels. These two types of error came to be called, respectively, *differential validity* and *differential prediction* (Linn, 1982).[27]

More than two decades ago the technical manuals of the two major undergraduate admissions testing programs reported a fairly consistent pattern of higher validity coefficients for women than for men. For example, Schrader (1971) found that the median validity coefficient for SAT and HSA combined was .62 for women and .55 for men. SAT and HSA alone showed the same pattern of higher validity for women. ACT findings were

---

[26]As Cleary is reported to have frequently pointed out, and as Anastasi (1988) noted, Humphreys (1952) was probably the first to suggest this definition of predictive bias.

[27]Strictly speaking, differential validity normally refers to differential correlations, but for simplicity in this illustration, we have avoided that complication by assuming equal standard deviations for predictor and criterion in Fig. 7.10. As Linn (1982) pointed out, it is the overall pattern of the regression system—including slope, intercept, and standard error of estimate—that should be evaluated. We follow here the conventional practice of focusing on differential validity and differential prediction, noting as did Linn, that the latter is the more important.

similar (ACT, 1973). Subsequent research has shown much the same result with different predictors and groups of students. Differential validity for females and males in recent data is illustrated by the two dashed lines in Fig. 7.10.[28]

Differential validity may advantage or disadvantage a subgroup, depending on whether critical decisions are more likely to be made at higher or lower score levels. Differential prediction, on the other hand, is usually considered the more important threat to noncomparable treatment because it can work to the disadvantage of a group throughout the score range. Early results based on test scores alone showed a substantial underprediction of women's freshman GPA. Linn (1973) studied data from 10 colleges and found an average underprediction of .36 based on the regression line for men (i.e., .18 underprediction for women and .18 overprediction for men). ACT (1973) reported an average underprediction of .27 for women in 19 colleges. Women were underpredicted by the test in each of the 29 colleges included in these two reports. As we will see, more recent research has shown considerably less differential prediction with the same tests.

Currently, researchers studying differential prediction more routinely include high school average as a second predictor, partly because it clearly makes a difference and partly because this is the measure that admissions tests are intended to complement in actual use. Another common feature of recent studies of differential prediction is to analyze the role of the criterion—specifically the effect of college grading variations. It is increasingly apparent that understanding either prediction or differential prediction is difficult, indeed, without careful examination of the college grade criterion.

Variations in Grading and the Effects on Prediction

Worries about variation in grading habits, patterns, and standards are not new. Two papers by Starch and Elliott (1912, 1913) established the tone early in this century. Having been accused of choosing a likely target by demonstrating wide variation in the grades that English teachers assigned to the same papers, these investigators repeated their research with a mathematics examination and reported the "alarming fact" of even wider

---

[28]The dashed lines in Fig. 7.10 are intended only to illustrate differential predictive validity. These are not regression lines because they do not include intercept differences; that is, differential prediction. These correlations of .60 and .55 take account of the possible effect of grading variations. The observed correlations gave similar results (.50 and .46), as did those correlations corrected for range restriction and criterion unreliability (.71 and .65).

variation. Over the years scholars have periodically provided useful accounts of grading and thoughtful commentaries on apparent incongruities in practices and their effects (Cureton, 1971; Fishman, 1958; Milton et al., 1986).

Grading patterns suggest the tendency for grades to take on the coloration of time and place. Drift in the difficulty of grading is a common problem; that is, "An A is not what it used to be." The 1950s to the early 1960s was a period of increasing stringency in grading. Due to the post-World War II baby boom, an expanding age cohort created a tightened selectivity in higher education and increasing proficiency of the freshman classes of many colleges—changes not accompanied by any adjustment in the average freshman grade assigned (Aiken, 1963; Webb, 1959; Willingham, 1963; Wilson, 1970). From the 1960s to the mid-1970s, a reverse trend—grade inflation—was well-documented (Bejar & Blew, 1981; Birnbaum, 1977). This trend leveled for a while (Ramist & Weiss, 1990), and then grade inflation evidently set in again in the 1990s (Ziomek & Svec, 1995).

Although such temporal trends in the level of grades assigned illustrate an easy slippage of standards, neither of these trends had any effect on prediction results, nor would such an effect be expected (Bejar & Blew, 1981; Willingham, 1990). If college grade inflation or deflation affects all students equally, it should not change the correlation between college grades and predictors.[29] Similarly, large variations in grading standards that are known to exist from college to college (Astin, 1971; Hills, 1964) are not likely to affect grade prediction within colleges. On the other hand, predictive accuracy could be affected by lack of *comparability* of grades within a class due to variation in standards among instructors, courses, or departments. A number of studies over the past two decades have confirmed that effect and clarified how it works.

First, it is clear that grades are not comparable across courses and departments, whether comparability is evaluated on the basis of test scores or simply by comparing grades of the same students in different courses (Elliott & Strenta, 1988; Goldman & Hewitt, 1975; Goldman, Schmidt, Hewitt, & Fisher, 1974; Goldman & Slaughter, 1976; Goldman & Widawski, 1976; Juola, 1968; Strenta & Elliott, 1987; Willingham, 1985). Students tend to earn lower grades than their test scores would suggest in quantitatively oriented courses like mathematics and science. Students in

---

[29]Grade inflation could affect predictive validity if the inflation results in a ceiling effect, although there was no sign of that in the inflationary period (Bejar & Blew, 1981). The important point is that noncomparability of grades is the larger threat to validity coefficients.

less quantitative areas like education and sociology tend to earn high grades in relation to their test scores. This pattern seems fairly consistent from institution to institution and study to study (Elliott & Strenta, 1988). An early and apparently correct explanation for these patterns is the tendency of faculty to adapt their grades to the ability level of their students (Goldman & Hewitt, 1975).

A number of investigators have demonstrated (a) reduced accuracy of grade prediction that is directly associated with noncomparability of grades across subject areas, and (b) improved grade prediction when grades are adjusted to make them more comparable (Elliott & Strenta, 1988; Goldman & Slaughter, 1976; Pennock-Roman, 1994; Ramist et al., 1990; Strenta & Elliott, 1987; Stricker, Rock, Burton, Muraki, & Jirele, 1994; Willingham, 1985; Young, 1990a). Two studies suggest situations in which grading variations may be so minor as to have little if any impact on grade prediction; for example, if students take much the same coursework, as in the first year of an engineering program (Willingham, 1963), or if grading is highly reliable and closely monitored, as may be the case in a military academy (Butler & McCauley, 1987).

The relationship between variation in grading standards and variation in predictability of the GPA criterion was further unraveled by a series of studies that were undertaken at ETS to understand changes in validity coefficients over time (Willingham et al., 1990). Changes over time were not due to changes in the admission test (Angoff, Pomplun, McHale, & Morgan, 1990). Had there been test effects they would likely have affected institutional coefficients similarly. In fact, Willingham and Lewis (1990) found substantial differences from college to college in both the absolute level of validity coefficients and in the character of yearly trends in those coefficients. Those college differences were traceable to the grade criterion. Ramist et al. (1990) demonstrated direct connections between changes in validity coefficients and changes in the pattern of course selection and course grading in individual institutions. For example, colleges that showed an increased variety in course selection by freshmen over several years tended to show declining validity coefficients in that period.

Finally, several studies have demonstrated that underprediction of women's freshman GPA is due in part to such grading variations and that underprediction is reduced by using a college grade criterion that is more comparable for women and men (Clark & Grandy, 1984; Elliott & Strenta, 1988; Gamache & Novick, 1985; Leonard & Jiang, 1995; McCornack & McLeod, 1988; Pennock-Roman, 1994; Ramist et al., 1994; Young, 1990b). In one other study (Stricker, Rock, & Burton, 1993), there was no reduction in underprediction for women with an adjusted GPA criterion, apparently because the adjustment method used was later shown to be less effective than other methods in correcting grade variations (Stricker et al., 1994). The study by Ramist and colleagues deserves some discussion because it was unusually comprehensive and broke new ground.

The Ramist, Lewis, and McCamley-Jenkins Study.   These authors extended their 1990 study of prediction trends to a detailed analysis of subgroup differences in prediction. The study involved grades of 46,379 students in 7,786 courses at 45 institutions. Using the SAT, high school average (HSA), and both measures together, predictions were carried out for grades within individual courses, grades by types of courses, and freshman GPA overall. The predictions were analyzed by gender, by ethnic and language group, by students with high and low academic composites (SAT plus HSA) at entry, and within more and less selective institutions.

As in other studies, grading tended to be stricter in more quantitative courses and more lenient in less quantitative courses. Weaker students (with lower academic composites) tended to take more leniently graded courses. As a result there was little relationship ($r = .12$) between the SAT mean and the grade mean from course to course. Three methods were used to correct for grading variations: (a) by using an additional predictor representing the average grading stringency in the courses selected by the student, (b) by predicting grades in individual courses, and (c) by predicting freshman GPA based on average course predictions in the particular courses that each student actually took. Each method builds on the assumption that individual students do not necessarily take the same courses or courses of comparable grading difficulty. All methods gave similar results.

The magnitude of the effect of grading variations on validity coefficients is indicated by the following comparison of observed freshman GPA predictions. Use of SAT alone yielded a validity coefficient of .36; adding HSA raised the coefficient to .48; basing the freshman GPA prediction on grade predictions for the particular courses that each student took raised the coefficient to .60—an increase of 25% in predictive effectiveness.[30]

This study also demonstrated that, without the criterion distortion of grading variations, the admissions test is actually a slightly more accurate grade predictor than is high school average. Across all colleges the average

---

[30]This result was based on the third correction method. The second method yielded a similar value, .58. Results for the second method were reported only with corrections for range restriction and are not comparable.

correlation with course grades was .60 for SAT and .58 for HSA. The difference was larger for women: .64 and .59 for SAT and HSA, respectively. These coefficients are somewhat higher than those in the preceding paragraph because Ramist et al. corrected all correlations with course grades to take account of the restricted range and unreliability of single course grades.

An equally striking finding was the enormous difference in validity coefficients for students with higher academic composites in more selective colleges (.83) compared with students who had lower academic composites in less selective colleges (.36).[31] The former is about as high a validity coefficient as one might reasonably expect to ever find. This result gives some doubt as to the likelihood that improved prediction will come from new tests—at least not in the case of better students in selective colleges.

In general, Ramist et al. found that validity coefficients for all predictors tended to be higher for females than for males. For example, in predicting freshman GPA from SAT and HSA, the correlations were .60 and .55 for women and men, respectively. The relatively small magnitude of that differential validity is illustrated by the two dashed diagonal lines in Fig. 7.10.

The findings regarding the more important differential prediction can be summarized as follows. For the 45 colleges, the average underprediction of women's freshman GPA based on the SAT alone was .09. This is half the amount estimated by Linn in 1973. Adding HSA to the SAT reduced the underprediction to .06.[32] Adding a correction for differences in grading stringency in the courses selected by women and men reduced the underprediction to .03. The corresponding overpredictions of men's grades were .10, .06, and .03, respectively. Figure 7.11 illustrates the under- and overprediction for women and men in the first and last of these three cases.

Predictions based on the SAT alone are shown in the top panel. Predictions based on SAT, HSA, and a grading correction are shown in the bottom panel. In the bottom panel the improvement in predictive validity (from .36 to .58) is reflected in a steeper slope of the regression line; the more closely spaced dashed lines also show a reduction in differential prediction for women and men. Because Fig. 7.11 is drawn to the same scale as Fig. 7.10, the magnitude of differential prediction can be evaluated in relation to the extent of prediction errors for students generally.

---

[31]These validity coefficients come from Table 11 in Ramist et al. (1994). Both are corrected for range restriction in order to make them comparable, one to the other, and to correlations based on a total class. The corresponding total class correlation was .63 (see their Table 5).

[32]ACT reported quite similar results (–.05 overprediction for men and .05 underprediction for women) based on four ACT tests and four high school grade averages (ACT, 1988, p. 66 and Table 4.27). The results are not strictly comparable because the ACT analysis was based on a cross-validation design.

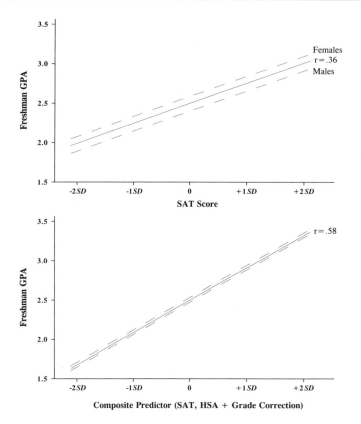

FIG. 7.11. Illustration of under- and overprediction for females and males when predictions are based on SAT alone or on a composite including SAT, HSA, and a grade correction. *SD* for both scales = .71.

As prediction errors vary for individuals, so does over- and underprediction for different groups. Ramist et al., reported differential prediction results using SAT and HSA to predict the course grade criterion for these six nonmajority subgroups based on gender, ethnicity, and language: women, .03; English not best language, .16; American Indian students, –.22; Asian American students, .08; Black students, –.12; Hispanic students, –.09. The positive numbers represent underprediction; the negative numbers represent overprediction.

Finally, differential prediction by gender was particularly associated with less selective institutions. Underprediction for women in more, average, and less selective colleges was .01, .02, and .05, respectively. In the more selective colleges, course grades of women were *under*predicted .04 with SAT alone, *over*predicted by .02 with HSA alone. There was zero differential prediction in these colleges when a measure of writing skills (TSWE) was added to SAT and HSA.

Implications for Test Use

In the previous section we reported data indicating that women, compared to men, do better on classroom grades than on tests by about one third of a standard deviation in each of the four subject areas examined. Given that result, it is no surprise that women's college freshman GPA tends to be underpredicted if the prediction is based on a test alone. But test results are routinely used with previous grades in selective admissions, and the *Standards* specifically note that all measures used in selection should be included in studies of differential prediction (AERA et al., 1985). We have seen that underprediction of freshman GPA largely goes away if the high school record and the college program of study are taken into account. The obvious implication regarding test fairness is that judgments of fairness need to be based on the measures actually used in selection and a criterion that is comparable. Otherwise, the picture is likely to be misleading. The obvious implication regarding test use is that scores should not be used alone in academic prediction.

What about the near zero, .03, underprediction that remains, on average, when such factors are taken into account? Assuming that result is accurate, does it suggest that the test should be somehow adjusted or changed? An important aspect of comparable test design and use is the feasibility of alternatives and possible consequences for other groups of examinees. For different gender, ethnic, and language groups, differential prediction varied from .16 to −.22. The corresponding estimate for women was .03, easily the smallest differential prediction among the six groups.

It seems clear that different factors will affect the grade performance of students in different subgroups and different institutions, and that one cannot reasonably expect to adjust a test so that all grade–score relationships come out even. The criterion and the situation is likely different for all students to some extent. These results give more evidence that tests are not surrogates for grades.

It is possible that other information or other tests can help to bring predicted and actual grades into optimal balance for some groups of students. As Linn and Werts (1971) demonstrated, under- and overprediction can easily result from the omission of key information about a group of students. For example, Stricker et al. (1993) showed that predictive validity was improved and underprediction for women was reduced by taking studiousness into account. Conversely, Gamache and Novick (1985) showed that underprediction for women was increased by including tests on which women scored lower but did not improve predictive validity. Also, recent research by Bridgeman and Lewis (1994) suggests that more emphasis on essay examinations would result in more gender-neutral differential prediction in some subject areas.

Summary: Topic 6

Prediction is related to test fairness because inaccurate predictions can influence selection decisions. Two types of accuracy were differentiated. When prediction studies are done separately for women and men, women's GPAs are typically predicted somewhat more accurately than those of men. When the same study is done with women and men in one group, the women's GPAs tend to be slightly underpredicted and the men's GPAs slightly overpredicted on average. This finding has been observed for many years, and the differential prediction now appears to be much smaller than it once was.

This result is parallel to the result for math course grades discussed in the previous section. The similar finding with regard to GPA is foreseeable from the fact that a gender difference in course grades versus test scores is not limited to mathematics. The same pattern was observed in other subject areas. The extent of underprediction of women's GPA varies somewhat among institutions, and it is partly due to differences in the severity of grading in courses that are taken more frequently by women and men. The most recent and extensive studies indicate that, overall, underprediction is quite small (.03 of a letter grade) when the GPA criterion is comparable for women and men and predictions are based on test scores and previous grade average.

In this section we found that the interpretation of test scores and high school grades in relation to performance in college is very nearly comparable for women and men. In the following section, we take up the next natural questions: Are test scores actually used in a comparable way in selection of women and men? How do we judge whether the decision process is equitable? What do we know about the outcome of selective admissions for women and men?

SELECTIVE ADMISSIONS

In the previous section we distinguished prediction from selection. Prediction involves an interpretation of what level of criterion performance one might expect on the basis of admissions measures, whereas selection refers to an action taken. Our objective here is to consider issues concerning fair actions in the use of academic predictors, and to report some admissions data that may be helpful in judging the fairness of the outcome for women and men. Thus, we approach the topic from two perspectives: what constitutes comparable selection in theory based only on grade predictions, and how comparable are selection outcomes in practice. We start by describing some so-called fair selection models. These models were proposed in response to general concerns regarding the meaning of fair test use, particularly minority–majority differences, but they apply equally well in principle to women and men.

Fair Selection Models

A number of hypothetical models have been developed in order to illustrate various issues or to argue points of view regarding fair selection. These models are not easy to follow, but they are worth the effort, because selection models offer a useful perspective on fair test use. They can be seen as achieving fair selection decisions through the use of different statistical strategies that amount to rival definitions of fairness. For our purposes, it will suffice to describe two such models. All share certain assumptions or characteristics.

The models assume that some applicants must be rejected, and that for that purpose, a comparable predictor is available for all applicants and an appropriate criterion can be used to distinguish "successes" and "failures." We also must assume that, in the past, all applicants were admitted irrespective of predictor score, making it possible to distinguish correct decisions (e.g., admitted students who succeeded) from incorrect decisions (e.g., admitted students who failed). Finally, we assume that for some subgroups the predictor may not be equally valid in some sense, or there may be justification for differential selection.

The Cleary Model.   Early concern about the fairness of tests focused particularly on whether predictions and selection decisions based on the majority group regression line underestimated the performance of minority students in college. On that basis Cleary (1968) defined test bias as systematic over- or underprediction of performance and carried out studies to evaluate predictions for Black students (see also Anastasi, 1968). The Cleary regression model was well-accepted and has been the method commonly used in studies of subgroup differences in prediction. This model is illustrated in Fig. 7.12.

The top portion of Fig. 7.12 shows Group I and Group II with an exaggerated difference on the predictor to make the illustration clearer. In

Regression Model (Cleary, 1968)

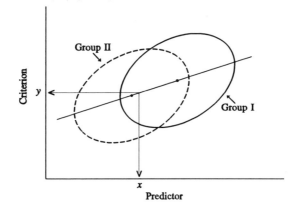

Conditional Probability Model (Cole, 1973)

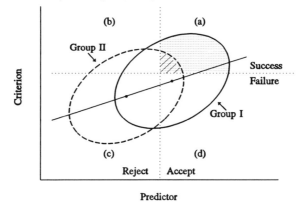

FIG. 7.12. Two fair selection models.

the case shown, the two groups share the same regression line. This means that those students with a predictor score *x* will, on average, earn the same criterion score *y*, regardless of group membership. In practice, grade predictions for Group I and Group II might differ, either because of difference in the subgroup regression lines or the amount of error around the regression line (see Fig. 7.10), or because of differential prediction (see Fig. 7.11). Under any of these conditions, fair selection is achieved by using separate regression equations for Group I and Group II, or as suggested by Einhorn and Bass (1971), computing probabilities of success separately for the two groups. Thus, according to this model, decisions based on the most accurate prediction for each group and each individual are the fairest decisions.

With Cleary's regression model, equal opportunity (i.e., comparability or fairness) is achieved through selecting those individuals, regardless of group membership, who are most likely to succeed. The model was uncontested for only 3 years, when it became evident that fairness could be viewed differently. Several authors introduced the notion of fair selection based on group parity (Cole, 1973; Darlington, 1971; Linn, 1973; Thorndike, 1971). The group parity models differ one from the other, but all are incompatible with the regression model in that what seems fair from one perspective is unfair from the other. We use Cole's model to illustrate the difference.

The Cole Model. The lower panel of Fig. 7.12 shows the same predictor–criterion relationships for Groups I and II as in the upper panel. The vertical dotted line separates those applicants who were hypothetically accepted or rejected. The horizontal dotted line distinguishes successful and failing students at a hypothetical passing score on the criterion. These lines create four quadrants: (a) and (c) where the prediction was correct, and (b) and (d) where the prediction was incorrect. According to Cole's definition, in fair selection the proportion of potentially successful students who are accepted should be the same in Group I and Group II. This means that the number of students in the region marked (a) divided by the number in regions (a) plus (b) should be the same for Group I and Group II.

However, as the figure clearly shows, those proportions are not the same in the two groups. Most of the potentially successful students in Group I were accepted (the stippled area), but of the students in Group II who might have succeeded, relatively few were accepted (the cross-hatched area). This discrepancy—this apparent unfairness in the acceptance rate for the two groups—has nothing to do with the nature of the predictor or the criterion or the students involved. It is a necessary statistical result whenever prediction is imperfect, and one group scores lower on the predictor than does the other group.

In the Cole model, fair selection requires an adjustment in the accept–reject points for the two groups so that the stippled and cross-hatched areas represent the same proportion of the "successful" students in their respective groups. Thus, the model can be seen as a psychometric rationale for affirmative action. But we have this dilemma: The method that seems fair to individuals is not fair to groups and the method that seems fair to groups is not fair to individuals. Other perspectives of group parity can be defined by various relationships among the numbers of people in the four quadrants (a) to (d).

In 1976 a series of papers were published in the *Journal of Educational Measurement* that keyed on Petersen and Novick's (1976) analysis of these various models. One result was the suggestion of additional models (Darlington, 1976; Novick & Petersen, 1976; Petersen & Novick, 1976; Sawyer, Cole, & Cole, 1976). There was general agreement that the fair selection models are often inconsistent, usually based on different value considerations, and sometimes affect different groups in contradictory or undesirable ways. The authors did not agree on a preferred model. That lack of consensus had been reflected 2 years earlier in the *Standards for Educational and Psychological Tests* (American Psychological Association, American Educational Research Association, & National Council on Measurement in Education [APA/AERA/NCME] 1974), which stated, "It is important to recognize that there are different definitions of fairness, and whether a given procedure is or is not fair may depend upon the definition accepted" (p. 44).

An important benefit of the fair selection models has been to provide rational bases for connecting affirmative action with different educational and social benefits associated with alternate selection strategies. Alternate strategies are neither right nor wrong; rather, they are based on positive values that may be in conflict; for example, treating people as equals, or according to developed abilities, or according to accomplishments (Deutsch, 1975; Rawls, 1971).

These potential conflicts illustrate why there can be instances when there is no clear answer to the question of what comparable treatment will result in fair test use. Such conflicts also imply the need for some formal means of debate and resolution. For that reason, there has been general agreement on Petersen and Novick's (1976) suggestion that fair selection models might prove more acceptable and less contradictory if they formally took into account the special value that might be associated with a particular selection outcome; for example, enrolling a potentially successful woman in an area, like physical science, where women are underrepresented (Cronbach, 1976; Linn, 1976; Sawyer et al., 1976).

Progress on this refinement has been limited, and it seems doubtful that there have been many instances in which fair selection models have been formally incorporated into the mechanics of the admissions process. There was a significant proposal to adjust employment test scores according to subgroup membership (Hartigan & Wigdor, 1989) that would have moderated disparate impact of selection on subgroups as suggested by the fair selection models. The practice was highly controversial and subsequently prohibited by the Civil Rights Act of 1991 (see Gottfredson, 1994, and Sackett & Wilk, 1994, for recent accounts.) Nevertheless, the thinking represented in the fair selection models has been influential, and they continue to be helpful in clarifying important issues regarding fair selection in practice. Several such issues deserve comment.

Practical Issues

Disagreement as to which selection model is fairer arises when groups differ on the predictors and because the predictors are fallible. The lower the predictive validity, the greater the potential problem. Several writers have described the distortion in apparent fairness or unfairness that can result from unreliable predictors, from missing predictors, or more specifically, from leaving out a predictor that is normally used in selection (Humphreys, 1986; Linn, 1983, 1984; Linn & Werts, 1971; Reilly, 1973).

The clearest and most important example of the effect of a missing predictor is the high school average. In selective admissions an applicant's test scores are routinely used in conjunction with the academic record. We saw in the earlier discussion of prediction that women and men consistently show a quite different pattern of mean performance on high school grades and test scores. As a consequence of that different pattern, HSA and test scores together always yield greater validity in predicting college GPA, and differential prediction varies noticeably when HSA is or is not included in the predictor composite. Furthermore, there are important instances (e.g., in predicting college math grades, or in predicting freshman GPA in selective institutions) in which HSA alone underpredicts for men much as test scores alone underpredict for women. Such results illustrate the complementary role that tests serve—as intended—in predicting academic performance. These considerations underscore the importance of evaluating selection fairness as specified in the *Standards* (AERA et al., 1985); that is, on the basis of the principal measures normally used in making decisions, not one measure in isolation.

In undergraduate admissions there is normally little difference in the average qualifications of female and male applicants because high school average and test scores are used together, and as we saw in chapters 3 and 4, the differential advantage of women on the former tends to cancel that of men on the latter. Thus, the contradictory implications of different fair selection models are not likely to apply generally at this level with respect to gender. Issues raised by these models could be pertinent to a particular institution or graduate field where women are underrepresented and tend to score somewhat lower on admissions measures.

Under close scrutiny, fair selection models also raise more fundamental educational issues. In considering fair selection models, it is usual to acknowledge possible shortcomings in the grade criterion (Linn, 1976; Petersen & Novick, 1976), but choice of the criterion can, in fact, be critical—not only because it may not be comparable for different groups, but because it may not even be the criterion on which one would prefer to make such judgments. For example, a broader criterion representing potential contribution to the college and to society could provide a better basis for judging fairness (Linn, 1984; Wild & Dwyer, 1980).

Colleges also have to judge fair test use on the basis of possible secondary effects. Fair selection models tend to be conceived and discussed as if they apply only to the two readily defined groups in question. In actual practice, any such decision rule that is formally incorporated into admissions procedures needs to withstand close scrutiny as to precisely who is in the group that profits. Aside from gender, other subgroups (e.g., based on race, language, disadvantage, or disability) typically pose difficult practical problems of fair identification (Duran, Enright, & Rock, 1985; Linn, 1976; Novick & Ellis, 1977; Willingham, 1988)

Furthermore, a selection rule affecting one group is likely to have rippling effects on other groups. To our knowledge there has been little if any systematic analysis of such effects. These various complications illustrate aspects of the larger context that must be taken into account if a particular instance of test use is to be comparable, everything considered. Meanwhile, selection continues and institutions endeavor to ensure fairness while serving diverse educational objectives.

Research results as well as descriptive accounts indicate that selective institutions place primary emphasis on academic promise in selecting their students (Breland et al., 1995; Skager, 1982; Wechsler, 1977; Willingham & Breland, 1982). Routinely, estimates of academic promise are based on prior academic performance and an admissions test score—hedged in individual cases by the judgment and experience of the admissions staff. There are two major mechanisms through which selective institutions adjust these decisions in the effort to make the selection process, in their judgment, as fair and valid as possible: (a) adjusting for evidence of differential prediction, and (b) affirmative action.

Throughout the history of grade prediction, it has been common practice to look for instances where groups of students habitually tend to achieve higher grades than routine prediction would lead one to expect, and to take such tendencies into account in selecting students. There are several advantages to adjustments for differential prediction, which is essentially the Cleary model. It tends to enhance validity and fairness to individual students. It is easy to apply in the case of large, readily identifiable groups like women and men. Major admissions testing programs typically offer free or low-cost validity study services that make it easy to use separate regression equations for subgroups where the institution believes it to be appropriate. As we have seen, there is little indication of underprediction of women's GPA, but it can obviously occur in a particular institution or program. Such adjustment for differential prediction is also a natural way to take into account evidence of special promise or unusual background that are known to presage higher performance in college for a particular group of students than traditional predictors would lead one to believe.

There are also definite disadvantages to blind correction for differential prediction. Over- or underprediction can result for a variety of reasons, such as unreliability of the predictor (Linn & Werts, 1971), or a missing predictor, such as poor schooling, may cause college grades to be overestimated. A group of students may be overpredicted for reasons that have quite different implications for the college; for example, because they were not well-prepared, took very difficult courses, devoted their talents to other important contributions to the institution, or spent their time in social pursuits, and so on.

Another compelling reason to be cautious regarding uncritical use of such adjusted predictions is that some results may run counter to other institutional objectives, such as enrolling more students from underrepresented groups. Results of differential prediction reported in the preceding section suggest that routine use of separate regression equations for subgroups would have the effect of selecting more Asian American applicants and students whose first language is not English, but fewer applicants among Black, Hispanic, and Native American groups. These latter groups are often the target of affirmative action programs, the second major mechanism for adjusting the selection process in order to carry out institutional policy.

Affirmative action programs have a different rationale—partly educational and partly social. There is positive educational benefit of diverse cultural representation and there is clear social need to redress the effects of social discrimination and economic disadvantage. As we have seen, fallible prediction inevitably leads to underrepresentation of potentially successful students in any group that tends to score lower than average on the composite measures used in selection. Appropriate affirmative action in selection and in the classroom has been the means of addressing such threats to fair selection since the late 1960s.

Then, as now, affirmative action has not proceeded without debate. In *Bakke*, one of the most widely discussed Supreme Court cases of modern times, the court delivered a verdict that was regarded, depending on the point of view, as either a ratification or a death knell for affirmative action (Regents of the University of California vs. *Bakke*). In a one-sentence decision, the court sanctioned the use of race as a factor in admissions decisions, but invalidated the special admissions program at the medical school of the University of California at Davis—principally because minority and majority students were admitted through a separate process, making race a controlling consideration (Powell, 1978). It was, in effect, a political compromise that had surprisingly little practical impact on institutional practice.

These various issues are important aspects of fair selection because they frame the larger context in which selection policy and practice are debated. The issues pertain in varying degree to different demographic groups, different cohorts, and different educational programs. Research and data on the outcomes of the selection process are helpful in judging where and how such issues may be relevant to gender differences—and to what extent the process appears to work fairly.

Outcomes of Selection

Enrollment of both women and men in higher education has increased greatly over the past four decades, but as Fig. 7.13 shows, their representation has shifted dramatically. From 1952 to 1992 total enrollment grew from 2.1 million to 14.5 million (NCES, 1994). Enrollment of men increased almost fivefold, but for women, the increase was tenfold. The female to male ratio shifted progressively in 10-year intervals from 1952 to 1992 as follows: .55, .61, .76, 1.06, and 1.22 (NCES, 1994). By far the largest shift in the F/M ratio (.76 to 1.06) occurred during the decade following the Title IX legislation in 1972.

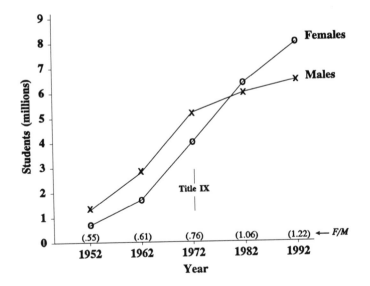

FIG. 7.13. Total fall enrollment of females and males in institutions of higher education—1952 to 1992. Source: *Digest of Education Statistics* (NCES, 1994). The points for 1962 are based on the averages of 1961 and 1963. *F/M* indicates the ratio of females to males for the years indicated.

TABLE 7.7

Outcome of the Admissions Process at Leading Public and Private Research Universities (Res I) and Selective Private Colleges

	Res I—Public (N=45)		Res I—Private (N=25)		Selective Private College (N=30)		Total (N=100)	
	F	M	F	M	F	M	F	M
Number of:								
Applications	274.4	276.6	120.5	135.8	55.1	51.0	450.1	463.4
Accepted applications	193.7	186.5	52.1	55.6	23.9	21.9	269.8	264.0
Enrolled freshmen	76.6	75.8	19.2	20.8	8.2	7.9	104.0	104.4
% of Applications accepted	71%	67%	43%	41%	43%	43%	60%	57%
F/M ratio for enrolled freshmen	1.01		.92		1.05		1.00	

Note. Based primarily on data published in 1995. Numbers in thousands. Multiple applications are included.

These data demonstrate a dramatic increase in the number of women in higher education, but they have little to say about admission to selective institutions and programs. While the gender balance among students in higher education changed over this period from almost twice as many males as females to about a fifth more females, other changes were taking place as well. Notably, this was an expanding period in higher education—one of diversification and democratization. Did women gain representation in the selective institutions, many of which had been heavily male? Citing institutional admissions data just prior to Title IX, Cross (1974) was critical of selective colleges that rejected well-qualified women while maintaining a substantial male majority in the student body.

Table 7.7 summarizes current admissions statistics regarding applications, accepted applications, and enrolled freshmen in 100 prominent higher institutions. These include 30 of the very selective private colleges and 70 major (Research I) universities that comprise many of the more selective and prestigious academic departments.[33] There are several noteworthy

---

[33]Research I universities were listed in the *Chronicle of Higher Education*, April 6, 1994; they include institutions that award 50 or more doctorates and receive $40 millon or more in federal support each year (Evangelauf, 1994). Selective private colleges were defined arbitrarily for this analysis as any undergraduate institution that met two of these three criteria: "most selective" in *Barron's Profiles* (Barron's Educational Series, 1994), most selective category in *Lovejoy's College Guide* (Straughn & Straughn, 1993), and reported less than 50% of applicants accepted in the *College Handbook 1995* (College Board, 1994a). Data on number of applicants, accepted applicants, and enrolled freshmen were obtained from the 1995 *Handbook* (or in a few instances the 1994 or 1993 *Handbook*; College Board, 1993a, 1992a) for 100 of 116 Research I or selective private institutions (86%). The tabled "% of applications accepted" was based on totals for each type of institution; the corresponding percentage was also computed for each institution and averaged. For each of the three types of institutions the amount of difference in the percentage accepted for males and females varied no more than 1% as computed by the two methods.

findings in the table. Somewhat more men than women applied to these institutions, but a slightly higher percentage of women were accepted (60% vs. 57%). As a result, almost exactly the same number of women and men (104,000 each) were enrolled as freshmen. Finally, each of the three types of institutions showed much the same pattern of application, accepted applications, and enrolled students.

These data do not speak directly to selection decisions, although they do allow an overall comparison of acceptance rates and enrollment rates for women and men with generally similar academic qualifications; that is, comparable average performance on the two predictors that are routinely used and about equally valid (Ramist et al., 1990). From data reported earlier, we can estimate the standard mean difference, D, for all college applicants to be about .17 for HSA and −.16 for admissions tests—opposite advantages for women and men that essentially cancel one another.[34] These data, linked with the near-zero differential prediction previously noted in selective institutions, suggests that selection in selective undergraduate institutions is very close to parity with respect to gender. In contrast, studies based on cohorts three to four decades ago showed sizable male advantage in college attendance after controlling for ability and background (Alexander & Ekland, 1974; Flanagan & Cooley, 1966; Folger, Astin, & Bayer, 1970).

This is not the complete picture. Results can vary in individual colleges because of differences in selection procedures or in applicant pools. In 11 of these 100 institutions, the acceptance rate differed by .10 or greater—in seven cases favoring women and four favoring men. Those different acceptance rates appear typically to represent an effort by the institution to achieve a more gender-balanced entering class in the face of an imbalance in its applicant pool. In the seven institutions with a higher acceptance rate for women, the F/M ratio was .64 in the pool and .72 in the entering class. In the four institutions with a higher acceptance rate for men, the F/M ratio was 1.50 in the pool and 1.28 in the entering class.

Furthermore, equal acceptance rates can still be questioned if there are different patterns in the average test score and HSA for female and male applicants. In a study involving nine selective private colleges, actual selection decisions were compared with predicted decisions based on applicants' HSA and SAT scores (Willingham & Breland, 1982). In one of those

---

[34]The test estimate, $D = -.16$, was obtained by averaging the Ds for ACT and SAT subtests in Table 3.2 and weighting the averages according to program volume. If the estimate is based on admissions tests that are as similar as possible, average Ds for verbal and quantitative (in Table 3.4) would yield almost the same figure, −.17. In the case of HSA, $D = .17$ is based on the weighted average for the ACT and SAT program samples shown in Table S-13.

institutions, the proportion of women accepted was .15 lower than expected, based on predictions undifferentiated by gender; in each of the other eight colleges, the acceptance rate for women differed from that predicted by no more than .02. In a similar recent study of 178 law schools, Wightman (1995) found the acceptance rate of women to be .03 higher than predictions based on male equations. Results were not reported by individual law school.

In addition to variation by institution or type of institution, selective admissions can vary substantially by field of study. It has been shown, for example, that acceptance rates can appear to favor men (or women) across a graduate division of a university, but look just the opposite when decisions are analyzed department by department (Bickel, Hammel, & O'Connell, 1975). Disciplines that require mathematical proficiency—mathematics, science (physical and biological), and engineering—are a particular concern because of a long history of underrepresentation by women. These are areas where group parity in selection becomes an issue because entry is typically restricted, and men tend to outnumber women among high scorers on difficult mathematical reasoning tests, a measure often judged to be important in these fields (Table 3.2).

Because entering freshmen typically apply to an institution rather than a particular department, a study of selection into undergraduate disciplines such as that already described is difficult if not impossible. Nonetheless, data on student plans and attainment provide useful information. Comparable data on baccalaureate degrees and graduate enrollment are most recently available for 1992. In that year, 8.5% of the women and 23.9% of the men who earned BA degrees received them in natural science, mathematics, and engineering. This gives an F/M ratio of .36 for BA recipients in science and technology (NCES, 1994). In that same year, 10.1% of the women and 30.9% of the men entering graduate school enrolled in those same fields giving an F/M ratio of .33 (Council of Graduate Schools, 1992). The small reduction in the relative number of women in science and technology from undergraduate to graduate school may be influenced by the migration of some women into medicine, a field not represented at the undergraduate level. Including medicine raises the F/M ratio at the graduate level to .40 (Association of American Medical Colleges [AAMC], 1992).

These ratios are generally similar to the ratio of women to men who say that they intend to major in mathematics, science, or engineering at the time they enter college. In 1990 the F/M ratio was .32 among students expressing such plans. Students are well-known for changing their plans during college, but the ratio gives some indication of relative interest among women and men in fields with more quantitative emphasis. The attraction of individual fields has changed for women as well as men over time, but the *F/M* ratio for students interested in these fields combined has not changed a great deal since 1966 when it was .29 (Dey et al., 1991).

Informative analysis of admission to doctoral programs has recently become possible due to the continuing assembly of student data under the aegis of the AAU/AGS Project for Research on Graduate Education. The project has focused its data gathering efforts on the following five disciplines: Biochemistry (41% F), Economics (29% F), English (61% F), Mathematics (25% F), and Mechanical Engineering (13% F). An analysis of fall 1990 applicants to 44 participating graduate schools (Russo & Montes, 1993) indicated considerable variation in the percentage of females among entering students (just shown in parentheses). Women had slightly lower acceptance rates than men in three fields and slightly higher rates in two fields. Were the acceptance rates comparable, considering qualifications?

Using the same database, a subsequent study (Attiyeh & Attiyeh, 1994) examined the comparability of admissions rates of different groups of applicants in these five graduate disciplines, taking into account their academic background (GRE General scores and undergraduate GPA[35]) and the selectivity of the departments to which they were applying. Figure 7.14 shows the results for women and men.

Conditional probability of admission can be interpreted as follows. Given a female and a male doctoral applicant who are similarly situated (same scores and undergraduate records applying to an equally selective department), what is the probability that each will be admitted? Any difference in the probabilities indicates that the selection committees gave some preference to the group with the higher conditional probability. An observed difference in female and male probabilities could have a variety of explanations—other qualifications not taken into account, affirmative action, unconscious selection preference, and so on. In all five fields the conditional probability was higher for women, although the differences were small and statistically significant only in the case of economics and English. The authors described these results as follows:

> It is clear that the substantial underrepresentation of women in economics, mathematics, and mechanical engineering is not a consequence of discriminatory admissions practices. At the same time, for mathematics and mechani-

---

[35]Undergraduate GPA was based on self-reported information provided to the Graduate Record Examinations Board when the student registered for the GRE General examination. The undergraduate GPA was adjusted for grading variations on the basis of average SAT scores at the undergraduate institution.

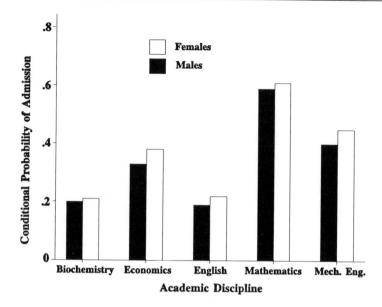

FIG. 7.14. Probability of admission for female and male doctoral candidates in five disciplines, conditional on their being similarly situated applicants. Source: Adaptation of Figure 2 on p. 4 from G. Attiyeh & R. Attiyeh (September, 1994). Are graduate admissions fair? *Program Profiles*, Vol. II(1). Princeton, NJ: Educational Testing Service, AAU/AGS Project for Research on Doctoral Education. Used with permission.

cal engineering, admissions committees do not appear to be making admissions decisions designed to compensate for the relatively small size of the female applicant pool in that the conditional probability of admission is not significantly greater for women. (Attiyeh & Attiyeh, 1994, p. 4)

This succinct statement brings together several important aspects of the preceding discussion. Judgments as to the fairness of an admissions process—that is, comparable treatment—must first take account of the standards and the measures on which selection decisions are mainly based. Admissions outcomes that appear comparable on that basis may or may not appear comparable in the broader context of institutional objectives that bear on subgroup parity.

Summary: Topic 7

The previous section considered whether academic predictions are comparably accurate for women and men. This section focused on the comparability of actions; that is, the outcome of selection decisions. The topic was approached from two perspectives: what constitutes comparable selection outcomes in theory, and how comparable selection outcomes are in practice.

Two "fair-selection" models were described in order to illustrate assumptions and contradictions as to what constitutes comparable treatment in selection. First, in judging whether a test is fair, it is essential to consider all predictors normally used and all subgroups of interest. In the generally accepted model, selection is fair when the individuals selected are those most likely to succeed, regardless of group membership. A second model illustrated that there are plausible alternate views of fair selection. When a subgroup has lower average scores on admissions measures, it was shown that selection decisions that seem fair to individuals do not necessarily produce outcomes that seem fair to groups. There has been no agreement on such alternate views of fair selection because they tend to yield contradictory results for different groups.

Enrollment data indicate a dramatic change in the gender balance in higher education—from a majority of men in the early 1970s to a majority of women in the early 1990s. Acceptance rates for women and men were compiled for 100 prominent undergraduate institutions—very selective private colleges and leading research universities. Somewhat more men than women applied to these institutions but a somewhat higher proportion of women were accepted. As a result, almost exactly the same number of women and men were enrolled. Several studies at the undergraduate and graduate level indicate that acceptance rates are very nearly the same for women and men who have comparable admissions qualifications.

Such data remind us that discussion of fair selection often focuses on important but limited information and concerns. In the larger context, institutions have additional priorities to balance, other issues to weigh, and other views of merit to consider. Our final topic examines fair selection in this larger context.

FAIR TEST USE IN CONTEXT

In practice, selective admissions is considerably more complex than the foregoing discussion would suggest. Institutions have a variety of social and educational interests to serve. They use a wide range of information about their applicants in an effort to serve those interests effectively and to serve them fairly for individual students as well as many subgroups. The use of such information and the procedures that are followed in selection opens many opportunities for making decisions that may be more fair or less fair.

Readers will appreciate that this topic is extraordinarily broad, engaging educational philosophy, the details of recruiting and processing applicants, the psychology of talent, the economics of education, state-mandated guidelines, legal constraints and protections, and so on. The purpose of this section is certainly not to cover all of this ground. Some important issues are noted only in passing. Our limited objective is to examine some implications of this broadened context for fair test use generally and for women and men particularly. To that end, we briefly address these topics: the nature of the admissions process, multiple views of talent, admissions decisions in action, and the weight on admissions tests.

The Nature of the Admissions Process

The Dean of Admissions at a prominent university once reflected on college admissions as follows (Hargadon, 1981):

> Foreign observers of higher education in this country generally find three particular aspects of our system remarkable: (a) its sheer size and scope; (b) its considerable variety and diversity; and (c) our lack of anything remotely approaching a common standard by which millions of students are admitted to college each year .... In no major system of higher education in the world is access to higher education less dependent on the results of a single examination or set of examinations than in the United States. (p. 112)

Diversity in the admissions process results only partly from diversity in the educational system. It is also clear from many descriptions of selective admissions that the process has multiple objectives (Beyers, 1986; Carnegie Commission on Higher Education, 1973; Carnegie Council on Policy Studies in Higher Education, 1977; College Board, 1992c; Kinkead, 1961; Moll, 1979; Thresher, 1966; Wechsler, 1977; Whitla, 1968; Wickenden, 1979). Moving students from a diverse set of schools to an even more diverse set of colleges is a complex procedure. For example, the process must:

- Match the demands of educational programs as well as possible with preparation, skills, and interests of individual students.
- Foster the educational opportunity in ways that encourage personal development and success for individuals as well as groups.
- Ensure fairness through objective evaluation in an admissions process that minimizes personal prejudice or favoritism, or unfair effects of differences in grading and curriculum among secondary schools.
- Serve academic as well as other goals of colleges such as enrolling a well-balanced class with diverse skills and interests.

- Encourage effective learning and teaching in secondary school through admissions policies that identify worthwhile learning outcomes and reward accomplishment.

Although an applicant's ability to succeed academically at an institution is normally the first requirement for admission, it clearly serves a college's vital interest also to admit students who are interested in the programs it offers, or students who can help produce a balanced class, or students who can bring important talents that serve the institution, regardless of whether such characteristics improve freshman grade prediction. Thus, a wide array of measures and information about applicants are likely to come into play: academic preparation, interests and plans, special skills and accomplishments, and so on. The admissions test provides one objective measure that is common for all students—an important element of fairness, aside from its predictive validity.

On what basis does one demonstrate the validity and fairness of such information for use in selection? Needless to say, it is more complicated than the psychometric models in the preceding discussion. A statistical association between test score and GPA does give strong evidence of a test's validity, but that is not the only basis for justifying the use of a test or other information in selection. An equally strong basis is evidence of balanced representation of those student skills, qualities, and other characteristics that are relevant to the academic programs and that best serve the goals of the institution and the admissions process generally. It is a justification based on logical argument as to the relevance of selection standards (AERA et al., 1985; Bowen, 1977; Carnegie Council on Policy Studies in Higher Education, 1977; Cole, 1990; College Board, 1992c; Cronbach, 1980; Manning, 1977; Messick, 1989; Wild & Dwyer, 1980). As Justice Powell (1978) argued in his influential opinion in the *Bakke* case, it is not only the institution's right to select its class, it is also appropriate—even desirable—to use multiple measures in selective admissions.

There is another important aspect of the broader context: Admissions is much more than selection. The essential institutional challenge is to maintain enrollment of an appropriate student body. This involves recruitment, application, selection, enrollment, and retention. Application and enrollment (and often, retention) are based on student decisions, which apparently have a much greater effect on the nature of the student body in most colleges than do selection decisions made by the institution. Based on their analysis of the National Longitudinal Study sample, Manski and Wise (1983) concluded as follows.

Do young men and women go to college largely at the discretion of admissions officers? ... We have found that individual application decisions are much more important than college admission decisions in the determination of attendance. Self-selection is the major determinant of attendance. (p. 4; see Willingham & Breland, 1982, for a similar conclusion.)

As Elliott and Strenta (1990) pointed out, the academic level of a class is heavily determined by the pool of applicants. For example, they reported a correlation of .91 between average SAT scores for applicants and entering students, even within a group of selective colleges. And among those applicants accepted, it is not unusual—even at selective colleges—for half or more to elect to go elsewhere (Willingham & Breland, 1982). More often than not, it is the more able student who accepts an offer from another college (Breland et al., 1995). Due to the importance of those student decisions and the competition among selective colleges, recruitment and enrollment planning have become critical endeavors—more important than selection for a great many colleges (Hossler, 1986; Zemsky & Oedel, 1983). Nonetheless, the use of tests and other information in selection obviously affects how institutions are viewed and how students make their decisions.

How does the selection process work? The first principle is that each institution decides on a process that suits its situation. Periodically, several of the major organizations involved in testing and admissions undertake a cooperative survey of admissions practices. The resulting data, based on some two thirds of the undergraduate institutions in the country, provide much useful detail on specific procedures in the admissions process as well as reports from admissions officers on how tests and other information are used in selection.

In the most recent survey (Breland et al., 1995), 4-year institutions reported that high school GPA or rank in class are the most important factors in reaching admissions decisions, followed by test scores, coursework, and the institution's evaluation of recommendations, interviews, and student essays. The latter types of credentials often give evidence on leadership, special accomplishments, initiative, and so on. Typically, such qualities were reported to be at least of some importance in about half of the public and three quarters of the private 4-year colleges and universities.

These institutions appeared to be about evenly split in reporting gender to be either a minor factor in admissions decisions or not a consideration. How much stress is placed on test scores versus the school record may be of more consequence in evaluating gender fairness because, as we have seen, female and male applicants tend to be differentially strong on those measures. Among 4-year institutions, about two of every five identified a single factor that they considered most important in their admissions process. High school GPA or rank in class was the single most important factor in 25.2% of the colleges and universities, another 5.5% indicated high school course-work, and 1.6% said that tests were most important.[36]

Even a quite comprehensive survey of policy and practice will not necessarily yield the same results as an empirical analysis of what influences actual selection decisions. We report some data pertinent to that point shortly. Also, an accounting of institutional policies and practices, useful as that may be, does not give much sense of the dynamics of the process. For example Skager (1982) postulated, "Most undergraduate colleges and universities use some variation of a three-category model in which applicants are initially classified into (a) presumptive-admit, (b) hold, and (c) presumptive-deny status" (p. 290).

Skager speculated that selection decision criteria may differ substantially for these three categories. In particular, he noted that colleges are likely to dip into the presumptive-deny category in order to meet affirmative action goals. Willingham (1983) described a similar but somewhat more elaborate "contin-gency" model (i.e., the nature of the decision is based on the characteristics of the applicant and the profile of the emerging accepted group). In his terms, an academic prediction model is used to identify applicants more or less likely to do well academically, but thereafter, that psychometric strategy does not serve the institution's needs too well. It is necessary to overlay another model; for example, a "mosaic" model through which particular qualified applicants in the uncertain decision area are selected in order to be sure that the college admits an adequate number of women, minority students, alumni legacies, hockey players, chemistry majors, students from key feeder schools, and so on.

In this later stage of the selection process, the coach, the orchestra director, and the development office hope to see their special prospects make the cut. This complex procedure is particularly associated with the private sector, but prominent public universities such as the University of California follow a similar tactic (University of California, 1995). The end of the selection process is also a time when a strong recommendation or an impressive interview may prove decisive. These more personalized credentials are particularly characteristic of the admissions process in graduate schools and medical schools, respectively.

This complex picture underscores the importance of context in under-standing selective admissions. As Cronbach (1980) emphasized, one cannot reasonably look only at the test to judge whether it is valid and used fairly. It is the whole selection process that must be justified. This means using the

---

[36]This detail was not included in the survey report. We are grateful to Hunter Breland for providing tallies of responses to Question 8, on which these percentages and Table 4.10 in Breland et al. (1995) are based.

right criteria as much as the right selection measures, and using a decision process that balances the various outcomes that may be individually desirable but collectively in competition. We look now at data that may give some sense of the interrelationships among some competing measures in admissions, how women and men score on these measures, and what role they play in selective admissions.

Multiple Views of Talent

There is a long history of research and writing that urges a broad view of talent and multiple measures of cognitive skills and achievement in selective admissions (Carnegie Commission on Higher Education, 1973; College Board, 1986; Frederiksen & Ward, 1978; Gardner, 1961; Holland & Astin, 1962; Richards, Holland, & Lutz, 1967; Shepard, 1992; Taber & Hackman, 1976; Wallach, 1976; Willingham, 1974b, 1980). In particular, evidence of special accomplishments of students in and outside of the classroom (e.g., in science, performing arts, and leadership) have received much attention in research literature for several reasons. Such accomplishments are often intrinsically meritorious, they represent quite different types of socially valued skills, and they bear only a limited relationship to traditional scholastic measures like grades and test scores.

For our purposes here, measures of student accomplishment have another very important attraction. Data on such accomplishments are available with HSA and test scores for the same nationally representative sample of students. This makes it possible to examine the relationship among skills, difference and similarity in the profile of skills for women and men, and changes in those profiles that might result from different selection strategies. Table 7.8 shows such data for seven categories of outstanding achievement among 11,269 high school seniors in the 1992 NELS follow-up sample. The achievements include high scores on the two traditional scholastic measures, HSA and a composite of the NELS tests, and five different types of accomplishment—all based on awards and honors won in high school.[37]

The percentage of students achieving each distinction varied, depending on the rarity or difficulty. The bottom lines of the table reflect a pattern

---

[37]Table 7.8 is based on 11,269 students on the NELS 1992 data tape who responded to the senior year questionnaire (49.4% female and 50.6% male). Nationally, females accounted for nearly 50% of high school graduates in 1992 (see footnote 2 in chapter 3). High performance on "HSA and test score" was defined as students in this sample who scored in the top 10% of a composite based on equally weighted grade average and test score average for four areas: math, English, science, and social studies. The other categories were defined on the basis of student self-reports that they had received awards or honors, were elected class officer, or received special recognition for high performance—all referred to here as "Awards and Honors." All results are based on weighted data.

TABLE 7.8

Intercorrelation Among Seven Types of Outstanding Achievement in High School, Percentage of Females and Males in Each Category

"Outstanding Achievement"	HSA	Test	Sports	Leader	Arts	Writing	Science
Scholastic measure							
HSA (Top 10%)	—	.70	.07	.23	.17	.21	.12
NELS test (Top 10%)	.71	—	.02	.06	.17	.27	.20
Awards & honors							
Sports	.03	−.16	—	.30	.02	.13	.28
Leadership	.32	.14	.27	—	.24	.28	.12
Performing arts	.14	.17	−.08	.32	—	.13	.03
Writing	.23	.22	.15	.36	.23	—	.25
Science/math	.30	.17	.26	.39	.21	.42	—
% High—Females	11.9	7.9	6.7	15.4	9.9	15.1	1.8
% High—Males	8.2	11.8	15.8	11.1	7.4	10.4	3.5
F/M	1.45	.67	.42	1.39	1.34	1.45	.51

Note. Tetrachoric correlations for females are above the diagonal,, males below. See footnote 37 for a description of the seven types of "outstanding achievement." Source: 1992 NELS second follow-up.

consistent with that described in chapters 3 and 4. More women were outstanding achievers on grades, leadership, performing arts, and writing. More men were outstanding achievers on tests, sports, and science and math.

Several aspects of the relationships among the achievements are noteworthy. The test score and HSA were highly related for both women and men; .70 and .71, respectively. However, these two scholastic measures typically had a relatively modest correlation with the other five performance-based accomplishments. As we have known for a long time, people who do well on scholastic measures are often not the same people who do well on performance measures (Holland & Richards, 1965). Also, the five different types of awards and honors are not highly correlated. This is mainly because quite different interests and skills are involved, but partly because students participate in some activities and not others. The pattern of intercorrelations is generally quite similar for women (above the diagonal) and men (below the diagonal). The F/M ratio in the bottom line of the table shows that all seven indicators of outstanding performance favor either the women or the men. Notice that each could be viewed as unfiar if it were the only measure used in college selection.

Table 7.9 is based on the same data but addresses a different question. If different strategies are used to select outstanding students, what is the effect on the number of women and men represented and on the profile of their talents? Wing and Wallach (1971) once did a similar analysis of applicants to Duke University. This table shows what happens when the top 10% of the national sample are "selected" by four methods: I—on HSA alone;

TABLE 7.9

Profiles of Outstanding Achievements in a Select Group of High School Seniors Identified by Each of Four Methods

	Percentage of Selected Group Who Were Outstanding Achievers											
	Method 1			*Method II*			*Method III*			*Method IV*		
Type of Outstanding Achievement	*Top 10%: HSA*			*Top 10%: Test*			*Top 10%: HSA, Test*			*Top 10%: HSA, Test, Marks*		
	F	*M*	*Total*	*F*	*M*	*Total*	*F*	*M*	*Total*	*F*	*M*	*Total*
Scholastic measure												
High on HSA	59	41	100	22	24	46	42	31	73	28	23	51
High on test	22	23	45	39	61	100	30	39	69	21	24	45
Awards & honors												
Science/math	2	4	6	2	4	5	1	4	6	4	10	15
Sports	5	7	12	3	6	9	4	6	10	13	21	34
Leadership	15	11	26	7	10	17	13	10	23	27	27	54
Performing arts	9	5	14	6	7	14	9	6	15	18	14	32
Writing	14	8	22	12	11	23	14	9	23	26	23	49
% of total group	59	41	100	39	61	100	52	48	100	50	50	100

Note. Source: 1992 NELS. See footnote 37.

II—on test composite alone; III—on HSA and test together; and IV—on the basis of the total number of high achievements, considering all seven. For each of the four panels, representing the four selection methods, the total column shows what percentage of the selected group was high on each outstanding achievement. The columns headed *F* and *M* indicate how many of those were female and male. In looking at this table it is also useful to think of individual students and how each might view the fairness and validity of the selection process. The table suggests several implications.

If a small proportion of students are selected only on the scholastic measures, relatively few of the awards and honors will be represented, and it does not make much difference whether HSA or the test gets more weight (Method I, II, or III). This is because neither HSA nor the test is strongly related to the performance measures—as we saw in the previous table. The big difference in the representation of awards and honors in the selected group comes only when those accomplishments are directly involved in the selection strategy; that is, Method IV. If selection is based on all seven achievements, the selected group loses about one third of the students who are high on HSA or test score, but gains two to three times as many students in each type of award and honor.

The choice of Method I, II, or III is not likely to make much difference to a student who has worked hard to earn one of the awards or honors. The pattern of these achievements represented in the selected group does not vary much across the three selection methods that are based on the scholastic measures. Also, the profile of awards and honors for women and men tends to be much the same with the three methods. On the other hand, giving more weight to a particular award or honor—say, sports or writing—could obviously have considerable effect on its representation in the selected group and on the number of women and men who are selected.

That fact is well-illustrated by comparing the outcome of Methods I and II. Putting more emphasis on HSA favors women; putting more emphasis on the test favors men. If selection were based only on HSA or only on the test, the result would be approximately 50% more women or men, respectively (i.e., about 60/40 in one direction or the other). Selecting on the scholastic measures, equally weighted, gives about the same proportion of women and men (52/48 based on HSA and test alone, 50/50 if the awards and honors are also considered). That result corresponds fairly well to the actual proportions of women and men among enrolled freshmen in Table 7.7. The equal weighting of HSA and test score also corresponds to the approximately equal predictive validity of the two types of measures (Ramist et al., 1994).[38]

The benefit of Tables 7.8 and 7.9 is to illustrate the dynamics of multiple measures and standards in a decision process much more complex than one predictor and one criterion. Needless to say, one can obtain quite different results with different assumptions as to what qualifications and standards are used in what manner. Another recent study from a somewhat different perspective also illustrates that point.

A more restricted sample of the NELS database was analyzed to estimate how many students might qualify for admission to a selective institution (Owings et al., 1995). High school seniors who were in academic programs were considered "qualified" if they had a HSA of 3.5, an SAT total of 1100, a specified strong pattern of academic courses, positive teacher comments, and two or more extracurricular activities. Again, more women met the HSA criterion, and more men met the SAT criterion. There were small

---

[38] Actually, the analysis by Ramist et al. (1994) provides fairly convincing evidence that the SAT is a slightly better predictor of course grades, whereas HSA is a slightly better predictor of freshman GPA. Corrected validity coefficients for SAT and HSA were, respectively: .57 and .61 for freshman GPA, and .60 and .58 for course grades (their Table 4). This pattern of coefficients represents a swing of .06 in predictive validity for the same very large sample. The difference apparently results from the fact that HSA incorporates the same types of grading variations as does freshman GPA. Correcting the criterion makes SAT the better predictor. The implication for selection depends on the value one places on the real GPA that appears on the transcript versus the real academic proficiency, not distorted by student selection of courses with different grading standards.

differences favoring women on the other qualifications. Relatively few students met all: 4.7% of the males and 6.9% of the females.

This result suggests that more women than men are so qualified and that perhaps more women should be admitted to selective institutions, but, of course, much depends on the criteria selected. The question of what is comparable and how large a role particular admissions criteria should play is surely a judgment that individual institutions must make. How many are accepted among the women, the men, or any other group of applicants depends on the pattern of actual decisions. We look now at a study that examined such decisions and their aftermath in some detail.

Admissions Decisions in Action

In 1978 the College Board and ETS initiated with nine private colleges a study of the role of personal qualities in the admissions process. More than 100 background characteristics, school achievements, personal interests, goals, and other measures were collected for 25,000 applicants to these colleges. This information was used to analyze the admissions decisions at each institution (Willingham & Breland, 1982). By following the students through 4 years, the study identified a number of different success criteria and the student qualities associated with each type of success (Willingham, 1985).

In choosing their students, the colleges gave three times as much weight to academic ratings of applicant folders as to personal ratings. The two main academic factors—high school rank (HSR) and SAT scores—were weighted equally in admissions decisions and proved equally valid in predicting freshman grades. A residual analysis was designed to evaluate how much preference in admissions decisions was associated with other student characteristics. Residual selection rates were defined as the actual percentage of a group that was accepted minus the percentage that was predicted to be accepted on the basis of HSR and SAT scores. Selected results are shown in Table 7.10.

Looking first at the overall residual rates in the righthand column, minority status and alumni ties showed the largest preferential effect of any student characteristic. There was no evidence that socially privileged students (i.e., those with high socioeconomic status)[39] received such prefer-

---

[39]Definitions of all measures and categories in Table 7.10 can be found in the *Supplement to Gender and Fair Assessment* and in Willingham and Breland (1982). The "follow-through" rating reflects productivity in out-of-class activities in high school. It was based on a pattern of persistent effort and successful achievement, preferably in more than one area over several years. "Diversity state" and "Close-tie school" are connected with recruiting priorities. "High SES" is here a composite of results for three characteristics of parents reported earlier: high occupational level, highly educated, and went to a selective college. "Outstanding interview" refers to a research staff rating of the interview protocol prepared by the admissions staff member who conducted the interview on campus.

TABLE 7.10

**Residual Selection Rates for Various Groups of Applicants—Within
Three Selection Zones and Overall**

| | Residual Selection Rate[a] | | | |
| | Low Selection Zone | Uncertain Selection Zone | High Selection Zone | Overall Residual Rate |
Characteristic				
Background				
Minority	45	30	5	31
Alumni parent	34	32	5	23
Close-tie school	8	1	3	4
Diversity state	7	7	0	4
Local resident	13	6	1	3
Disadvantaged	7	0	−1	1
High SES	2	1	0	0
Women	1	−8	0	−2
Accomplishments				
Academic honors	−3	13	1	4
Follow-through	−1	7	0	4
Leadership	0	7	1	3
Athletic achievement	1	4	1	2
Creative talent	0	10	0	2
Community activities	−6	2	0	0
Testimony				
Outstanding interview	28	28	7	21
Student statement	3	14	4	7
School report	1	14	2	6

Note. Adapted and reprinted with permission from Willingham, W., & Breland, H., *Personal Qualities and College Admissions.* Copyright © 1982 by The College Entrance Examination Board. All rights reserved.

[a]Entries are actual percentage of group accepted minus percentage that would be selected only on the basis of HSR and SAT. The three selection zones are defined as score ranges on a composite of HSR and SAT where probability of acceptance was $\leq .25$ (low), .26 to .74 (uncertain), and $\geq .75$ (high). Residual rates were computed by college and pooled. See footnote 39.

ence. Overall, outstanding accomplishments had limited effect on admissions decisions,[40] but an outstanding campus interview had quite a strong effect on selection decisions in some colleges. Neither of these latter two effects was consistent with policy intentions of the colleges and came as a surprise to the admissions staffs.

For the total pool of applicants, the residual selection rate for women was near zero, but there was a small negative residual (−.08) among those applicants in the "uncertain" zone where the accept–reject decision could go either way. Three quarters of that negative residual is due to decisions at

---

[40]This result seems counterintuitive in the case of athletic achievement, considering the well-known tendency of many colleges to actively recruit athletes. The explanation apparently lies in the fact that a substantial proportion of applicants presented evidence of an athletic achievement. In smaller groups flagged by coaching staffs, the residual selection rate was above .10 at three colleges.

one college, the only one of the nine where the overall residual for women was larger than plus or minus .02.

The dynamics of the selection process are well-illustrated by the results in the first three columns of Table 7.10. These data confirmed the admissions officers' accounts that the decision process is very different for those applicants where the likelihood of acceptance is low, uncertain, or high. Applicants high on HSR and SAT were accepted largely on that basis. Personal qualities came into play when acceptance was less certain or unlikely on academic measures alone. In that case, critical background characteristics like minority status and alumni ties provided a basis for affirmative admissions preference (often early in the process).

On the other hand, evidence of personal achievement (e.g., leadership, outstanding school references) tended to be used mainly as a late tie-breaker among applicants still in the running with good but similar academic credentials. The strong positive residual for "outstanding interview" is especially interesting. It apparently represents the advocacy of individual admissions staff for individual applicants. One cannot help wondering how those students pan out.

Naturally, these results do not necessarily apply to a particular institution. In fact, this study showed that the more selective the institution, the more it drew on personal qualities in making selection decisions. An analysis of universities or public institutions would undoubtedly show important differences.[41] The main point, however, is that selective educational programs are likely to use a variety of information in different ways to serve multiple objectives. Whether a given applicant is accepted may well depend on the individual's particular characteristics, where she or he stands in the competition, and how the construction of the incoming class is proceeding. Obviously, many competing objectives must be balanced, and the process necessarily involves much considered judgment and many small exceptions, all of which makes any simple evaluation of the fairness of those decisions a chancy matter. An important question is what happens over 4 years. Does the selection process look generally valid and fair in light of student experience and success?

---

[41]The main policy differences are likely to be between the less selective public and private institutions with respect to measures other than HSR and test scores, which almost all 4-year institutions say are important. In their stated policies, private colleges in general place much more emphasis on recommendations, interviews, extracurricular accomplishments, and so on than do public institutions (College Board, 1994d). But as the data in Breland et al. (1995) show, the very selective 4-year institutions express rather similar admissions policies, regardless of control. As the data of Willingham and Breland (1982) suggest, the less selective college may be more inclined to exercise its limited rejections on applicants that it judges unlikely to be able to cope with the academic standards of the institution's programs.

The criterion has been called the Achilles' heel of predictor-criterion validity evidence (Linn, 1976, 1984). In the Personal Qualities study, the colleges collected considerable evidence regarding student success over 4 years (Willingham, 1985). But what type of success is most important? As Cronbach (1980) asked, "What justifies *this* criterion? What biases does it have?" (p. 103). One strategy was to group a number of success measures into three broad types: scholastic honors, leadership positions, and significant accomplishments. Also, the colleges were asked to select those seniors whom they considered their most successful overall, based on the college's definition of success.

Figure 7.15 summarizes the results. The size and placement of the circles indicates the number of seniors in each category and the overlap among the three types of success, which were only moderately related. One striking result was that the colleges gave very nearly equal emphasis to scholarship, leadership, and accomplishments when they picked their most successful students. The three types of success correlated .43, .46, and .47, respectively, with the "most successful" nomination. Note also the overrepresentation of women in most categories—40% more women than men won scholarship honors, and 28% more women were designated most successful overall. Figure 4.9 in chapter 4 provides further detail.

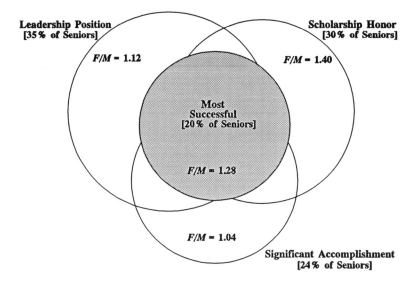

FIG. 7.15. Success in college: Percentage of seniors who won recognition in either of three areas or were nominated most successful overall—female to male ratio (*F/M*) in each group. Reprinted with permission from W. Willingham, *Success in college: The role of personal qualities and academic ability.* Copyright © 1985 by The College Entrance Examination Board. All rights reserved.

What forecast these different types of success? High school rank and test scores were by far the best predictors of scholarship. Additional measures added very little useful information for that purpose. On the other hand, it was mainly other measures that were useful in predicting "leadership position" and "significant accomplishment." Furthermore, additional measures beyond HSR and SAT were necessary to select optimally those students that the colleges considered most successful overall. The one that added most effectively to HSR and SAT was "follow through," a measure of persistent and successful extracurricular accomplishment in secondary school. High school honors, the student's personal statement, and the school reference also added. The admissions interview, which had a strong influence on selection decisions, added nothing to HSR and SAT in predicting success—not success in scholarship, leadership, or significant accomplishments in college.

Overall, the admissions process at such institutions gives strong evidence of valid policy and careful execution. Nonetheless, there were some apparent inconsistencies that vary from one institution to another: admissions policy intentions versus actual decision outcomes, the relative amount of emphasis on personal achievements in selecting applicants versus identifying successful college seniors, the ratio of women to men accepted versus the ratio of women to men judged most successful after 4 years, and the impact of the personal interview on admissions decisions versus its lack of predictive usefulness. In varying degree, each could affect gender fairness.

These apparent inconsistencies illustrate possible threats to validity and fairness that are discernable only in an examination of selection decisions in context; that is, when considering the multiple objectives, measures, and procedures that selection typically involves in practice. Such difficulties encountered in the fair use of multiple measures in selective admissions reveal an underlying value dilemma. A selection process can be "individualized and fair" by using different measures with individual students to recognize their different strengths. The process can be "objective and fair" by basing decisions on the same measures for everyone. A selection process cannot have full benefit of both of these virtues at the same time.

A related concern, especially in literature critical of test use practices (Connor & Vargyas, 1992; Rosser, 1989; Wellesley College, 1992), is the amount of weight a test or other admissions standard receives in high-stakes decisions. We close this chapter by considering aspects of test use that bear on that question.

The Weight on the Test

There are a number of ways in which a test score or any other measure or characteristic of an applicant can receive heavy weight or little weight in actual selection decisions. Clearly, there may be fairness implications for women and men if a measure so affected also shows a mean gender difference. We have just seen unintentional instances of increased or decreased actual weight on measures in selection, not always consistent with validity evidence or policy intention. Two aspects of test use have received considerable attention in writings on test use because they can have important effects: one is the use of cut scores, another is basing decisions on a single measure. We consider these in turn, noting that each is a complex topic much beyond the scope of this already lengthy chapter.

Cut Scores. Ordinarily a passing score or *cut score* refers to a particular score on a single measure or a composite measure that differentially determines a decision, such as accept or reject. The primary issue posed by the use of a cut score is the exclusion of other factors in the decision—other measures that may improve the validity of the process, other relevant evidence, mitigating factors, and so on. Deciding yes or no on the basis of the cut score—even if it is a composite of several measures—has the effect of placing all of the weight on that score. Accordingly, standards of test use routinely urge caution in defining and using cut scores (AERA et al., 1985; ETS, 1987; Joint Committee on Testing Practices, 1988). Much depends, however, on the purpose of the test and the circumstances of use.

Setting the passing score on a school-leaving examination or an examination for course credit is based on requirements of knowledge and skill determined by educational objectives. This places a heavy burden on the content of the test, but allowing decisions to be influenced by factors other than the designated score on that content threatens fairness and runs the risk of defeating the purpose of the test. A difficult task is deciding how high or low that score should be. As Dwyer (1995) made clear, it is always a judgment of informed users, and there is no "true" answer.

The situation is quite different when educational decisions are based on a student's demonstrated capability to profit from a particular academic program; for example, grade placement and classification in the lower grades, or selective admissions to higher education. In these instances, cut scores may place undue weight on the particular measures used because additional skills and characteristics may be necessary in order to reach valid and fair decisions.

Do colleges use cut scores in admissions? Surveys of admissions policy indicate that some 30% to 40% set a minimum qualification on ACT, SAT, and HSR. Those percentages did not vary much in the 1979, 1985, and 1992 surveys; nor have they varied much between public and private institutions. In 1992, the percentage of colleges setting a minimum on high school *grade average* was about 20 points higher for both public and private institutions (Breland et al., 1995).

The minimum standards typically used in 1992 were about 2.1 for high school GPA, 750 to 800 for total SAT, and 17 to 18 for ACT composite. The standards were up slightly from the 1979 survey (American Association of Collegiate Registrars and Admissions Officers [AACRAO] & College Board, 1980). In his review of test use in admissions for the National Research Council, Skager (1982) concluded, "the mean cut-off scores used by these institutions were surprisingly low" (p. 293). A low cut score is very different from a high cut score because the low score excludes relatively few candidates—in the main, those who are not likely to succeed. Also, if a low cut score represents only a minimum requirement, applicants may be selected or rejected largely on the basis of additional information.

Do selective colleges actually follow this stated policy, and accept significant numbers of applicants with modest test scores and school grades? Unpublished data on admit decisions for applicants to the nine colleges in the Personal Qualities study showed a quite consistent picture for both the HSR and the SAT. In all instances the probability of admission dropped smoothly as test score or school rank declined. In none of 18 graphs was there an abrupt drop, which would indicate that no applicants were accepted below a particular score. Furthermore, all colleges accepted some students with average SAT scores in the 300s, and all accepted some students even in the bottom 1% to 2% in the distribution of applicants' test scores.

We know of no comparable information on graduate admissions. Skager (1982) reported that, "There are apparently some instances in which GRE scores are used as cut-offs but this does not appear to be the norm" (p. 300). The GRE Board advises score recipients to justify carefully the use of any composite cut-off and never to base a cut-off on GRE scores alone (GRE Board, 1991a).

Decisions Based on One Measure.   In a sense, using tests alone in making educational decisions is a corollary to using a cut score. Depending on the nature of the test and its purpose, both types of use can put more weight on the test than was intended or is desirable. One result can be an adverse effect on a subgroup of examinees—more often on women than on men. The point deserves special attention because we saw it manifested several times in this chapter and in earlier chapters as well. We know, for example, that:

- If tests are used as a graduation requirement, the choice of which tests—writing versus science, for example—can make a substantial difference in the proportion of women and men who fail to receive a diploma.
- Whether previous grades and other types of accomplishments are included can make a significant difference in the relative number of women and men who are admitted by a selective college.
- Mathematical reasoning tests, used without taking account of previous math grades, are likely to underestimate the performance of women in college freshman mathematics courses (although not in more advanced technical courses).
- Tests in general—not just in mathematics—tend to underestimate women's academic performance if used alone, without some measure of previous grades.
- Taking into account both grades and test score in academic prediction is fairer to all students because predictive validity is substantially higher with both.

The arguments as to when it might be appropriate to use a test alone and why that might be undesirable in other situations are much the same as with the use of cut scores. There is a special problem with regard to selective admissions because one cannot possibly put everything into the test that is relevant. There is no disagreement on this point, and it is not a new idea. This point of view is stressed in accounts of selective admissions previously cited. Also, measurement professionals writing specifically about test misuse warn of the *"hazard of the single indicator"* (Anastasi, 1990, p. 19, italics in original), and the problems inherent in "using test scores in isolation for decision making" (Gardner, 1982, p. 323.).

Organizations that develop and sponsor prominent national testing programs have often encouraged users to draw on multiple sources of information in order to ensure fairness and to balance the limitations of any single measure (ACT, 1992; College Board, 1988; ETS, 1987; GRE Board, 1991a). For many years, testing programs have also sought to broaden the use of different test formats in order to draw on different skills—sometimes with great success, as was the case with AP (Turner, 1967), sometimes less so, as was the early experience with writing (French, 1966).

In this review we have seen little evidence of selection decisions being based exclusively on tests. There are particular situations, however, where there may be practical problems in using additional measures or information that might be desirable. For example, the National Merit Scholarships have long been awarded on the basis of extensive information about each semifinalist.[42] The semifinal group is initially identified only on the PSAT/NMSQT because of serious difficulty in obtaining reliable and detailed data on a preliminary pool of more than 1 million students. Concern has centered on the possibility that an overrepresentation of males among the semifinalists may influence a similar overrepresentation among the winners (Bracey, 1993).

This same issue applies more generally to other situations in which there may be a large number of applicants. Collection and evaluation of detailed information on thousands of candidates for admissions may be beyond the resources of a large university. The problem is exacerbated by the difficulty in obtaining accurate information that is valid and reliable. Tests are an efficient way of adding objectivity, but that gain in fairness should not be offset by overreliance on the test.

When using tests for educational selection, the desirability of considering past grades is unambiguous, although the noncomparability of grades from teacher to teacher and school to school could be a major source of unfairness if grades were used alone. Similarly, the need to avoid excessive weight on a test and the desirability of representing fully the skills and characteristics that might be important does not give free rein to using any measures that sound good. Adding measures just to be adding something can easily introduce even more serious threats to fairness. Any test, performance or otherwise, must meet acceptable standards of reliability, validity, security, and practicality. What we have called personal qualities are particularly promising and—judging from the data cited on the interview—can also be particularly suspect.

Uncritical reliance on personal testimony, informal evidence, or unvalidated information can open the door to arbitrariness, personal prejudice, and manipulation. In the larger view of validity and fairness, such problems can engage serious ethical issues (Messick, 1964) and undermine the social effectiveness of the admissions process (Glazer, 1970). Strict selection rules are clearly a weakness in trying to take account of unusual situations and recognize unique talents. Strict rules are also clearly a strength of an open and objective admissions system—yet another example of the inherent difficulty in deciding what constitutes comparable treatment.

---

[42]The most extensive early research on multiple talents and how to measure them in a national testing program was undertaken by the National Merit Scholarship Corporation in the early 1960s (Holland, 1961; Holland & Astin, 1962). That groundbreaking work was an impetus for collecting detailed information about coursework and special accomplishments of students, which is now common in national admissions testing programs.

Summary: Topic 8

Evaluating the validity and fairness of tests used in high-stakes decisions almost always requires a broader view than the immediate purpose to which the test is put. Selective admissions to higher education was used to illustrate this principle. Tests are used with a variety of other information about students in order to serve a variety of institutional and social goals. What measures are used with what emphasis can have an important bearing on what learning and accomplishment are encouraged among young people and what talents they develop.

Illustrative data were used to demonstrate that students differ in their qualifications and accomplishments, and that comparable treatment in test use often requires taking other measures into account. Emphasis on different measures can result in a quite different profile of selected students and a different ratio of women and men. Furthermore, emphasis on some measures has rippling effects on the apparent weight on still other measures in selection. Thus, fairness depends on the reasonableness of the whole process. It was shown that selective colleges do use a variety of measures in selecting students, although not always in a manner that is either consistent with their policy intentions or as effective as it might be in enrolling the types of students that the college identifies as most successful after 4 years. Women tended to be overrepresented among the most successful students, academically and otherwise.

That different types of evidence may be relevant to a complex, high-stakes decision like selective admissions further illustrates the fairness inherent in multiple measures. Putting too much weight on one measure can challenge fairness in a variety of ways. This principle was illustrated with examples of cut scores and test scores used alone.

CONCLUDING OBSERVATIONS

This chapter has examined eight selected topics that are especially important with respect to the fairness of test design and use for women and men. We have closed the discussion of each of those topics with a brief summary. The following chapter summarizes those findings along with the results of other chapters. A few comments may provide a useful bridge to the final chapter.

The first important decision in test design is choice of constructs and how to measure them. Those choices should be determined mainly by the purpose of the test and its overall validity, although there may well be plausible alternative measures. Because the mean performance of women and men may differ on those alternatives, the choices can have differential impact on their mean score levels. Testing format can have important effects, but they are by no means simple and predictable. The multiple-choice format does not, in itself, seem to be an important source of gender difference. What constructs to measure—what knowledge and skills—appears to be the salient issue. This is also why we see the connection between test design and test use as critical in evaluating fairness issues. Writing and mathematics are two key areas where design and use interact.

Writing is perhaps the most generally relevant academic skill that is not routinely included in high-stakes admissions tests. Writing also shows the largest gender difference among high school seniors of any generally relevant academic skill. Furthermore, in some subjects, it can be reasoned that the ability to write about a topic—to organize and support an argument—is intrinsic to its understanding; in other words, an important part of the construct of interest.

Mathematics is widely assumed to be a critical skill in many technical disciplines and is often included in high-stakes tests. Whether the mathematics test emphasizes reasoning or computation and general mathematical knowledge bears on its educational relevance as well as the mean performance of women and men. Although math knowledge and computation skills may be useful indicators of performance in a particular initial college math course, mathematical reasoning is more pertinent to an admissions test due to its wider and longer term applicability to academic work. Many students are still inclined to avoid advanced work in mathematics as soon as they have the option, women more often than men.

Writing and mathematical reasoning are key skills because of their importance in education and their opposite pattern of mean gender difference. Spatial-mechanical skills have received less attention but also show significant gender differences that appear to be reflected in figural test material and some aspects of science. If science tests unnecessarily include spatial-mechanical tasks, they penalize females unfairly. On the other hand, if some science concepts rest fundamentally on spatial-mechanical reasoning, then a valid test should include such skills in proportion to their importance so that instruction can try and rectify any resulting gender difference.

Any of these three—writing, math reasoning, and spatial-mechanical—can be an important construct component in a more complex test. Understanding component skills in a test is important for three reasons: to better appreciate the nature and implications of individual and group differences, to design valid tests that connect effectively with the educational process, and to ensure that such skills are neither under- nor overrepresented so tests are as fair as possible.[43]

The tendency for women to do relatively better on class grades and men to do relatively better on test scores was a consistent finding across different testing programs and in different subject areas. This phenomenon makes clear that tests and grades are overlapping constructs, not merely surrogates of one another. A second clear implication is that grade performance of women is likely to be underestimated if based on test scores alone. The generality of those relationships has not received sufficient attention.

Over the past 20 years there has been a substantial shift from more men than women in higher education to the opposite pattern. Are women selected fairly into the undergraduate and graduate programs that are most sought after? Although the answer appears to be generally yes, much obviously depends on what one means by fairly selected. Any close analysis of selective admissions suggests that institutions use a variety of measures and applicant characteristics in different ways to serve multiple objectives. For that reason, it is important to evaluate the fairness of the whole process rather than individual measures in isolation.

---

[43]There have been several lines of informative work during the past few years in the study of gender differences through analysis of test components or latent factors. The use of latent analysis to improve understanding of test fairness issues seems promising for more than one reason. The most obvious is the possibility of differentiating sources of construct-relevant subgroup differences that have educational implications. Snow and Ennis (1996) and Rosen (1995) provide examples. (See footnote 5 in chapter 3 for additional references.) Mislevy (1993) gave a useful account of various test models based on cognitive analysis of underlying knowledge and skill—models that might also be turned to effective analysis of fairness issues. Another potential application of such latent analysis is the development of a better means of differentiating construct-relevant and construct-irrelevant factors among test items. As chapter 6 suggests, subtle context effects may not be consistently detected through DIF analysis, but items should not be rejected solely in order to lessen group differences. One could thereby weaken the validity and usefulness of a test for students generally if group differences stem from lower proficiency on cognitive skills that have critical educational connections.

8

Summary and Implications

This final chapter has three parts. First, there is a brief summary of our principal findings based on previous research and the new data presented here. In the second section we offer some observations on the evidence concerning gender difference and similarity, commenting in particular on what we see as significant patterns and possible educational connections. Finally, we consider implications for assessment, especially regarding several complex fairness issues. None of these issues invite simple solutions, but all we believe, are amenable to improvement.

PRINCIPAL FINDINGS

This study had two purposes. One was to improve our understanding of gender difference and similarity in test performance and related achievements. The other was to examine what implications those findings might have for fair assessment, which includes considering what effect the assessment process itself might have on the test performance of women and men. Research evidence concerning gender difference and similarity was presented in chapters 3 and 4. Chapter 3 was based largely on test performance data from major testing programs and large national surveys. Chapter 4 was based on published descriptive information from a number of testing programs and national surveys, plus several special analyses of those data. Chapters 6 and 7 presented a variety of information pertaining to test fairness. Both relied heavily on published research; the latter also included a number of special analyses.

Findings on Gender Difference and Similarity

Test Performance.   A principal objective in our analysis of gender differences was to disentangle the overlapping effects of differences among samples, cohorts, and constructs—the term we have used to refer to a domain of knowledge and skills. In a key analysis, test performance of women and men was compared on a wide range of commonly used tests in large, nationally representative samples for very nearly the same age cohort of students. The results showed no gender difference in the overall average test performance. Furthermore, on most of the 74 individual tests, the mean gender difference was negligible or would be characterized as "small" on standards commonly used. Most commonly, at Grade 12 the difference between the average score for females and males accounted for no more than 1% of all score variation. In these respects females and males performed similarly on the cognitive tests that are commonly administered to general populations of students at the end of secondary school.

This finding is qualified by some variation in the profile of different types of knowledge and skills for women and men. On average, women tended to do well on verbal tests, especially writing, which showed the largest mean gender difference among the 10 categories of traditionally academic tests. Men tended to do well in technical subjects, such as natural science and particularly mechanical—electronics, a special skill that can be highly relevant to work in some academic areas. Test results for Grade 4 to Grade 12 showed an increasing gender differentiation reflecting that pattern, but in all cases, score distributions for females and males overlapped substantially, and there were wide individual differences within each group.

Another qualification to the overall pattern of gender similarity was a tendency to somewhat greater variability in the scores of males than in those of females in most test categories. A relative increase in the variability of male scores from Grade 4 to Grade 12 represented a second form of gender differentiation through the school years. The effect of these two types of differentiation was reflected in unequal representation of high-scoring females and males in representative samples of 12th graders. For example, one and one half to two times more males than females scored in the top 10% on mathematics and science tests because of the combined effects of mean differences and greater variability. Females showed a similar over-representation in the top 10% on reading and writing, mostly because of their higher mean scores in these areas.

In another group of 55 advanced tests that are administered to self-selected samples of high school seniors, there was a small mean score difference favoring males, as contrasted to no mean gender difference in tests administered to representative samples of all seniors. This difference did not appear to result from the types of tests employed, but from the statistical effects of restricting the samples to higher scoring students where males tend to outnumber females. A detailed analysis of this phenomenon indicated that three factors are at work in sample restriction: the tendency to greater variability in male scores, restriction in the range of scores that comes from testing mostly higher scoring students, and the relative number of females and males in the selected group.

There appears to be a slightly greater difference favoring males in mean test scores at the graduate as compared to the undergraduate level, but that result is very difficult to interpret. It does not signify that females or males gain relatively more knowledge and skill during the college years because the data are not comparable. The nature of the tests and the samples of students taking them vary considerably at the two levels. The pattern of gender difference and similarity varied somewhat from one graduate and professional field to another, and there was noticeably less gender difference within disciplines than across the graduate group overall.

Within nationally representative populations, gender differences in test performance did not vary with any consistency from one ethnic group to another. There was some variation in the pattern of gender difference within ethnic groups on some selective tests, particularly among Black students. Black women were more likely to take undergraduate admissions tests and more likely to do well compared to Black men than was true in other groups. Also, a much larger proportion of Black women in high school took AP examinations than did Black men, but scored just as well.

Previously published data on national samples of students suggest that several decades ago there were substantially larger gender differences among Grade 12 students on some tests, notably mathematics and science, than is currently the case. Several large sets of data were analyzed to determine what changes in patterns of gender difference may have occurred in recent years; that is, on the same or comparable tests administered in the early 1980s and the early 1990s. Some tests, in representative as well as selected samples, showed a small but significant shift to relatively higher female performance by the end of that decade. The most noticeable change in this period was an increase in the representation of women among high school students demonstrating college-level proficiency in science and mathematics.

Grades and Other Measures. Moving beyond test performance, females and males show broad similarity as well as distinctive patterns of difference. Using a wide variety of indices, girls and women tend to have stronger academic records than boys and men throughout all levels of education. Females tend to have stronger academic work habits and more positive indicators of attitude and effort. Compared to males, they tend to show stronger interests in academic and intellectual endeavor. Girls' grades are higher than those of boys overall. As a group, girls earn their highest grades in English and their lowest grades in mathematics.

Both females and males show a wide range of other accomplishments and proficiencies. In secondary school women tend to excel in leadership, writing, and academic activities. Men tend to excel in scientific activities, technical pursuits, and sports. There is some evidence that women are more often considered outstanding in college, partly because of such out-of-class achievements and partly because of earning academic honors more frequently.

Evidence of gender difference and similarity was examined in related measures of interests and values. Summary data for such measures indicate that females and males tend to have distinct patterns of values and interests in academic and leisure activities, as well as in occupational preferences. When girls and women exercise personal choice, as a group they tend to prefer the arts, humanities, and social sciences as their academic, leisure, and career interests. Females are more likely than males to avoid mathematics and science when they have a choice.

The profile of men's and women's achievements and interests is rather consistent across age levels, ethnic groups, and historic cohorts. There is, however, substantial overlap between females and males on such measures, as well as wide individual differences within groups of women and men. Furthermore, there are indications that the picture varies under different circumstances. For example, gender differences favoring girls tend to be greater among Black students than among White students. Also, girls and women in other countries do not always show the distaste for mathematics and science expressed by many women in this country.

Findings on Fairness Issues in Assessment

In this study we have viewed test fairness as comparable assessment for each examinee. Comparability means somewhat different things at different stages in the assessment process and must be judged on the basis of all measures, including tests, that are used in making decisions about students. Fair test design implies comparable opportunity to demonstrate relevant knowledge and skills. In test development and administration, a fair test should provide comparable tasks, testing conditions, and scaled scores for all examinees. Fair test use should result in comparable treatment of examinees. Chapters 6 and 7 reviewed research evidence and reported additional special analyses in order to examine evidence of such comparability. Findings from the four stages—design, development, administration, and use—are reviewed in that order in the following paragraphs.

Test Design. The first important decision in designing a test is the choice of constructs to measure. That choice is determined primarily by the purpose of the test, although there may be reasonable alternatives; that is, choices as to which construct is preferable and how best to define it. Mean performance of women and men may differ on these alternatives. In a hypothetical example, it was shown that plausible choices in designing a testing program can affect overall score levels for women and men and impact the outcome of educational decisions based on those scores.

Choice of assessment format is another important decision in test design. In order to evaluate possible gender-related implications in alternate forms of assessment, score patterns of women and men were examined for a number of tests that provided free-response and multiple-choice scores for the same sample on ostensibly similar constructs. Different free-response formats sometimes showed consequential gender effects. Men tended to score relatively higher on *figural* free-response questions than on multiple-choice questions. Women tended to score relatively higher on *written* free-response questions than on multiple-choice questions in science and geopolitical subjects, but not in mathematics or language and literature. This pattern was rather consistent on advanced tests in this country and in England as well. There is insufficient evidence, however, to distinguish among several possible reasons for gender differences in some written assessment results and not others.

The use of the multiple-choice format places limitations on what can be assessed. On the other hand, a review of 12 studies found little evidence that the multiple-choice format is, itself, a significant source of gender difference in test results. Removing the answer alternatives from a MC question and requiring the examinee to produce the answer unaided appears to have little if any effect on what is measured or on the relative performance of females and males. Whether format makes a difference in what is measured may turn on whether a question has a best answer or, by its nature, has more than one possible answer or requires an extended response.

Test Development and Administration. The general character of a test is established with the choice of construct and format at the design stage of the assessment process. Fairness of test content remains an issue, however, in the selection of specific content for a given administration of the test. The analysis of DIF has strengthened our ability to select items that are comparable for different groups of examinees. Systematic DIF analysis of many tests over the past decade has shown that relatively few questions must be discarded after preliminary testing because they are not comparable for women and men. Nonetheless, DIF has proven to be a useful screen for deleting individual draft items that may not be comparable and for developing guidelines to avoid use of certain types of test material that have features unrelated to what is being measured but can negatively influence responses of women or men (e.g., mathematics test items couched in a military or sports context).

Selection of material for performance tests poses much more serious problems because of the difficulty in balancing material fairly when a given test may contain only a few exercises, and choice of one over another may noticeably affect subgroup performance. That problem might be lessened by giving examinees more opportunity to choose among assessment exercises, although we do not yet know how to ensure that the resulting scores are adequately comparable from student to student.

Other comparability issues arise in test administration. Most tests are timed, for practical considerations if nothing else. It may also be the case that a time limit has an intrinsic relationship to the construct being tested. The effect of a time limit is somewhat lessened on traditional paper-and-pencil tests by the fact that high scorers tend to finish early and low scorers tend soon to run out of items at their level of proficiency. In determining whether speededness is a fairness issue for women, as sometimes has been suggested, the critical question is whether a less speeded version of the same test would tend to favor women. Research on this question does not indicate that women gain more score points relative to men when both have more time—on either multiple-choice or essay tests.

Studies have examined possible gender differences due to various aspects of test wiseness or test-taking strategies. In some test situations, women tend to be slightly less prone than men to guess when not sure of the answer. Several lines of evidence indicate, however, that neither differential guessing nor use of test formats that can have different consequences for guessing have any significant effect on observed gender difference. Nor do studies of answer changing indicate differential effect on female and male scores. Research findings do not suggest that women or men are differentially test wise, or that they gain differentially from coaching. Finally, available evidence gives no indication that taking tests by computer significantly affects gender differences, but in time computers will introduce more variety in test administration and more potential threats to comparability that will need to be evaluated.

Anxiety in the test situation is another reason why a test may not be comparable for all examinees. Although there is evidence that anxiety does affect scores, it is uncertain what level of anxiety is functional or dysfunctional on what types of tests. Women more frequently report being test anxious, although it is not clear whether females and males are equally likely to report anxiety when they feel it. The fact that gender difference appears to be almost identical when the same test is administered under high- and low-stakes conditions makes it doubtful that anxiety is an important source of test unfairness for women.

Test Use.   Writing is perhaps the most generally relevant academic skill that is not routinely used in high-stakes admissions tests. Writing also shows the largest gender difference among high school seniors of any generally relevant academic skill. Available data indicate that the inclusion of writing in a testing program will tend to balance the number of women and men who score at a high level in situations where men would otherwise outnumber women.

In representative samples of 13-year-olds, girls score as well or better than boys on math knowledge or computation tests, but among gifted students in that age range, high-scoring boys outnumber high-scoring girls on math reasoning tests. In representative samples at the end of high school, males tend to score better than females on math tests, apparently because the tests put more stress on reasoning and males tend to take more advanced math courses. Several studies have indicated that a math reasoning test, used alone, is likely to underpredict women's college freshman math grades. Underprediction of math grades is largely eliminated when high school average is used together with test scores.

When test scores and school grades are compared for the same samples of students, the tendency for women to make somewhat better grades and men to make somewhat better scores was a consistent finding across different testing programs and in different subject areas. This phenomenon suggests that freshman GPAs of women are likely to be underestimated if estimates are based on test scores alone. Extensive recent analyses show little if any over- or underprediction for either gender when predictions are based on both high school record and test scores, especially when college grade criteria are comparable for women and men.

Over the past 20 years there has been a substantial shift from a majority of men to a majority of women in higher education. Are women selected fairly into the undergraduate and graduate programs that are most sought after? An analysis of admissions at 100 prominent undergraduate colleges and universities indicated that acceptance rates for women and men were approximately the same and that they were equally represented in the entering classes. Other studies found that female and male applicants with equal test scores and previous grades were equally likely to be accepted in a group of selective private colleges, in law schools, and in five graduate disciplines. There was only limited evidence that women were any more likely than similarly qualified men to be accepted in those graduate programs where women are currently underrepresented.

Close analysis of selective admissions suggests that colleges use a variety of measures in different ways to serve multiple objectives of the institution. A threat to fairness can certainly arise if the college places too much emphasis on a particular measure, be it a test or a personal judgment. Women and men, as well as other groups, show quite different profiles on different predictors and on different success criteria. Available data clearly suggest that institutions strive to balance their individual admissions decisions to achieve an overall result that is as valid and fair as possible. Because of the complexity of such decision processes, it is doubtful that individual measures can be used fairly or evaluated accurately in isolation.

OBSERVATIONS ON GENDER DIFFERENCE AND SIMILARITY

Taking one step beyond the foregoing summary of findings, we comment now on several aspects of the results regarding gender difference and similarity. Some patterns seem particularly important in understanding gender differences. The patterns are also helpful, we think, in raising questions about the education of young people. First, a reminder regarding the need for caution. This study deliberately cast a wide net, and the results are based on many different tests and other measures of achievement. Nonetheless, we focused on prominent testing programs and large representative samples, and were therefore constrained by the measures that are presently available. It is important to remember when we refer to constructs, abilities, and so on, that we are always referring to performance on those particular measures. With these cautions, we point to five important patterns in the findings.

Significant Patterns

Similarity and Overlap. The dominant pattern in the test performance of females and males is similarity. Gender differences in achievement are typically small on most individual measures, and the overlap of female and male scores is substantial. Average results say nothing about individuals, or how particular groups of women and men might do on a given test, or whether individual women or men should be encouraged to pursue a given area of study or line of work. Great care is necessary to avoid stereotyping or implying social policy on the basis of small group differences. On the other hand, it is important to understand the challenge that score differences may represent, and it is essential to ensure that score differences, even though small, do not result from unfair testing.

Profile Distinctions. That the profile of female and male test perform- ance and other achievements at Grade 12 should show some differences is not news. On the other hand, it is often assumed that cognitive achieve- ments of girls and women are pretty much the same as those of boys and men because there is little if any overall difference in test scores, and mean differences for a given measure are typically not large. Our findings make it clearer why choosing one type of achievement or another in an assessment program can make a difference in the relative score levels of females and males. This is not only the case across broad areas like verbal and mathe- matics, but also within areas. For example, an assumption that has gained some currency in recent years is that there is no gender difference in verbal ability. For Grade 12 women, that assumption is generally accurate as to word knowledge, but on average, women score better than men on word usage and much better on writing.

Linkage of Interests and Test Performance. Another significant finding is the strong pattern of connections between types of test performance of females and males in chapter 3 and types of interest and other accomplishments in chapter 4. There are wide individual differences and substantial overlap for girls and boys, but also much evidence that, on average, girls tend to prefer and value social and aesthetic activities, whereas boys tend to be more oriented to technical and scientific activities. These interests are clearly reflected in the experiences of females and males and in the academic and career preferences that they express. Interest patterns appear to be surprisingly stable over several decades. These are certainly not one-to-one relationships, although there are clear similarities between patterns of test performance and evidence as to how young women and men appear to spend their time.

Differentiation Through the Grades. The differentiation that was ob- served in the test performance of girls and boys from Grade 4 to Grade 12 is significant partly because it reflects patterns similar to interest differences—girls improving relatively more in reading and writing, boys improving more in technical subjects like science and mathematics. Since girls and boys take much the same coursework through most of the school years, these different relative gains in school subjects suggest that test performance is influenced by interests and activities out of class. Certainly learning is not restricted to school. The

1986 NAEP Science Assessment asked Grade 11 students several questions that illustrate differences in how females and males spend their time. When asked whether they had ever tried to figure out what was wrong with an unhealthy animal, 31% of girls and 26% of boys answered "many times." What percentage had tried many times to fix something electrical? Only 8% of girls, but 46% of boys (Mullis & Jenkins, 1988).

Differential Variability.   Recent writers have shown that differential variability is common on many tests; that is, male scores tend to spread out more at the top and the bottom than do female scores (Feingold, 1992b; Hedges & Nowell, 1995). Those results are confirmed by our data in chapter 3. When it occurs, differential variability is important because it means that there will be more males at extreme score levels—more low-performing males at the bottom and more high-performing males at the top—even if there is no mean gender difference. Differential variability also means that, in a selected group of outstanding students, high-scoring males will tend to outnumber high-scoring females. Similarly, in a selected group of remedial students, males will tend to outnumber females.

What accounts for these five patterns? As we said at the outset in chapter 1, our objective has been to describe the nature of gender difference and similarity in more useful detail so that implications for fair assessment would become clearer. Beyond that descriptive effort, we have not aspired to unravel the antecedent factors that lead to some gender differentiation in achievement. There is a very large literature on this topic, only briefly mentioned in chapter 2. As part of our collective effort on this project, Wilder (1997) provided a detailed review of the research on possible factors—social, psychological, educational, and biological—that might explain the observed patterns of gender difference and similarity.

Although we did not set out to explain antecedents, any success at better description is, by definition, some progress on explanation. The study did disentangle to some extent the effects of constructs, samples, and cohorts. It is our impression that the effort has been helpful in making clearer the connections between the different interests of girls and boys and their somewhat different patterns of activities, special accomplishments, and performance on tests. With so much evidence of differences in the preferences of girls and boys as well as differences in their nontest achievements, it is no surprise that there are also some differences also in their patterns of test performance. As we have noted, gender differences in some key areas, such as mathematics and science, are now considerably smaller among Grade 12 students than was true three decades ago.

Understanding the reasons for differences in score variability is an important new challenge. There may be quite different explanations for more males at the top and at the bottom of a score distribution. Chapter 2 cited some of the research literature on how and why males are more frequently dysfunctional for physiological reasons. Cognitive psychologists and researchers interested in women's issues provide some clues as to why males are overrepresented among extreme scorers in some subjects. These investigators have stressed the necessity of extensive time-on-task in order to develop the automaticity and cognitive maps that facilitate, in turn, strategic skills and high performance (Dreyfus & Dreyfus, 1986; Fennema & Peterson, 1985; Posner, 1978).

Other writers suggest complementary clues. Mann (1994) described age 12 as a turning point for girls, a time when they become more concerned with relationships and not being seen as different. This syndrome, she speculated, discourages the intense devotion to task that develops cognitive skills, and also discourages the deviant behavior that sometimes gets boys off track altogether. Similarly, Noddings (1992) noted that females are still encouraged toward a "nice girl" norm, and generally conform sufficiently to avoid landing at the bottom of any distribution. Many of the brightest girls feel pressed not to exhibit superior capabilities.

Educational Connections

Our findings reinforce one assumption that has guided efforts in recent years to ensure gender equity in education. Young people, regardless of gender, develop talent and proficiency in particular areas when they devote the time it takes. Programs that encourage less gender-specific experience, training, and careers have succeeded to a remarkable degree, and more of that effort will be needed. A key issue is the habitual pattern of experiences that can result from differential interest and social roles. Due to those channeling influences, equal opportunity cannot be ensured through passive means. If young women and men are not encouraged and accepted into fields of work and study at levels beyond current underrepresented norms, then their opportunity in those fields is likely to be defined by the status quo.

Are educational programs doing enough to compensate for negative influences and underrepresentation of females and males where it exists in major career lines, especially for women in scientific and technical areas? Such efforts are probably uneven. Their effectiveness might be improved with better information, from field to field, as to how well reservoirs of potentially interested and qualified students are being encouraged, recruited, and accepted.

Information in earlier chapters demonstrates that, even on conventional measures, achievements of young people are quite varied. Placing emphasis on only some of their relevant accomplishments can advantage some students and not others. Institutions espouse broad values but normally focus on relatively narrow and traditional criteria of academic merit. Are we sometimes more impressed with the theoretical need for different types of talent and proficiency in society than with the practical worth of different versions of excellence in a group of admitted freshmen?

On the other hand, there are gender differences on traditional measures of intellectual skill that play a critical role in some important areas of study and work. Mathematical reasoning is such a skill in many fields. Improvements in the representation of young women in advanced high school mathematics courses is a positive development, but fewer girls than boys develop high-level math skills at younger ages. How to change that imbalance—even as both groups are taking much the same courses—is an important educational problem.

Finally, the data on test performance suggest a gender-differentiated neglect in the development of cognitive skills: Girls tend to fall behind in the development of spatial-mechanical skills as reflected in performance on figural material; boys tend to fall behind in the development of writing skills. It seems obvious that deficiencies in these skills can hamper proficient performance in particular fields. It is less obvious in what ways such skills may be generally important in the acquisition of knowledge. In any event, learning how better to foster the development of both skills will help to put all students on an equal footing.

IMPLICATIONS FOR ASSESSMENT

Primarily, we use tests in making decisions about students and programs in order to enhance the effectiveness of some aspect of the educational system. A test's validity in serving that purpose is its primary justification, although other important consequences of use must be considered as well. In a larger sense—with what we earlier called a systemic view of fairness—one must also ask whether a test has long-term beneficial effects, whether it is a fair challenge to examinees, and whether it affects their lives in fair and constructive ways.

A corollary purpose of educational tests is to ensure objectivity in making decisions about people and programs. Thus, comparability is an essential requirement for validity and an organizing principle for fair assessment. Tests need to be used with other measures in ways that are as comparable as possible for all examinees in several senses—comparable opportunity to demonstrate proficiency, comparable assessment tasks and scores, and comparable treatment resulting from use.

If examinees have varied interests and experience, their ability to score well will certainly vary. Comparable opportunity to demonstrate skills is not the same as comparable opportunity to acquire skills. Test fairness can only address the former. Although our educational goal may properly be a comparable opportunity to acquire skills, the assessment goal is not equality of group scores. Indeed, a valid and fair test must show group score differences that appropriately reflect differences in interests and experience. As outlined in the foregoing pages, a very large amount of data on many measures and samples confirms that women and men are much more similar than dissimilar, but they also show some patterns of difference. These patterns are sufficiently consistent, involving so many tests and samples, that we see little grounds for attributing these differences to unfair tests.

Although the focus here is on gender fairness, note that we improve test fairness most by improving test validity in all respects for all examinees. How do fairness issues get resolved? A modification that makes a test more fair in one sense may make the same test less fair in another sense. Consideration of the test's overall usefulness, its fairness to all examinees, and its practicality all play necessary roles.

What types of assessment decisions seem most consequential with respect to fairness to women and men? In test development and administration, the second and third stages of assessment, test fairness turns especially on implementing a test design so that scores are as comparable as possible across all individuals and groups. Based on our review of research findings, we see relatively little evidence of threats to gender fairness in these two stages of assessment with present tests. Standardization of tests and testing conditions appears to be doing its intended job in making present tests objective and comparable. Procedures to control threats to fairness for performance assessment at these two middle stages in the assessment process are less well-resolved and will need continuing work. New modes of assessment often require us to rethink what test standardization must mean in order to ensure useful and comparable assessment for all examinees.

Test design and test use pose quite different issues. Currently the test creation process emphasizes the use of independent policy-setting groups that bring a breadth of perspective to the determination of a test's purpose, its general nature, and its proper use (ETS, 1991). On the other hand, fairness issues have received less research attention in test design and use than in test development and administration. In the following paragraphs we consider seven areas for which our findings have implications for fair assessment. Six of the seven concern design and use in one way or another.

Construct Choice.   Test validity is the primary consideration in choosing constructs to include in a testing program. The validity of an educational test depends on multiple features such as representation of relevant knowledge and skills, predictive power, long-term social and educational importance, and beneficial effects on students and their learning. Fairness considerations and practical concerns play an important role as well. Depending on the function of the test, construct choice may entail plausible alternatives. Choices turn partly on what other information is available and what knowledge and skills might better be assessed through means other than tests. Taking any such additional measures into account, a gender-fair assessment design should provide comparable opportunity for women and men to demonstrate knowledge and skills relevant to the purpose of the test. Our findings confirm the importance of careful attention early in test design to the pattern of gender difference and similarity likely to result from valid construct alternatives and whether those patterns seem consistent with other relevant information. It is important to advance our understanding of such construct differences and their educational implications beyond the content characteristics that are usually emphasized in test specifications.

Tested constructs are often complex and include important component skills that may not be immediately obvious in the test or in the observed score. Writing, mathematical reasoning, and spatial-mechanical skills are examples of skills that can be components of tests. Such skills may play a critical role in acquiring and demonstrating proficiency in broad academic areas or in particular subjects. Often, they also show important gender differences. Test designers should take care that such component skills are neither over- nor underrepresented in choosing constructs that effectively reflect the purpose of the test.

If the domain of interest is even more complex—say, promise for graduate study—it is not likely to be feasible to field test all possible alternate test designs nor practical to assume that all relevant knowledge and skills can be tested. It is a reasonable expectation, however, that designs for new tests should routinely consider plausible choices among possible constructs—their usefulness in serving the purpose of the test, how they might complement other available information, and patterns of test performance for women and men (or other groups) that would likely result. The objective should never be to balance arbitrarily the mean scores of groups of examinees but to design valid assessments that are consistent, overall, with other information that is relevant to the purpose of the test.

Assessing Mathematics.   At younger ages, on math tests that stress computation and knowledge, girls tend to score as well or better than boys. At older ages, on more advanced tests that stress problem solving and reasoning, men tend to score better than women. Tests intended to assess outcomes of instruction should certainly be keyed to specific course objectives. But in high-stakes testing programs that serve broad educational purposes, what is the appropriate emphasis on math? What types of mathematics should be emphasized?

The observed gender difference on advanced math reasoning tests takes on importance because the ability to use math skills is critical to many areas of study and a number of career lines. For that reason, mathematics typically is, and deserves to be, an important component in tests that are used for selective admissions to diverse programs. When a mathematics test serves a broad assessment function of that type, its design must take account of immediate purpose as well as long-term benefits and possible effects on instruction. It seems clear that an advanced test must assess higher order skills. As is always the case in test use, it is important to decide how much weight is appropriate to place on math skills in a given situation.

Assessing Writing.   The assessment of writing proficiency is important primarily because of its educational implications. Considering the central role that this complex skill plays in academic work and adult life, samples of actual writing have been underused in many testing programs. The relevance of writing along with the pattern of gender difference that is typically observed suggest that excluding writing poses both validity and fairness questions. This work has convinced us that writing proficiency should always be considered in the design of an assessment intended to serve broad educational purposes. Indirect measures of writing may be better than none at all, but the educational benefit of requiring students to write seems apparent. It is important, however, to be sure that including writing in a testing program does not create imbalances in overall test performance that are inconsistent with other evidence.

An equally important question is how the use of writing affects the assessment of knowledge and skills in different subject areas. When is writing an intrinsic part of the construct of interest—say, knowledge of American history, or chemistry, or mathematics? If writing is part of the construct, what does writing add, and what implication does that have for fair assessment? For instance, women tend to score better, relative to men, on written than on multiple-choice tests in some subjects. Is this due simply to better writing, or clearer articulation of understanding, or superior understanding? These questions are all part of a broader need to understand better the educational implications of alternate assessment formats.

Free-Response Assessment. Some free-response formats sometimes favor women; others sometimes favor men. The attraction of performance assessment and other free-response formats is the possibility of measuring a broader range of more complex proficiencies that more closely match school learning and educational objectives. Complex proficiencies are based on many skills, and alternate assessment formats can tap different skills. Thus, multiple formats have the potential to improve overall validity as well as fairness.

On the other hand, free-response tests usually have time for only a few complex questions, which means that both the nature of the test and its difficulty are more dependent on what particular questions were included than is the case with MC tests. Our review of studies that directly compared MC and FR versions of the same test indicates that MC tests are not inherently unfair. Moreover, MC tests have other advantages. The MC format is not only highly efficient in time and cost; it also makes it possible to cover effectively a broad subject domain and to measure reliably a wide variety of skills at different levels of complexity. For those reasons, MC is likely to remain a method of choice in most assessment programs where comparability of scores is important.

Nonetheless, performance assessments—and FR formats generally—provide an important complement to MC formats. Because FR formats hold such promise for improving the range of measurement, we need to work actively to improve their technical quality and their representation in testing programs. Proposals for new testing programs would be much improved by a benefit analysis of the strengths and weaknesses of alternate formats, giving particular attention to likely construct differences and their effects on validity and fairness. We also need more systematic research to develop a better working understanding of construct–format connections, especially those that involve writing.

Selecting Test Content. Choosing a construct still leaves issues of specific content to be resolved. As our data amply show, women and men will not necessarily score the same on a given construct. For that reason, material for a test cannot be selected with an intent to show no gender difference where there is likely to be a real difference. Furthermore, our results show important gender differences in interests and experience. We have this dual requirement in selecting test content: (a) to accurately reflect the construct, even if that produces gender differences; and (b) to avoid content that is not relevant to the construct but could affect gender differences.

DIF analysis is very helpful in achieving these objectives, but in our results we see further reason to urge more concerted attention to two issues. The first is the possibility of small context effects that do not show consistently in individual item results. One could guard against such effects by specifically considering gender differences within pools of appropriate items, if effects on the construct measured and on other groups could be adequately controlled. Or, following common practice, one can avoid questions that are set in contexts that are irrelevant to what is being measured but may affect performance because that context is less familiar to some groups (e.g., war and football in the case of women). A more rigorous method of handling this problem would be desirable. A second issue of equal importance is the need for improved methods of selecting comparable sets of free-response test material. For example, the limited number of exercises typically included in a performance test precludes use of the usual DIF methods that serve that purpose. As a result, gender difference is likely to fluctuate more on a performance test than on a MC test.

Using Grades and Scores. When test scores are properly used in academic prediction, research has shown almost no difference in the average grade predicted for women and the average grade actually earned. In particular institutions or situations, there may be some variation from that overall result, favoring either women or men. In the past, some institutions have chosen to correct any such difference by using separate predictions for women and men. We have emphasized that grades and test scores have different strengths and weaknesses and often represent somewhat different skills. Grades and test scores serve a complementary role in predicting grades, and the use of either alone can incur problems. We believe that test agencies should undertake more energetic information programs to clarify this issue and to discourage use of tests alone in academic prediction unless that is justified by other considerations or evidence.

Measures Used in Selection. When tests are used in admissions and other forms of educational selection, it is useful to think carefully about what is *not* included in the test. What is not included for students generally; what unusual skills of individual applicants may be overlooked? Tests provide objective measures of important cognitive abilities that apply quite generally to academic work, but everything considered, they play a limited role. Tests make no pretense of measuring motivation, character, background, or even unusual skills and accomplishments that may be directly relevant to potential success in an educational program or to potential contributions to that program.

There have always been sound educational and social reasons for viewing talent broadly. Fair selection is part of that rationale. Two requirements are important for valid use of multiple measures in selection. One is to be certain that the measures used in admissions adequately cover what is important to the institution. Recent research suggests that, with a good college GPA criterion not entangled with grading variations, prediction based on an admissions test and previous grade average is surprisingly accurate. If this finding is generally true, it means that when a college sticks only to a GPA criterion, it is not likely to find new admissions measures that will much improve prediction of success so defined. Selection can change to the advantage of the college if it recognizes student characteristics and criteria of success other than GPA and thereby establishes a broader basis for admitting qualified applicants that serve the goals of the institution.

A second requirement is to give students credit for strengths that are relevant. Men and women show different profiles of accomplishment in college. Selective institutions have multiple objectives. Both considerations argue strongly against a narrow view of talent when admitting students or validating selection measures. It is the full set of measures normally used in admissions—not tests alone—that should ensure that students have a fair chance to demonstrate their relevant knowledge and skill. The same principle applies to grade placement in the primary grades, to high school leaving examinations, and in other situations where tests are used in making important educational decisions. An important challenge for those who develop testing programs is to help make relevant nontest information as salient and easy to use as are test scores.

The central role of the construct tested is now more evident. Continued progress on the fairness issues in each of these seven areas of assessment depends on understanding constructs and their connection to the educational process. As emphasized in the discussion of chapter 5, most fairness issues come down to being as clear as we can about what we want to assess for what reason, and carrying out that assessment in ways that are as valid as possible for all students.

Constraint and Resolution

This volume amply illustrates the variety and complexity of fairness issues in assessment. Designing a test and justifying its use means resolving those issues within constraints. One type of constraint is that solutions to different fairness issues or their effects on different groups may be in conflict. We have emphasized that test fairness should mean comparable validity for all examinees.

Constraints are often posed by the larger context in which tests are used. Tests have to be fair, but they also have to be useful and practical. These constraints are interrelated because there are different types of assessment concerns. With a high-stakes admissions test, for example, educators and the public are concerned that scores accurately represent proficiency, that the test fairly reflects and beneficially influences school learning, and that the assessment process is objective. If a test is important, the public is rightly concerned about many aspects of objectivity; particularly that scores should be influenced as little as possible by security breaches, inconsistent scoring, or coaching tricks.

Different types of tests may have quite contrasting implications for these different aspects of test fairness. A college admissions test that closely mirrors the high school curriculum may beneficially focus students on learning that curriculum. However, it may simultaneously be more susceptible to curriculum–test mismatches than would be a test focused on developed skills that are more generally applicable to a wider range of academic work.

Furthermore, different examinees, groups of examinees, or parties to the assessment process may see these issues through different lenses. Different views, each based on desirable but different values, are likely to suggest different priorities for fair assessment. Users must often balance such competing values in judging the usefulness, fairness, and practicality of a test. Testing organizations have a responsibility to make evidence available that is relevant to such judgments and to clarify principles of fair use.

We have necessarily examined gender differences and issues of fairness for testing as it is today. As we discussed in chapter 7, testing is a field in the midst of change, triggered by the desire for more effective assessment and by the capabilities of technology. Looking to the future, we have examined not just specific issues but also principles that may help to clarify fairness issues within new forms of assessment. For many years, test design has too often been either neglected or a perfunctory exercise that mimics earlier designs. With new assessment possibilities, test design takes on a more critical role and requires the attention given here. We hope this book will contribute to an improved understanding of gender and fair testing as testing changes in the future.

References

Ackerman, T. A., & Smith, P. L. (1988). A comparison of the information provided by essay, multiple-choice, and free-response writing tests. *Applied Psychological Measurement, 12,* 117–128.

Adler, T. (1995, March). Prized projects win Westinghouse honors. *Science News, 147,* 166.

Admissions Testing Program, The College Board. (1992). *Profile of SAT and Achievement Test takers.* New York: College Entrance Examination Board.

Advanced Placement Program, The College Board. (1992). *National summary reports.* New York: College Entrance Examination Board.

Advisory Committee on Testing in Chapter 1. (1993, May). *Reinforcing the promise, reforming the paradigm.* Washington, DC: U.S. Department of Education.

Aiken, L. R. (1963). The grading behavior of a college faculty. *Educational and Psychological Measurement, 23,* 319–322.

Aiken, L. R. (1986–1987). Sex differences in mathematical ability: A review of the literature. *Educational Research Quarterly, 10*(4), 25–35.

Alderson, J. C., & Wall, D. (1993). Does washback exist? *Applied Linguistics, 14,* 115–129.

Alexander, K. L., & Eckland, B. (1974). Sex differences in the educational attainment process. *American Sociological Review, 39,* 668–682.

Allport, G. W., Vernon, P. E., & Lindzey, G. (1970). *Study of Values—A scale for measuring the dominant interests in personality* (3rd ed.). New York: Houghton Mifflin.

Alpert, R., & Haber, R. (1960). Anxiety in academic achievement situations. *Journal of Abnormal and Social Psychology, 61*(2), 207–215.

Alsalam, N., Ogle, L., Rogers, G., & Smith, T. (1992). *The condition of education 1992* (NCES 92-096). Washington, DC: U.S. Department of Education, National Center for Education Statistics.

Alverno College Faculty. (1994). *Student assessment-as-learning.* Milwaukee, WI: Alverno College Institute.

American Association of Collegiate Registrars and Admissions Officers & The College Board. (1980). *Undergraduate admissions: The realities of institutional policies, practices, and procedures.* New York: College Entrance Examination Board.

American Association for the Advancement of Science. (1989). Women (not) in math. *Science, 246,* 574.

American College Testing Program. (1966). *College student profiles: Norms for the ACT assessment.* Iowa City, IA: Author.

American College Testing Program. (1972). *College student profiles: Norms for the ACT assessment: Assessing students on the way to college* (Vol. 2). Iowa City, IA: Author.

American College Testing Program. (1973). *Assessing students on the way to college: Technical report for the ACT assessment program* (Vol. 1). Iowa City, IA: Author.

American College Testing Program. (1988). *ACT assessment program technical manual*. Iowa City, IA: Author.

American College Testing Program. (1992). *ACT assessment user handbook, 1992–93*. Iowa City, IA: Author.

American College Testing Program. (1993). *Reference norms for spring 1992 ACT tested h. s. graduates*. Iowa City, IA: Author.

American Educational Research Association, American Psychological Association, & National Council on Measurement in Education. (1985). *Standards for educational and psychological testing*. Washington, DC: American Psychological Association.

American Psychological Association, American Educational Research Association, & National Council on Measurement in Education. (1974). *Standards for educational and psychological tests*. Washington, DC: American Psychological Association.

Anastasi, A. (1968). *Psychological testing* (3rd ed.). New York: Macmillan.

Anastasi, A. (1988). *Psychological testing* (6th ed.). New York: Macmillan.

Anastasi, A. (1990). What is test misuse? Perspectives of a measurement expert. In Educational Testing Service, *The uses of standardized tests in American education: Proceedings of the 1989 ETS Invitational Conference* (pp. 15–25). Princeton, NJ: Educational Testing Service.

Anastasi, A., & Foley, J. P., Jr. (1949). *Differential psychology: Individual and group differences in behavior*. New York: Macmillan.

Angoff, W. H. (Ed.). (1971a). *The College Board Admissions Testing Program: A technical report on research and development activities relating to the Scholastic Aptitude Test and Achievement Tests*. New York: College Entrance Examination Board.

Angoff, W. H. (1971b). Scales, norms, and equivalent scores. In R. L. Thorndike (Ed.), *Educational measurement* (2nd ed., pp. 508–600). Washington DC: American Council on Education.

Angoff, W. H. (1989). Does guessing really help? *Journal of Educational Measurement, 26*, 323–336.

Angoff, W. H., Pomplun, M., McHale, F., & Morgan, R. (1990). Comparative study of factors related to the predictive validities of 1974–75 and 1984–85 forms of the SAT. In W. W. Willingham, C. Lewis, R. Morgan, & L. Ramist (Eds.), *Predicting college grades: An analysis of institutional trends over two decades* (pp. 195–212). Princeton, NJ: Educational Testing Service.

Angoff, W. H., & Schrader, W. B. (1984). A study of hypotheses basic to the use of rights and formula scores. *Journal of Educational Measurement, 21*(1), 1–17.

Applebee, A. N., Langer, J. A., Jenkins, L. B., Mullis, I. V., & Foertsch, M. A. (1990). *Learning to write in our nation's schools: Instruction and achievement in 1988 at grades 4, 8, and 12* (NAEP 19-W-02). Princeton, NJ: Educational Testing Service, National Assessment of Educational Progress.

Applebee, A. N., Langer, J. A., & Mullis, I. V. (1986). *Writing: Trends across the decade 1974–84*. Princeton, NJ: Educational Testing Service, National Assessment of Educational Progress.

Applebee, A. N., Langer, J. A., Mullis, I. V., Latham, A. S., & Gentile, C. A. (1994). *NAEP 1992 writing report card*. Princeton, NJ: Educational Testing Service, National Assessment of Educational Progress.

Archbald, D. A., & Newmann, F. M. (1988). *Beyond standardized testing: Assessing authentic academic achievement in the secondary school*. Reston, VA: National Association of Secondary School Principals.

Armstrong, J. M. (1985). A national assessment of participation and achievement of women in mathematics. In S. F. Chipman, L. R. Brush, & D. M. Wilson (Eds.), *Women and mathematics: Balancing the equation* (pp. 59–94). Hillsdale, NJ: Lawrence Erlbaum Associates.

Association of American Medical Colleges. (1992, October 20). *Facts: Applicants, matriculants and graduates—1986 to 1992.* Washington, DC: Author.

Association for Measurement and Evaluation in Counseling and Development. (1992). *Responsibilities of users of standardized tests.* Alexandria, VA: American Association for Counseling and Development.

Astin, A. W. (1971). *Predicting academic performance in college.* New York: The Free Press.

Astin, A. W. (1993). *What matters in college? Four critical years revisited.* San Francisco: Jossey-Bass.

Attiyeh, G., & Attiyeh, R. (1994). Are graduate admissions fair? *Program Profiles, II*(1). Princeton, NJ: Educational Testing Service, AAU/AGS Project for Research on Doctoral Education.

Ayres, L. P. (1909). *Laggards in our schools: A study of retardation and elimination in city school systems.* New York: Russell Sage.

Backman, M. E. (1979). Patterns of mental abilities of adolescent males and females from different ethnic and socioeconomic backgrounds. In L. Willerman & R. G. Turner (Eds.), *Readings about individual and group differences* (pp. 261–265). San Francisco: Freeman.

Baker, D. P., & Jones, D. P. (1992). Opportunity and performance: A sociological explanation for gender differences in academic mathematics. In J. Wrigley (Ed.), *Education and gender equality* (pp. 193–203). London: Falmer.

Baker, E. L. (1994). Learning-based assessments of history understanding. *Educational Psychologist, 29,* 97–106.

Baker, E. L., Aschbacher, P. R., Niemi, D., & Sato, E. (1992). *CRESST performance assessment models: Assessing content area explanations.* Los Angeles: University of California, Center for Research on Evaluation, Standards, and Student Testing.

Baker, E. L., O'Neil, H. F., Jr., & Linn, R. L. (1993). Policy and validity prospects for performance-based assessment. *American Psychologist, 48*(12), 1210–1218.

Baker, M. A. (Ed.). (1987). *Sex differences in human performance.* Chichester, England: Wiley.

Barron's Educational Series. (Ed.). (1994). *Barron's profiles of American colleges* (20th ed). Hauppauge, NY: Author.

Barton, P. E., & Coley, R. J. (1993). *Performance assessment sampler: A workbook.* Princeton, NJ: Policy Information Center, Educational Testing Service.

Barton, P. E., & Coley, R. J. (1994). *Testing in America's schools.* Princeton, NJ: Policy Information Center, Educational Testing Service.

Becker, B. J. (1990). Item characteristics and gender differences on the SAT-M for mathematically able youths. *American Educational Research Journal, 27,* 65–87.

Becker, B. J., & Hedges, L. V. (1988). Commentary: The effects of selection and variability in studies of gender differences. *Behavioral and Brain Sciences, 11,* 183–184.

Becker, D. F., & Forsyth, R. A. (1990, April). *Gender differences in academic achievement in grades 3 through 12: A longitudinal analysis.* Paper presented at the annual meeting of the American Educational Research Association, Boston, MA.

Bejar, I. I., & Blew, E. O. (1981). *Grade inflation and the validity of the Scholastic Aptitude Test* (CB Rep. No. 81-3). New York: College Entrance Examination Board.

Bejar, I. I., & Braun, H. I. (1994). On the synergy between assessment and instruction: Early lessons from computer-based simulations. *Machine-Mediated Learning, 4,* 5–25.

Bell, R. C., & Hay, J. A. (1987). Differences and biases in English language examination formats. *British Journal of Educational Psychology, 57,* 212–220.

Beller, M., & Gafni, N. (1995). *International perspectives on the schooling and learning achievement of girls and boys as revealed in the 1991 International Assessment of Educational Progress (IAEP).* Jerusalem: National Institute for Testing and Evaluation.

Beller, M., & Gafni, N. (1996a). *Can item format (multiple-choice vs. open-ended) account for gender differences in mathematics achievement?* Jerusalem: National Institute for Testing and Evaluation.

Beller, M., & Gafni, N. (1996b). The 1991 International Assessment of Educational Progress in mathematics and sciences: The gender differences perspective. *Journal of Educational Psychology, 88*(2), 365–377.

Benbow, C. P. (1986). Physiological correlates of extreme intellectual precocity. *Neuropsychologia, 24,* 719–725.

Benbow, C. P. (1988a). Neuropsychological perspectives on mathematical talent. In L. K. Obler & D. Fein (Eds.), *The exceptional brain: Neuropsychology of talent and special abilities* (pp. 48–69). New York: Guilford.

Benbow, C. P. (1988b). Sex differences in mathematical reasoning ability in intellectually talented preadolescents: Their nature, effects, and possible causes. *Behavioral and Brain Sciences, 11,* 169–232.

Benbow, C. P. (1990). Gender differences: Searching for facts. *American Psychologist, 45,* 988.

Benbow, C. P., & Stanley, J. C. (1980). Sex differences in mathematical ability: Fact or artifact? *Science, 210,* 1262–1264.

Benbow, C. P., & Stanley, J. C. (1982). Consequences in high school and college of sex differences in mathematical reasoning ability: A longitudinal perspective. *American Educational Research Journal, 19,* 598–622.

Benbow, C. P., & Stanley, J. C. (1983). Differential course-taking hypothesis revisited. *American Educational Research Journal, 20,* 469–573.

Bennett, R. E., Rock, D. A., Braun, H. I., Frye, D., Spohrer, J. C., & Soloway, E. (1990). The relationship of expert-system scored constrained free-response items to multiple-choice and open-ended items. *Applied Psychological Measurement, 14,* 151–162.

Bennett, R. E., Rock, D. A., & Wang, M. (1991). Equivalence of free-response and multiple-choice items. *Journal of Educational Measurement, 28,* 77–92.

Bennett, R. E., & Ward, W. C. (Eds.). (1993). *Construction versus choice in cognitive measurement: Issues in constructed response, performance testing, and portfolio assessment.* Hillsdale, NJ: Lawrence Erlbaum Associates.

Ben-Shakhar, G., & Sinai, Y. (1991). Gender differences in multiple-choice tests: The role of differential guessing tendencies. *Journal of Educational Measurement, 28,* 23–35.

Bersoff, D. N. (1981). Testing and the law. *American Psychologist, 36,* 1047–1056.

Beyers, B. (1986, November 12). Admit scholars with constancy, faculty advised. *Campus Report,* Stanford University, p. 1.

Bickel, P. J., Hammel, E. A., & O'Connell, J. W. (1975). Sex bias in graduate admissions: Data from Berkeley. *Science, 187,* 398–404.

Birnbaum, R. (1977). Factors related to university grade inflation. *Journal of Higher Education, 48*(5), 519–539.

Block, J. H. (1976a). Debatable conclusions about sex differences [Review of *The psychology of sex differences*]. *Contemporary Psychology, 21*(8), 517–522.

Block, J. H. (1976b). Issues, problems, and pitfalls in assessing sex differences: A critical review of the psychology of sex differences. *Merrill-Palmer Quarterly, 22,* 283–308.

Bloom, B. S. (Ed.). (1956). *Taxonomy of educational objectives. The classification of educational goals. Handbook 1: Cognitive domain.* New York: David McKay.

Board of Senior Secondary School Studies. (1995). *Queensland Core Skills (QCS) test: Test specifications.* Spring Hill, Queensland, Australia: Author.

Bolger, N., & Kellaghan, T. (1990). Method of measurement and gender differences in scholastic achievement. *Journal of Educational Measurement, 27,* 165–174.

Bowen, W. G. (1977). Admissions and the relevance of race. *Educational Record, 58*(4), 333–349.

Bowles, F. (1965). *Access to higher education: Vol. I. The international study of university admissions.* Paris: United Nations Educational, Scientific and Cultural Organization, and International Association of Universities.

Bracey, G. W. (1993, January). Sex, math, and SATs. *Phi Delta Kappan, 74*(5), 415–417.

Braun, H. I., Centra, J., & King, B. F. (1987). *Verbal and mathematical ability of high school juniors and seniors in 1983: A norm study of the PSAT/NMSQT and the SAT.* Unpublished manuscript, Educational Testing Service.

Breland, H. M. (1996). *Writing skill assessment: Problems and prospects.* Princeton, NJ: Educational Testing Service, Policy Information Center.

Breland, H. M., Bonner, M. W., & Kubota, M. Y. (1996). *Factors in performance on brief, impromptu essay examinations* (CB Rep. No. 95-4; ETS RR-95-41). New York: College Entrance Examination Board.

Breland, H. M., Camp, R., Jones, R. J., Morris, M. M., & Rock, D. A. (1987). *Assessing writing skill* (College Board Research Monograph No. 11). New York: College Entrance Examination Board.

Breland, H. M., Danos, D. O., Kahn, H. D., Kubota, M. Y., & Bonner, M. W. (1994). Performance versus objective testing and gender: An exploratory study of an Advanced Placement history examination. *Journal of Educational Measurement, 31,* 275–293.

Breland, H. M., Danos, D. O., Kahn, H. D., Kubota, M. Y., & Sudlow, M. W. (1991). *A study of gender and performance on Advanced Placement History examinations* (CB Rep. No. 91-4; ETS RR-91-61). New York: College Entrance Examination Board.

Breland, H. M., & Griswold, P. A. (1982). Use of a performance test as a criterion in a differential validity study. *Journal of Educational Psychology, 74,* 713–721.

Breland, H. M., & Jones, R. J. (1982). *Perceptions of writing skills* (College Board Rep. No. 82-4; ETS RR-82-47). New York: College Entrance Examination Board.

Breland, H. M., Jones, R. J., & Jenkins, L. (1994). *The College Board vocabulary study* (CB Rep. No. 94-4; ETS RR-89-50). New York: College Entrance Examination Board.

Breland, H. M., Maxey, J., McLure, G. T., Valiga, M. J., Boatwright, M. A., Ganley, V. L., & Jenkins, L. M. (1995). *Challenges in college admissions: A report of a survey of undergraduate admissions policies, practices, and procedures.* Washington, DC: American Association of Collegiate Registrars and Admissions Officers.

Bridgeman, B. (1991). *Essays and multiple-choice tests as predictors of college freshman GPA* (ETS RR-91-3). Princeton, NJ: Educational Testing Service.

Bridgeman, B. (1992). A comparison of quantitative questions in open-ended and multiple-choice formats. *Journal of Educational Measurement, 29*(3), 253–271.

Bridgeman, B. (1993). *A comparison of open-ended and multiple-choice question formats for the quantitative section of the Graduate Record Examinations General Test* (GRE Rep. No. 88-13P; ETS RR-91-35). Princeton, NJ: Educational Testing Service.

Bridgeman, B., Hale, G. A., Lewis, C., Pollack, J., & Wang, M. (1992). *Placement validity of a prototype SAT with an essay* (ETS RR-92-28). Princeton, NJ: Educational Testing Service.

Bridgeman, B., Harvey, A., & Braswell, J. (1995). Effects of calculator use on scores on a test of mathematical reasoning. *Journal of Educational Measurement, 32,* 323–340.

Bridgeman, B., & Lewis, C. (1994). The relationship of essay and multiple-choice scores with grades in college courses. *Journal of Educational Measurement, 31,* 37–50.

Bridgeman, B., & Lewis, C. (1996). Gender differences in college mathematics grades and SAT-M scores: A reanalysis of Wainer and Steinberg. *Journal of Educational Measurement, 33,* 257–270.

Bridgeman, B., & McHale, F. (1996). *Gender and ethnic group differences on the GMAT analytical writing assessment* (ETS RR-96-2). Princeton, NJ: Educational Testing Service.

Bridgeman, B., & Rock, D. A. (1993). *Development and evaluation of computer-administered analytical questions for the Graduate Record Examinations General Test* (GRE Rep. No. 88-06P; ETS RR-92-49). Princeton, NJ: Educational Testing Service.

Bridgeman, B., & Schaeffer, G. (1995, April). *A comparison of gender differences on paper-and-pencil and computer-adaptive versions of the Graduate Record Examination.* Paper presented at the annual meeting of the American Educational Research Association, San Francisco.

Bridgeman, B., & Wendler, C. (1989). *Prediction of grades in college mathematics courses as a component of the placement validity of SAT-Mathematics scores* (CB Rep. No. 89-9; ETS RR-89-50). New York: College Entrance Examination Board.

Bridgeman, B., & Wendler, C. (1991). Gender differences in predictors of college mathematics performance and in college mathematics course grades. *Journal of Educational Psychology, 83*, 275–284.

Briggs, D. (1980). A study of the influence of handwriting upon grades using examination scripts. *Educational Review, 32*, 185–193.

Bunch, M. B. (1993). *Georgia high school graduation test results of administration of performance items.* Athens, GA: Measurement Incorporated.

Burton, N. W., Lewis, C., & Robertson, N. (1988). *Sex differences in SAT scores* (CB Rep. No. 88-9; ETS RR-88-58). New York: College Entrance Examination Board.

Butler, R., & McCauley, C. (1987). Extraordinary stability and ordinary predictability of academic success at the United States Military Academy. *Journal of Educational Psychology, 79*, 83–86.

Camp, R. (1993). Changing the model for the direct assessment of writing. In M. M. Williamson & B. A. Huot (Eds.), *Validating holistic scoring for writing assessment: Theoretical and empirical foundations* (pp. 45–78). Cresskill, NJ: Hampton Press.

Campbell, D. T., & Fiske, D. W. (1959). Convergent and discriminant validation by the multitrait-multimethod matrix. *Psychological Bulletin, 56*, 81–105.

Campbell, P. B. (1988). *Who's better? Who's worse? Research and the search for differences.* Groton, MA: Author.

Campbell, P. B., & Greenberg, S. (1993). Equity issues in educational research methods. In S. K. Biklen & D. Pollard (Eds.), *Gender and education: Ninety-second yearbook of the National Society for the Study of Education, Part I* (pp. 64–89). Chicago: University of Chicago.

Caplan, P. J., MacPherson, G. M., & Tobin, P. (1985). Do sex-related differences in spatial abilities exist? A multilevel critique with new data. *American Psychologist, 40*, 786–799.

Carlton, S. T., & Harris, A. M. (1992). *Characteristics associated with differential item performance on the Scholastic Aptitude Test: Gender and majority/minority group comparisons* (ETS RR-92-64). Princeton, NJ: Educational Testing Service.

Carnegie Commission on Higher Education. (1973). *Continuity and discontinuity: Higher education and the schools.* New York: McGraw-Hill.

Carnegie Council on Policy Studies in Higher Education. (1977). *Selective admissions in higher education: Comment and recommendations and two reports.* San Francisco: Jossey-Bass.

Carroll, J. B. (1993). *Human cognitive abilities: A survey of the factor-analytic studies.* New York: Cambridge University Press.

Casserly, P. L. (1980). Factors affecting female participation in Advanced Placement programs in mathematics, chemistry, and physics. In L. H. Fox, L. Brody, & D. Tobin (Eds.), *Women and the mathematical mystique: Proceedings of the Eighth Annual Hyman Blumberg Symposium on Research in Early Childhood Education* (pp. 138–163). Baltimore: Johns Hopkins University.

Center for Research on Evaluation, Standards, and Student Testing. (1995, Spring). *The CRESST Line Newsletter.* Los Angeles: UCLA Graduate School of Education.

Chase, C. I. (1986). Essay test scoring: Interaction of relevant variables. *Journal of Educational Measurement, 23*(1), 33–41.

Cherry, R. D., & Meyer, P. R. (1993). Reliability issues in holistic assessment. In M. M. Williamson & B. A. Huot (Eds.), *Validating holistic scoring for writing assessment: Theoretical and empirical foundations* (pp. 109–141). Cresskill, NJ: Hampton Press.

Chi, M., Glaser, R., & Farr, M. (Eds.). (1988). *The nature of expertise.* Hillsdale, NJ: Lawrence Erlbaum Associates.

Chickering, A. W. (1969). *Education and identity.* San Francisco: Jossey-Bass.

Chickering, A. W. (1983). Grades: One more tilt at the windmill. *AAHE Bulletin, 35*(8), 10–13.

Chipman, S. F. (1988). Far too sexy a topic [Review of *The psychology of gender: Advances through meta-analysis*]. *Educational Researcher, 17*(3), 46–49.

Chipman, S. F., Brush, L. R., & Wilson, D. M. (1985). *Women and mathematics: Balancing the equation.* Hillsdale, NJ: Lawrence Erlbaum Associates.

Chronicle of Higher Education. (1994, April 6). Carnegie Foundation's classification of 3,600 institutions of higher education, pp. A18ff.

Cizek, G. J. (1993a). The place of psychometricians' beliefs in educational reform: A rejoinder to Shepard. *Educational Researcher, 22*(4), 14–15.

Cizek, G. J. (1993b). Rethinking psychometricians' beliefs about learning. *Educational Researcher, 22*(4), 4–9.

Clark, M. J., & Grandy, J. (1984). *Sex differences in the academic performance of Scholastic Aptitude Test takers* (CB Rep. No. 84-8, ETS RR-84-43). New York: College Entrance Examination Board.

Cleary, T. A. (1968). Test bias: Prediction of grades of Negro and White students in integrated colleges. *Journal of Educational Measurement, 5*(2), 115–124.

Cleary, T. A. (1992). Gender differences in aptitude and achievement test scores. In *Sex equity in educational opportunity, achievement, and testing: Proceedings of the 1991 ETS Invitational Conference* (pp. 51–90). Princeton, NJ: Educational Testing Service.

Code of Fair Testing Practices in Education. (1988). Washington, DC: Joint Committee on Testing Practices.

Cohen, J. (1988). *Statistical power analysis for the behavioral sciences* (2nd ed.). Hillsdale, NJ: Lawrence Erlbaum Associates.

Cohen, J. (1994). The Earth is round ($p < .05$). *American Psychologist, 49,* 997–1003.

Colangelo, N., Assouline, S. G., & Ambroson, D. L. (Eds). (1992). *Talent development: Proceedings from the 1991 Henry B. and Jocelyn Wallace National Research Symposium on Talent Development.* Unionville, NY: Trillium.

Cole, N. S. (1973). Bias in selection. *Journal of Educational Measurement, 10*(4), 237–255.

Cole, N. S. (1981). Bias in testing. *American Psychologist, 36*(10), 1067–1077.

Cole, N. S. (1984). Testing and the "crisis" in education. *Educational Measurement: Issues and Practices, 3*(3), 4–8.

Cole, N. S. (1990, April). *Gender differences and admission policies: Implications for test use.* Paper presented at a Symposium: Fairness, Justice, and Equity in Admissions and Employment Testing: Validity in the Trenches, conducted at the annual meeting of the American Educational Research Association, Boston.

Cole, N. S., & Moss, P. A. (1989). Bias in test use. In R. L. Linn (Ed.), *Educational measurement* (3rd ed., pp. 201–219). New York: American Council on Education & Macmillan.

Coley, R. J., & Goertz, M. E. (1990). *Educational standards in the 50 states: 1990* (ETS RR-90-15). Princeton, NJ: Educational Testing Service.

College Board. (1984). *College-bound seniors: Eleven years of national data from the College Board's Admissions Testing Program, 1973–1983*. New York: College Entrance Examination Board.

College Board. (1986). *Measures in the college admissions process: A College Board colloquium*. New York: College Entrance Examination Board.

College Board. (1988). *Guidelines on the uses of College Board test scores and related data*. New York: College Entrance Examination Board.

College Board. (1992a). *The college handbook, 1993* (30th ed.). New York: College Entrance Examination Board.

College Board. (1992b). *College-bound seniors: 1992 profile of SAT and Achievement Test takers*. Princeton, NJ: Educational Testing Service Board.

College Board. (1992c). *The great sorting: A report on the College Board's admission study colloquium*. New York: Author.

College Board. (1993a). *The college handbook, 1994* (31st ed.). New York: College Entrance Examination Board.

College Board, Admissions Testing Program. (1993b). *College-bound seniors: 1993 profile of SAT and Achievement Test takers*. New York: College Entrance Examination Board.

College Board. (1994a). *The college handbook, 1995* (32nd ed.). New York: College Entrance Examination Board.

College Board. (1994b). *1994 AP Mathematics free-response scoring guide and sample student answers. Calculus AB—Calculus BC*. New York: College Entrance Examination Board & Educational Testing Service.

College Board. (1994c). *1994 AP Physics C: Free-response scoring guide and sample student answers*. New York: College Entrance Examination Board & Educational Testing Service.

College Board. (1994d). *Summary statistics: Annual survey of colleges, 1992–93 and 1993–94*. New York: College Entrance Examination Board.

College Board. (1995). *Taking the SAT I Reasoning Test: The official guide to the SAT I*. New York: Author.

Commission on Standards for School Mathematics of the National Council of Teachers of Mathematics. (1989, March). *Curriculum and evaluation standards for school mathematics*. Reston, VA: National Council of Teachers of Mathematics.

Connor, K., & Vargyas, E. J. (1992). The legal implications of gender bias in standardized testing. *Berkeley Women's Law Journal, 7*, 13–89.

Conrad, L., Trismen, D., & Miller, R. (1977). *Graduate Record Examinations technical manual*. Princeton, NJ: Educational Testing Service.

Cook, L. L., & Petersen, N. S. (1987). Problems related to the use of conventional and item response theory equating methods in less than optimal circumstances. *Applied Psychological Measurement, 11*, 225–244.

Council of Graduate Schools. (1992). *CGS/GRE survey of graduate enrollment* [selected data run on November 17, 1995]. Washington, DC: Author.

Cronbach, L. J. (1976). Equity in selection—Where psychometrics and political philosophy meet. *Journal of Educational Measurement, 13*(1), 31–41.

Cronbach, L. J. (1980). Validity on parole: How can we go straight? In W. B. Schrader (Ed.), *New directions for testing and measurement, 5. Measuring achievement over a decade. Proceedings of the 1979 ETS Invitational Conference* (pp. 99–108). San Francisco: Jossey-Bass.

Cross, K. P. (1974). The woman student. In W. T. Furniss & P. A. Graham (Eds.), *Women in higher education* (pp. 29–49). Washington, DC: American Council on Education.

Cross, K. P., Valley, J. R., & Associates. (1974). *Planning non-traditional programs*. San Francisco: Jossey-Bass.

Cross, L. H., & Frary, R. B. (1977). An empirical test of Lord's theoretical results regarding formula scoring of multiple-choice tests. *Journal of Educational Measurement, 14*(4), 313–321.

Cruise, P. I., & Kimmel, E. W. (1990). *Changes in the SAT-Verbal: A study of trends in content and gender references 1961–1987* (CB Rep. No. 90-1, ETS RR-89-17). New York: College Entrance Examination Board.

CTB. (1991). *CTBS Comprehensive Tests of Basic Skills technical report* (4th ed.). Monterey, CA: Author, Macmillan/McGraw-Hill.

Cureton, L. W. (1971). The history of grading practices. *Measurement in Education, 2*(4), 1–8.

Curley, W. E., & Schmitt, A. P. (1993). *Revising SAT-Verbal items to eliminate differential item functioning* (CB Rep. No. 93-2; ETS RR-93-61). New York: College Entrance Examination Board.

Darling-Hammond, L. (1994). Performance-based assessment and educational equity. *Harvard Educational Review, 64*(1), 5–30.

Darlington, R. B. (1971). Another look at "cultural fairness." *Journal of Educational Measurement, 8*(2), 71–82.

Darlington, R. B. (1976). A defense of "rational" personnel selection, and two new methods. *Journal of Educational Measurement, 13*(1), 43–52.

Deaux, K. (1985). Sex and gender. *Annual Review of Psychology, 36*, 49–81.

DeMauro, G. E., & Olson, J. F. (1989, March). *The impact of differential speededness on DIF.* Paper presented at the annual meeting of the National Council on Measurement in Education, San Francisco.

Denno, D. (1982). Sex differences in cognition: A review and critique of the longitudinal evidence. *Adolescence, 17*, 779–788.

Department of Health, Education, and Welfare. (1977). Nondiscrimination on the basis of handicap in programs and activities receiving or benefiting from federal financial assistance. *Federal Register, 42*, 22676–22702.

Deutsch, M. (1975). Equity, equality and need: What determines which value will be used as the basis of distributive justice? *Journal of Social Issues, 31*(3), 137–149.

Dewey, J. (1902). *The child and the curriculum.* Chicago: University of Chicago Press.

Dey, E. L., Astin, A. W., & Korn, W. S. (1991). *The American freshman: Twenty-five year trends.* Los Angeles: University of California, Higher Education Research Institute.

Dey, E. L., Astin, A. W., Korn, W. S., & Riggs, E. R. (1992). *The American freshman: National norms for fall 1992.* Los Angeles: Higher Education Research Institute, University of California, Los Angeles.

Diederich, P. B. (1974). *Measuring growth in English.* National Council of Teachers of English.

Dijkstra, B. (1986). *Idols of perversity: Fantasies of feminine evil in fin-de-siecle culture.* New York: Oxford University.

Donlon, T. F. (Ed.). (1984). *The College Board technical handbook for the Scholastic Aptitude Test and Achievement Tests.* New York: College Entrance Examination Board.

Donlon, T. F., Ekstrom, R. B., Lockheed, M. E., & Harris, A. (1977). *Performance consequences of sex bias in the content of major achievement batteries* (ETS PR-77-11). Princeton, NJ: Educational Testing Service.

Doolittle, A. E. (1989). Gender differences in performance on mathematics achievement items. *Applied Measurement in Education, 2*, 161–177.

Doolittle, A. E., & Cleary, T. A. (1987). Gender-based differential item performance in mathematics achievement items. *Journal of Educational Measurement, 24*, 157–166.

Doolittle, A. E., & Welch, C. (1989). *Gender differences in performance on a college-level achievement test* (ACT Research Rep. Series 89-9). Iowa City, IA: American College Testing Program.

Dorans, N. J., & Holland, P. W. (1993). DIF detection and description: Mantel-Haenszel and standardization. In P. W. Holland & H. Wainer (Eds.), *Differential item functioning* (pp. 35–66). Hillsdale, NJ: Lawrence Erlbaum Associates.

Dorans, N. J., & Kulick, E. (1983). *Assessing unexpected differential item performance of female candidates on SAT and TSWE forms administered in December 1977: An application of the standardization approach* (ETS RR-83-9). Princeton, NJ: Educational Testing Service.

Dorans, N. J., & Kulick, E. (1986). Demonstrating the utility of the standardization approach to assessing unexpected differential item performance on the Scholastic Aptitude Test. *Journal of Educational Measurement, 23,* 355–368.

Dorans, N. J., Schmitt, A. P., & Bleistein, C. A. (1992). The standardization approach to assessing comprehensive differential item functioning. *Journal of Educational Measurement, 29,* 309–319.

Dorans, N. J., Schmitt, A. P., & Curley, W. E. (1996). *Differential speededness: Some items have DIF because of where they are, not what they are.* Manuscript submitted for publication.

Dossey, J. A., Mullis, I. V., & Jones, C. O. (1993). *Can students do mathematical problem solving? Results from constructed-response questions in NAEP's 1992 mathematics assessment.* Princeton, NJ: Educational Testing Service, National Assessment of Educational Progress.

Dossey, J. A., Mullis, I. V., Lindquist, M. M., & Chambers, D. L. (1988). *The mathematics report card: Are we measuring up?* Princeton, NJ: Educational Testing Service, National Assessment of Educational Progress.

Dreyden, J. I., & Gallagher, S. A. (1989). The effects of time and direction changes on the SAT performance of academically talented adolescents. *Journal for the Education of the Gifted, 12*(3), 187–204.

Dreyfus, H., & Dreyfus, S. (1986). *Mind over machine.* New York: The Free Press.

Dunbar, S. B. (1987, April). *Comparability of indirect assessments of writing skill as predictors of writing performance across demographic groups.* Paper presented at the annual meeting of the American Educational Research Association, Washington, DC.

Dunbar, S. B., Koretz, D., & Hoover, H. D. (1991). Quality control in the development and use of performance assessments. *Applied Measurement in Education, 4*(4), 289–304.

Dunteman, G. H., Wisenbaker, J., & Taylor, M. E. (1979). *Race and sex differences in college science program participation.* Washington, DC: National Science Foundation.

Duran, R. P., Enright, M. K., & Rock, D. A. (1985). *Language factors and Hispanic freshmen's student profile* (CB Rep. No. 85-3; ETS RR-85-44). New York: College Entrance Examination Board.

Dwyer, C. A. (1974). Influence of children's sex role standards on reading and arithmetic achievement. *Journal of Educational Psychology, 66,* 811–815.

Dwyer, C. A. (1979). The role of tests and their construction in producing apparent sex-related differences. In M. A. Wittig & A. C. Petersen (Eds.), *Sex-related differences in cognitive functioning* (pp. 335–353). New York: Academic Press.

Dwyer, C. A. (1993). Teaching and diversity: Meeting the challenges for innovative teacher assessment. *Journal of Teacher Education, 44*(2), 119–129.

Dwyer, C. A. (1995, August). Cut scores and testing: Statistics, judgment, truth, and error. In R. L. Lowman (Chair), *What every psychologist should know about measurement—and doesn't.* Symposium conducted at the annual convention of the American Psychological Association, New York.

Dwyer, C. A., & Ramsey, P. A. (1995). Equity issues in teacher assessment. In M. T. Nettles & A. L. Nettles (Chair), *Equity and excellence in educational testing and assessment.* Symposium conducted at the annual convention of the American Psychological Association, New York.

Eagly, A. H. (1995). The science and politics of comparing women and men. *American Psychologist, 50,* 145–158.

Eccles, J. S. (1987). Gender roles and women's achievement-related decisions. *Psychology of Women Quarterly, 11,* 135–172.

Eccles (Parsons), J., Adler, T. F., Futterman, R., Goff, S. B., Kaczala, C. M., Meece, J. L., & Midgley, C. (1983). Expectancies, values, and academic behaviors. In J. T. Spence (Ed.), *Achievement and achievement motives: Psychological and sociological approaches* (pp. 75–146). San Francisco: Freeman.

Eccles, J. S., & Jacobs, J. E. (1986). Social forces shape math attitudes and performance. *Signs: Journal of Women in Culture and Society, 11,* 367–380.

Educational Testing Service. (1986). *ETS sensitivity review process: Guidelines and procedures.* Princeton, NJ: Author.

Educational Testing Service. (1987). *ETS standards for quality and fairness.* Princeton, NJ: Author.

Educational Testing Service. (1991). *How can we judge the fairness of tests* (ETS Board of Trustees Public Accountability Report). Princeton, NJ: Author.

Educational Testing Service. (1992). Three new reports on gender differences in standardized testing. *ETS Developments, 37*(3), 4–7.

Educational Testing Service. (1994). DIF procedures (1994 supplement). In *Test development manual.* Princeton, NJ: Author.

Einhorn, H. J., & Bass, A. R. (1971). Methodological considerations relevant to discrimination in employment testing. *Psychological Bulletin, 75,* 261–269.

Ekstrom, R. B. (1964). *Colleges' use and evaluation of the CEEB writing sample* (RB-64-4). Princeton, NJ: Educational Testing Service.

Ekstrom, R. B. (1994). *Gender differences in high school grades: An exploratory study* (CB Rep. No. 94-3; ETS RR-94-25). New York: College Entrance Examination Board.

Ekstrom, R. B., Goertz, M. E., & Rock, D. A. (1988). *Education and American youth: The impact of the high school experience.* London: Falmer.

Elliott, R., & Strenta, A. C. (1988). Effects of improving the reliability of the GPA on prediction generally and on comparative predictions for gender and race particularly. *Journal of Educational Measurement, 25,* 333–347.

Elliott, R., & Strenta, A. C. (1990). *Is the SAT redundant with high school record in college selection?* (Research and Development Update). New York: The College Board.

Evangelauf, J. (1994, April). A new "Carnegie classification": Academe is "healthy and expanding," the updated edition shows. *The Chronicle of Higher Education, Personal & Professional,* A17, A25–A26.

Evans, F. R. (1980). *A study of the relationships among speed and power aptitude test scores, and ethnic identity.* Princeton, NJ: Educational Testing Service.

Eyde, L. D., Robertson, G. J., Krug, S. E., Moreland, K. L., Robertson, A. G., Shewan, C. M., Harrison, P. L., Porch, B. E., Hammer, A. L., & Primoff, E. S. (1993). *Responsible test use: Case studies for assessing human behavior.* Washington, DC: American Psychological Association.

Eysenck, H. J. (1981). In H. J. Eysenck & L. J. Kamin, *The intelligence controversy: H. J. Eysenck vs. Leon Kamin* (pp. 11–89, 157–172). New York: Wiley.

Fausto-Sterling, A. (1985). *Myths of gender: Biological theories about women and men.* New York: Basic Books.

Feingold, A. (1988). Cognitive gender differences are disappearing. *American Psychologist, 43*(2), 95–103.

Feingold, A. (1992a). The greater male variability controversy: Science versus politics. *Review of Educational Research, 62*(1), 89–90.

Feingold, A. (1992b). Sex differences in variability in intellectual abilities: A new look at an old controversy. *Review of Educational Research, 62*(1), 61–84.

Feingold, A. (1993a). Cognitive gender differences: A developmental perspective. *Sex Roles, 29,* 91–112.

Feingold, A. (1993b). Joint effects of gender differences in central tendency and gender differences in variability. *Review of Educational Research, 63*(1), 106–109.

Feingold, A. (1994). Gender differences in variability in intellectual abilities: A cross-cultural perspective. *Sex Roles, 30,* 81–92.

Feingold, A. (1995). The additive effects of differences in central tendency and variability are important in comparisons between groups. *American Psychologist, 50*(1), 5–13.

Fennema, E. (1974). Mathematics learning and the sexes: A review. *Journal for Research in Mathematics Education, 5,* 126–139.

Fennema, E., & Peterson, P. (1985). Autonomous learning behavior: A possible explanation of gender-related differences in mathematics. In L. C. Wilkinson & C. B. Marrett (Eds.), *Gender influences in classroom interaction* (pp. 17–35). Orlando, FL: Academic Press.

Fennema, E. H., & Carpenter, T. P. (1981). Sex-related differences in mathematics: Results from national assessment. *The Mathematics Teacher, 74,* 554–559.

Fennema, E. H., & Sherman, J. A. (1977). Sex-related differences in mathematics achievement, spatial visualization, and sociocultural factors. *Journal of Educational Research, 14,* 51–71.

Fennema, E. H., & Sherman, J. A. (1978). Sex-related differences in mathematics achievement and related factors: A further study. *Journal for Research in Mathematics Education, 9,* 189–203.

Fennema, E. H., & Tartre, L. A. (1985). The use of spatial visualization in mathematics by girls and boys. *Journal for Research in Mathematics Education, 16*(3), 184–206.

Feryok, N. J., & Wright, N. K. (1993, April). *Design of the 1992 SAT and PSAT/NMSQT field trial.* Paper presented at the annual meeting of the National Council on Measurement in Education, Atlanta, GA.

Finn, J. D. (1972). Expectations and the educational environment. *Review of Educational Research, 72,* 387–410.

Fishman, J. A. (1958). Unsolved criterion problems in the selection of college students. *Harvard Educational Review, 28*(4), 340–349.

Flanagan, J. C., & Cooley, W. W. (1966). *Project TALENT: One-year follow-up studies* (Final Report for Cooperative Research Project No. 2333, U.S. Office of Education). Pittsburgh, PA: University of Pittsburgh.

Flanagan, J. C., Dailey, J. T., Shaycoft, M. F., Gorham, W. A., Orr, D. B., & Goldberg, I. (1962). *Project Talent: Design for a study of American youth* (American Institute for Research). Boston: Houghton Mifflin.

Flanagan, J. C., Davis, F. B., Dailey, J. T., Shaycoft, M. F., Orr, D. B., Goldberg, I., & Neyman, C. A., Jr. (1964). *Project TALENT: The American high-school student* (Final Report for Cooperative Research Project No. 635, U.S. Office of Education). Pittsburgh, PA: University of Pittsburgh.

Folger, J. K., Astin, H. S., & Bayer, A. E. (1970). *Human resources and higher education: Staff report of the Commission on Human Resources and Advanced Education.* New York: Russell Sage Foundation.

Fox, L. H., & Denham, S. A. (1974). Values and career interests of mathematically and scientifically precocious youth. In J. C. Stanley, D. P. Keating, & L. H. Fox (Eds.), *Mathematical talent: Discovery, description, and development. Proceedings of the Third Annual Hyman Blumberg Symposium on Research in Early Childhood Education* (pp. 140–175). Baltimore: Johns Hopkins University.

Frederiksen, J. R., & Collins, A. (1989). A systems approach to educational testing. *Educational Researcher, 18*(9), 27–32.

Frederiksen, N. (1984). The real test bias: Influences of testing on teaching and learning. *American Psychologist, 39*, 193–202.

Frederiksen, N., & Ward, W. C. (1978). Measures for the study of creativity in scientific problem solving. *Applied Psychological Measurement, 2*, 1–24.

French, J. W. (1966). Schools of thought in judging excellence of English themes. In A. Anastasi (Ed.), *Testing problems in perspective: Twenty-fifth anniversary volume of topical readings from the Invitational Conference on Testing Problems* (pp. 587–596). Washington, DC: American Council on Education.

Friedman, L. (1989). Mathematics and the gender gap: A meta-analysis of recent studies on sex differences in mathematical tasks. *Review of Educational Research, 59*, 185–213.

Gallagher, A. M. (1990). *Sex differences in the performance of high-scoring examinees on the SAT-M* (CB Rep No. 90-3; ETS RR-90-27). New York: College Entrance Examination Board.

Gallagher, A. M. (1992). *Sex differences in problem-solving strategies used by high-scoring examinees on the SAT-M* (CB Rep. No. 92-2; ETS RR-92-33). New York: College Entrance Examination Board.

Gallagher, A. M., & De Lisi, R. (1994). Gender differences in the Scholastic Aptitude Test Mathematics problem solving among high ability students. *Journal of Educational Psychology, 86*, 204–211.

Gamache, L. M., & Novick, M. R. (1985). Choice of variables and gender differentiated prediction within selected academic programs. *Journal of Educational Measurement, 22*(1), 53–70.

Gardner, E. (1982). Some aspects of the use and misuse of standardized aptitude and achievement tests. In A. Wigdor & W. Garner (Eds.), *Ability testing: Uses, consequences and controversies* (Vol. II, pp. 315–332). Washington, DC: National Academy Press.

Gardner, H. (1983). *Frames of mind: The theory of multiple intelligences.* New York: Basic Books.

Gardner, J. W. (1961). *Excellence: Can we be equal and excellent too?* New York: Harper & Row.

Geisinger, K. F. (1982). Marking systems. In H. E. Mitzell (Ed.), *Encyclopedia of educational research* (5th ed., pp. 1139–1149). New York: The Free Press.

Gipps, C., & Murphy, P. (1994). *A fair test? Assessment, achievement and equity.* Buckingham, England: Open University.

Glaser, R. (1963). Instructional technology and the measurement of learning outcomes: Some questions. *American Psychologist, 18*, 519–521.

Glass, G. V. (1976). Primary, secondary, and meta-analysis of research. *Educational Researcher, 5*(10), 3–8.

Glass, G. V., McGaw, B., & Smith, M. L. (1981). *Meta-analysis in social research.* Beverly Hills, CA: Sage.

Glazer, N. (1970, November–December). Are academic standards obsolete? *Change, 38*–44.

Goals 2000. (1994). Educate America act of 1994, Pub. L. 103–227, Sec. 1 et seq. 108 Stat. 125.

Godshalk, F. I., Swineford, F., & Coffman, W. E. (1966). *The measurement of writing ability* (Research Monograph No. 6). New York: College Entrance Examination Board.

Goldman, R. D., & Hewitt, B. N. (1975). Adaptation-level as an explanation for differential standards in college grading. *Journal of Educational Measurement, 12*(3), 149–161.

Goldman, R. D., Schmidt, D. E., Hewitt, B. N., & Fisher, R. (1974). Grading practices in different major fields. *American Educational Research Journal, 11*(4), 343–357.

Goldman, R. D., & Slaughter, R. E. (1976). Why college grade point average is difficult to predict. *Journal of Educational Psychology, 68*(1), 9–14.

Goldman, R. D., & Widawski, M. H. (1976). A within-subjects technique for comparing college grading standards: Implications in the validity of the evaluation of college achievement. *Educational and Psychological Measurement, 36,* 381–390.

Goodison, M. B. (1982). *A summary of data collected from Graduate Record Examinations test-takers during 1980–1981* (Data Summary Rep. No. 6). Princeton, NJ: Educational Testing Service.

Goodison, M. B. (1983). *A summary of data collected from Graduate Record Examinations test-takers during 1981–1982* (Data Summary Rep. No. 7). Princeton, NJ: Educational Testing Service.

Gordon, E. W. (in press). Human diversity and equitable assessment. In S. Messick (Ed.), *Assessment in higher education: Issues of access, quality, student development, and public policy.* Mahwah, NJ: Lawrence Erlbaum Associates.

Goslin, D. A. (1967). What's wrong with tests and testing? *College Board Review,* Part I (65), 12–18; Part II (66), 33–37.

Gottfredson, L. S. (1994). The science and politics of race-norming. *American Psychologist, 49,* 955–963.

Graduate Record Examinations Board. (1991a). *Guidelines for the use of GRE scores.* Princeton, NJ: Educational Testing Service.

Graduate Record Examinations Board. (1991b). *Sex, race, ethnicity, and performance on the GRE General Test* (Questions and answers). Princeton, NJ: Educational Testing Service.

Graduate Record Examinations Board. (1991c). *Sex, race, ethnicity, and performance on the GRE General Test* (A technical report). Princeton, NJ: Educational Testing Service.

Graduate Record Examinations Board. (1992). *GRE 1992–93 guide to the use of the Graduate Record Examinations program.* Princeton, NJ: Educational Testing Service.

Grandy, J. (1987). *Characteristics of examinees who leave questions unanswered on the GRE General Test under rights-only scoring* (GRE Board Professional Rep. No. 83-16P; ETS RR-87-38). Princeton, NJ: Educational Testing Service.

Grandy, J. (1994a). *Gender and ethnic differences among science and engineering majors: Experiences, achievements, and expectations* (GRE No. 92-03; ETS RR-94-30). Princeton, NJ: Educational Testing Service.

Grandy, J. (1994b). *GRE—Trends & profiles: Statistics about General Test examinees by sex and ethnicity* (ETS RR-94-1) and *Supplementary tables* (ETS RR-94-1A). Princeton, NJ: Educational Testing Service.

Gray, D. J. (1988, June). Writing across the college curriculum. *Phi Delta Kappan,* 729–733.

Guilford, J. P., & Hoepfner, R. (1971). *The analysis of intelligence.* New York: McGraw-Hill.

Guion, R. M. (1974). Open a new window: Validities and values in psychological measurement. *American Psychologist, 29,* 287–296.

Gustafsson, J. E. (1992). The relevance of factor analysis for the study of group differences. *Multivariate Behavioral Research, 27*(2), 239–247.

Guttman, L. (1969). Integration of test design. In *Toward a theory of achievement measurement: Proceedings of the 1969 Invitational Conference on Testing Problems* (pp. 53–65). Princeton, NJ: Educational Testing Service.

Hall, J. A., & Halberstadt, A. G. (1986). Smiling and gazing. In J. S. Hyde & M. C. Linn (Eds.), *The psychology of gender: Advances through meta-analysis* (pp. 136–158). Baltimore: Johns Hopkins University.

Halpern, D. F. (1989). Comment: The disappearance of cognitive gender differences: What you see depends on where you look. *American Psychologist, 44*(8), 1156–1158.

Halpern, D. F. (1992). *Sex differences in cognitive abilities* (2nd ed.). Hillsdale, NJ: Lawrence Erlbaum Associates.

Hambleton, R. K., & Jones, R. W. (1994). Comparison of empirical and judgmental procedures for detecting differential item functioning. *Educational Research Quarterly, 18,* 21–36.

Hamilton, L. S., Nussbaum, M., Kupermintz, H., Kerkhoven, J. I., & Snow, R. E. (1995). Enhancing the validity and usefulness of large-scale educational assessments: II. NELS:88 science achievement. *American Educational Research Journal, 32*(3), 555–581.

Han, L., Cleary, T. A., & Rakaskietisak, S. (1992). *Gender differences on achievement tests: A trend study based on nationally representative samples.* Unpublished manuscript, University of Iowa.

Haney, W. (1981). Validity, vaudeville, and values: A short history of social concerns over standardized testing. *American Psychologist, 36,* 1021–1034.

Hansen, J. C., & Campbell, D. P. (1985). *Manual for the SVIB-SCII. Strong-Campbell interest inventory—Form T325 of the Strong Vocational Interest Blank* (4th ed.). Stanford, CA: Stanford University.

Hare-Mustin, R. T., & Marecek, J. (1988). The meaning of difference: Gender theory, post-modernism, and psychology. *American Psychologist, 43*(6), 455–464.

Hargadon, F. (1981). Tests and college admissions. *American Psychologist, 36*(10), 1112–1119.

Harnqvist, K. (in press). Gender and grade differences in latent ability variables. *Scandinavian Journal of Psychology, 38*(1), 55–62.

Harris, A. M., & Carlton, S. T. (1993). Patterns of gender differences on mathematic items on the Scholastic Aptitude Test. *Applied Measurement in Education, 6,* 137–151.

Hartigan, J. A., & Wigdor, A. K. (Eds.). (1989). *Fairness in employment testing: Validity generalization, minority issues, and the general aptitude test battery* (Committee on the General Aptitude Test Battery, Commission on Behavioral and Social Sciences and Education, National Research Council). Washington, DC: National Academy.

Haynie, K. A., & Way, W. D. (1994). *NCLEX dif analysis report for the April 1994 operational and July 1994 pretest item pools.* Unpublished manuscript, Educational Testing Service.

Hedges, L. V., & Becker, B. J. (1986). Statistical methods in the meta-analysis of research on gender differences. In J. S. Hyde & M. C. Linn (Eds.), *The psychology of gender: Advances through meta-analysis* (pp. 14–50). Baltimore: Johns Hopkins University.

Hedges, L. V., & Friedman, L. (1993a). Computing gender difference effects in tails of distributions: The consequences of differences in tail size, effect size, and variance ratio. *Review of Educational Research, 63*(1), 110–112.

Hedges, L. V., & Friedman, L. (1993b). Gender differences in variability in intellectual abilities: A reanalysis of Feingold's results. *Review of Educational Research, 63*(1), 94–105.

Hedges, L. V., & Nowell, A. (1995). Sex differences in mental test scores, variability, and numbers of high-scoring individuals. *Science, 269,* 41–45.

Hedges, L. V., & Olkin, I. (1985). *Statistical methods for meta-analysis.* Orlando, FL: Academic Press.

Hellekant, J. (1994). Are multiple-choice tests unfair to girls? *System, 22*(3), 349–352.

Hembree, R. (1988). Correlates, causes, effects and treatment of test anxiety. *Review of Educational Research, 58,* 47–77.

Hills, J. R. (1964). Prediction of college grades for all public colleges of a state. *Journal of Educational Measurement, 1,* 155–159.

Hilton, T. L., & Berglund, G. W. (1974). Sex differences in mathematics achievement—A longitudinal study. *Journal of Educational Research, 67,* 231–237.

Hoffman, B. (1962). *The tyranny of testing.* New York: Crowell-Collier.

Hogan, T. P. (1981). *Relationship between free-response and choice-type tests of achievement: A review of the literature.* Green Bay: University of Wisconsin. (ERIC Document Reproduction Service No. ED 224 811)

Hogrebe, M. C., Nist, S. L., & Newman, I. (1985). Are there gender differences in reading achievement? An investigation using the High School and Beyond data. *Journal of Educational Psychology, 77*(6), 716–724.

Holland, J. L. (1961). Creative and academic performance among talented adolescents. *Journal of Educational Psychology, 52*, 136–147.

Holland, J. L. (1966). *The psychology of vocational choice: A theory of personality types and model environments.* Waltham, MA: Blaisdell.

Holland, J. L. (1973). *Making vocational choice: A theory of careers.* Englewood Cliffs, NJ: Prentice-Hall.

Holland, J. L., & Astin, A. W. (1962). The prediction of the academic, artistic, scientific, and social achievement of undergraduates of superior scholastic aptitude. *Journal of Educational Psychology, 53*, 132–143.

Holland, J. L., & Richards, J. M. (1965). Academic and nonacademic accomplishment: Correlated or uncorrelated? *Journal of Educational Psychology, 56*(4), 165–174.

Holland, P. W., & Thayer, D. T. (1988). Differential item performance and the Mantel-Haenszel procedure. In H. Wainer & H. Braun (Eds.), *Test validity* (pp. 129–145). Hillsdale, NJ: Lawrence Erlbaum Associates.

Hollingworth, L. S. (1914). Variability as related to sex differences in achievement: A critique. *American Journal of Sociology, 19*, 510–530.

Holloway, M. (1993). A lab of her own. *Scientific American, 269*(5), 94–103.

Hoover, H. D., & Han, L. (1995, April). *The effect of differential selection on gender differences in college admission test scores.* Paper presented at the annual meeting of the American Educational Research Association, San Francisco.

Horn, J. L. (1972). Structure of intellect: Primary abilities. In R. M. Dreger (Ed.), *Multivariate personality research: Contributions to the understanding of personality in honor of Raymond B. Cattell* (pp. 451–511). Baton Rouge, LA: Claitor.

Hossler, D. (1986). *Creating effective enrollment management systems.* New York: College Entrance Examination Board.

Hough, L. (in press). Personality at work: Issues & evidence. In M. Hakel (Ed.), *Beyond multiple choice: Evaluating alternatives to traditional testing for selection.* Mahwah, NJ: Lawrence Erlbaum Associates.

Hudson, L. (1986). Item-level analysis of sex differences in mathematics achievement test performance. *Dissertation Abstracts International, 47*(02), 850-B (Order No. AAD86-07283).

Hughes, D. C., Keeling, B., & Tuck, B. F. (1983). Effects of achievement expectations and handwriting quality on scoring essays. *Journal of Educational Measurement, 20*, 65–70.

Humphreys, L. G. (1952). Individual differences. *Annual Review of Psychology, 3*, 131–150.

Humphreys, L. G. (1986). An analysis and evaluation of test and item bias in the prediction context. *Journal of Applied Psychology, 71*(2), 327–333.

Humphreys, L. G. (1988). Sex differences in variability may be more important than sex differences in means. *Behavioral and Brain Sciences, 11*(2), 195–196.

Hunter, J. E., Schmidt, F. L., & Jackson, G. B. (1982). *Meta-analysis: Cumulating research findings across studies.* Beverly Hills, CA: Sage.

Hyde, J. S. (1981). How large are cognitive gender differences? A meta-analysis using w^2 and d. *American Psychologist, 36*(8), 892–901.

Hyde, J. S. (1986). Introduction: Meta-analysis and the psychology of gender. In J. S. Hyde & M. C. Linn (Eds.), *The psychology of gender: Advances through meta-analysis* (pp. 1–13). Baltimore: Johns Hopkins University.

Hyde, J. S. (1991). *Half the human experience: The psychology of women* (4th ed.). Lexington, MA: D. C. Heath.

Hyde, J. S. (1994). Can meta-analysis make feminist transformations in psychology? *Psychology of Women Quarterly, 18*, 451–462.

Hyde, J. S., Fennema, E., & Lamon, S. J. (1990). Gender differences in mathematics performance: A meta-analysis. *Psychological Bulletin, 107*, 139–155.

Hyde, J. S., & Linn, M. C. (Eds.). (1986). *The psychology of gender: Advances through meta-analysis.* Baltimore: Johns Hopkins University.

Hyde, J. S., & Linn, M. C. (1988). Gender differences in verbal ability: A meta-analysis. *Psychological Bulletin, 104*(1), 53–69.

Irvine, J. J. (1990). *Black students and school failure: Policies, practices, and prescriptions.* Westport, CT: Greenwood.

Jacklin, C. N. (1989). Female and male: Issues of gender. *American Psychologist, 44*(2), 127–133.

Jackson, C. A. (1992, April). *An analysis of factors related to male/female differential item functioning on percent questions on the SAT.* Paper presented at the annual meeting of the American Educational Research Association/National Council on Measurement in Education, San Francisco.

Jacobs, J. E., & Eccles, J. S. (1985). Gender differences in math ability: The impact of media reports on parents. *Educational Researcher, 14*(3), 20–25.

Jensen, A. R. (1971). The race x sex x ability interaction. In R. Cancro (Ed.), *Intelligence: Genetic and environmental influences* (pp. 107–161). New York: Grune & Stratton.

Joint Committee on Testing Practices. (1988). *Code of fair testing practices in education.* Washington, DC: Author.

Jones, L. R., Mullis, I. V., Raizen, S. A., Weiss, I. R., & Weston, E. A. (1992). *The 1990 science report card: NAEP'S assessment of fourth, eighth, and twelfth graders.* Princeton, NJ: Educational Testing Service, National Assessment of Educational Progress.

Jones, L. V. (1987). The influence on mathematics test scores, by ethnicity and sex, of prior achievement and high school mathematics courses. *Journal for Research in Mathematics Education, 18*, 180–186.

Jones, R., & Comprone, J. J. (1993). Where do we go next in writing across the curriculum? *College Composition and Communication, 44*(1), 59–68.

Juola, A. E. (1968). Illustrative problems in college-level grading. *Personnel and Guidance Journal, 47*(1), 29–33.

Kamin, L. J. (1981). In H. J. Eysenck & L. J. Kamin, *The intelligence controversy: H. J. Eysenck vs. Leon Kamin* (pp. 90–157, 172–187). New York: Wiley.

Kane, M. T. (1992). An argument-based approach to validity. *Psychological Bulletin, 112*, 527–535.

Kansas State Board of Education. (1993). *Kansas mathematics curriculum standards.* Topeka, KS: Author.

Kaplan, R., & Burstein, J. (Eds.). (1994). *Educational Testing Service conference on natural language processing techniques and technology in assessment and education. Proceedings of the Conference, May 17–18, 1994.* Princeton, NJ: Educational Testing Service.

Katz, I. R., Friedman, D. E., Bennett, R. E., & Berger, A. E. (1996). *Differences in strategies used to solve stem-equivalent constructed-response and multiple-choice SAT-mathematics items* (CB Rep. No. 93-3; ETS RR-96-20).

Keeton, M. T., & Associates. (1976). *Experiential learning: Rationale, characteristics, and assessment.* San Francisco: Jossey-Bass.

Kentucky Department of Education. (1995, July). *KIRIS accountability cycle I technical manual. Based on the analysis of data from the 1991–92 through 1993–94 school years.* Frankfurt, KY: Author.

Kimball, M. M. (1989). A new perspective on women's math achievement. *Psychological Bulletin, 105*, 198–214.

Kinkead, K. T. (1961). *How an ivy league college decides on admissions*. New York: Norton.

Kirsch, I. S., Jungeblut, A., Jenkins, L., & Kolstad, A. (1993). *Adult literacy in America: A first look at the National Adult Literacy Survey*. Washington, DC: U.S. Department of Education, National Center for Education Statistics.

Kitzinger, C. (Ed.). (1994). Should psychologists study sex differences [Special Feature]. *Feminism & Psychology, 4*(4), 501–546.

Klein, S. P. (1981). *The effect of time limits, item sequence, and question format on applicant performance on the California Bar Examination*. San Francisco: Committee of Bar Examiners of the State Bar of California and the National Conference of Bar Examiners.

Klein, S. P., & Bolus, R. (1984). *An analysis of the performance test on the July 1983 California bar examination* (PR-84-2). San Francisco: Committee of Bar Examiners of the State Bar of California.

Klein, S. S. (Ed.). (1985). *Handbook for achieving sex equity through education*. Baltimore: Johns Hopkins University.

Koretz, D., Stecher, B., & Deibert, E. (1992). *The Vermont portfolio assessment program: Interim report on implementation and impact, 1991–92 school year* (CSE Tech. Rep. No. 350). Los Angeles: University of California, National Center for Research on Evaluation, Standards, and Student Testing.

Koretz, D., Stecher, B., Klein, S., & McCaffrey, D. (1994, Fall). The Vermont portfolio assessment program: Findings and implications. *Educational Measurement: Issues and Practice, 13*(3), 5–16.

Kuhl, J., & Kraska, K. (1989). Self-regulation and metamotivation: Computational mechanisms, development, and assessment. In R. Kanfer, P. L. Ackerman, & R. Cudeck (Eds.), *Abilities, motivation, and methodology: The Minnesota Symposium on Learning and Individual Differences* (pp. 343–374). Hillsdale, NJ: Lawrence Erlbaum Associates.

Kupermintz, H., Ennis, M. M., Hamilton, L. S., Talbert, J. E., & Snow, R. E. (1995). Enhancing the validity and usefulness of large-scale educational assessments: I. NELS:88 mathematics achievement. *American Educational Research Journal, 32*, 525–554.

Laing, J., Engen, H., & Maxey, J. (1987). *Relationships between ACT test scores and high school courses* (ACT RR 87-3). Iowa City, IA: American College Testing Program.

Langer, J. A., Campbell, J. R., Neumann, S. B., Mullis, I. V., Persky, H. R., & Donahue, P. L. (1995). *Reading assessment redesigned: Authentic texts and innovative instruments in NAEP's 1992 survey* (Rep. No. 23-FR-07). Princeton, NJ: Educational Testing Service, National Assessment of Educational Progress.

Lawrence, I. M. (1993). *The effect of test speededness on subgroup performance* (ETS RR-93-49). Princeton, NJ: Educational Testing Service.

Lawrence, I. M., & Curley, W. E. (1989). *Differential item functioning for males and females on SAT-Verbal reading subscore items: Follow-up study* (ETS RR-89-22). Princeton, NJ: Educational Testing Service.

Lawrence, I. M., Curley, W. E., & McHale, F. J. (1988). *Differential item functioning for males and females on SAT-Verbal reading subscore items* (CB Rep. No. 88-4; ETS RR-88-10). New York: College Entrance Examination Board.

Lawrence, I. M., Lyu, C. F., & Feigenbaum, M. D. (1995). *DIF data on free-response SAT I mathematical items* (ETS RR-95-22). Princeton, NJ: Educational Testing Service.

Lehman, J. D., & Lawrence, I. M. (1992). *A score change study of the PSAT/NMSQT* (unpublished ETS Statistical Report, SR-91-99). Princeton, NJ: Educational Testing Service.

Leonard, D. K., & Jiang, J. (1995, April). *Gender bias in the college predictions of the SAT.* Paper presented at the annual meeting of the American Educational Research Association, San Francisco.

Lewis, C., & Willingham, W. W. (1995). *The effects of sample restriction on gender differences* (ETS RR-95-13). Princeton, NJ: Educational Testing Service.

Liben, L. S. (1995). Psychology meets geography: Exploring the gender gap on the National Geography Bee. *Psychological Science Agenda, 8*(1), 8–9.

Linn, M. C. (1986). Meta-analysis of studies of gender differences: Implications and future directions. In J. S. Hyde & M. C. Linn (Eds.), *The psychology of gender: Advances through meta-analysis* (pp. 210–231). Baltimore: Johns Hopkins University.

Linn, M. C. (1992). Gender differences in educational achievement. In *Sex equity in educational opportunity, achievement, and testing: Proceedings of the 1991 ETS Invitational Conference* (pp. 11–50). Princeton, NJ: Educational Testing Service.

Linn, M. C., & Hyde, J. S. (1989). Gender, mathematics, and science. *Educational Researcher, 18*, 17–27.

Linn, M. C., & Petersen, A. C. (1985a). Emergence and characterization of sex differences in spatial ability: A meta-analysis. *Child Development, 56*, 1479–1498.

Linn, M. C., & Petersen, A. C. (1985b). Facts and assumptions about the nature of sex differences. In S. Klein (Ed.), *Handbook for achieving sex equity through education* (pp. 53–77). Baltimore: Johns Hopkins University.

Linn, M. C., & Petersen, A. C. (1986). A meta-analysis of gender differences in spatial ability: Implications for mathematics and science achievement. In J. Hyde & M. Linn (Eds.), *The psychology of gender: Advances through meta-analysis* (pp. 67–101). Baltimore: Johns Hopkins University.

Linn, R. L. (1973). Fair test use in selection. *Review of Educational Research, 43*, 140–161.

Linn, R. L. (1976). In search of fair selection procedures. *Journal of Educational Measurement, 13*(1), 53–58.

Linn, R. L. (1978). Single group validity, differential validity and differential prediction. *Journal of Applied Psychology, 63*, 507–512.

Linn, R. L. (1982). Ability testing: Individual differences, prediction, and differential prediction. In A. Wigdor & W. Garner (Eds.), *Ability testing: Uses, consequences, and controversies, Part II: Report of the National Academy of Sciences Committee on Ability Testing* (pp. 335–388). Washington, DC: National Academy Press.

Linn, R. L. (1983). Predictive bias as an artifact of selection procedures. In H. Wainer & S. Messick (Eds.), *Principals of modern psychological measurement: A festschrift for Frederic M. Lord* (pp. 27–40). Hillsdale, NJ: Lawrence Erlbaum Associates.

Linn, R. L. (1984). Selection bias: Multiple meanings. *Journal of Educational Measurement, 21*(1), 33–47.

Linn, R. L. (1993a). Educational assessment: Expanded expectations and challenges. *Educational Evaluation and Policy Analysis, 15*(1), 1–16.

Linn, R. L. (1993b). *Educational assessment: Expanded expectations and challenges* (CSE Tech. Rep. 351). Los Angeles: University of California, National Center for Research on Evaluation, Standards, and Student Testing (CRESST).

Linn, R. L. (1993c). The use of differential item functioning statistics: A discussion of current practice and future implications. In P. W. Holland & H. Wainer (Eds.), *Differential item functioning* (pp. 349–366). Hillsdale, NJ: Lawrence Erlbaum Associates.

Linn, R. L. (1994). Performance assessment: Policy promises and technical measurement standards. *Educational Researcher, 23*(9), 4–14.

Linn, R. L., Baker, E. L., & Dunbar, S. B. (1991). Complex, performance-based assessment: Expectations and validation criteria. *Educational Researcher, 20*(8), 15–21.

Linn, R. L., & Burton, E. (1994). Performance-based assessment: Implications of task specificity. *Educational Measurement: Issues and Practice, 13*(1), 5–8, 15.

Linn, R. L., Kiplinger, V. L., Chapman, C. W., & LeMahieu, P. G. (1991). Cross-state comparability of judgments of student writing: Results from the New Standards Project. *Applied Measurement in Education, 5,* 89–110.

Linn, R. L., & Werts, C. E. (1971). Considerations for studies of test bias. *Journal of Educational Measurement, 8*(1), 1–4.

Lohman, D. F. (1994). Spatially gifted, verbally inconvenienced. In N. Colangelo, S. G. Assouline, & D. L. Ambroson (Eds.), *Talent development: Vol. II. Proceedings from the 1993 Henry B. and Jocelyn Wallace National Research Symposium on Talent Development* (pp. 251–263). Dayton: Ohio Psychology Press.

Lord, F. M. (1980). *Applications of item response theory to practical testing problems.* Hillsdale, NJ: Lawrence Erlbaum Associates.

Lubinski, D., & Humphreys, L. G. (1990). A broadly based analysis of mathematical giftedness. *Intelligence, 14,* 327–355.

Lupkowski, A. E. (1992). Gender differences on the Differential Aptitude Tests. In N. Colangelo, S. G. Assouline, & D. L. Ambroson (Eds.), *Talent development: Proceedings from the 1991 Henry B. and Jocelyn Wallace National Research Symposium on Talent Development* (pp. 46–48). Unionville, NY: Trillium.

Maccoby, E. E., & Jacklin, C. N. (1974). *The psychology of sex differences.* Stanford, CA: Stanford University.

Madaus, G. F. (1994). A technological and historical consideration of equity issues associated with proposals to change the nation's testing policy. *Harvard Educational Review, 64*(1), 76–96.

Makitalo, A. (1994). *Non-comparability of female and male admission test takers* (Evaluation Through Follow-up: Rep. No. 1994:06). Molndal, Sweden: Goteborg University, Department of Education and Educational Research.

Mann, J. (1994). *The difference: Growing up female in America.* New York: Warner.

Manning, W. H. (1977). The pursuit of fairness in admissions to higher education. In *Selective admissions in higher education: Comment and recommendations and two reports: A report of the Carnegie Council on Policy Studies in Higher Education* (pp. 20–64). San Francisco: Jossey-Bass.

Manski, C. F., & Wise, D. A. (1983). *College choice in America.* Cambridge, MA: Harvard University.

Mantel, N., & Haenszel, W. (1959). Statistical aspects of the analysis of data from retrospective studies of disease. *Journal of the National Cancer Institute, 22,* 719–748.

Marsh, H. W. (1989). Sex differences in the development of verbal and mathematics constructs: The High School and Beyond study. *American Educational Research Journal, 26*(2), 191–225.

Marshall, S. P., & Smith, J. D. (1987). Sex differences in learning mathematics: A longitudinal study with item and error analyses. *Journal of Educational Psychology, 79*(4), 372–383.

Martin, D. J., & Hoover, H. D. (1987). Sex differences in educational achievement: A longitudinal study [Special issue]. *Journal of Early Adolescence, 7*(1), 65–83.

MathCounts Foundation. (1993). *MathCounts News, 9*(1).

Mazzeo, J., Schmitt, A. P., & Bleistein, C. A. (1991, April). *Do women perform better, relative to men, on constructed-response tests or multiple-choice tests? Evidence from the Advanced Placement examinations.* Paper presented at the annual meeting of the National Council of Measurement in Education, Chicago.

Mazzeo, J., Schmitt, A. P., & Bleistein, C. A. (1993). *Sex-related performance differences on constructed-response and multiple-choice sections of Advanced Placement examinations* (CB Rep. No. 92-7; ETS RR-93-5). New York: College Entrance Examination Board.

McClelland, D. C. (1973). Testing for competence rather than for "intelligence." *American Psychologist, 28,* 1–14.

McCornack, R. L., & McLeod, M. M. (1988). Gender bias in the prediction of college course performance. *Journal of Educational Measurement, 25,* 321–331.

McGrath, E. J. (Ed.). (1966). *Universal higher education.* New York: McGraw-Hill.

McNemar, Q., & Terman, L. M. (1936). Sex differences in variational tendency. *Genetic Psychology Monographs, 18*(1), 1–65.

McPeek, W. M., & Wild, C. L. (1992). *Identifying differentially functioning items in the NTE core battery* (ETS RR-92-62). Princeton, NJ: Educational Testing Service.

Mehrens, W. A. (1992). Using performance assessment for accountability purposes. *Educational Measurement: Issues and Practice, 11*(1), 3–9, 20.

Messick, S. (1964). Personality measurement and college performance. *Proceedings of the 1963 Invitational Conference on Testing Problems* (pp. 110–129). Princeton, NJ: Educational Testing Service. (Reprinted in A. Anastasi [Ed.]. [1966]. *Testing problems in perspective* [pp. 557–572]. Washington, DC: American Council on Education.)

Messick, S. (1975). The standard problem: Meaning and values in measurement and evaluation. *American Psychologist, 30,* 955–966.

Messick, S. (1980). *The effectiveness of coaching for the SAT: Review and reanalysis of research from the fifties to the FTC.* Princeton, NJ: Educational Testing Service.

Messick, S. (1984). Abilities and knowledge in educational achievement testing: An assessment of dynamic cognitive structures. In B. S. Plake (Ed.), *Social and technical issues in testing: Implications for test construction and usage* (pp. 155–169). Hillsdale, NJ: Lawrence Erlbaum Associates.

Messick, S. (1989). Validity. In R. L. Linn (Ed.), *Educational measurement* (3rd ed., pp. 13–103). New York: American Council on Education & Macmillan.

Messick, S. (1992). Multiple intelligences or multilevel intelligence? Selective emphasis on distinctive properties of hierarchy: On Gardners' *Frames of Mind* and Sternberg's *Beyond IQ* in the context of theory and research on the structure of human abilities [Review of *Frames of mind: The theory of multiple intelligences* and *Beyond IQ: A triarchic theory of human intelligence*]. *Psychological Inquiry, 3,* 365–384.

Messick, S. (1994a). *Alternative modes of assessment, uniform standards of validity* (ETS RR-94-60). Princeton, NJ: Educational Testing Service.

Messick, S. (1994b). The interplay of evidence and consequences in the validation of performance assessments. *Educational Researcher, 23*(2), 13–23.

Messick, S. (1994c). The matter of style: Manifestations of personality in cognition, learning, and teaching. *Educational Psychologist, 29*(3), 121–136.

Messick, S. (1994d). *Standards-based score interpretation: Establishing valid grounds for valid inferences* (ETS RR-94-57). Princeton, NJ: Educational Testing Service.

Messick, S. (1996). *Validity and washback in language testing* (ETS RR-96-17). Princeton, NJ: Educational Testing Service.

Mickelson, R. A. (1984). *Race, class, and gender differences in adolescent academic achievement attitudes and behaviors.* Unpublished doctoral dissertation, University of California at Los Angeles.

Mickelson, R. A. (1989). Why does Jane read and write so well? The anomaly of women's achievement. *Sociology of Education, 62*(1), 47–63.

Millar, S. (1968). *The psychology of play.* Baltimore: Penguin Books.

Miller, T. R., & Welch, C. J. (1993, April). *Issues and problems in assessing differential item functioning in performance assessments.* Paper presented at the annual convention of the National Council on Measurement in Education, Atlanta, GA.

Millman, J., Bishop, C. H., & Ebel, R. (1965). An analysis of test-wiseness. *Educational and Psychological Measurement, 25*(3), 707–726.

Milton, O., Pollio, H. R., & Eison, J. A. (1986). *Making sense of college grades.* San Francisco: Jossey-Bass.

Mislevy, R. J. (1993). A framework for studying differences between multiple-choice and free-response test items. In R. E. Bennett & W. C. Ward (Eds.), *Construction versus choice in cognitive measurement* (pp. 75–106). Hillsdale, NJ: Lawrence Erlbaum Associates.

Mislevy, R. J. (1995). *Test theory reconceived* (ETS RR-94-2-ONR). Princeton, NJ: Educational Testing Service.

Moll, R. (1979). *Playing the private college admissions game.* New York: Times Books.

Moore, E. G., & Smith, A. W. (1987). Sex and ethnic group differences in mathematics achievement: Results from the National Longitudinal Study. *Journal for Research in Mathematics Education, 18*(1), 25–36.

Morgan, R. (1989). *An examination of the relationships of academic coursework with admissions test performance* (CB Rep. No. 89-6; ETS RR-89-38). New York: College Entrance Examination Board.

Morgan, R. (1994). *College Board 1993 Advanced Placement test analyses—Forms 3PBP* (Statistical Rep. No. SR-94-04). Princeton, NJ: Educational Testing Service.

Morgan, R. (1995). *College Board 1994 Advanced Placement test analyses—Forms 3QBP* (Statistical Rep. No. SR-95-02). Princeton, NJ: Educational Testing Service.

Morgan, R., Pomplun, M., & Nellikunnel, A. (1993). *Choice in Advanced Placement tests and subgroup equity* (Statistical Rep. No. SR-93-167). Princeton, NJ: Educational Testing Service.

Mueller, D. J., & Wasser, V. (1977). Implications of changing answers on objective test items. *Journal of Educational Measurement, 14*(1), 9–13.

Mullis, I. V., Dossey, J. A., Foertsch, M. A., Jones, L. R., & Gentile, C. A. (1991). *Trends in academic progress* (Rep. No. 21-T-01). Washington, DC: U.S. Government Printing Office.

Mullis, I. V., Dossey, J., Owen, E., & Phillips, G. (1991). *The STATE of mathematics achievement—NAEP's 1990 assessment of the nation and the trial assessment of the states* (Rep. No. 21-ST-04). Princeton, NJ: Educational Testing Service, National Assessment of Educational Progress.

Mullis, I. V., Dossey, J., Owen, E., & Phillips, G. (1993). *NAEP 1992 mathematics report card for the nation and the states—Data from the national and trial state assessments* (Rep. No. 23-ST-02). Princeton, NJ: Educational Testing Service, National Assessment of Educational Progress.

Mullis, I. V., & Jenkins, L. B. (1988). *The science report card: Elements of risk and recovery. Trends and achievement based on the 1986 national assessment.* Princeton, NJ: Educational Testing Service, National Assessment of Educational Progress.

Mullis, I. V., Owen, E. H., & Phillips, G. W. (1990). *America's challenge: Accelerating academic achievement—A summary of findings from 20 years of NAEP.* Princeton, NJ: Educational Testing Service, National Assessment of Educational Progress.

Murphy, R. J. (1980). Sex differences in GCE examination entry statistics and success rates. *Education Studies, 6*(2), 169–178.

Murphy, R. J. (1982). Sex differences in objective test performance. *British Journal of Educational Psychology, 52*, 213–219.

National Assessment Governing Board, U.S. Department of Education. (1995). *Mathematics framework for the 1996 National Assessment of Educational Progress: NAEP mathematics consensus project.* Washington, DC: Author.

National Center for Education Statistics, U.S. Department of Education. (1993). *Digest of education statistics 1993* (NCES 93-292). Washington, DC: U.S. Government Printing Office.

National Center for Education Statistics. (1994). *Digest for education statistics.* Washington, DC: U.S. Government Printing Office.

National Council on Education Standards and Testing. (1992). *Raising standards for American education: A report to Congress, the Secretary of Education, the National Education Goals Panel, and the American people.* Washington, DC: U.S. Government Printing Office.

National Council on Measurement in Education Ad Hoc Committee on the Development of a Code of Ethics. (1995). *Code of professional responsibilities in educational measurement.* Washington, DC: National Council on Measurement in Education.

National Council of Teachers of Mathematics. (1989). *Curriculum and evaluation standards for school mathematics.* Reston, VA: Author.

National Science Foundation. (1990, January). *Women and minorities in science and engineering* (NSF 90-301). Washington, DC: Author.

Neisser, U. (Chair), et al. (1996). Intelligence: Knowns and unknowns. *American Psychologist, 51*(2), 77–101.

Nelson-Le Gall, S. (1992). The condition of sex equity in education: Sex, race, and ethnicity. In *Sex equity in educational opportunity, achievement, and testing: Proceedings of the 1991 ETS Invitational Conference* (pp. 91–102). Princeton, NJ: Educational Testing Service.

Newcombe, N., & Dubas, J. S. (1987). Individual differences in cognitive ability: Are they related to timing of puberty? In R. M. Lerner & T. T. Foch (Eds.), *Biological-psychosocial interactions in early adolescence* (pp. 249–302). Hillsdale, NJ: Lawrence Erlbaum Associates.

Noble, J. P. (1991). *Predicting college grades from ACT assessment scores and high school course work and grade information* (ACT Research Rep. Series, 91–3). Iowa City, IA: American College Testing Program.

Noble, J., & McNabb, T. (1989, August). *Differential coursework and grades in high school: Implications for performance on the ACT assessment* (ACT Research Rep. Series, 89-5). Iowa City, IA: American College Testing Program.

Noble, J. P., & Sawyer, R. (1987). *Predicting grades in specific college freshman courses from ACT test scores and self-reported high school grades* (ACT Research Rep. Series, 87-20). Iowa City, IA: American College Testing Program.

Noddings, N. (1992). Variability: A pernicious hypothesis. *Review of Educational Research, 62*(1), 85–88.

Novick, M. R., & Ellis, D. D. (1977). Equal opportunity in educational and employment selection. *American Psychologist, 32*(5), 306–320.

Novick, M. R., & Petersen, N. S. (1976). Towards equalizing educational and employment opportunity. *Journal of Educational Measurement, 13*(1), 77–88.

O'Neill, K. A., & McPeek, W. M. (1993). Item and test characteristics that are associated with differential item functioning. In P. W. Holland & H. Wainer (Eds.), *Differential item functioning* (pp. 255–276). Hillsdale, NJ: Lawrence Erlbaum Associates.

O'Neill, K. A., McPeek, W. M., & Wild, C. L. (1993, August). *Differential item functioning on the Graduate Management Admission Test* (ETS RR-93-35). Princeton, NJ: Educational Testing Service.

O'Neill, K. A., Wild, C. L., & McPeek, W. M. (1989). *Gender-related differential item performance on graduate admissions tests.* Paper presented at the annual meeting of the American Educational Research Association, San Francisco.

O'Neill, K. A., Wild, C. L., & McPeek, W. M. (1995). *Identifying differentially functioning items on the Graduate Record Examination General Test.* Manuscript submitted for publication.

Organisation for Economic Co-Operation and Development. (1986). *Girls and women in education: A cross-national study of sex inequalities in upbringing and in schools and colleges.* Paris: Author.

Owings, J., McMillen, M., Burkett, J., & Pinkerton, B. D. (1995). *Making the cut: Who meets highly selective college entrance criteria?* (NCES 95-732). Washington, DC: U.S. Department of Education, National Center for Education Statistics.

Pallas, A. M., & Alexander, K. L. (1983). Sex differences in quantitative SAT performance: New evidence on the differential coursework hypothesis. *American Educational Research Journal, 20,* 165–182.

Pattison, P., & Grieve, N. (1984). Do spatial skills contribute to sex differences in different types of mathematical problems? *Journal of Educational Psychology, 76(4),* 678–689.

Pennock-Roman, M. (1994). *College major effects and gender differences in the prediction of college grades* (CB Rep. No. 94-2; ETS RR-94-24). New York: College Entrance Examination Board.

Petersen, N. S., & Livingston, S. A. (1982). *English Composition Test with essay: A descriptive study of the relationship between essay and objective scores by ethnic group and sex* (ETS SR 82-96). Princeton, NJ: Educational Testing Service.

Petersen, N. S., & Novick, M. R. (1976). An evaluation of some models for culture-fair selection. *Journal of Educational Measurement, 13(1),* 3–29.

Peterson, P. L., & Fennema, E. (1985). Effective teaching, student engagement in classroom activities, and sex-related differences in learning mathematics. *American Educational Research Journal, 22(3),* 309–335.

Policy Information Center, Educational Testing Service. (1989a). The gender gap in education: How early and how large? *ETS Policy Notes, 2(1),* 1–5.

Policy Information Center, Educational Testing Service. (1989b). Sex differences in test performance: A synthesis of research. *ETS Policy Notes, 2(1),* 7.

Pollack, J. M., & Rock, D. A. (in press). *Constructed response tests in the NELS:88 school effects study.* Washington, DC: National Center for Education Statistics.

Pollard, D. S. (1993). Gender, achievement, and African-American students' perceptions of their school experience. *Educational Psychologist, 28,* 341–356.

Pomplun, M., Morgan, R., & Nellikunnel, A. (1992). *Choice in Advanced Placement tests* (Statistical Rep. No. SR-92-51). Princeton, NJ: Educational Testing Service.

Pomplun, M., Wright, D., Oleka, N., & Sudlow, M. (1992). *An Analysis of English Composition Test essay prompts for differential difficulty* (CB Rep. No. 92-4; ETS RR-92-34). New York: College Entrance Examination Board.

Posner, M. I. (1978). *Chronometric explorations of mind.* Hillsdale, NJ: Lawrence Erlbaum Associates.

Powell, L. F. J. (1978). Opinion in *Regents of the University of California vs. Bakke,* 438 U.S. 265, 98 ct. 2377, 57 L.Ed. 2d 750.

Powers, D. E. (1993). Coaching for the SAT: A summary of the summaries and an update. *Educational Measurement: Issues and Practice, 12(2),* 24–30, 39.

Powers, D. E., Fowles, M. E., Farnum, M., & Ramsey, P. (1994). Will they think less of my handwritten essay if others word process theirs? Effects on essay scores of intermingling handwritten and word-processed essay. *Journal of Educational Measurement, 31(3),* 220–233.

Powers, D. E., Fowles, M. E., & Willard, A. E. (1994). Direct assessment, direct validation? An example from the assessment of writing. *Educational Assessment, 2,* 89–100.

Quellmalz, E. S., Capell, F. J., & Chou, C. P. (1982). Effects of discourse and response mode on the measurement of writing competence. *Journal of Educational Measurement, 19*(4), 241–258.

Raffalli, M. (1994, January 9). Why so few women physicists? *New York Times Education Life,* pp. 26, 28.

Ramist, L., & Arbeiter, S. (1986). *Profiles, college-bound seniors, 1985.* New York: College Entrance Examination Board.

Ramist, L., Lewis, C., & McCamley, L. (1990). Implications of using freshman GPA as the criterion for the predictive validity of the SAT. In W. W. Willingham, C. Lewis, R. Morgan, & L. Ramist (Eds.), *Predicting college grades: An analysis of institutional trends over two decades* (pp. 253–288). Princeton, NJ: Educational Testing Service.

Ramist, L., Lewis, C., & McCamley-Jenkins, L. (1994). *Student group differences in predicting college grades: Sex, language, and ethnic group* (CB Rep. No. 93-1; ETS RR-94-27). New York: College Entrance Examination Board.

Ramist, L., & Weiss, G. (1990). The predictive validity of the SAT, 1964 to 1988. In W. W. Willingham, C. Lewis, R. Morgan, & L. Ramist (Eds.), *Predicting college grades: An analysis of institutional trends over two decades* (pp. 225–238). Princeton, NJ: Educational Testing Service.

Ramsey, P. A. (1993). Sensitivity review: The ETS experience as a case study. In P. W. Holland & H. Wainer (Eds.), *Differential item functioning* (pp. 367–388). Hillsdale, NJ: Lawrence Erlbaum Associates.

Rasinski, K. A., Ingels, S. J., Rock, D. A., Pollack, J. M., & Wu, S. C. (1993, June). *America's high school sophomores: A ten year comparison* (NCES 93-087). Washington, DC: U.S. Department of Education, National Center for Education Statistics.

Ravitch, D. (1995). *National standards in American education: A citizen's guide.* Washington, DC: Brookings Institution.

Rawls, J. (1971). *A theory of justice.* Cambridge, MA: Harvard University.

Regents of the University of California v. Bakke, 438 U.S. 265, 98 C.t. 2377 57L.Ed. 2d750 (1978).

Rehabilitation Act of 1973. (1973, September 26) PL 93-112; 87 Stat. 355.

Reilly, R. R. (1973). A note on minority group bias studies. *Psychological Bulletin, 80,* 130–133.

Resnick, L. B., & Resnick, D. P. (1992). Assessing the thinking curriculum: New tools for educational reform. In B. R. Gifford & M. C. O'Connor (Eds.), *Changing assessments: Alternative views of aptitude, achievement, and instruction* (pp. 37–75). Boston: Kluwer.

Richards, J. M., Jr., Holland, J. L., & Lutz, S. W. (1967). Prediction of student accomplishment in college. *Journal of Educational Psychology, 58*(6), 343–355.

Rindler, S. E. (1979). Pitfalls in assessing test speededness. *Journal of Educational Measurement, 16*(4), 261–270.

Rock, D. A., Ekstrom, R. B., Goertz, M. E., & Pollack, J. (1986). *Study of excellence in high school education: Longitudinal study, 1980-82 final report.* Washington, DC: U.S. Department of Education, Center for Statistics, Office of Educational Research and Improvement.

Rock, D. A., & Pollack, J. M. (1992, April). *Gains in the tested achievement of NELS:88 students.* Paper presented at the annual meeting of the American Educational Research Association, San Francisco.

Rock, D. A., Pollack, J. M., Owings, J., & Hafner, A. (1990). *Psychometric report for the NELS:88 base year test battery* (NCES 90-468). Washington, DC: U.S. Department of Education, National Center for Education Statistics, Office of Educational Research and Improvement.

Rosen, M. (1995). Gender differences in structure, means and variances of hierarchically ordered ability dimensions. *Learning and Instruction, 5*(1), 37–62.

Rosenthal, R., & Rubin, D. B. (1982a). Further meta-analytic procedures for assessing cognitive gender differences. *Journal of Educational Psychology, 74*(5), 708–712.

Rosenthal, R., & Rubin, D. B. (1982b). A simple, general purpose display of magnitude of experimental effect. *Journal of Educational Psychology, 74,* 166–169.

Rosser, P. (1989). *The SAT gender gap: Identifying the causes.* Washington, DC: Center for Women Policy Studies.

Rothman, R. (1994, Winter). *Evaluation comment. Assessment questions: Equity answers. Proceeding of the 1993 CRESST Conference.* Los Angeles: UCLA Graduate School of Education.

Russo, R., & Montes, G. (1993). Participation in doctoral education at major research universities by U.S. citizens, women, and underrepresented minorities. *Program Profiles, 1.* Princeton, NJ: Educational Testing Service, AAU/AGS Project for Research on Doctoral Education.

Sackett, P. R., & Wilk, S. L. (1994). Within-group norming and other forms of score adjustment in preemployment testing. *American Psychologist, 49,* 929–954.

Sadker, M., & Sadker, D. (1994). *Failing at fairness: How America's schools cheat girls.* New York: Scribner's.

Sarason, S., & Mandler, G. (1952). Some correlates of test anxiety. *Journal of Abnormal and Social Psychology, 47,* 810–817.

Sarnacki, R. E. (1979). An examination of test-wiseness in the cognitive test domain. *Review of Educational Research, 49*(2), 252–279.

Sawyer, R. L., Cole, N. S., & Cole, J. W. (1976). Utilities and the issue of fairness in a decision theoretic model for selection. *Journal of Educational Measurement, 13*(1), 59–76.

Schaeffer, G. A., Reese, C. M., Steffen, M., McKinley, R. L., & Mills, C. N. (1993). Field test of a computer-based GRE General Test (GRE Report No. 88-08P, ETS RR-93-07). Princeton, NJ: Educational Testing Service.

Schaeffer, G. A. Steffen, M., Golub-Smith, M. L., Mills, C. N., & Durso, R. (1995). The introduction and comparability of the computer adaptive GRE General Test (GRE Report No. 88-08aP, ETS RR-95-20). Princeton, NJ: Educational Testing Service.

Schau, C. G., & Scott, K. P. (1984). Impact of gender characteristics of instructional materials: An integration of the research literature. *Journal of Educational Psychology, 76,* 190.

Scheuneman, J. D. (1987). An experimental exploratory study of causes of bias in test items. *Journal of Educational Measurement, 24,* 97–118.

Scheuneman, J. D., & Gerritz, K. (1990). Using differential item functioning procedures to explore sources of item difficulty and group performance characteristics. *Journal of Educational Measurement, 27,* 109–131.

Schmitt, A. P. (1995, April). *Performance of gender, ethnic and language groups on the verbal and math content of the new PSAT/NMSQT.* Paper presented at the annual meeting of the National Council on Measurement in Education, San Francisco.

Schmitt, A. P., & Crone, C. R. (1991). *Alternative mathematical aptitude item types: DIF issues* (ETS RR-91-42). Princeton, NJ: Educational Testing Service.

Schmitt, A. P., Curley, W. E., Bleistein, C. A., & Dorans, N. J. (1988, April). *Experimental evaluation of language and interest factors related to differential item functioning for Hispanic examinees on the SAT-Verbal.* Paper presented at the annual meeting of the National Council on Measurement in Education, New Orleans, LA.

Schmitt, A. P., Dorans, N. J., Crone, C. R., & Maneckshana, B. T. (1991, August). *Differential speededness and item omit patterns on the SAT* (ETS RR-91-50). Princeton, NJ: Educational Testing Service.

Schrader, W. B. (1971). The predictive validity of College Board admissions tests. In W. H. Angoff (Ed.), *The College Board Admissions Testing Program: A technical report on research and development activities relating to the Scholastic Aptitude Test and Achievement Tests* (pp. 117–145). New York: College Entrance Examination Board.

Schwarz, S. P., McMorris, R. F., & DeMers, L. P. (1991). Reasons for changing answers: An evaluation using personal interviews. *Journal of Educational Measurement, 28*(2), 163–171.

Scott, K. P., Dwyer, C. A., & Lieb-Brilhart, B. (1985). Sex equity in reading and communication skills. In S. S. Klein (Ed.), *Handbook for achieving sex equity through education* (pp. 269–279). Baltimore: Johns Hopkins University.

Sharf, J. C. (1988). Litigating personnel measurement policy. *Journal of Vocational Behavior, 33*(3), 235–271.

Shavelson, R. J., Baxter, G. P., & Gao, X. (1993). Sampling variability of performance assessments. *Journal of Educational Measurement, 30,* 215–232.

Shepard, L. A. (1990). Inflated test score gains: Is the problem old norms or teaching the test? *Educational Measurement: Issues and Practice, 9,* 15–22.

Shepard, L. A. (1991). Psychometricians' beliefs about learning. *Educational Researcher, 20,* 2–16.

Shepard, L. A. (1992). Commentary: What policy makers who mandate tests should know about the new psychology of intellectual ability and learning. In B. R. Gifford & M. C. O'Connor (Eds.), *Changing assessments: Alternative views of aptitude, achievement and instruction* (pp. 301–328). Boston: Kluwer.

Shepard, L. A. (1993). The place of testing reform in educational reform: A reply to Cizek. *Educational Researcher, 22*(4), 10–13.

Sherman, J. A. (1967). Problem of sex differences in space perception and aspects of intellectual functioning. *Psychological Review, 74*(4), 290–299.

Sherman, J. A. (1978). *Sex-related cognitive differences: An essay on theory and evidence.* Springfield, IL: Thomas.

Skager, R. (1982). On the use and importance of tests of ability in admission to postsecondary education. In A. K. Wigdor & W. R. Garner (Eds.), *Ability testing: Uses, consequences, and controversies, Part II: Documentation section* (pp. 286–314). Washington, DC: National Academy Press.

Slakter, M. J. (1967). Risk taking on objective examinations. *American Educational Research Journal, 4*(1), 31–43.

Slakter, M. J. (1968a). The effect of guessing strategy on objective test scores. *Journal of Educational Measurement, 5*(3), 217–222.

Slakter, M. J. (1968b). The penalty for not guessing. *Journal of Educational Measurement, 5*(2), 141–144.

Slakter, M. J., Koehler, R. A., & Hampton, S. H. (1970). Grade level, sex, and selected aspects of test-wiseness. *Journal of Educational Measurement, 7*(2), 119–122.

Slakter, M. J., Koehler, R. A., Hampton, S. H., & Grennell, R. L. (1971). Sex, grade level, and risk taking on objective examinations. *The Journal of Experimental Education, 39*(3), 65–68.

Smith, A. Z., & Dobbin, J. E. (1960). Marks and marking systems. In C. W. Harris (Ed.), *Encyclopedia of educational research* (3rd. ed., pp. 783–791). New York: Macmillan.

Smith, M. L. (1991). Put to the test: The effects of external testing on teachers. *Educational Researcher, 20*(5), 8–11.

Smyth, F. L. (1990). SAT coaching: What *really* happens to scores and how we are led to expect more. *Journal of College Admissions, 129,* 7–17.

Snow, R., & Ennis, M. (1996). Correlates of high mathematical ability in a national sample of eighth graders. In C. Benbow & D. Lubinski (Eds.), *Intellectual talent: Psychometric and social issues* (pp. 301–327). Baltimore: Johns Hopkins University Press.

Snyder, T. D. (Ed.). (1993, January). *120 years of American education: A statistical portrait.* Washington, DC: U.S. Department of Education, National Center for Education Statistics.

Stage, E. K., Kreinberg, N., Eccles, J., & Becker, J. R. (1985). Increasing the participation and achievement of girls and women in mathematics, science, and engineering. In S. Klein (Ed.), *Handbook for achieving sex equity through education* (pp. 237–268). Baltimore: Johns Hopkins University.

Stanley, J. C. (1992). Differences on the College Board Achievement Tests and the Advanced Placement examinations: Effect sizes versus some upper-tail ratios. In N. Colangelo, S. G. Assouline, & D. L. Ambroson (Eds.), *Talent development: Proceedings from the 1991 Henry B. and Jocelyn Wallace National Research Symposium on Talent Development* (pp. 52–59). Unionville, NY: Trillium.

Stanley, J. C. (1993). Boys and girls who reason well mathematically. In G. R. Bock & K. Ackrill (Eds.), Ciba Foundation Symposium 178, *The origins and development of high ability* (pp. 119–138). Chichester, England: Wiley.

Stanley, J. C., Benbow, C. P., Brody, L. E., Dauber, S., & Lupkowski, A. E. (1992). Gender differences on eighty-six nationally standardized aptitude and achievement tests. In N. Colangelo, S. G. Assouline, & D. L. Ambroson (Eds.), *Talent development: Proceedings from the 1991 Henry B. and Jocelyn Wallace National Research Symposium on Talent Development* (pp. 41–48). Unionville, NY: Trillium.

Stanley, J. C., Fox, L. H., & Keating, D. P. (1972, October). *Annual report to the Spencer Foundation.* Baltimore: Johns Hopkins University.

Starch, D., & Elliott, E. C. (1912). Reliability of the grading of high-school work in English. *The School Review, 20,* 442–457.

Starch, D., & Elliott, E. C. (1913). Reliability of grading work in mathematics. *The School Review, 21*(5), 254–296.

Sternberg, R. J. (1985). *Beyond IQ: A triarchic theory of human intelligence.* New York: Cambridge University Press.

Stobart, G., Elwood, J., & Quinlan, M. (1992). Gender bias in examinations: How equal are the opportunities? *British Educational Research Journal, 18,* 261–276.

Stockard, J., & Wood, J. (1984). The myth of female underachievement: A reexamination of sex differences in academic underachievement. *American Educational Research Journal, 21,* 825–838.

Straughn, C. T., II, & Straughn, B. L. (Eds.). (1993). *Lovejoy's college guide* (22nd ed.). New York: Prentice-Hall.

Strenta, A. C., & Elliott, R. (1987). Differential grading standards revisited. *Journal of Educational Measurement, 24*(4), 281–291.

Stricker, L. J., Rock, D. A., & Burton, N. W. (1993). Sex differences in predictions of college grades from Scholastic Aptitude Test scores. *Journal of Educational Psychology, 85*(4), 710–718.

Stricker, L. J., Rock, D. A., & Burton, N. W., Muraki, E., & Jirele, T. J. (1994). Adjusting college grade point average criteria for variations in grading standards: A comparison of methods. *Journal of Applied Psychology, 79*(2), 178–183.

Stroud, T. W. (1980). Reanalysis of the Federal Trade Commission study of commercial coaching for the SAT. In S. Messick (Ed.), *The effectiveness of coaching for the SAT: Review and reanalysis of research from the fifties to the FTC* (pp. 97–121). Princeton, NJ: Educational Testing Service.

Stumpf, H., & Stanley, J. C. (1996). Gender-related differences on the College Board's Advanced Placement and Achievement Tests, 1982–1992. *Journal of Educational Psychology, 88*(2), 353–364.

Subotnik, R., & Arnold, K. (Eds.). (1994). *Beyond Terman: Contemporary longitudinal studies of giftedness and talent.* Norwood, NJ: Ablex.

Sue, S., & Abe, J. (1988). *Predictors of academic achievement among Asian American and White students* (CB Rep. No. 88-11). New York: College Entrance Examination Board.

Suter, L. E. (Ed.). (1993). *Indicators of science and mathematics education 1992* (NSF 93-95). Washington, DC: National Science Foundation, Division of Research, Evaluation and Dissemination.

Swanson, D. B., Norman, G. R., & Linn, R. L. (1995). Performance-based assessment: Lessons from the health professions. *Educational Researcher, 24*(5), 5–11, 35.

Swim, J., Borgida, E., Maruyama, G., & Myers, D. G. (1989). Joan McKay versus John McKay: Do gender stereotypes bias evaluations? *Psychological Bulletin, 105*(3), 409–429.

Swineford, F. (1974). *The test analysis manual* (ETS SR 74-06). Princeton, NJ: Educational Testing Service.

Taber, T. D., & Hackman, J. D. (1976). Dimensions of undergraduate college performance. *Journal of Applied Psychology, 61*(5), 546–558.

Taylor, C. (1995). Responsible test use: Case studies for assessing human behavior [Review of *Responsible test use: Case studies for assessing human behavior*]. *Journal of Educational Measurement, 32*, 217–221.

Thorndike, E. L. (1910). *Educational psychology* (2nd ed.). New York: Teachers College, Columbia University.

Thorndike, R. L. (1971). Concepts of culture-fairness. *Journal of Educational Measurement, 8*(2), 63–70.

Thresher, A. (1966). *College admissions and the public interest.* New York: College Entrance Examination Board.

Tobias, S. (1985). Test anxiety: Interference, defective skills, and cognitive capacity. *Educational Psychologist, 20*(3), 135–142.

TOEFL Program. (1992a). *Test of Spoken English manual for score users* (4th ed.). Princeton, NJ: Educational Testing Program.

TOEFL Program. (1992b). *Test of Written English guide* (3rd ed.). Princeton, NJ: Educational Testing Service.

Traub, R. E. (1993). On the equivalence of the traits assessed by multiple-choice and constructed-response tests. In R. E. Bennett & W. C. Ward (Eds.), *Construction versus choice in cognitive measurement: Issues in constructed response, performance testing, and portfolio assessment* (pp. 29–44). Hillsdale, NJ: Lawrence Erlbaum Associates.

Traub, R. E., & Fisher, C. W. (1977). On the equivalence of constructed-response and multiple-choice tests. *Applied Psychological Measurement, 1*, 355–369.

Traub, R. E., & MacRury, K. (1990). Multiple-choice vs. free-response in the testing of scholastic achievement [Antwort-auswahl vs. freie-antwort-aufgaben bei lerner-folgstestes]. In K. Ingenkamp (Ed.), *Yearbook on educational measurement* [*Test und trends 8: Jarbuch der paedagogischen diagnostik*]. Weinheim, Germany: Beltz-Verlag.

Turner, A. R. (1967). New developments in the Spanish Advanced Placement Program of the College Entrance Examination Board. In G. J. Edberg (Ed.), *Foreign language currents, Hispania, L*(2), 348–353.

Tyler, L. E. (1947). *The psychology of human differences.* New York: Appleton-Century-Crofts.

Tyler, L. E. (1961). Research explorations in the realm of choice. *Journal of Counseling Psychology, 8*(3), 195–201.

Tyler, L. E. (1965). *The psychology of human differences* (3rd ed.). New York: Appleton-Century-Crofts.

Tyler, R. W., & White, S. H. (Eds.). (1979). *Testing, teaching and learning: Report of a conference on research on testing, August 17–26, 1979.* Washington, DC: National Institute of Education.

United Nations. (1995). *The world's women 1995: Trends and statistics* (Social Statistics Indicators, Series K, No. 12). New York: Author.

University of California. (1995). *Introducing the University 1996–1997.* Oakland: Author.

U. S. Department of Education. (1988). *Education directory: Higher education 1987–88.* Washington, DC: U.S. Government Printing Office.

Valentine, J. A. (1962, Winter). The first year of the Writing Sample. *College Board Review,* (No. 46), 22–26.

van den Bergh, H. (1990). On the construct validity of multiple–choice items for reading comprehension. *Applied Psychological Measurement, 14,* 1–12.

Wah, D. M., & Robinson, D. S. (1990). *Examinee and score trends for the GRE General Test: 1977–78, 1982–83, 1986–87, and 1987–88.* Princeton, NJ: Educational Testing Service.

Wainer, H., & Steinberg, L. S. (1991). *Sex differences in performance on the mathematics section of the Scholastic Aptitude Test: A bidirectional validity study* (PSRTR No. 91-12; ETS RR-91-45). Princeton, NJ: Educational Testing Service.

Wainer, H., & Steinberg, L. S. (1992). Sex differences in performance on the mathematics section of the Scholastic Aptitude Test: A bidirectional validity study. *Harvard Educational Review, 62,* 323–336.

Wainer, H., & Thissen, D. (1994). On examinee choice in educational testing. *Review of Educational Research, 64,* 159–195.

Wallach, M. A. (1976). Psychology of talent and graduate education. In S. Messick & Associates, *Individuality in learning* (pp. 178–210). San Francisco: Jossey-Bass.

Ward, W. C. (1982). A comparison of free-response and multiple-choice forms of verbal aptitude tests. *Applied Psychological Measurement, 6,* 1–11.

Ward, W. C., Dupree, D., & Carlson, S. B. (1987). *A comparison of free-response and multiple-choice questions in the assessment of reading comprehension* (ETS RR-87-20). Princeton, NJ: Educational Testing Service.

Ward, W. C., Frederiksen, N., & Carlson, S. B. (1980). Construct validity of free-response and machine-scorable forms of a test. *Journal of Educational Measurement, 17,* 11–29.

Way, W. D. (1994). *A simulation study of the Mantel-Haenszel procedure for detecting DIF with the NCLEX using CAT.* Manuscript submitted for publication.

Webb, S. C. (1959). Measured changes in college grading standards. *College Board Review,* 39, 27–30.

Wechsler, H. S. (1977). *The qualified student: A history of selective college admissions in America.* New York: Wiley.

Weinberg, S. L. (1993). The Hedges and Friedman index: Two-tailed significance. *Review of Educational Research, 63,* 527–529.

Wellesley College Center for Research on Women. (1992). *The AAUW report: How schools shortchange girls: A study of major findings on girls and education.* Washington, DC: American Association of University Women Educational Foundation and National Education Association.

Wendler, C. L., & Carlton, S. T. (1987, April). *An examination of SAT Verbal items for differential performance by women and men: An exploratory study.* Paper presented at the annual meeting of the American Educational Research Association, Washington, DC.

Werts, C. E., Breland, H. M., Grandy, J., & Rock, D. A. (1980). Using longitudinal data to estimate reliability in the presence of correlated measurement errors. *Educational and Psychological Measurement, 40*(1), 19–29.

Westinghouse Electric Corporation & Science Service. (1993a). *The 53rd annual Westing-house science talent search: 1993–94 facts and official entry form*. Washington, DC: Science Service.

Westinghouse Electric Corporation & Science Service. (1993b). *Finalists of the 52nd annual Westinghouse science talent search*. Washington, DC: Science Service.

Westinghouse Electric Corporation & Science Service. (1996). *Finalists of the 55th annual Westinghouse science talent search*. Washington, DC: Science Service.

Wheeler, P., & Harris, A. (1981). *Comparison of male and female performance on the ATP Physics test* (CB Rep. No. 81-4). New York: College Entrance Examination Board.

Whitaker, U. (1989). *Assessing learning: Standards, principles, & procedures*. Philadelphia: Council for Adult and Experiential Learning.

White, E. M. (1994). *Teaching and assessing writing: Recent advances in understanding, evaluating, and improving student performance* (2nd ed.). San Francisco: Jossey-Bass.

Whitla, D. K. (1968). Evaluation of decision making: A study of college admissions. In D. K. Whitla (Ed.), *Handbook of measurement and assessment in behavioral sciences* (pp. 456–491). Reading, MA: Addison-Wesley.

Wickenden, J. W. (1979, October 22). Memorandum to all Princeton alumni on the admissions process. *Princeton Alumni Weekly*.

Wiggins, G. (1989). A true test: Toward more authentic and equitable assessment. *Phi Delta Kappan, 70*, 703–713.

Wiggins, G. (1993). Assessment: Authenticity, context, and validity. *Phi Delta Kappan 75* (3), 200–214.

Wightman, L. F. (1995). *Analysis of LSAT performance and patterns of application for male and female law school applicants* (LSAC Research Rep. 94-02). Newtown, PA: Law School Admission Council.

Wild, C. L., & Durso, R. (1979). *Effect of increased test-taking time on test scores by ethnic and gender subgroups* (GRE No. 76-06R). Princeton, NJ: Educational Testing Service.

Wild, C. L., & Dwyer, C. A. (1980). Sex bias in selection. In L. J. van der Kamp, W. F. Langerak, & D. N. de Gruijter (Eds.), *Psychometrics for educational debates* (pp. 153–168). New York: Wiley.

Wild, C. L., & McPeek, W. M. (1986, August). *Performance of the Mantel–Haenszel statistic in identifying differentially functioning items*. Paper presented at the annual meeting of the American Psychological Association, Washington, DC.

Wilder, G. Z. (1997). Antecedents of gender differences. In *Supplement to Gender and fair assessment*. Princeton, NJ: Educational Testing Service.

Wilder, G. Z., & Powell, K. (1989). *Sex differences in test performance: A survey of the literature* (CB Rep. No. 89-3; ETS RR-89-4). New York: College Entrance Examination Board.

Willingham, W. W. (1963). *A comparison of the entering classes of 1957 through 1962* (Research Memorandum 63-2, Evaluation Studies, Vol. III). Atlanta: Georgia Institute of Technology, Office of the Dean of Faculties.

Willingham, W. W. (1974a). *College placement and exemption*. New York: College Entrance Examination Board.

Willingham, W. W. (1974b). Predicting success in graduate education. *Science, 183*, 273–278.

Willingham, W. W. (1980, Summer). The case for personal qualities in admissions. *College Board Review*, No. 116, A1–A8.

Willingham, W. W. (1983). Measuring personal qualities in admissions: The context and the purpose. In R. B. Ekstrom (Ed.), *Measurement, technology, and individuality in education* (New Directions for Testing and Measurement 17). San Francisco: Jossey-Bass.

Willingham, W. W. (1985). *Success in college: The role of personal qualities and academic ability*. New York: College Entrance Examination Board.

Willingham, W. W. (1988). Testing handicapped people—The validity issue. In H. Wainer & H. I. Braun (Eds.), *Test validity* (pp. 89–103). Hillsdale, NJ: Lawrence Erlbaum Associates.

Willingham, W. W. (1990). Understanding yearly trends: A synthesis of research findings. In W. W. Willingham, C. Lewis, R. Morgan, & L. Ramist (Eds.), *Predicting college grades: An analysis of institutional trends over two decades* (pp. 23–82). Princeton, NJ: Educational Testing Service.

Willingham, W. W. (in press). A systemic view of test fairness. In S. Messick (Ed.), *Assessment in higher education: Issues of access, quality, student development, and public policy.* Mahwah, NJ: Lawrence Erlbaum Associates.

Willingham, W. W., & Breland, H. M. (1982). *Personal qualities and college admissions.* New York: College Entrance Examination Board.

Willingham, W. W., & Lewis, C. (1990). Institutional differences in prediction trends. In W. W. Willingham, C. Lewis, R. Morgan, & L. Ramist (Eds.), *Predicting college grades: An analysis of institutional trends over two decades* (pp. 141–158). Princeton, NJ: Educational Testing Service.

Willingham, W. W., Lewis, C., Morgan, R., & Ramist, L. (1990). *Predicting college grades: An analysis of institutional trends over two decades.* Princeton, NJ: Educational Testing Service.

Willingham, W. W., & Morris, M. (1986). *Four years later: A longitudinal study of Advanced Placement students in college* (CB Rep. No. 86-2; ETS RR-85-46). New York: College Entrance Examination Board.

Willingham, W. W., Ragosta, M., Bennett, R. E., Braun, H., Rock, D. A., & Powers, D. E. (1988). *Testing handicapped people.* Boston: Allyn & Bacon.

Willis, S. (1993). Are letter grades obsolete? *Association for Supervision and Curriculum Development (ASCD) Update, 35*(7), 1, 4, 8.

Wilson, K. M. (1970, Fall). Increased selectivity and institutional grading standards. *College and University,* 46–53.

Wilson, K. M. (1983). A review of research on the prediction of academic performance after the freshman year (CB Rep. No. 83-2; ETS RR-83-11). New York: College Entrance Examination Board.

Wine, J. (1971). Test anxiety and direction of attention. *Psychological Bulletin, 76*(2), 92–104.

Wing, C. W., & Wallach, M. A. (1971). *College admissions and the psychology of talent.* New York: Holt, Rinehart, & Winston.

Wise, L. L. (1985). Project TALENT: Mathematics course participation in the 1960s and its career consequences. In S. F. Chipman, L. R. Brush, & D. M. Wilson (Eds.), *Women and mathematics: Balancing the equation* (pp. 25–58). Hillsdale, NJ: Lawrence Erlbaum Associates.

Wood, R. (1978). Sex differences in answers to English language comprehension items, *Educational Studies, 4,* 157–164.

Young, J. W. (1990a). Adjusting the cumulative GPA using item response theory. *Journal of Educational Measurement, 27*(2), 175–186.

Young, J. W. (1990b, April). *Gender bias in predicting college academic performance: A new approach using item response theory.* Paper presented at the annual meeting of the American Educational Research Association, Boston, MA.

Zemsky, R., & Oedel, P. (1983). *The structure of college choice.* New York: College Entrance Examination Board.

Ziomek, R. L., & Svec, J. C. (1995). *High school grades and achievement: Evidence of grade inflation* (ACT Research Rep. Series 95-3). Iowa City, IA: American College Testing Program.

Author Index

Subject Index